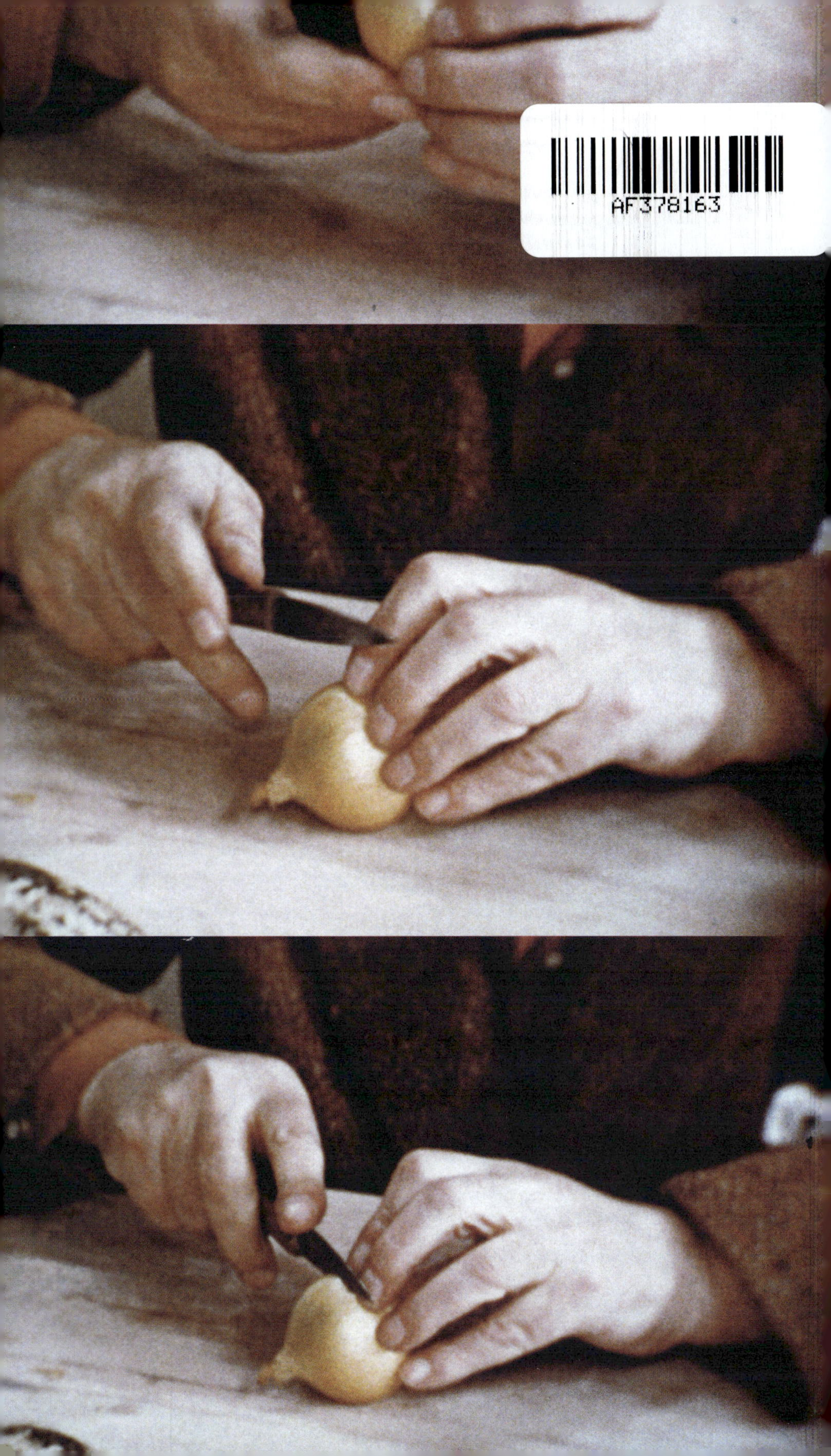

AF378163

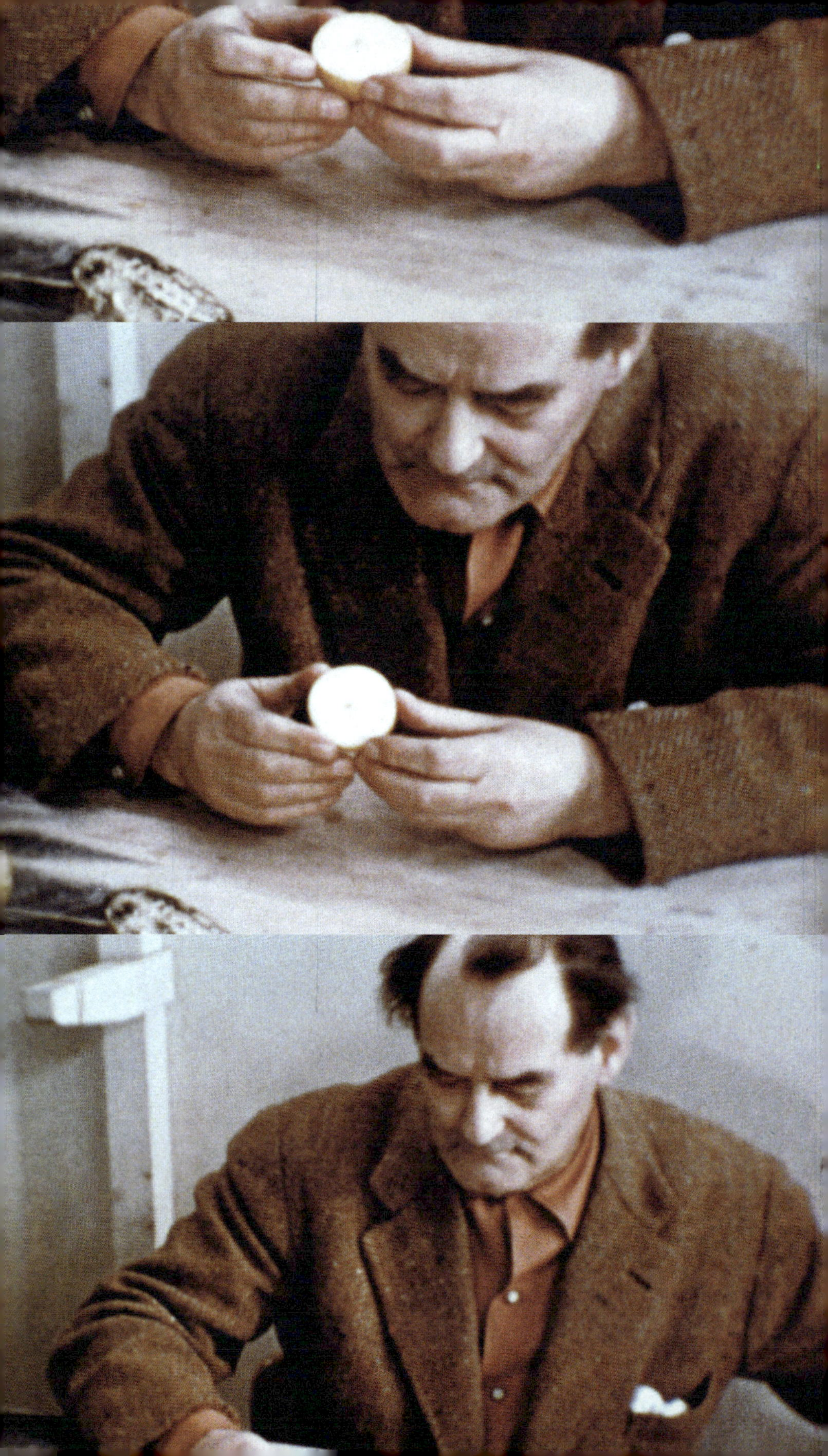

Playing with Fire

*Edmund de Waal
and Axel Salto*

press

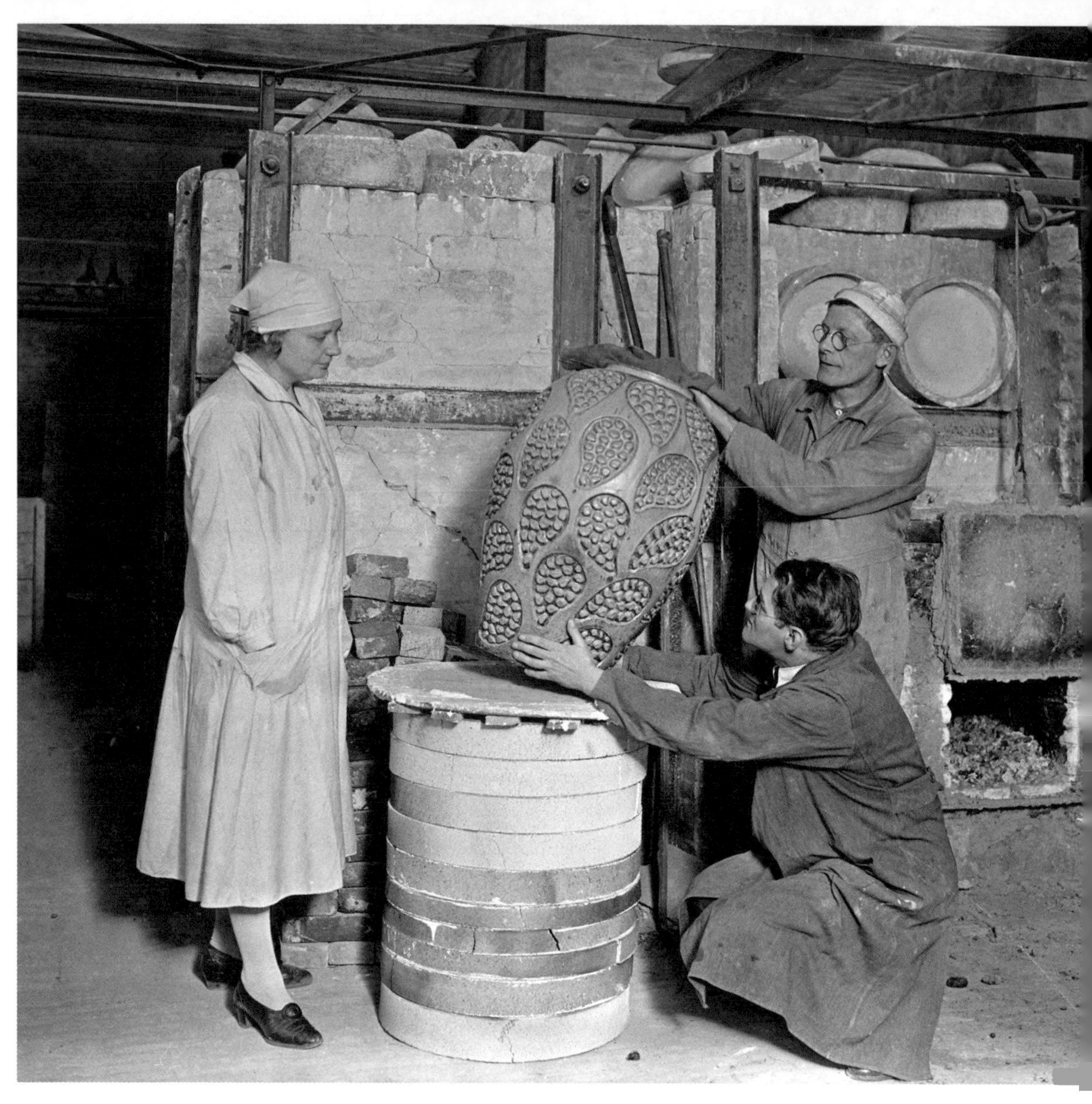

Interior from the SAXBO workshop, 1932
Nathalie Krebs, Axel Salto and Oscar Olsen
have just taken *The Grape Vase* out of the kiln
Ritzau Scanpix

Contents

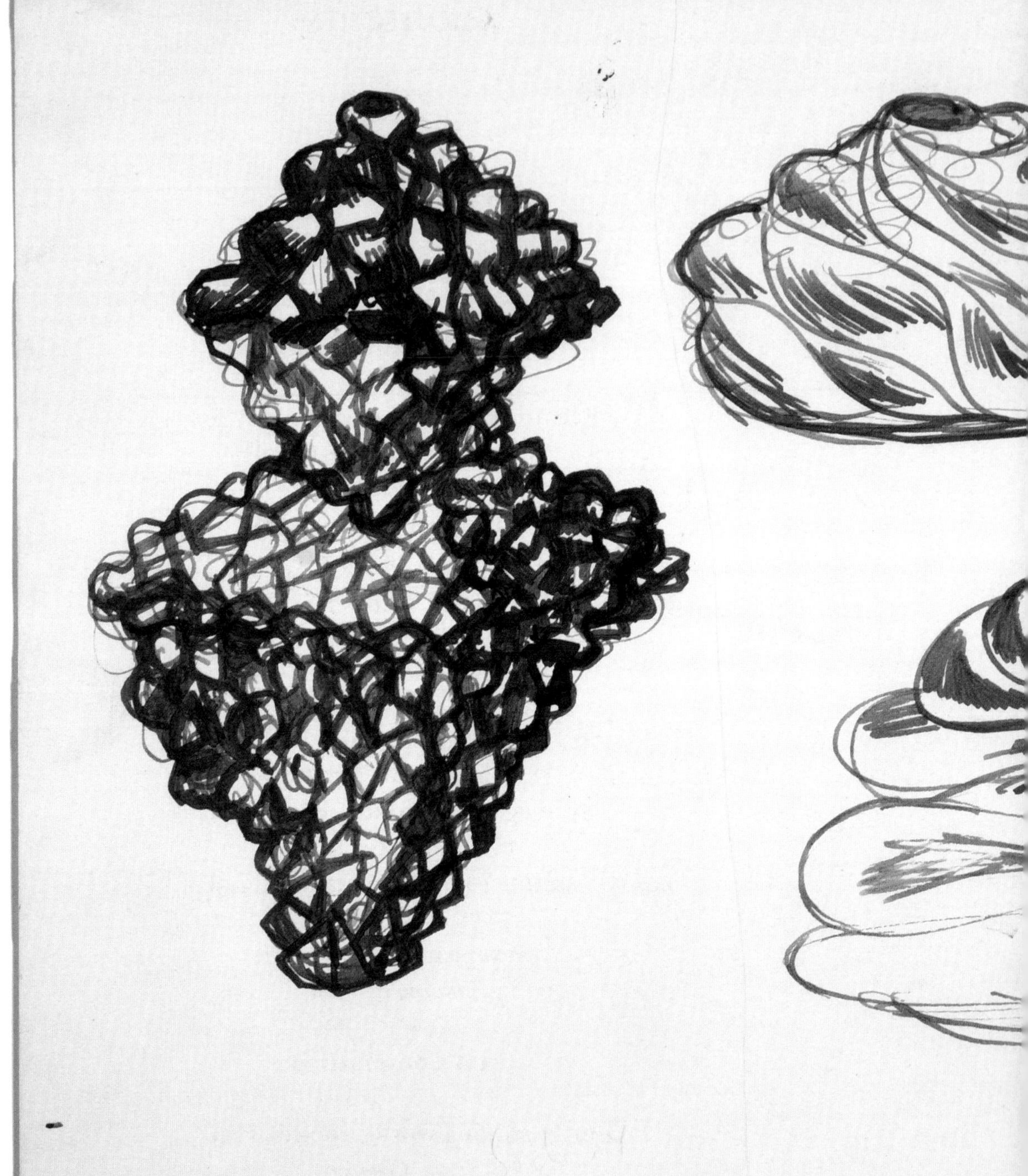

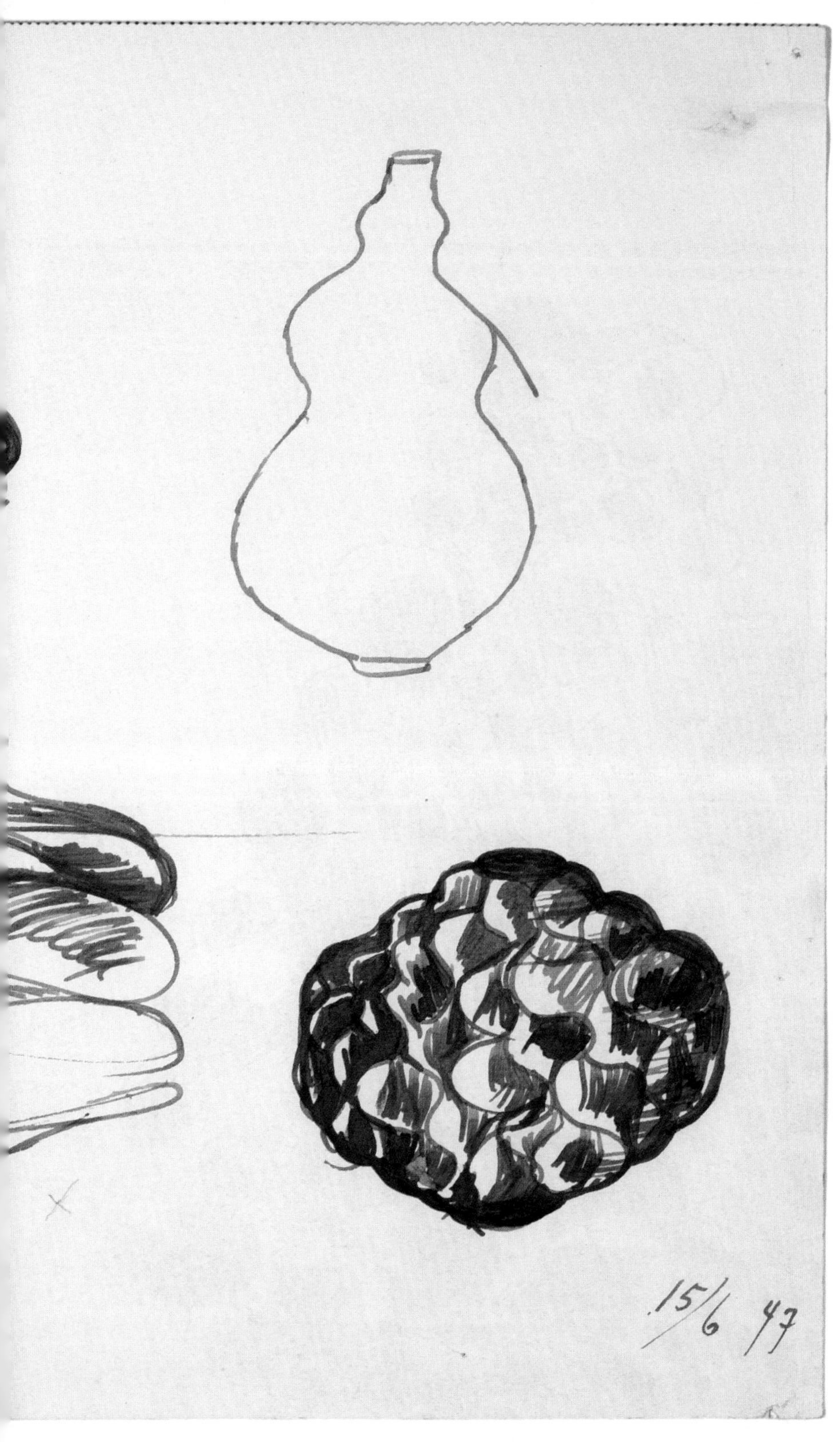

Axel Salto
Studies of various vessels, 1947
Ink on paper, 292 × 416 mm
CLAY / The Royal Copenhagen Collection

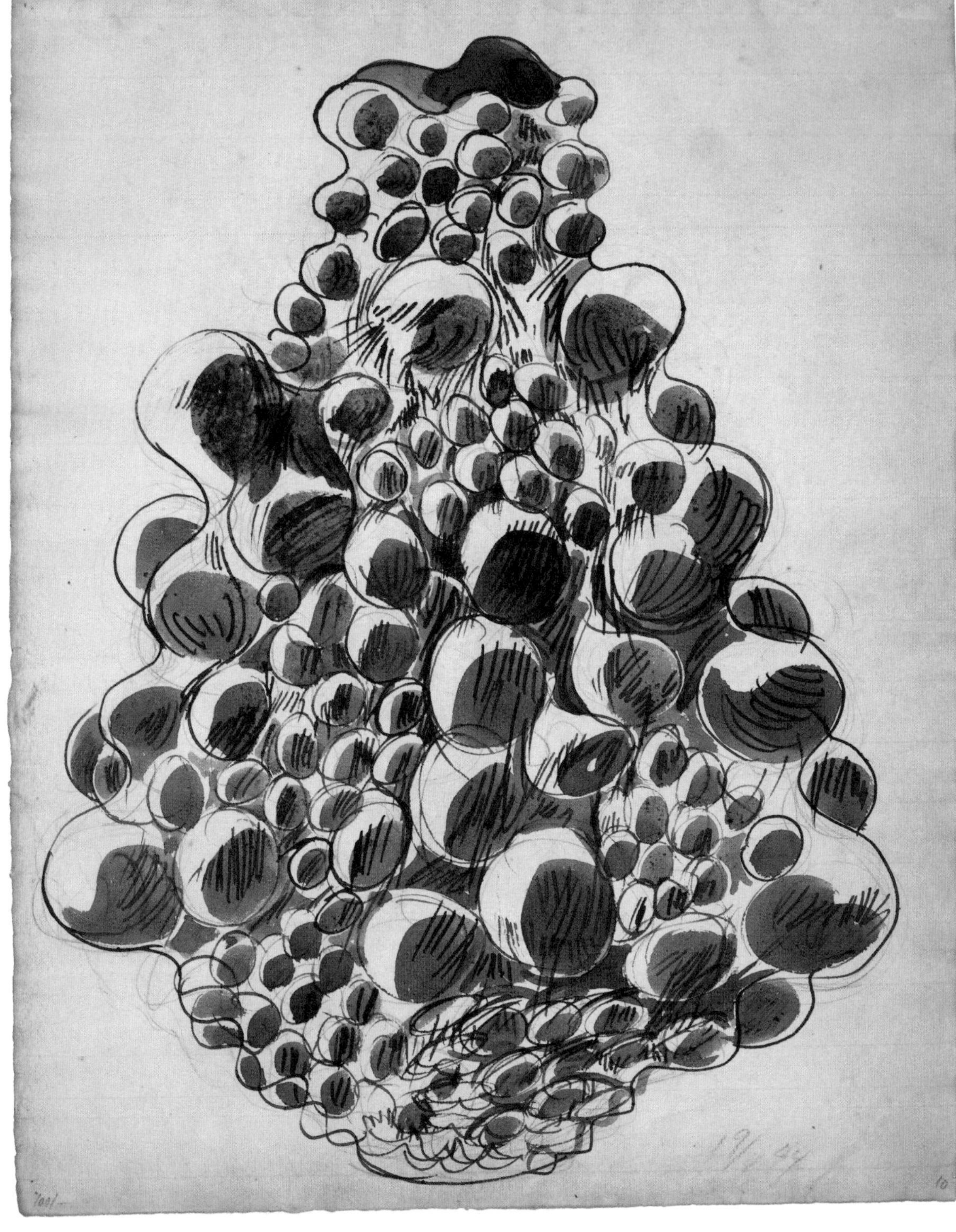

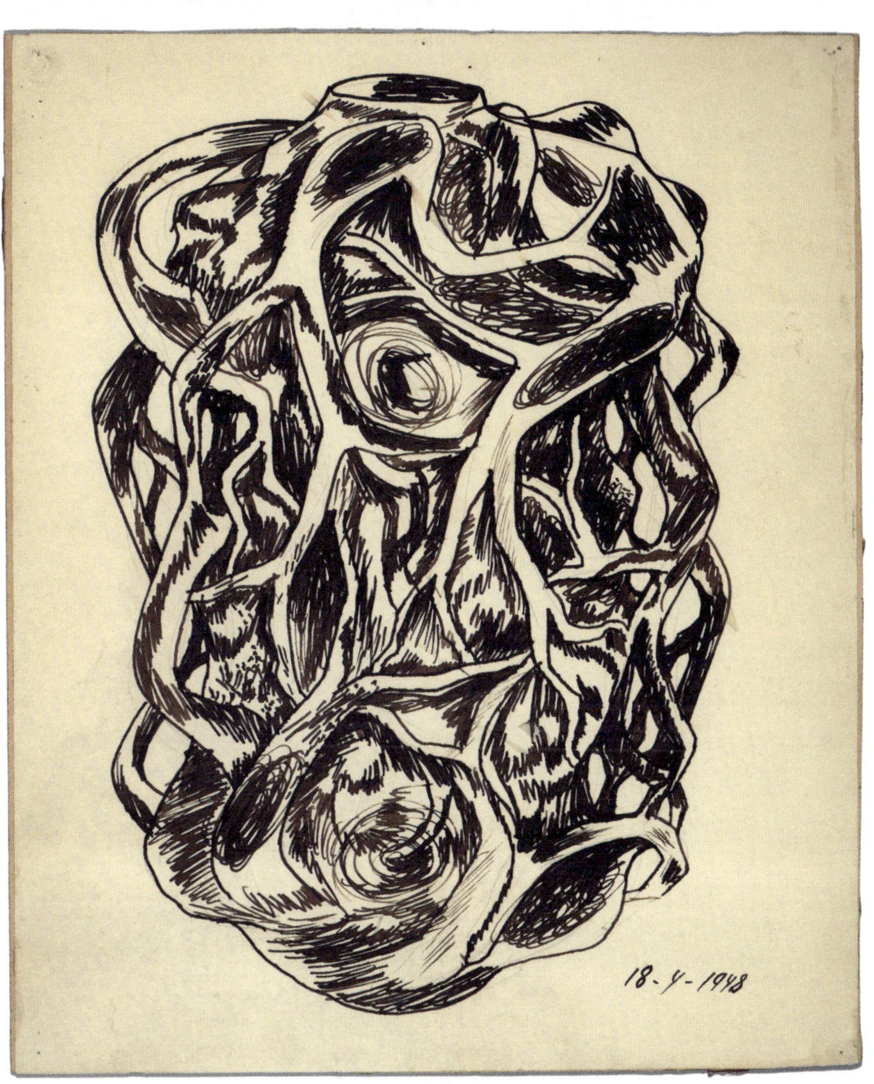

Axel Salto
Sketch of vase, 1944
Watercolour on paper, 575 × 440 mm
CLAY/The Royal Copenhagen Collection

Axel Salto
Sketch of vase, 1948
Graphite and ink on paper, 520 × 425 mm
CLAY/The Royal Copenhagen Collection

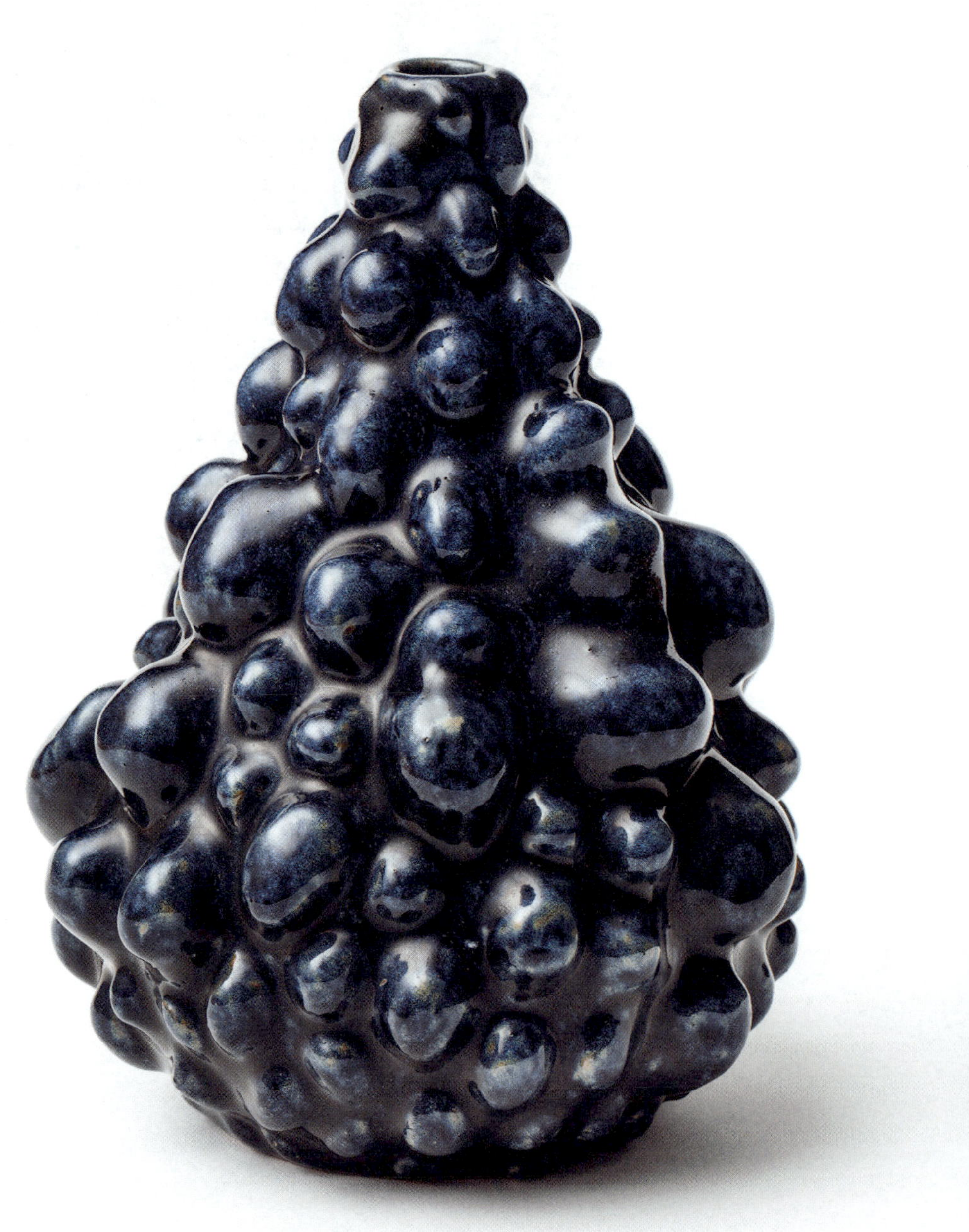

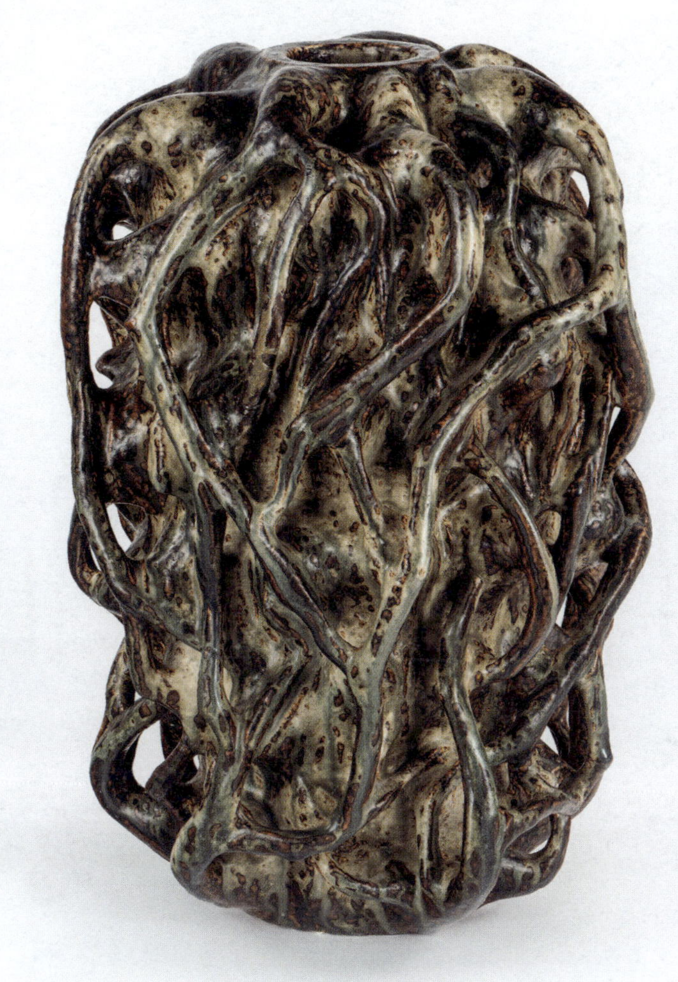

Axel Salto
Vase, 1957
Stoneware with Blue Mussel glaze, H: 23 cm
CLAY/The Erik Veistrup Collection

Axel Salto
Vase, 1949
Stoneware with Sung glaze, H: 43 cm
The Tangen Collection/Kunstsilo

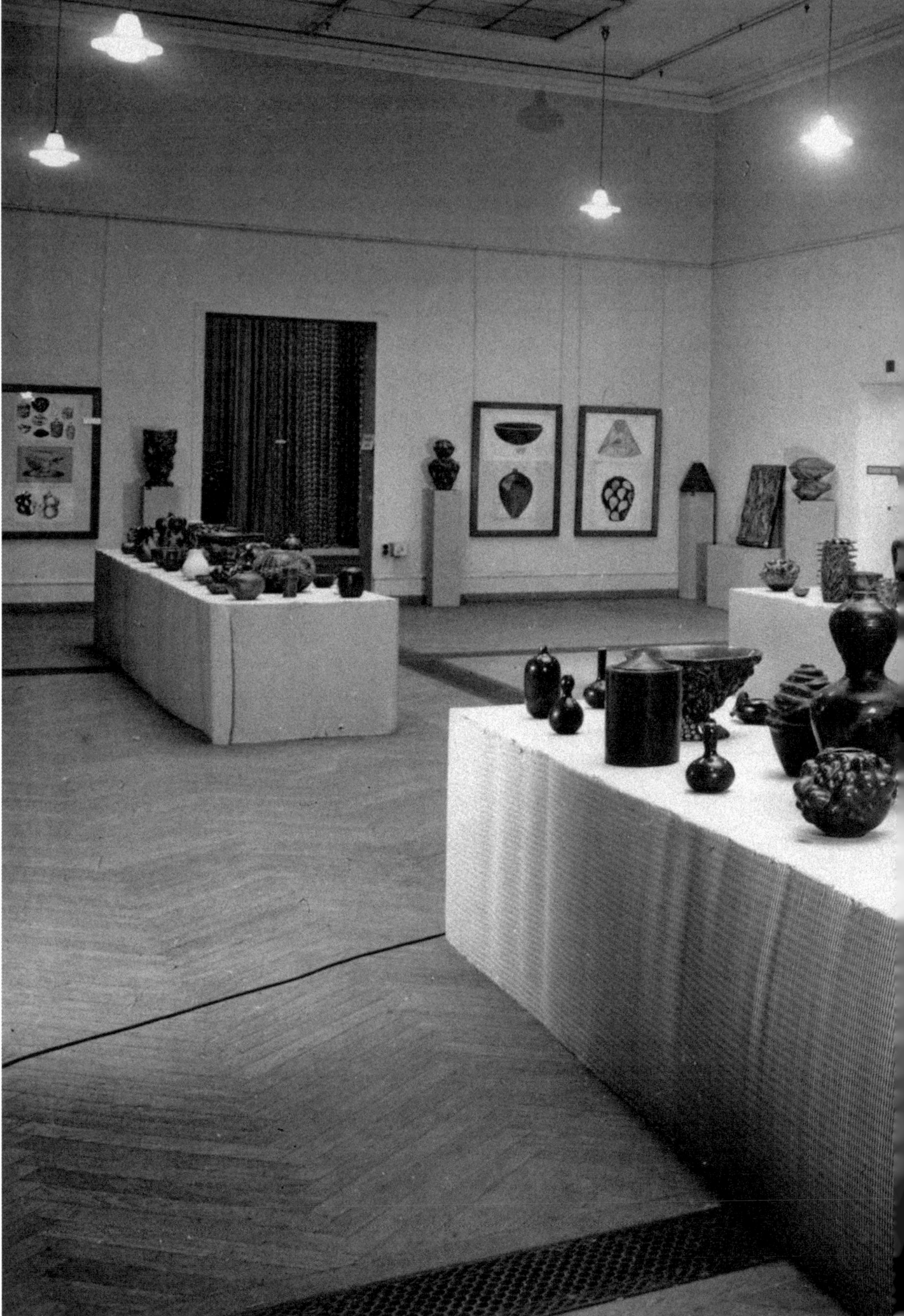

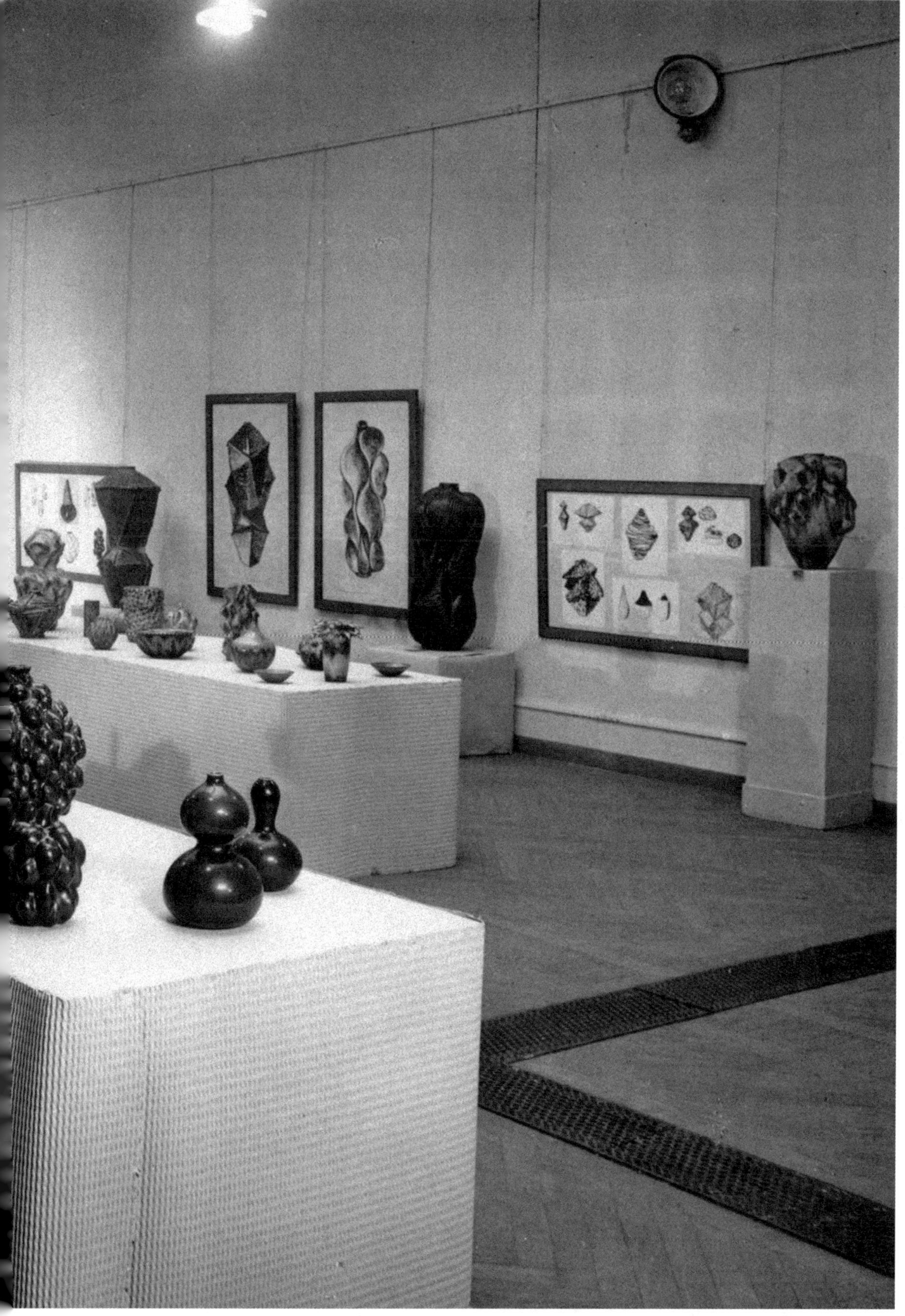

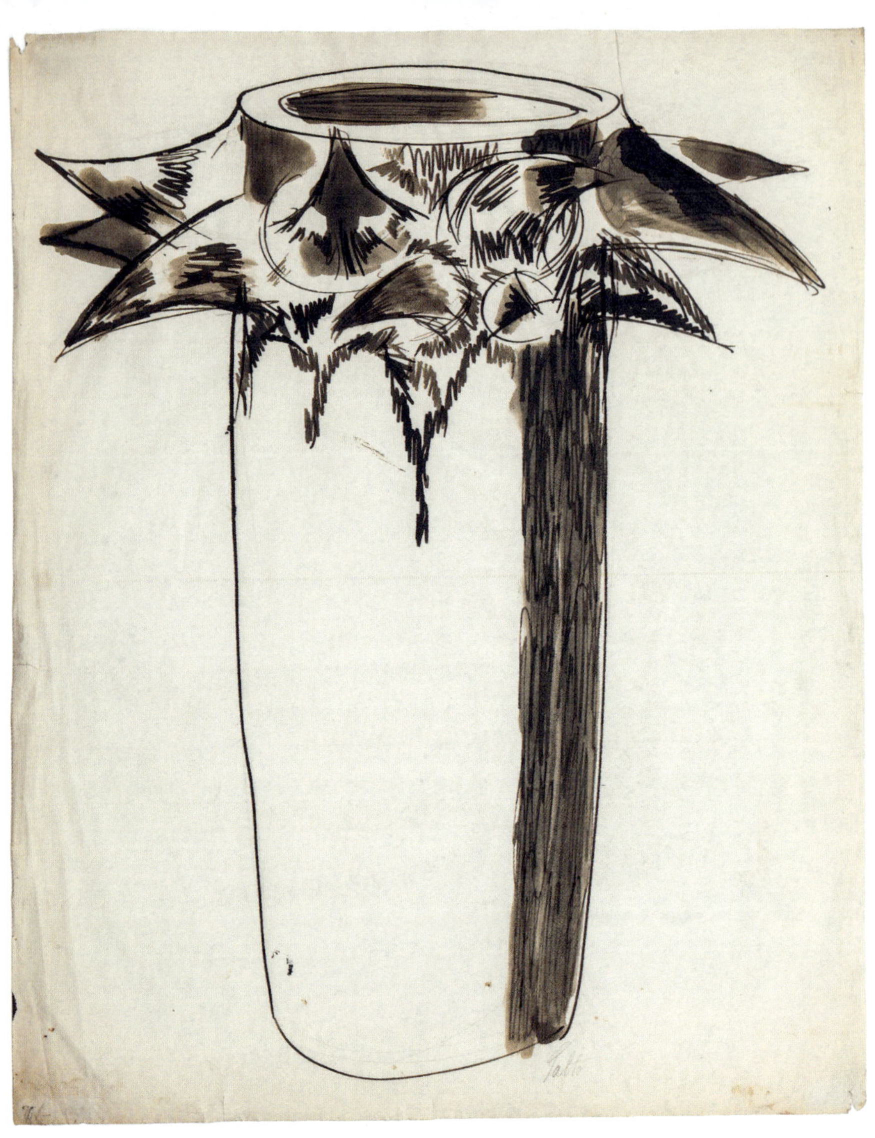

Above
Axel Salto
Sketch of vase, n.d.
Ink on paper, 567 × 441 mm
CLAY/The Royal Copenhagen Collection

Previous spread
Axel Salto exhibition
Charlottenborg, 1949
Copenhagen
CLAY/The Royal Copenhagen Collection

Right
Axel Salto
Sketch of vase, 1943
Watercolour on paper, 460 × 600 mm
CLAY/The Royal Copenhagen Collection

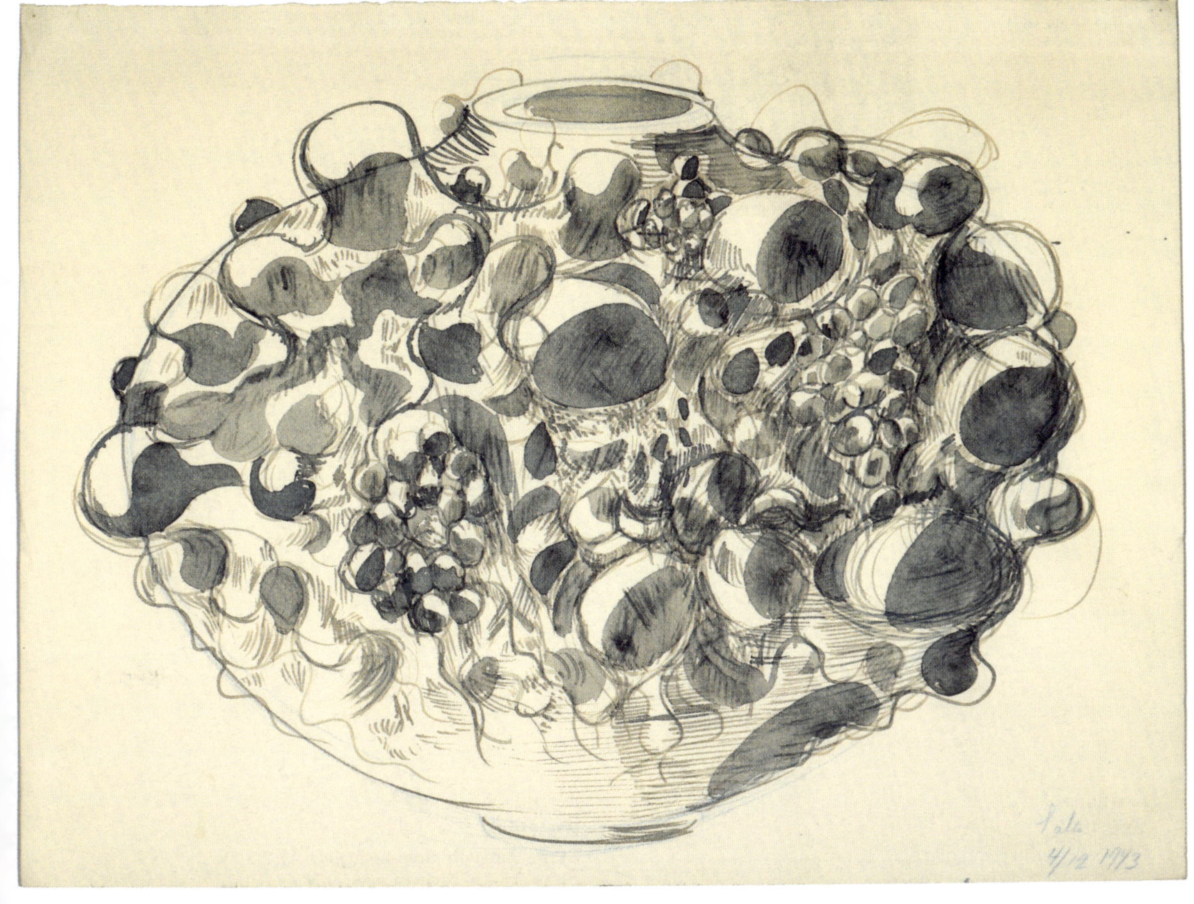

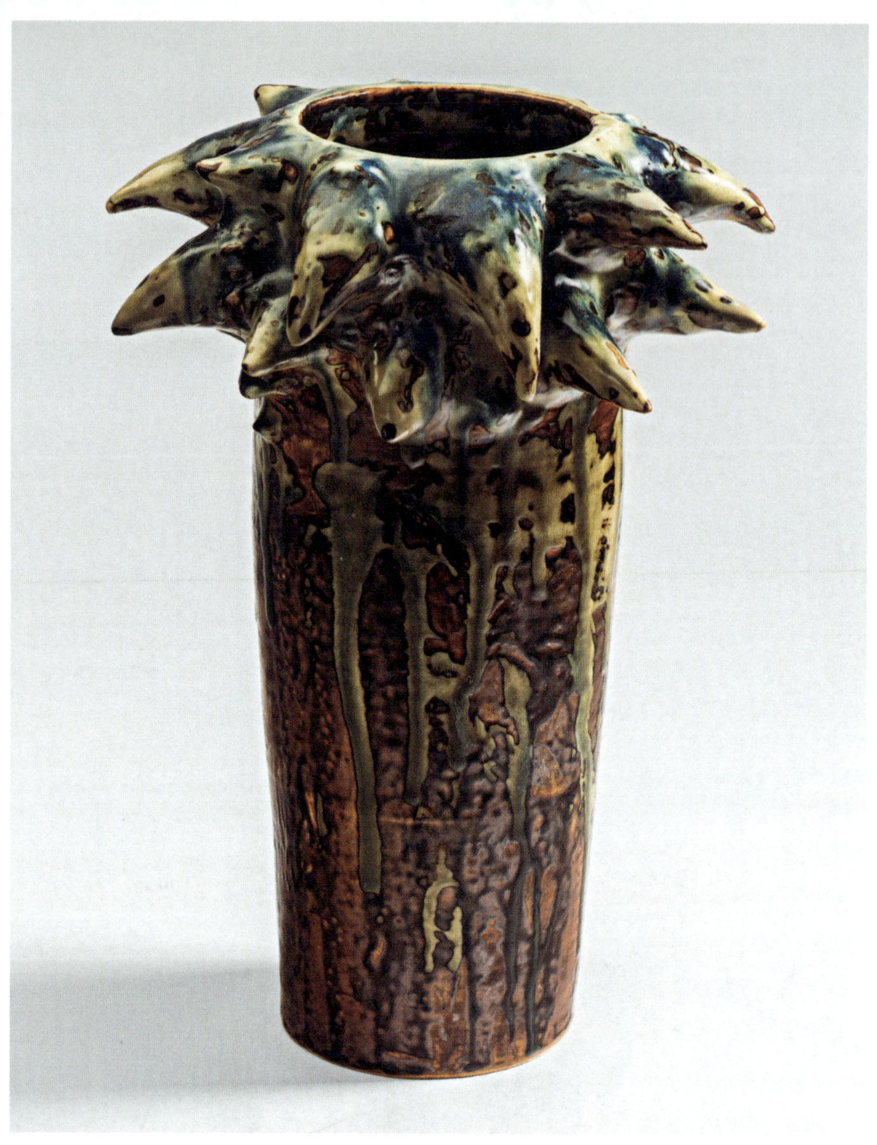

Axel Salto
Vase, 1942
Stoneware with Sung glaze, H: 35 cm
The Tangen Collection/Kunstsilo

Axel Salto
Vase, 1943
Stoneware with Solfatara glaze, H: 20 cm
CLAY/The Royal Copenhagen Collection

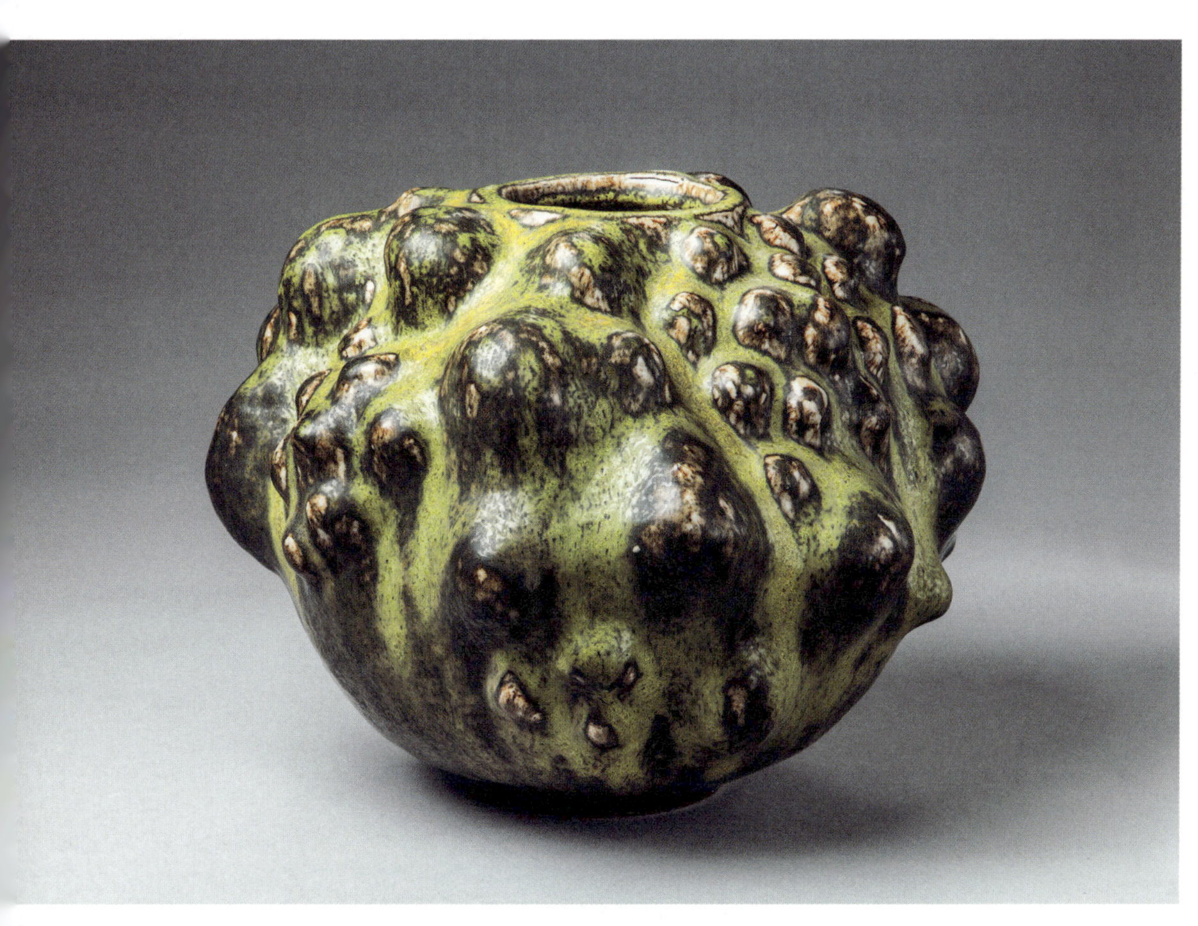

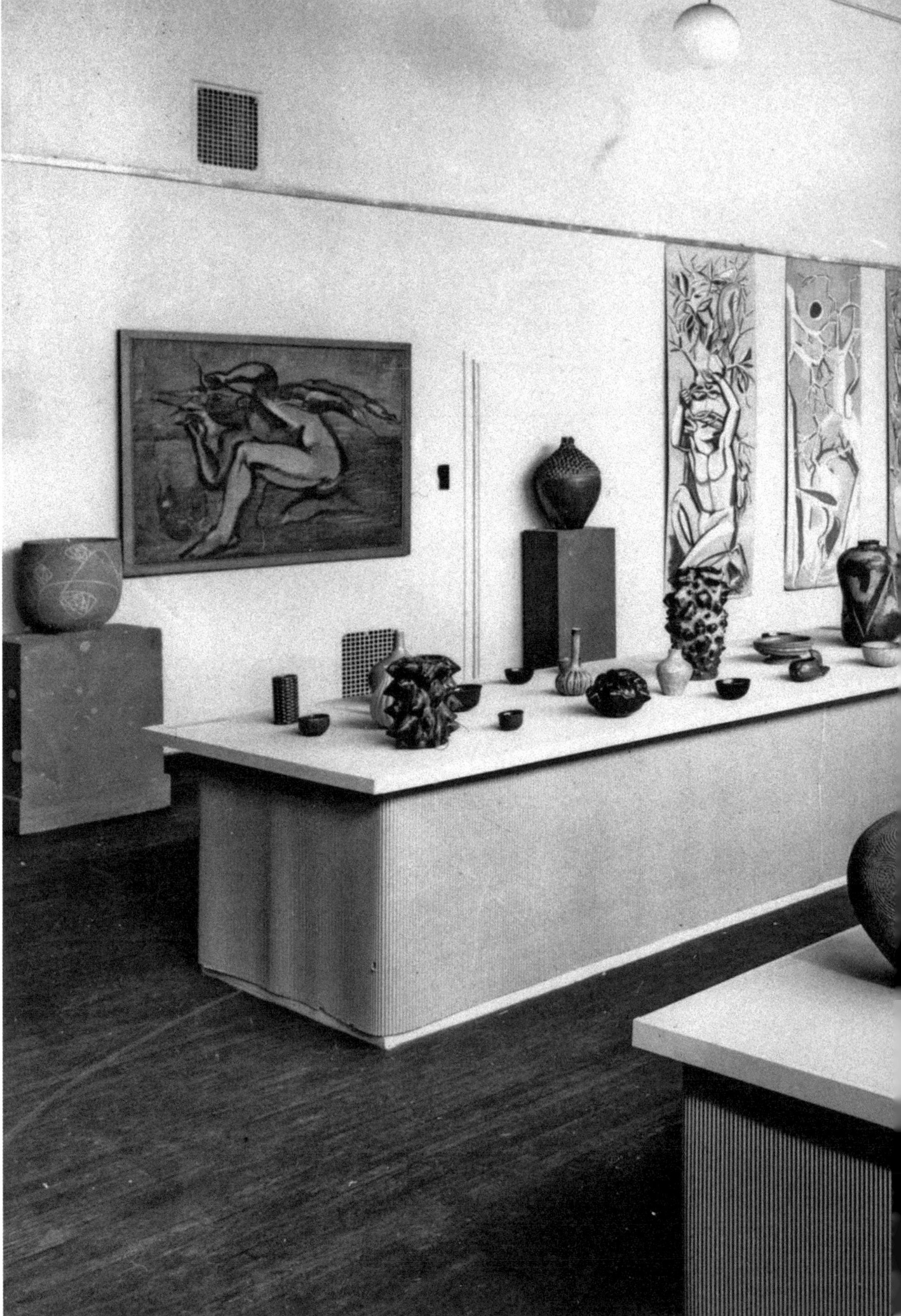

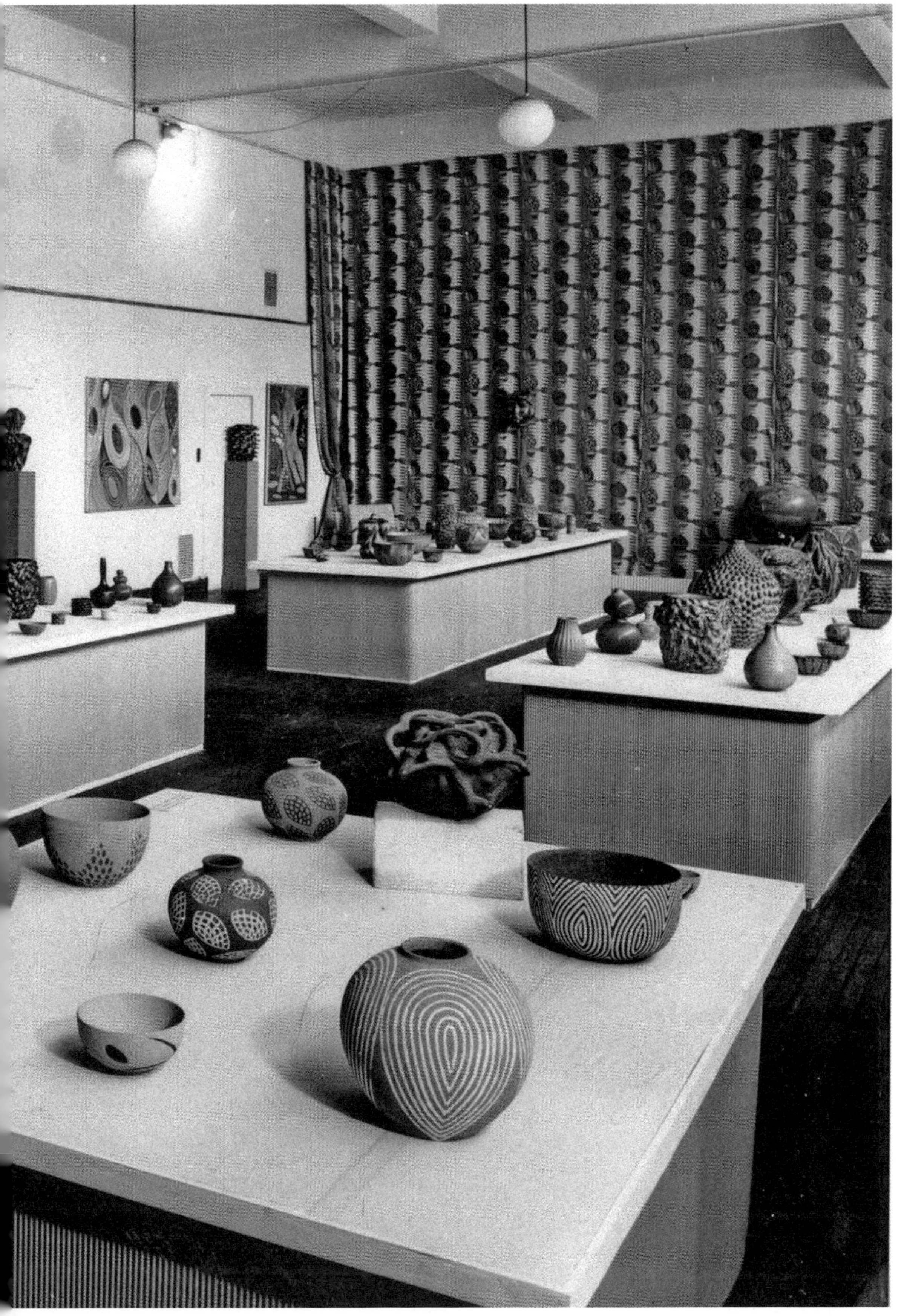

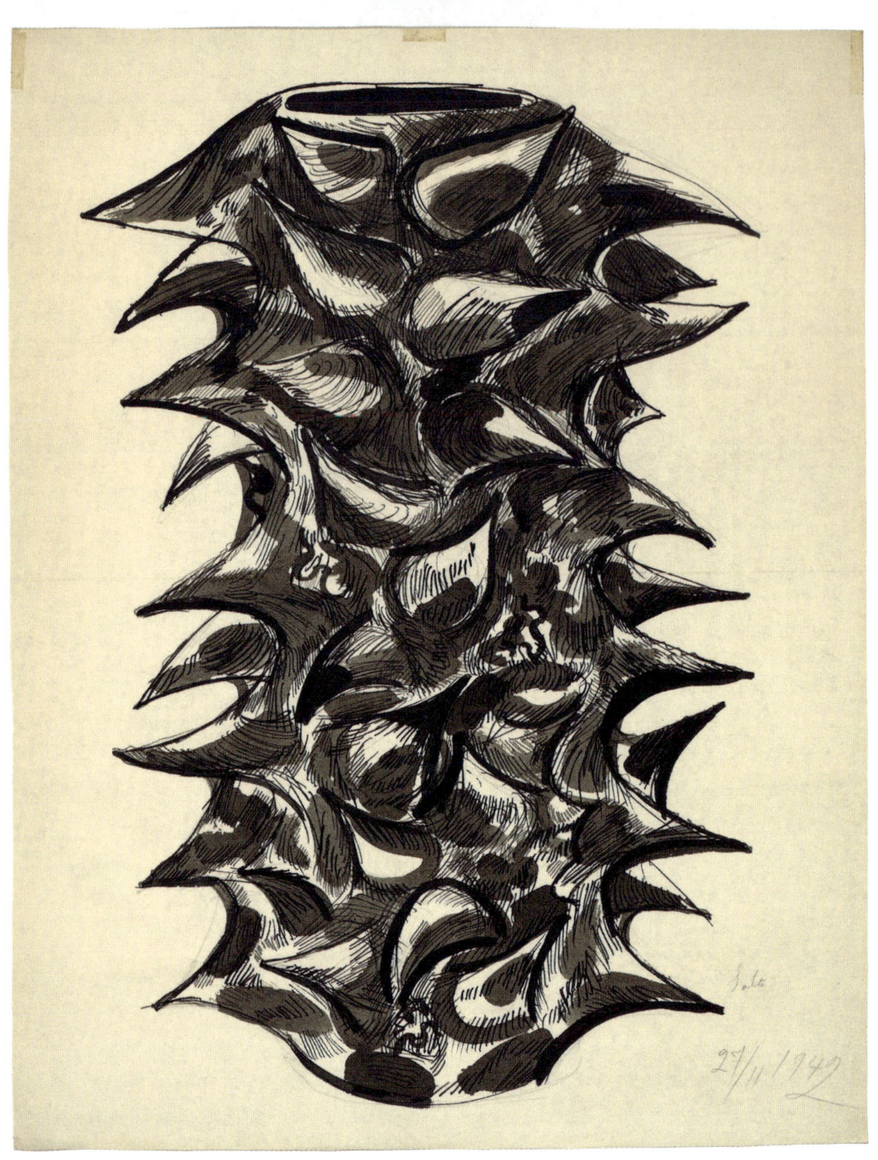

Above
Axel Salto
Sketch of vase, 1942
Ink on paper, 595 × 452 mm
CLAY/The Royal Copenhagen Collection

Right
Axel Salto
Vase, 1940's
Stoneware with Sung glaze, H: 37 cm
CLAY/The Royal Copenhagen Collection

Previous spread
Axel Salto exhibition
Nasjonalmuseet Oslo, 1950
CLAY/The Royal Copenhagen Collection

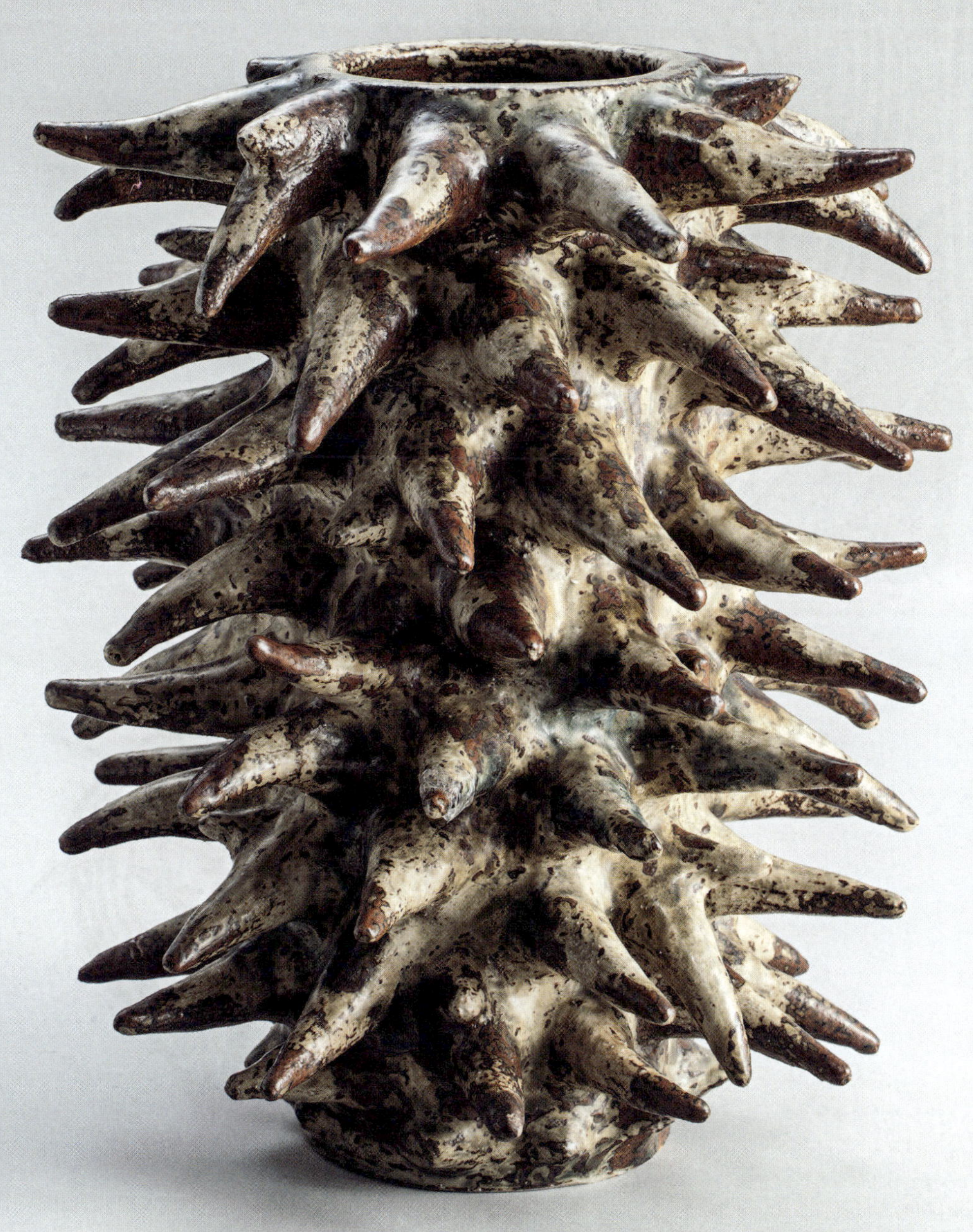

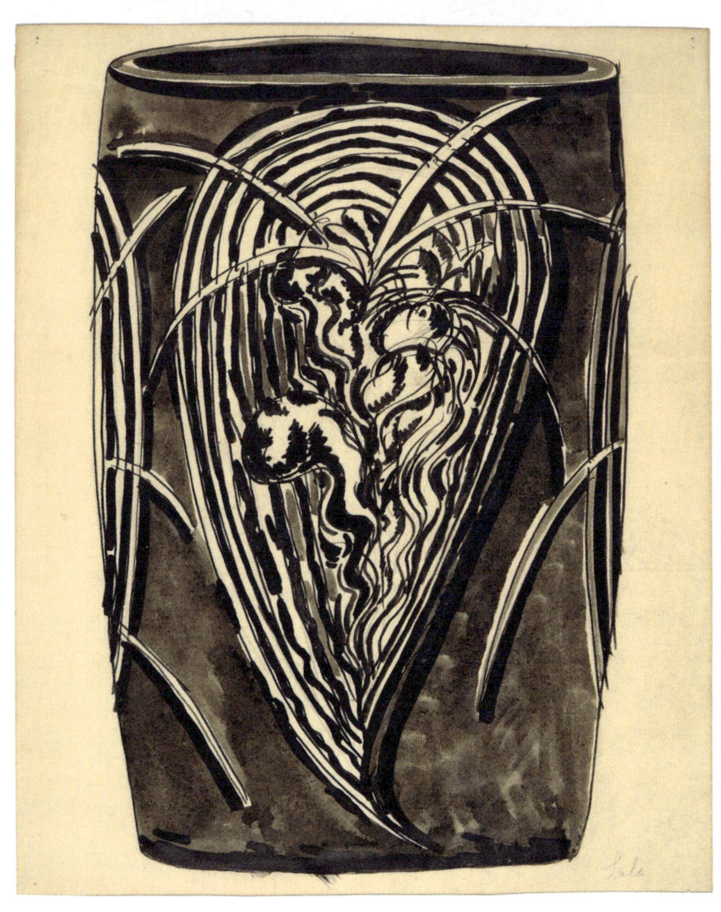

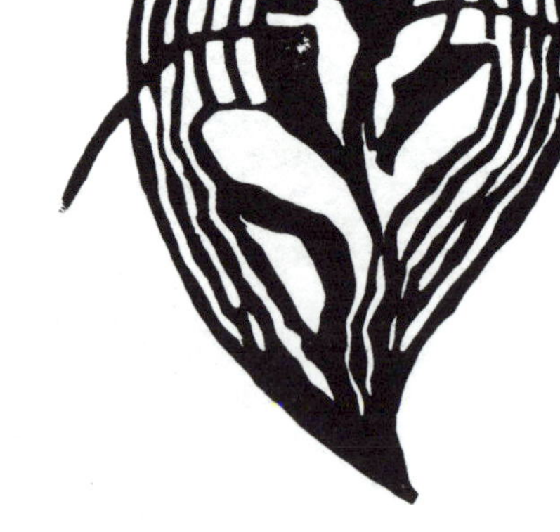

Top
Axel Salto
Sketch of vase, n.d.
Motif *The Living Stone*
Ink on paper, 466 × 372 mm
CLAY/The Royal Copenhagen Collection

Bottom
Axel Salto
Print, n.d.
Motif *The Living Stone*
Woodcut on paper, 200 × 210 mm
CLAY/The Royal Copenhagen Collection

Right
Axel Salto
Vase, n.d.
Motif *The Living Stone*
Stoneware with Sung glaze, H: 38 cm
CLAY/The Erik Veistrup Collection

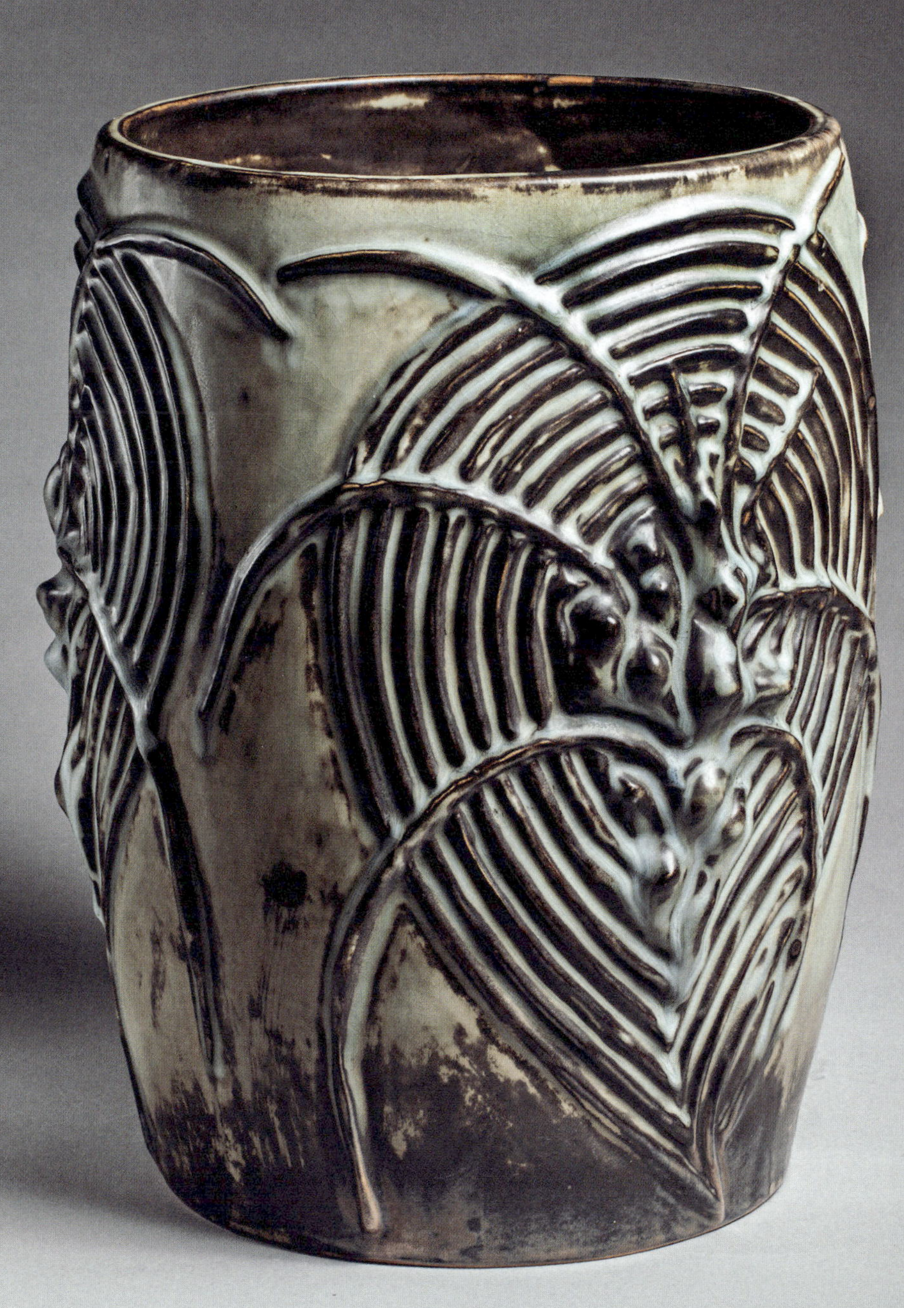

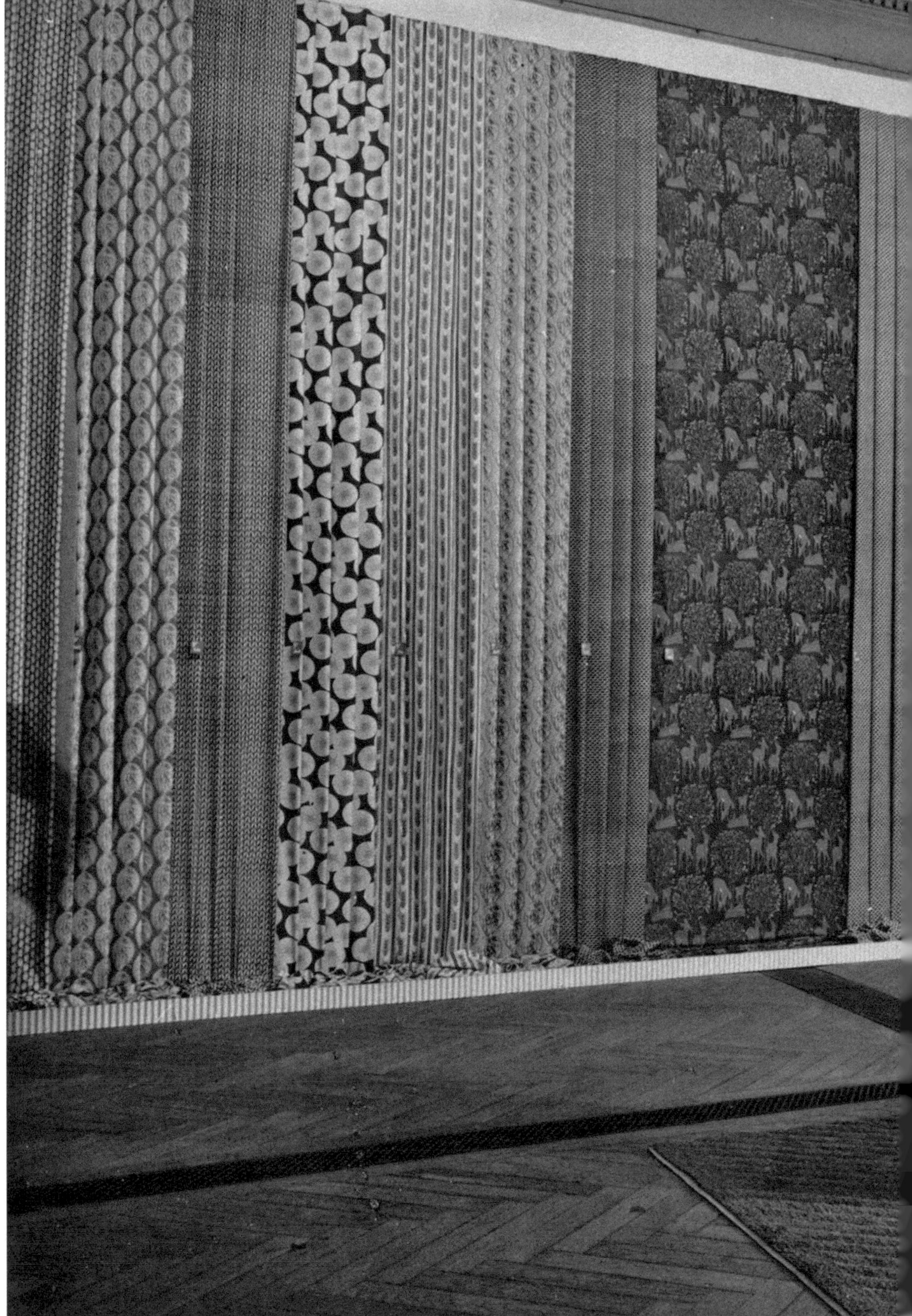

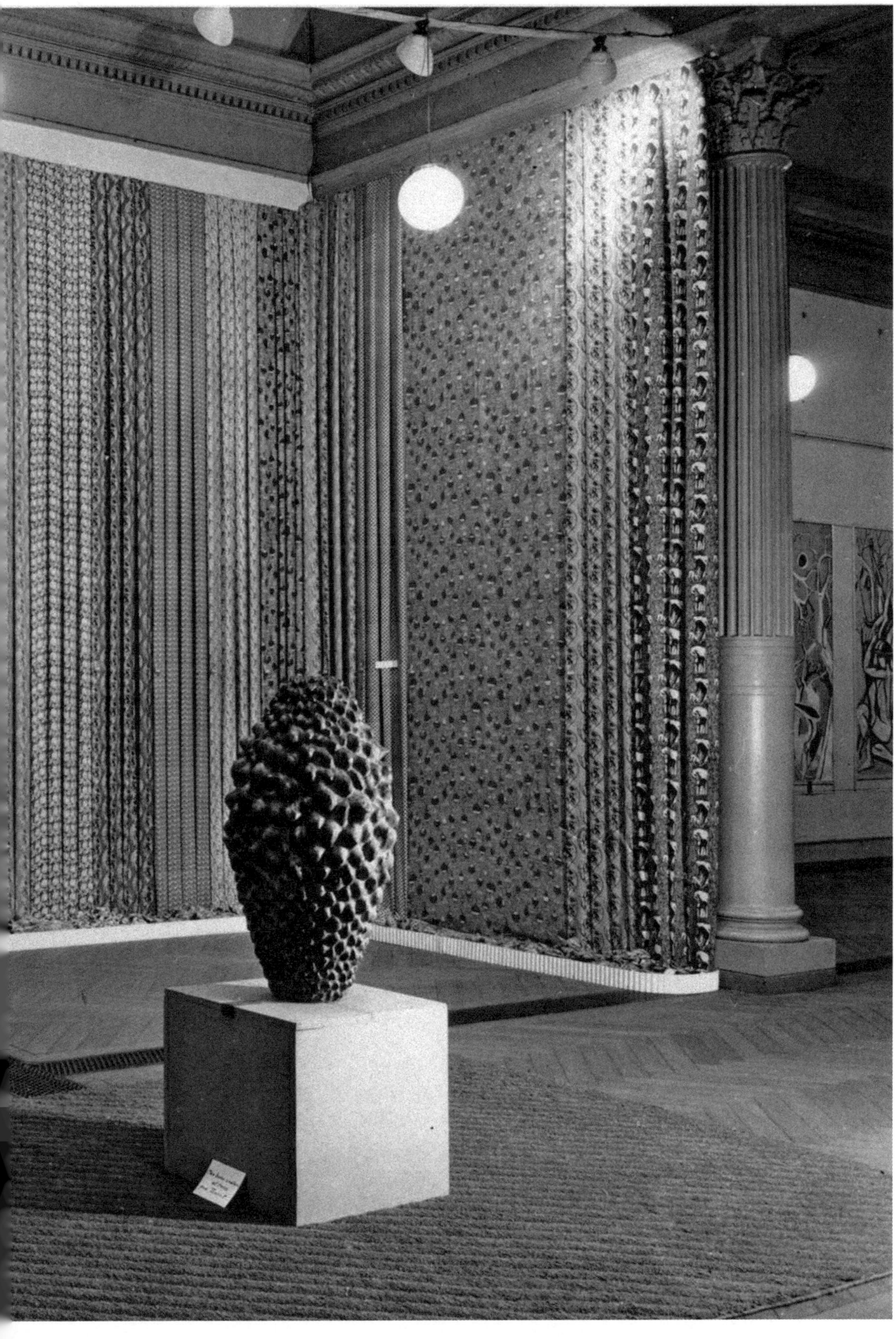

Previous spread
Axel Salto exhibition
Charlottenborg, 1949
Copenhagen
CLAY/The Royal Copenhagen Collection

Axel Salto
Excerpts

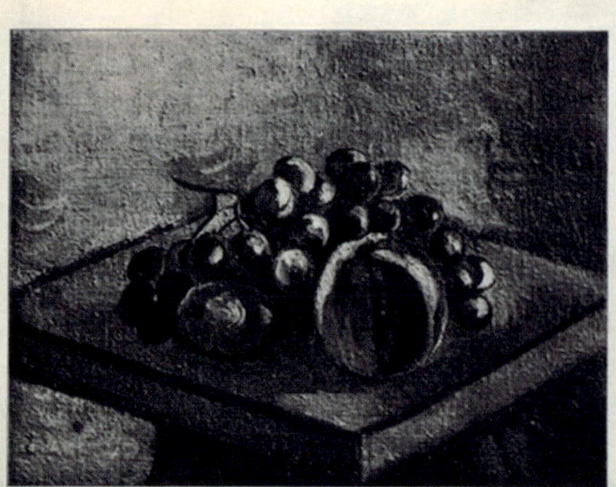

OPTEGNELSER FRA EN REJSE I ITALIEN

AF AXEL SALTO

FRA det gustent tynde Tyskland, hvor Togene trods Revolution og Borgerkrig føres planmæssigt igennem, kom vi over Frankfurt til Basel. Efter Tyskland er Sweitz paafaldende friskmalet med gode, glade Mennesker, Hjemstedet for Mælkechokolade og ædruelige Troubekendelser; her første Gang i lange Tider saa vi igen store hvide Sølvpenge. Med Luzern begynder det rigtige Postkortsweitz: blaa Himmel og Hornkvæg, Vierwaldstädterseen i Solskin og Rigis snuklædte Kegle. Gennem St. Gotthard fog vi med en Snestorm ned i Italien, hvor Posletten som et blomstret Tæppe strækker sig under Piletræer og hængende Vinhaver. I Toscana bliver Landskabet bjergfuldt; vi gør første Gang Ophold i *Firenze* og her bliver Lundstrøm syg. Foden, der hele Tiden har smertet, faar en Betændelse; han maa lade den operere og holde Sengen. Dette Uheld foreger paa en naturlig Maade hans Had til Italien. Naar om Natten Firenzes krydrede Duft af Pin og Blomster fylder Værelset og de unge Mænd

nede paa Gaden spiller Serenader og leger som Gedekid, ligger Lundstrøm under Forhandeler og venter paa Helbredelse for at komme ned og slaa ihjel. Italienerne er iøvrigt ogsaa narngtige Mennesker. De elsker Katte, Elskov og Iskager og som alle farvede smasker de. Mændene er parfumerede Løpse med brogede Veste, Armbaand og Kastratstemmer. Jeg har mens jeg malede i Rom talt paa een Gang 19 Tenorer i det samme Hus, alle sang *Cavalleria* med kælen Skabagtighed.

Visne Ejendommeligheder, som virker uvant paa nordiske Tilhørere, synes at udmærke italiensk Opera. I Rom overværede vi en Opførelse af Tosca. Hvergang Kunstmaleren kom til et Bravursted glemte han Rollens Fordring til Agtren, stillede sig op frontalt mod Publikum, let skrævende og med bøjede Knæ. I denne Stilling, der vel befordrer Toendannelsen, sang han sit Nummer, tog Bifald og gav paa staaende Fod Dacapo mens Stykket udenom gik helt i Staa. Ved en anden Lejlighed døde

Records From a Journey to Italy

*Optegnelser fra
en rejse til Italien*
Essay in *Klingen*, 1920, 3. yr. no 10/11/12
Private collection

Axel Salto was the founder of the magazine *Klingen*, which he self-financed and published in 1917–20 and edited in collaboration with the art critic Poul Uttenreitter and architect Poul Henningsen, among others. The purpose of the magazine was to promote knowledge of graphic art and new trends in the art world, in addition to its function as a voice for modernism.

Records From a
Journey to Italy
(1920)

Excerpt

"During our stay in Pompeii we climbed Mount Vesuvius. [...]
As we neared the summit the air got cooler. The view from up
there is stunning; one can see, as from an aeroplane, down to
the bottom of the green gulf where clouds come and go. Woods
and towns lie scattered in the sunshine, and among them the
solidified lava flows appear as black lines. At the very top the view
is obscured by a veil of mist that always hovers over the peak;
it is cold up there, and the noxious sulphur gases suffocating.
From the rim we descended some way into the crater, a rather
precarious walk, as the pumice stone slips and slides downwards,
making the climb back up difficult. The actual crater bottom is a
viscous, moving mass, its metallic colours flickering uncannily.
Steam rises up through the magma with a fizzing sound like
simmering porridge. Small cone-shaped vents poke through
the lava lake, expelling stones and fire with a thunderous roar.
Here is the entrance to hell itself; we drank a bottle of Lacryma
to lift the mood. Our descent was quick and careless, with many
visits to the taverns along the way. We swerved expertly into
Torre Annunziata and shook off the memory of the volcano's
cold and poisonous breath."

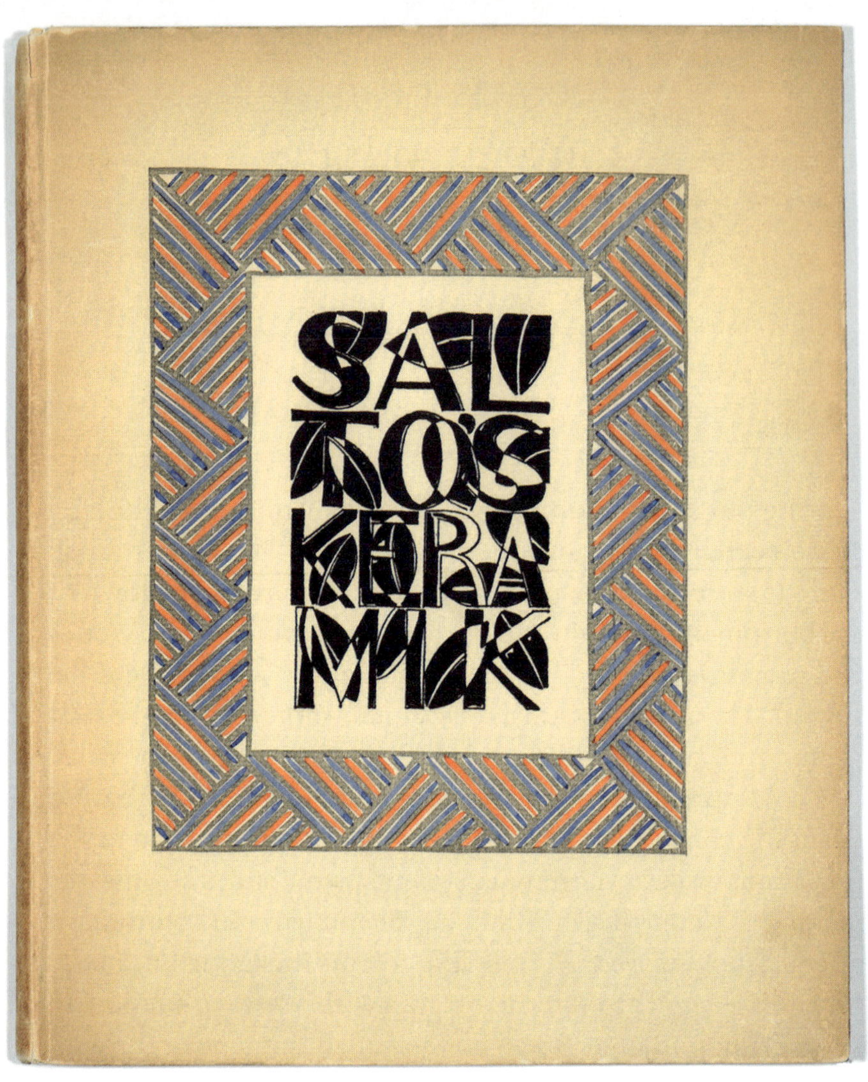

Salto's Ceramics

Salto's Keramik
1930, Copenhagen
Det Berlingske Bogtrykkeri, 74 p.
CLAY / The Royal Copenhagen Collection

This book was published after Salto's period in ceramist Carl Halier's studio in Copenhagen. With the book, Salto enters the world of ceramics as an artist with full intent. He presents his first works of stoneware and pieces in both fluted and budding styles, all derived from the patterns and structures of nature. The book comes in an experimental design with photos and illustrations running out towards the edge of the page.

Salto's Ceramics
(1930)

Excerpts

"In May 1929 I began my stoneware production in cooperation with ceramist Carl Halier. Halier was born on May 1st 1873 in the old potters' town of Ziesar in Saxony where he learned his craft. After working at the earthenware factory in Hamburg, Halier moved to Denmark in 1898 to work for G. Brack in Roskilde. In 1913 he found employment at The Royal Copenhagen Porcelain Manufactory in the stoneware department where he has worked ever since, for a time with the late Patrick Nordstrøm. In July 1926, Halier built his own kiln at Frederiksberg Bredegade, where in the evenings he fires his own ceramic pieces.

It is a long process before the finished piece of ceramic stands on its base. The clay must be moistened, dried, kneaded – and beaten, to expel the air. Halier kneads his clay the old-fashioned way, with his bare feet, like a baker's apprentice – and then places it on the wheel. Once dried, the shaped piece is ready for the kiln. Stoneware is fired twice, first at 900 degrees in the so-called biscuit firing, making it sufficiently hard to receive the wet glaze. It is then glazed and fired at 1300 degrees in the final glost firing. The firing process is controlled through two pipes, one on each side, leading from the outside into the heart of the kiln. The openings of these pipes are covered with mica due to the outgoing heat. Right by the second opening inside the kiln are three cones, each melting individually at 1260 degrees, 1280 degrees and 1300 degrees. When the 1260-degree cone collapses, one knows that the firing is soon complete. With the 1280-degree cone down too, and the 1300-degree one beginning to wobble, it is time to stop feeding the fire and close the kiln, which is then

"

left to cool down for a couple of days. And now! The long-awaited moment has come, the potter's romance, when the stoneware is brought out, scorching hot, creaking beneath the cooling glaze. The excitement, joy and disappointment of this moment are all worth the two months of preparatory work: right there are a hundred ceramic pieces!"

[...]

"What is the starting point for an artist when creating a piece of stoneware? What are his goals, and what can he achieve? To answer these questions I shall quote the ceramists Niels Hansen Jacobsen and Carl Halier, as I roughly recall their words. I consider a piece of stoneware to be good, says Hansen Jacobsen, when in its essence it resembles lava, a bit of the Earth's prime matter, having broken loose during an eruption. His ceramic pieces emerge contorted and colourful from the repeated firings. They have sacrificed all formal structure but gained a pure glow, a wide spectrum of shimmering stuff, genuine splinters from the volcano's furnace. In Halier's view a piece of stoneware is perfect when it looks and feels like a stone having been rounded by the surf. Here too, there is correspondence between words and actions, one only has to pick up one of his bright yellow glazed pieces to feel its cool smoothness."

[...]

"If I were to explain what I strive for in my own ceramics, it could be described as follows: I take as a starting point a stalk, a leaf, a piece of fruit, a fossil, or ivy climbing a tree trunk; I work these motifs, or rather the motion in them, into the ceramic piece, so that they, without imposing themselves as imitations of nature, imperceptibly rest in the ceramic and thus elicit, through the memory of something once seen, a pleasant emotional response in the beholder."

[...]

"It is more important for an artist to create in the spirit of nature than to imitate its outward appearance. In art, as in everything, it is the coherence, the larger vision that counts. Ornamentation must be experienced, and not rest unmediated on lotus or papyrus."

[...]

"In the nature that surrounds us and rejuvenates the mind, the artist finds his finest inspirations, so much dearer to him because they stem from the fresh experience of the moment. It is a settling of accounts between the ceramist and the beautifully fluted seashell on the beach. The joy of finding this rare object obliges him to give back this find in the shape of a bowl. There can be no greater satisfaction than to make a beautiful moment eternal; then one senses a likely coherence between things and takes delight in life."

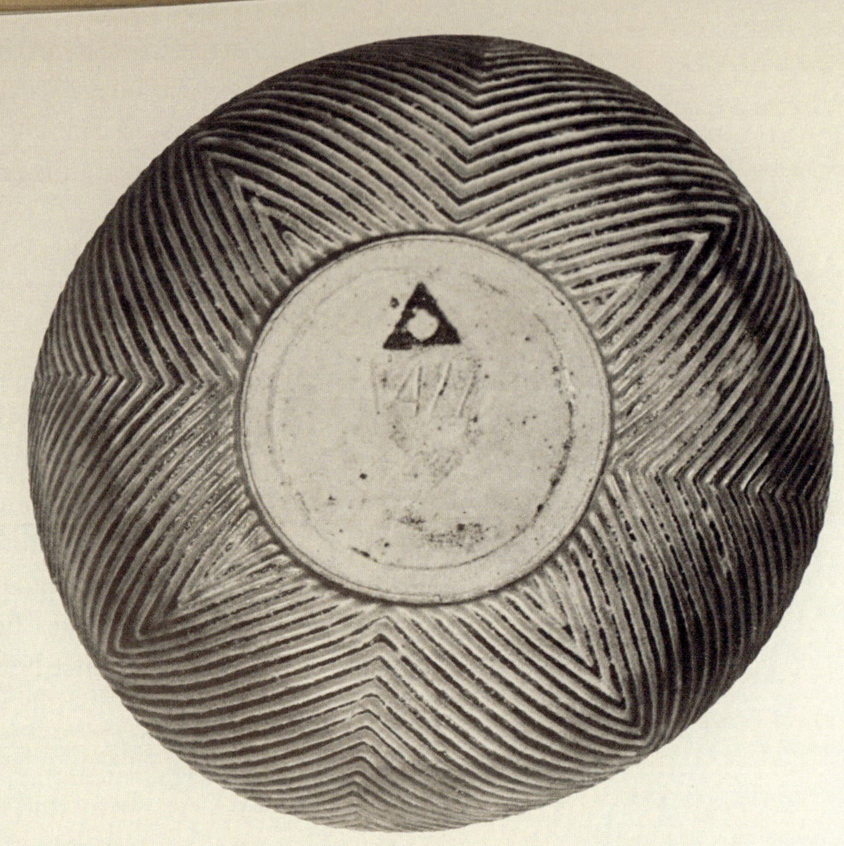

Fig. 7

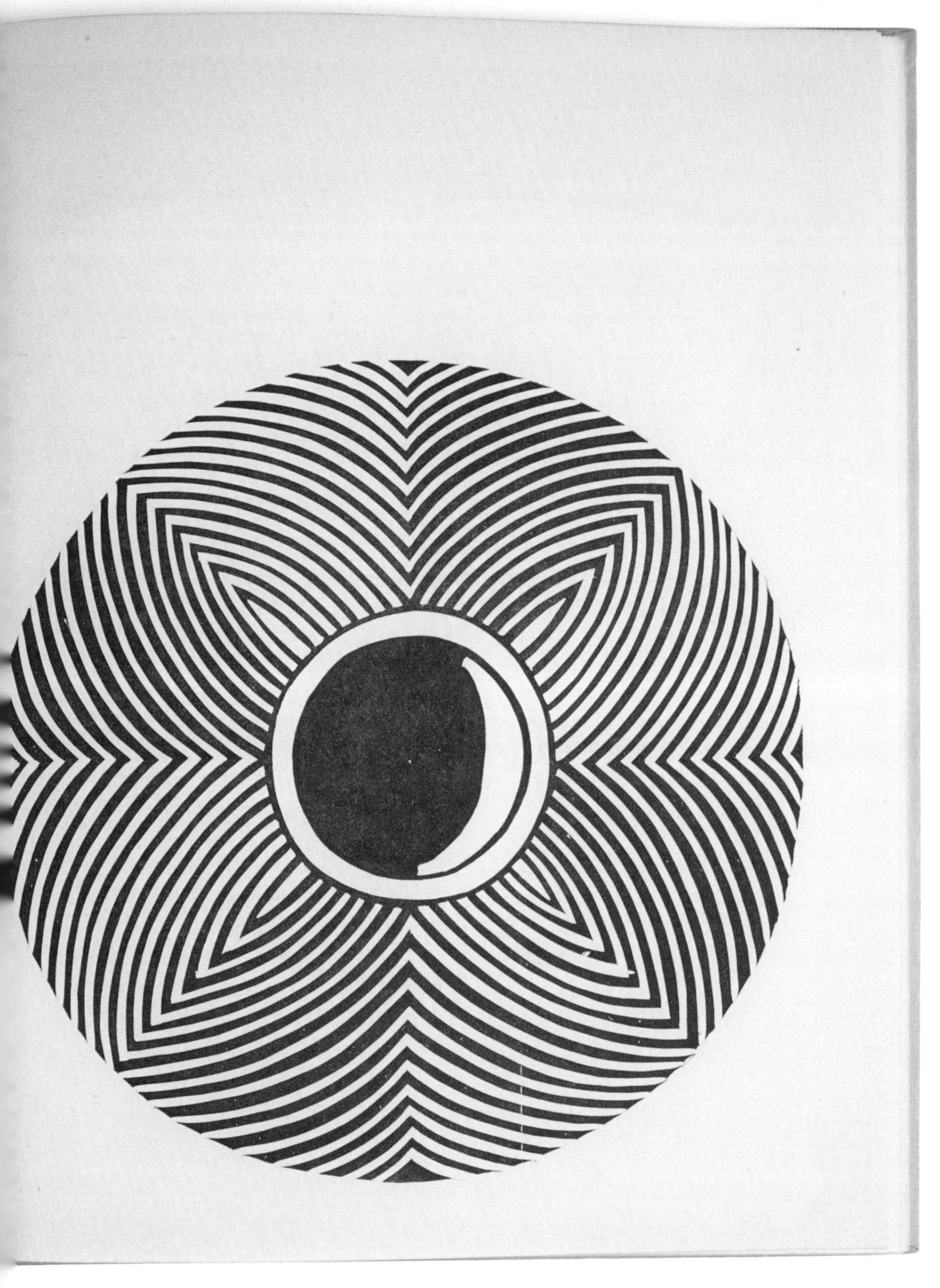

Spread from
Salto's Keramik, 1930

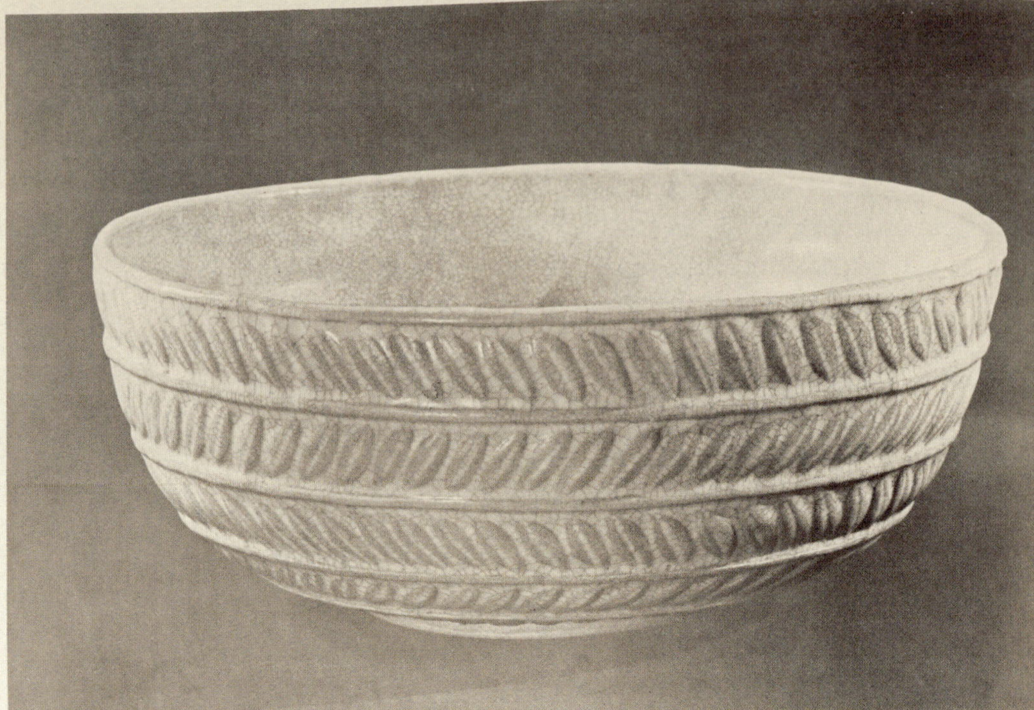

Fig. 9

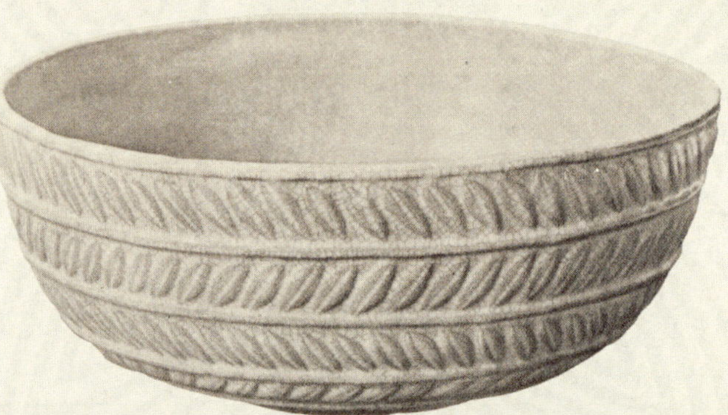

Fig. 10

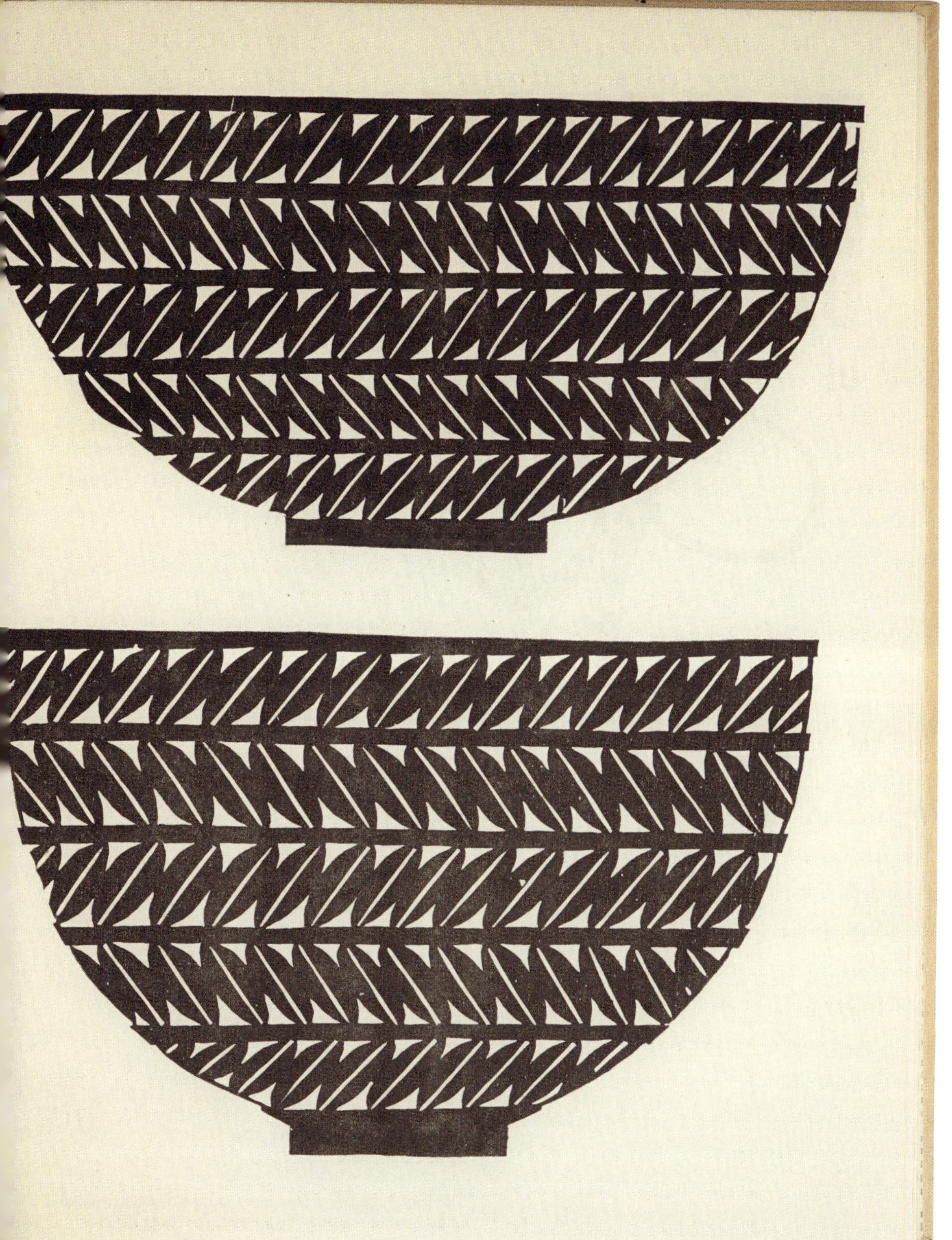

Spread from
Salto's Keramik, 1930

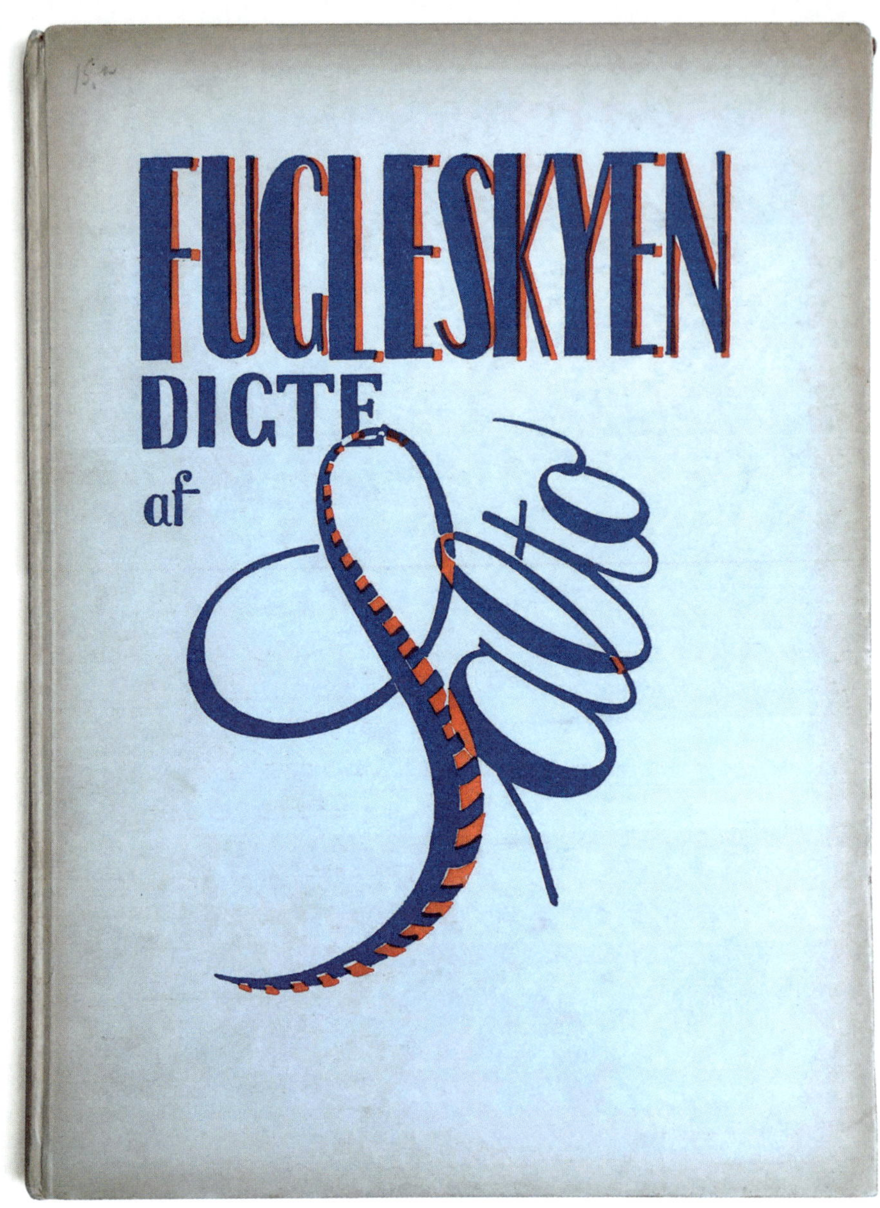

To a Bowl

Til en Skaal
Poem in *Fugleskyen*
1935, Copenhagen
Det Berlingske Bogtrykkeri, 40 p.
Private collection

The book *Fugleskyen (The Bird Cloud)* is made up of poems
and illustrations and is the first of Salto's publications
in which he strives for a symbiosis between typography
and content. The long poem *Fugleskyen* approaches the
rhythms of night and day, and of life, by way of a stream of
natural sensations, emotions and references to mythology.
Reflecting later on his work in the book *The Sprouting Style*
(1949), Salto describes *Fugleskyen* as 'the quivering of the
sprouting style transposed into words'.

To a Bowl
(1935)

Onto your side I plant
seed by seed, those round, plump, firm, smooth ones
I found on the forest floor.
In ceramic repose seed next to seed become stone,
and balmy blows the wind again
onto the little dour men.
There they dream a stone's
heavy dreams, yearning, close like
swallows into the earthly twilight.
Contemplative eyes follow the
tide as it rises, falls,
rises again and ebbs away on the Shore of the Hour,
while with split sides the abandoned
brothers moulder under the June Moon.

See in the starry night a
fire script displaying its oracular speech,
sentences aflame, blazing
night loathing from the kiln's coal mouth –
the distant voice is heard clearly –
uttering strange knowledge
about a relative long gone
who on all vessels sowed seeds
and with ingenuity burned
a silent and gruff mien
onto the acorn saved:

"The acorn, which the widely travelled
  Greek used as his drinking cup,
shall be dug out by a late Odysseus
from this room's
mythical kitchen midden."

Time flies, good bowl, like shabby old
clothes these bright days fall from me,
soon I am quite naked.
You are still on your shelf,
silently staring at the centuries turning
in circular motion around your hard curvature.
You would think, vessel, though always
the position is retained. Eternal peace, League of
Nations, not for a second do you lose your composure.
The moon caught in a net, navigated
the star, you are none the wiser and happy,
standing in silence, looking out.
But one thing you remember, in your
clay body the stone heart gently moves:
me you remember, who once
placed you on the shelf.

AXEL SALTO

FUGLESKYEN

DIGTE OG RADERINGER

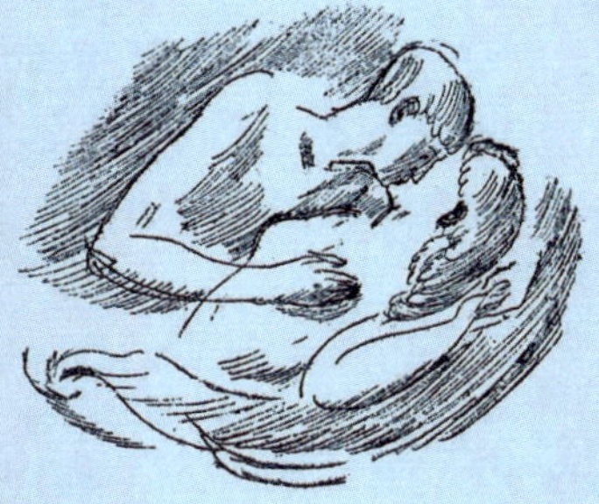

KØBENHAVN
DET BERLINGSKE BOGTRYKKERI
1935

Spread from
Fugleskyen, 1935

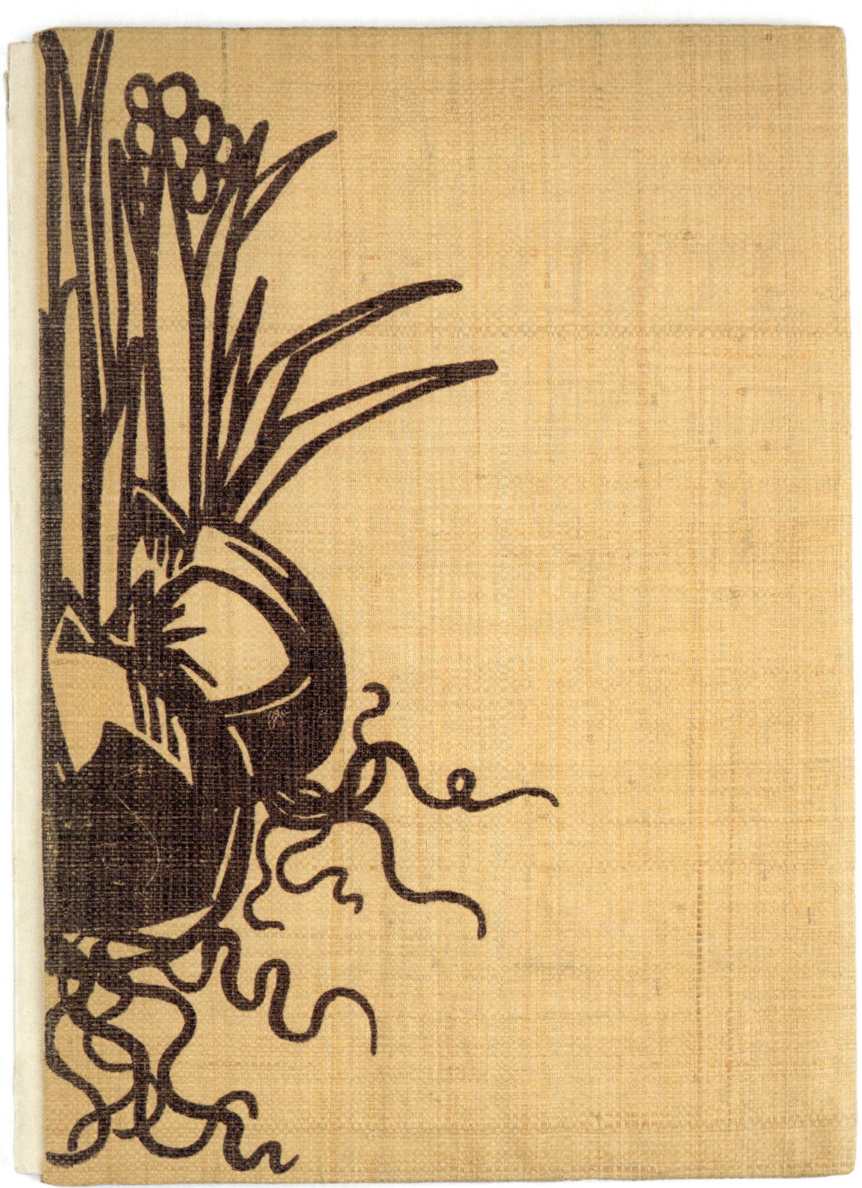

The Burning Now

Det brændende Nu
1938, Copenhagen
Grafisk Cirkel, 16 p.
Private collection

Salto produced this concise publication for foreman Aage Wantzin of the newly founded Grafisk Cirkel, a small group of experimental typographers. The book was issued in just 25 copies and bound in bast, with Salto's print of sprouting bulbs drawn all the way to the edge of the panel. The book elaborates upon Salto's concept 'the burning now' in both words and woodcuts.

The Burning Now
(1938)

Excerpts

"There is a great deal of discussion about the social function of art; it is the refrain of the moment, history may smile at it. It is therefore tempting to point out something which does not bear the imprimatur of fashion: to achieve personal fulfilment, recognise and exploit those peculiarities in the realm of one's power is precisely the artist's nature and his obligation, indeed his sole possibility of putting a penny and not a trouser button in the Purse of Ideas: art is irrational, a reserve of mental strength in those who truly embrace life. One man finds relief in barrows, another loves water jugs and deer, a third is passionate about bicycles and free love. One should not interfere with a man and his inspiration: only the warmth and ability one gives to things have validity; in a hundred years, however, all will be forgotten. What one seeks in a work of art, that which profoundly moves one, is the mind, the human mind must be concealed in the images. It is a question of filling one's matter with spirit."

[...]

"I have discovered the art of photography, high-speed photography and moving images of flowers unfolding, legumes releasing their seeds, that kind of thing. I believe it is possible to create surprising visual art from these photographic tricks."

[...]

"I am working on a painting of cups falling off a tray. The picture is a representation of *The Burning Now*, the tense, uneasy yet strangely enchanted second between when the cups start to slide and then smash as they hit the ground. The falling, turning cups hover for a short moment in mid-air, like a bush that grows from the bottom cup that has already splintered upon contact with the floor, but whose shards still hang upright in the air, in reaction to the moment of the blasting. This further outward movement of the shards serves to augment the momentary life, which is the whole point of the painting. A motif like this is directly inspired by photographs taken using ultra-short exposure time. In these, for example, one sees a fired rifle bullet traversing a sheet of glass or a cup of hot chocolate, smashing it and displaying its liquid content as a solid mass amidst the already broken shards clinging to the chocolate, the contours of the cup still manifest. Aside from the nerve-wracking moment prior to the devastation, which seems strangely thrilling to modern man who, from driving cars, is familiar with the sweet danger of a split second, there appear in these concentrated motifs hitherto-undreamt-of figures and movements that form an ornamentation which may contribute to an understanding of the nature of things. In this context I would just like to mention a photograph of a running tap, shot at 1/50,000 of a second, with the water jet wriggling like a worm out of the spout; now, this is what water looks like in reality.

The eruptive woodcut with its emerging bulbs was inspired by moving images of flower buds unfolding or a chrysalis splitting open and the butterfly escaping. These films, where a movement or an act that normally may take several days unfolds on the screen in the course of a few minutes, can truly teach us something. Here, the natural world reveals itself, and it dawns upon us in ways large and small, how expedient and adapted to its function everything is, and through this one may learn something about oneself. The woodcut with the bulbs shows these at the exact moment when they sprout from the ground, reaching for the light.

Taking place over several days, the plant's sprouting process is concentrated in the moment of breaking through. The bulbs are sucked up through the roots as they twist and turn in anticipation – their blind fumbling around can be witnessed too on these films; everything rises and erupts like a volcano.

You cannot ask for a simpler, more clear presentation of the wonders of plant growth, of cause and effect. Motifs like this and several others are the gift of technology for artists. If the artist knows how to use this gift with imagination, he may one day inspire a scientific mindset; thus humans advance in the best possible way, hand in hand.

A third woodcut represents Actaeon who turns into a deer, his transformation happening at the very moment of viewing, "neither rain nor sun, but the weather changing". These transformations have always fascinated me, I have drawn and painted them since I read Ovid at school. The motifs are dramatic in themselves; by making the transformation happen as one views the picture this dramatic life is multiplied enormously. It is not that Actaeon runs away as a human and comes back as a deer, but that the wonder happens in its very horror there and then, like a machine with its cogs and wheels turning. The feet are wrapped up in hard hooves and Actaeon buckles down on his four animal legs. The terrible reduction of the human form and human mind tears through the poor fellow, his tortured brain seeks in vain to hold on to the disintegrating human way of thinking for another moment yet, and then he is all animal, and a howl roars from his throat. This is drama, not just an external plot, a fable, but an internal development, recreating the external form, making everything more fluid, blurring the contours, as a hand in just a second turns into a hoof."

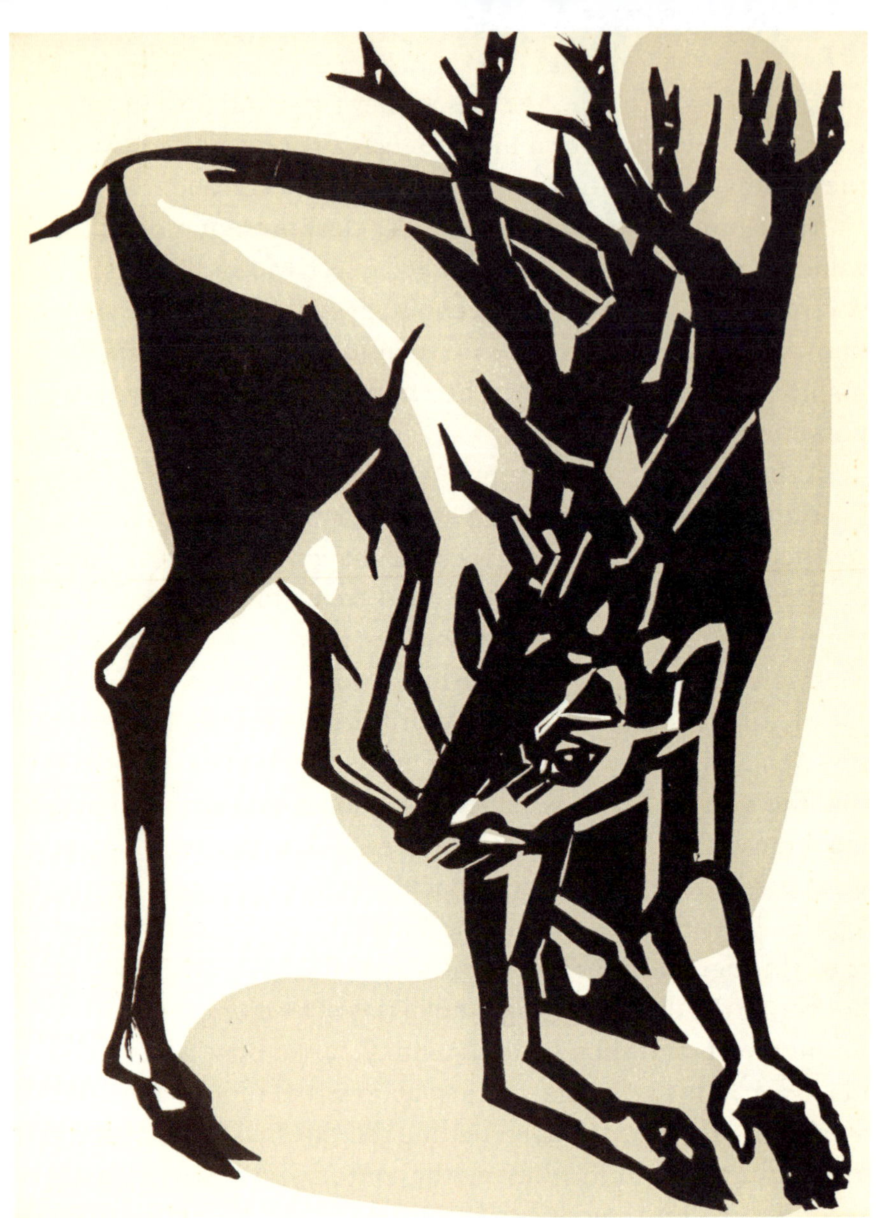

Left and right
Illustrations from
Det brændende Nu, 1938

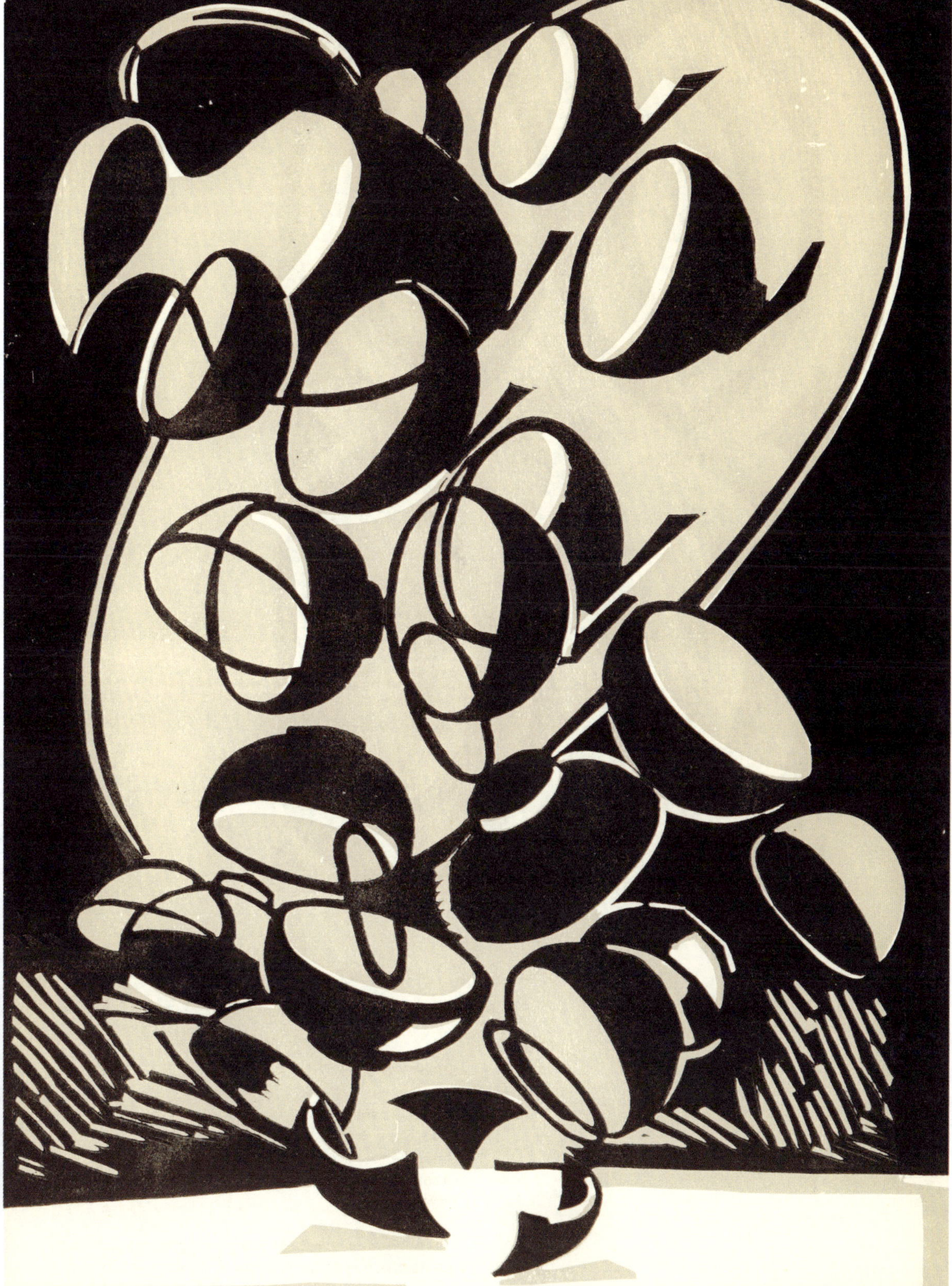

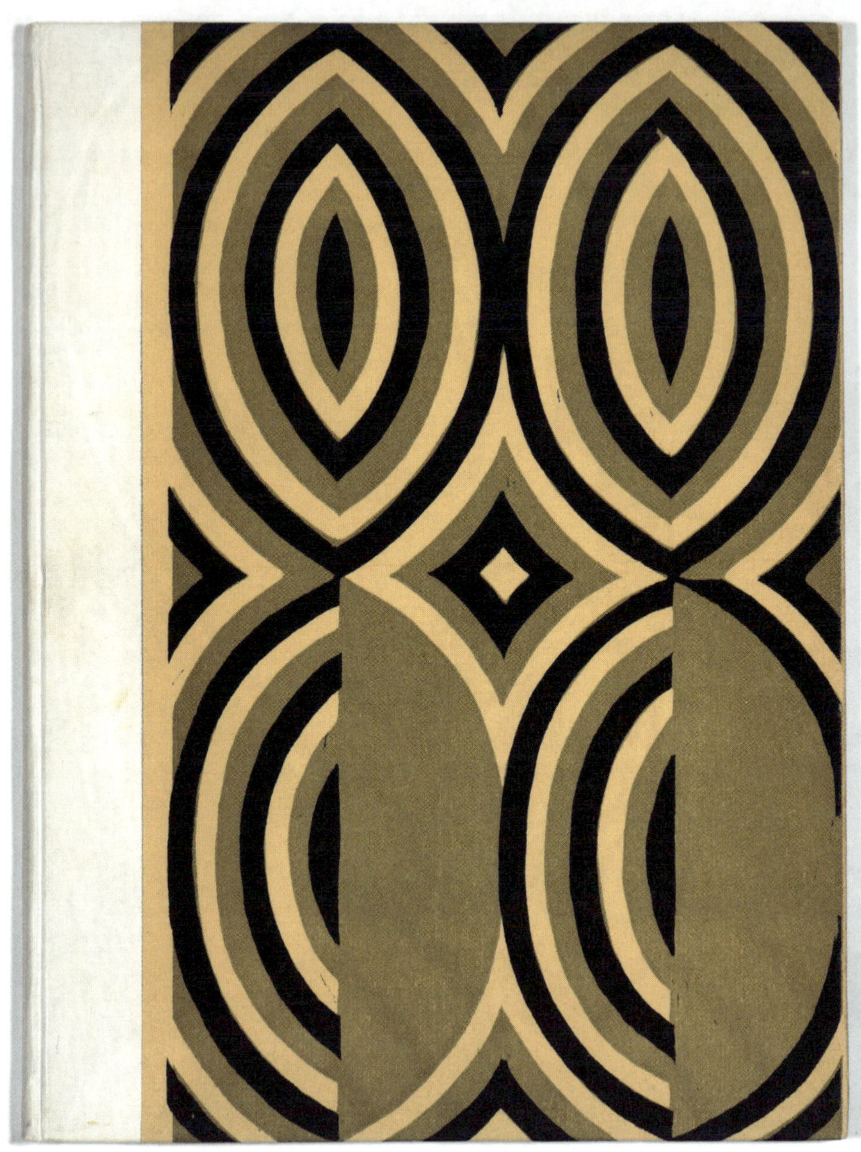

Salto's Woodcuts

Salto's Træsnit
1940, Copenhagen
Det Hoffenbergske
Etablissement, 48 p.
Private collection

This book cover reveals Salto's growing interest in investigating dynamic patterns on paper. Salto's text in the book is broken down into three parts: the first on the history of the woodcut, the second on its techniques, and the third a reflection on his motifs and artistic process. At the back there is an essay on Salto's woodcuts written by his good friend, the poet Paul la Cour.

Salto's Woodcuts
(1940)

Excerpt

"The concept of 'metamorphosis' has intrigued me right from my schooldays when they sneaked into my consciousness via lovely Ovidian poems that for me became more than just grotesque fables for children. In them I see symbols of the variability of life, the changing seasons, germination, growth and death. First and foremost they show the fate behind all things, the fate assigning everyone their lot, not blindly but exactly what he, she, they deserve, be it reward or punishment in a fantastic prolongation of the narrative. The licentious turns into a pig, the hunted virgin into a tree, and the crier becomes free-flowing like a spring. Does one not, by the way, sense both humour and irritation among the mighty gods? I shall not elaborate further on this delightful theme, the importance of poetic natural mysticism resides, for the artist of today, in the fundamental observations of the material: no living thing is complete in itself, everything is in motion, rising or falling. It is the Actaeon myth most of all that has stirred my imagination. May I say a few words about this? Actaeon spies on the bathing Diana and, as punishment, is turned into a deer and torn apart by his own dogs. Actaeon becomes a stag, the primal instinct releases an avalanche in him, I imagine the change having occurred quickly and having many pictorial aspects: a human mind becomes animalistic, a wretched act, accomplished on the spot, as the will of the goddess has the power and suddenness of lightning. The destruction of the soul is a high-ranking motif, psychologically the reduction of human to animal is interesting, of almost pathological complexity. As for the first aspect of the motif, it is in the power of visual art to give it full expression. The deer-like crescendo, the waning humanness is, for the colourist, a lovely theme. More important though are the expressionistic values of the motif: the antlers breaking through the perplexed forehead, like a fast-growing palm tree, hands and feet, encased now in sharp cloven hooves, and the back, arching, becoming curved. This play of forms in transition within the outline of the double-animal, at once agitated and frozen as a statue, is an immensely rich source of inspiration."

Axel Salto at work
1944
Royal Danish Library

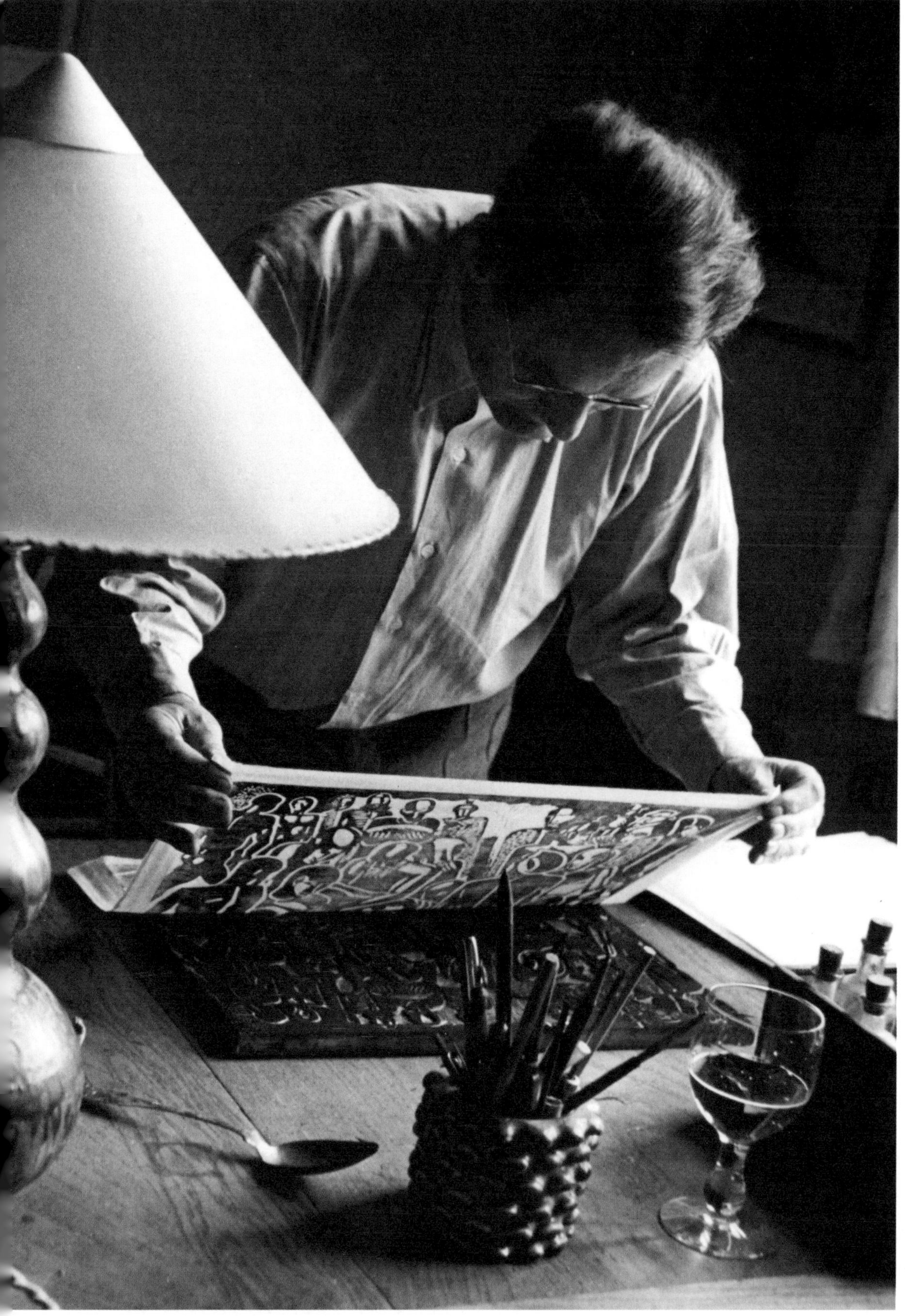

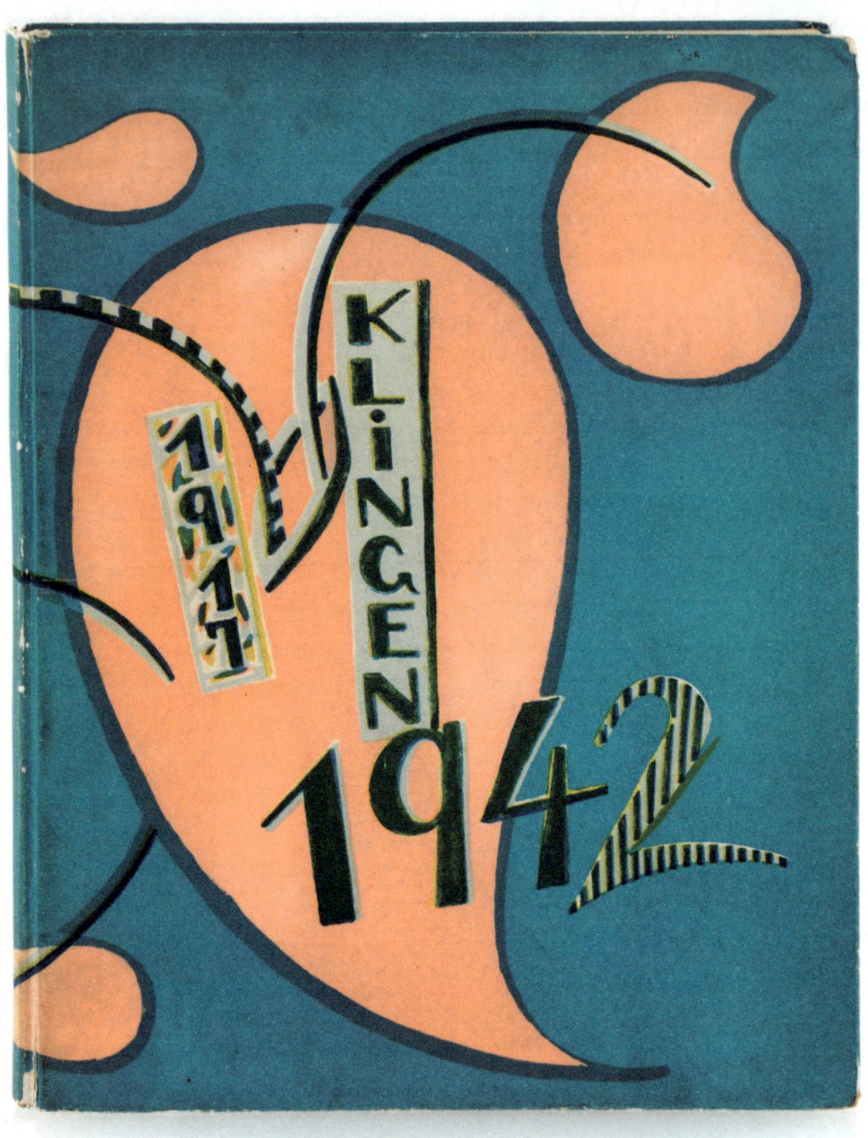

The Sprouting Style

Den spirende Stil
in *Klingen*
1942, Copenhagen
Fischers Forlag
Private collection

This article originates from a special edition of *Klingen* published in 1942 for the 25th anniversary of the magazine's founding. In the essay, Salto introduces the concept of 'the sprouting style', which marks a significant new expressive direction for his ceramics. The book is bound in one of Salto's lithographs, which is based on an abstraction of the motif *The Living Stone*.

The Sprouting Style
(1942)

If you ask me why I continually write about myself, explaining things which probably, without lecturing, are very easy to understand, I would answer: because I enjoy it. I quite simply take great pleasure in bringing words together to form sentences, just like others enjoy playing dice or going to amusement parks. And, if one must write about something, it seems natural to write about oneself, simply because it is the only thing one really knows anything about. It is amusing, and so all is well. "In art no seriousness can assert itself, here joy is the safest guide." Yesterday at the factory, a ceramist said to me, displeased: "But you are just playing!" Yes, there we have it! That is exactly what I was doing, letting the clay slip through my fingers, work and play had merged, happiness in a nutshell. Feeling uplifted, I got the idea of sticking long horns onto the vases, my resoluteness making me somewhat alarmed and pleased at the same time. However, I knew deep down that something had happened that day.

There is among the Salto Stoneware a category which I, boasting a little, call 'the sprouting style'. As these pieces in their concept differ quite significantly from the other ornamental characters, I would like to talk a little about them. The fluted and the budding modes are directly modelled on nature's diverse small, subtle details, on the recollection of the chestnut's spiky shell, of the acorn, eucalyptus, beechnut, pineapple and seashell's fluted surface, whose principle is fused as a non-naturalistic but recognisable function into the ceramic here, I feel solidarity with Bernard Palissy in my joy over these natural elements, but employ them in a different way. Rather, 'the sprouting style' does not rest on isolated observations of fruit and conches. It delineates a movement, growth. It is thus the sprouting branch that becomes this style's naturalistic model, the 'miracle of growth', this pressure from within, something pushing itself forward, wanting to get out. In this way I have made vases that grow on the spot, as it were, breaking it, and this mobility in the sides of the vase makes the glaze come alive as well, as it is forced to either condense or avoid the spikes. This is why I consciously use only stoneware for these motifs.

Thus spring seems to be sprouting from the vase, life is forcing its way through, but when should we stop the growth? In the garden, twigs and leaves unfold from the branch, and yes, we create in the spirit of nature while the vase obeys its own law. So let us follow the irrepressible spring as far as possible. Let the sprouting power strike out in all directions; we venture as far as we dare, to precisely where the balance between the core of the vase and the horns of power is not upset, so that it all feels physically natural. It demands a subtle perception in the fingertips, as it is exactly the last little "further out" that determines the artwork's decisive boldness. It is a matter of millimetres. Is the material over-stretched in these sprouting vases? Probably not, although they are brittle and may perhaps not pass into eternity. They find themselves in dangerous situations at times, but then so do little fragile porcelain figurines during their neat life, and yet in what other material would one want them? The worse moment has got to be when the vase is taken out of the kiln, but then again, that is true for all life. These vases are not to be transported in a cab or turned this way and that, no, you are hardly allowed to touch them. They are to remain quietly in one place for a thousand years, being disquieting.

Although this unusual sight should, in theory, stir the beholder's attention and receptiveness, nobody seems entirely comfortable with these beak-studded and ominous vases, despite them being a quite logical continuation of the sprouting style, the "two weeks on" style. They are bordering on the downright distasteful, where in fact so much of the best work resides. They are classic, aggressive, perhaps even hysterical, yes, what would a Freudian deduct from them, I wonder? Yet they radiate a willpower which in the end will conquer the obstinate. They should not be compared to anything else, perhaps not even be considered as art. They belong to a demonic family.

I once found in my garden a spider's web hidden in the raspberry bushes, a metre-long lace sail, wafting in the raw September morning wind, heavy dew weighing it down. When the light breeze caught the web, a rainbow-coloured fire flickered across it, as though filtering the morning sun's first rays, and the spider, that withered little homunculus, came running to see if there was anything to do. This fly trap strewn with diamonds, so simply and naturally formed, so fragile and disregarded, appeared to me as perfection itself, a bold manifestation in an inconspicuous dimness of nature's extravagance. I do not recall any work of art having resonated as strongly with me, all at once. This web was a demonic thing.

What exactly provoked this panicked reaction? The general situation, probably, a heightened receptivity that lonely early morning, those very last raspberries, the net's size and construction jumping out at me, because the thick web covered in dew had somewhat become part of the permanent world, and finally, the officious spider, death itself, the point of it all. The first time I saw the stela with the *Code of Hammurabi* in the Louvre, I had the feeling of standing before a phenomenon which eluded all assessment; it almost looked like a black severed finger with its nail. This stela could not be linked to anything else known and assimilated in our world; it was utterly alone and enclosed in a mysterious aura of essential wisdom.

It had, like the spiderweb and its deadly intent, a dimension beyond the tangible. One could set much store by other artefacts, often very much indeed, and I never withhold my admiration from something worthy of it. But in comparison with Hammurabi's basalt stela everything else seemed strangely unimportant. It was the strongest, most penetrating object one could imagine; an atmosphere of the deep and remote emanated from it. By virtue of its message and its wild calm, of those thoughts having gone towards it and those eyes having rested upon it, of the supreme will of the ruler speaking through it, it was demonic; and it was wonderful because it was demonic, and not the other way around.

I am entertaining these vague immeasurable concepts in order to come up with some kind of explanation of the inexplicable; not in order to elbow my way towards an interesting attitude, but to give a flickering and uncertain outline of a feeling of some deep and undefinable coherence which the uniformity of my reactions suggest. An uncertain testimony, a placeless and timeless unrest, so to speak. When one is weeping, it may be with both sorrow and joy, and when I am strongly moved by essentially different things and in very different settings, it does not necessarily mean that I brush up against the riddle of life every time, but it may be worth noting that when I become greatly excited in this way, my mind unleashes the same airy notion which, always with the same accuracy, traverses the same path, stopping at the same points; every time I remind myself that I have had a similar experience before, like having lived the same moment before – and then the train of thought disappears completely, without a trace it withdraws into itself like the bird in a cuckoo clock. After all it is the concept of universal connection that we are all tracing in everything we do. For the conclusive determination of phenomena, science is yet to give us a finer instrument than our own instinct.

And now the vase, the preposterous manifestation from Smallegade! Here I am, seeing it as some hostile and astonishing fact. Embedded in it, undoubtedly, are both my feeling of happiness with being in tune with the creative spirit of spring and my fear of nature's ever-present fury. By God, the old hallucination is rummaging through my mind, I can feel it as I sit here. Definitely: the horned and heathen vase is possessed just like the spiderweb and the stela.

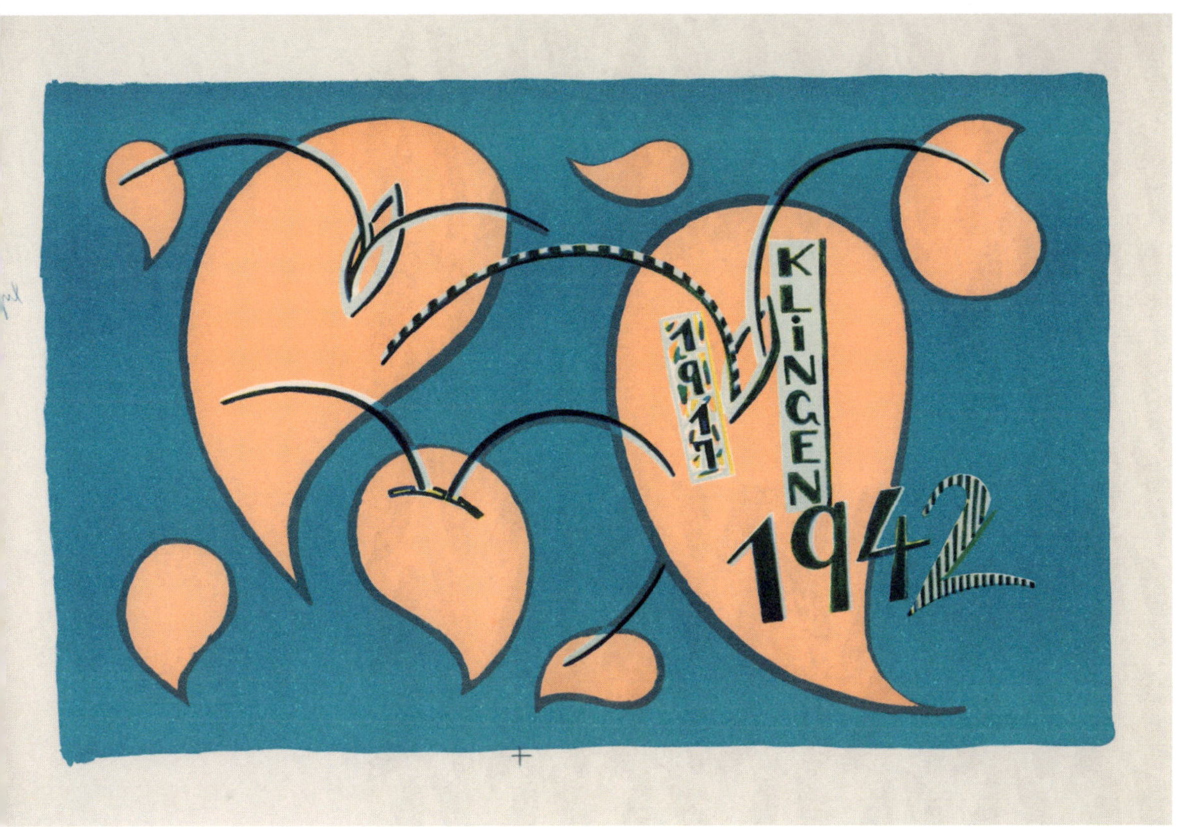

Axel Salto
Illustration for the cover of *Klingen,* 1942
Lithography, 451 × 616 mm
Statens Museum for Kunst

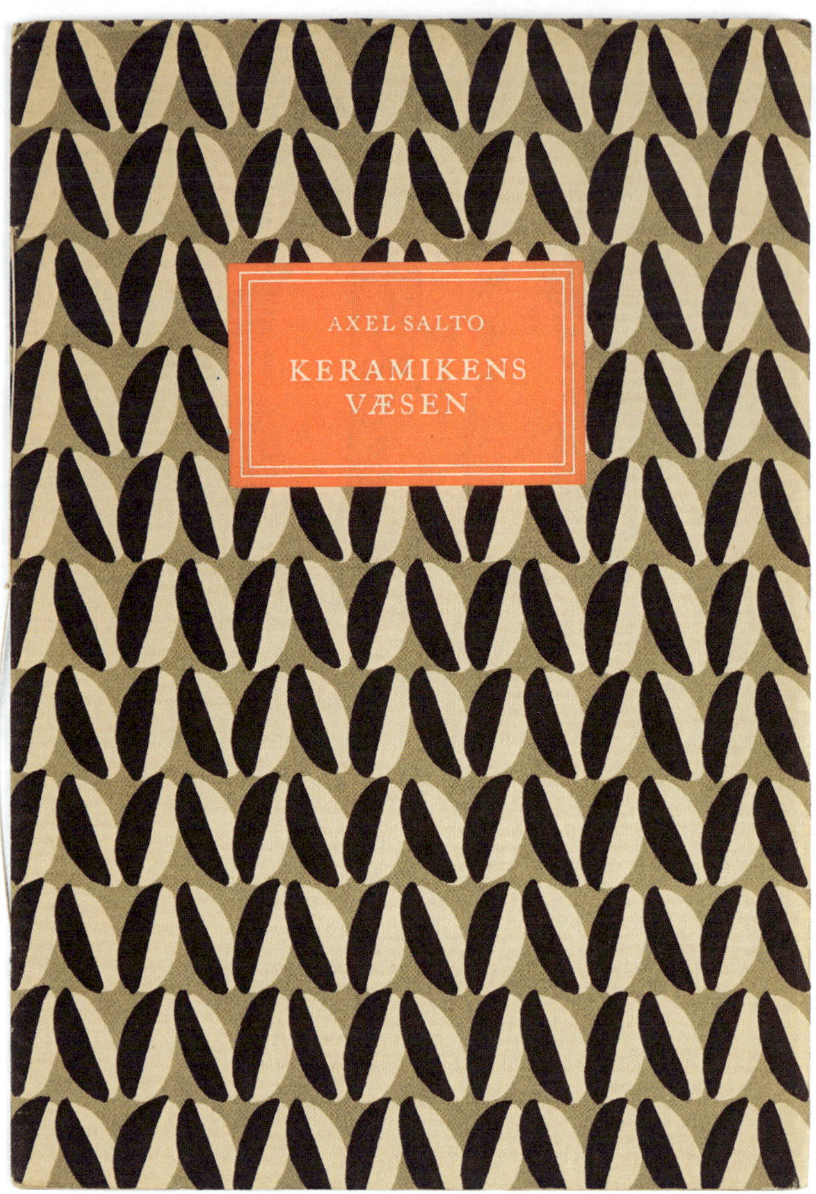

The Nature of Ceramics

Keramikens Væsen
1946, Copenhagen
Den Kongelige
Porcelainsfabrik, 12 p.
Private collection

The Royal Copenhagen Porcelain Manufactory published this short book to coincide with Salto's exhibition at Nordiska Kompaniet in Stockholm. The text summarises Salto's reflections on clay, ceramics and his three fluted, budding and sprouting styles. The cover is made from Salto's *Kornax* paper.

The Nature of Ceramics
(1946)

Excerpt

"The present collection of stoneware was produced in 1945–46 at The Royal Copenhagen Porcelain Manufactory in collaboration with the ceramist Carl Halier, chief engineer Madslund, foreman Mathiesen and other excellent colleagues. As we all step forward and bow, I would like to acknowledge my friends; the exhibition is, in the best sense of the word, a group exhibition.

Many different disciplines are mastered in the ceramic practice, they are very rarely contained within one head: wheel throwing, chemistry, a feeling for the material, kiln routine and that vague concept: artistic sensibility. For me the crucial skill is to take a free imaginative approach to the clay, to make the ceramic ornament the bearer of an idea, to become the buried matter. A number of skilled ceramists in Denmark have in recent years developed stoneware glazes of a very high and beautiful quality, both with reference to Chinese glazing and in their very own experimental design – at the Royal, Madslund's Solfatara and Mathiesen's olivine glazes – the instrument is built, now play it! The ceramist's world is wonderfully varied, and in the fired and glazed clay, thoughts can be expressed of which neither painting nor sculpture are capable, we are only at the beginning. The material must be approached with imagination, as those who aimed highest always did. The Chinese and the Persians, perhaps the most accomplished of all ceramists, were the poets of clay – they elevated the craft to art.

The Chinese, who kept a thousand kilns in a thousand cities firing for a thousand years, took the path of patience and perseverance and ended up knowing absolutely everything about

clay. They clad their ceramics in poetry, engraved an ingenious
world of symbols onto it; even the supreme spirit, Tao, took up
residence in their vases. Their approach to the work was cere-
monial, resulting in noble art.

The Persians treated the clay with reverence. The prophet
and his descendants sanctified it with their bodies in their graves.
All living matter goes into the earth, becomes earth and shall rise
again. Omar Khayyam expresses the thought in his Rubáiyát:

Yesterday at the bazaar,
I saw a potter pounding his clay,
when the clay, in its language, said to him:
"Easy now! Like you, I was once flesh and blood"

or like this:

Day and night alternated long before you and I were born,
and the sky arched over life and death.
Tread lightly, the dust on the road may well be
a woman's eye, once glowing with life.

I myself have tried:

Look at the bowl in my hand, clay of the grave.
With flame-bitten, tempered and pure forms
rose from vanity's musty blanket
the tense, tinkling sides, the young girl's breast.–
You long dead girl, entering among us,
from a thousand cheerless lost springs,
now springtime strokes your breast afresh,
you are with me again in all your warmth.
It is, for the mind, a gentle wonder of resurrection
that the girl rises in her clay, sounding like a bell.

The historic example of an an all-round ceramist, the Frenchman
Bernard Palissy in the sixteenth century, gained his proficiency
through an infinite effort, and he wanted to encompass the whole

world. In his home-built kilns he would fire his faience, thrown by himself and covered with his self-invented glazes, again and again. In the end he succeeded in depicting on a large dish "the entire earth with the river Okeanos in the middle, brimming with weird little water creatures and with soil to nourish worms and snails, butterflies and all kinds of insects". On one plate!

With the invention of the potter's wheel, the use of clay became universal and ceramics found the source of knowledge of bygone cultures; but long before, there were jars shaped by hand and with a much greater rhythmic beauty than thrown jars; then, left-handedness was able to do itself justice. The magnificent hand-shaped jars from the later Stone Age have never been surpassed. Undoubtedly the potter's wheel has destroyed the art of ceramics and run it into a craft-based sidetrack, even though the bowl is still the most obvious design from a lump of clay. I am holding it in my hand, the bowl, the only bowl which is me, myself. Smooth inside, fluted on the outside, functional as a fruit bowl and simple as a pilgrim's tool. It is a truly great thing to make a bowl, and so begins and ends ceramics.

But even though our sense of form still needs the stimulus of the bowl, over time many other usable materials have been invented, and it may now be time to focus on clay's other physical properties: one is able to improvise with it, be imaginative and solidify the imagined in the fire. Clay body and glaze fired together, concealing and accentuating each other, is a special art form with its own possibilities. With this material the Chinese created rolling clifftops and della Robbia colourful bunches of fruit whilst Palissy wrote his world of small creatures into his faience. The playful and spontaneous is the ceramist's domain, this is my Rhodes where I dance.

My motifs range from variations of flowers and fruits to sculptural landscapes, spread out on the roundness of the vase; from 'living stones' – a decorative figure, illustrating the idea that stones are alive, have organs, that stones may fall ill and die – to the sprouting vases and Actaeon's anxiety. The points of departure for the applied ornamentation are observations of natural occurrences which are melded into the ceramic, without this appearing naturalistic. A stem, a leaf, a fruit, the star pattern of a fossilised sea urchin are all motifs embedded imperceptibly in the stoneware, and through the memory of something once seen they elicit the pleasure of recognition in the beholder.

At the same time, these fluted and budding features offer the glazes various possibilities for effect as they become denser or thinner, depending on their flow across the obstacles; and now the clay body takes charge. Clay body and glaze, stoneware's masterful dialogue.

Later 'the sprouting style' developed. The fluted and budding manner draws directly upon nature's diverse details, on the memory of the chestnut's spiky shell – as opposed to its creamy white inside – on the acorn, the eucalyptus fruit and the fluted seashell. The sprouting style describes movement, *growth*. [...] It begins as something brewing on the side of the jar trembling increasingly, and then, one day in May in Smallegade, the smouldering force finally breaking out as long heathen horns.

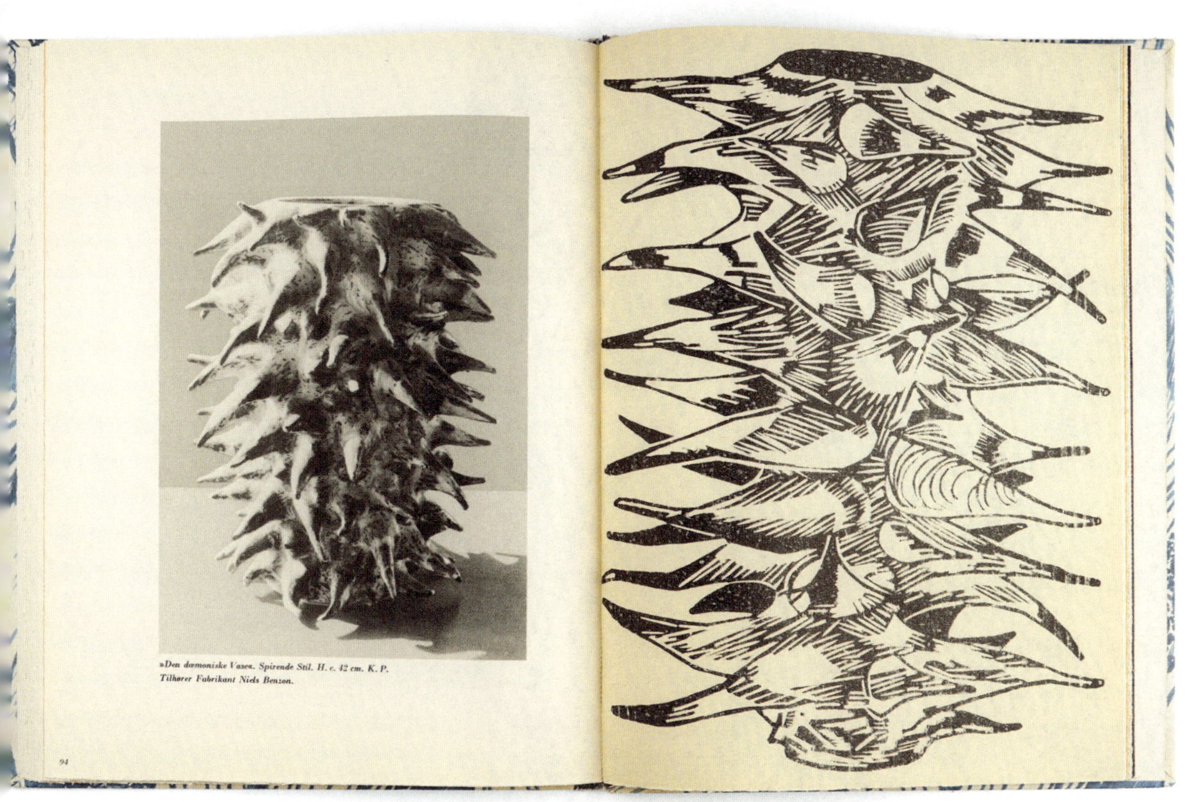

»Den dæmoniske Vase«. Spirende Stil. H. c. 42 cm. K. P.
Tilhører Fabrikant Niels Benzon.

Spread showing
The Demonic Vase
from *Den spirende Stil,* 1949 , see p. 64

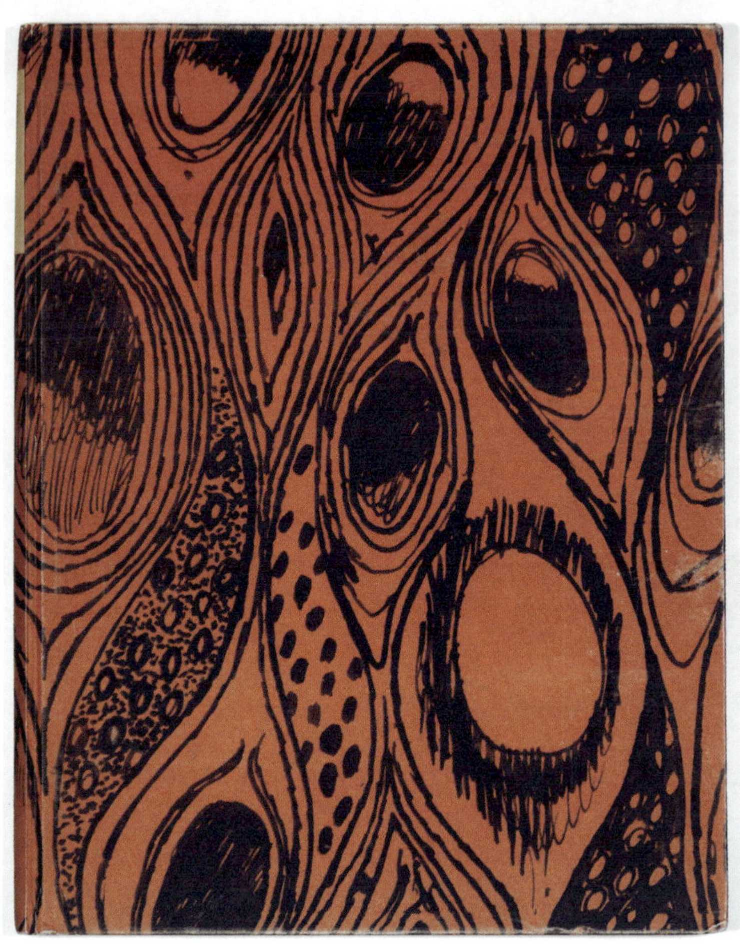

The Sprouting Style

Den spirende Stil
1949, Copenhagen
Grafisk Cirkel, 130 p.
Private collection

This book was published in two editions for Salto's 60th
birthday and the 15th anniversary of Grafisk Cirkel.
Salto reflects on his inspirations, motifs, materials and
collaborators, and the book functions as a retrospective,
particularly of his ceramic practice. The book also contains a
prose presentation of the poem *Fugleskyen*, first published
in 1935.

The Sprouting Style
(1949)

Excerpts

"Events of recent years have, more vigorously than has happened for a long time, reminded us of the inherent power of things. The splitting of the atom pointed out the enormous sensitivity of the solar system, without it amazing us though; but for someone already oriented towards the sprouting style it is not a cause for concern to assimilate with the power of the material, the innocent walks on water. In the sprouting style I sense the throbbing pulse of life, a cliché denoting a heading towards the light, a belief in freedom at last, and safety for people, a belief which I nonetheless do not hesitate to embrace. It stands for buoyancy; we poor must have hope."

[...]

"As science continually changes our idea of the world, so do the developments quite naturally change people's demands as to the form and content of art. The stationary Ptolemaic crystal ball system, to which angels and stars were fastened with pins, corresponds to the medieval theological constraint, the cathedral, arching over its own mysticism. As scientific knowledge tends towards a definition of all matter as frequency, the underlying principle of movement must impose itself as artistic leitmotif, forces flowing, the transition from one form to another, transformation. Thus it seems that access to an irrational world has been given, or one might say, that one is leaving a fictive perception behind, replacing it with a real one, real in 1949. It turns out that there was a far more sophisticated understanding of nature in the 'everything is in flux' of antiquity than in the medieval puppet theatre. Greater truth and therefore greater beauty."

[...]

"Art and science advance in parallel and sparks of inspiration fly between them; today's proven fact was only guessed at yesterday. When both are present in one individual: Goethe, we have the seer, or prophet, the highest form of homo sapiens. With the Indian scientist Bose's investigations into the reactions of metals and the conscious life of plants we are right in the middle of the unconscious basis of abstract art. My ornaments entitled *The Living Stone*, I owe to him. *Sir Jagadish Chandra Bose* (1858–1937) was the first Indian to gain European fame for his scientific work. He obtained a degree from Cambridge University and from University College London, but lived and worked in India, lastly at the Bose Institute, built for him in Calcutta (Kolkata).

Bose did experimental work with electromagnetic radiations. His investigations into the reactions of plants are ground-breaking. In his preface to Plant Autographs and Their Revelations, he writes: "In pursuing investigations on the border regions of physics and physiology, I was amazed to find boundary lines vanishing and points of contact emerge between the realms of the living and non-living. Metals are found to respond to stimuli; they are subject to fatigue, stimulated by certain drugs and killed by poisons.

Between inorganic matter at one extreme end and animal life at the other, there is spread out the vast expanse of the silent life of plants. I have been able to make the dumb plant the most eloquent chronicler of its inner life and experiences by making it write down its own history. The self-made records thus show that there is no life-reaction in even the highest animal that has not been foreshadowed in the life of the plant. The plant and the animal appear as a multiform unity in a single ocean of being. That vision crushes out of him all self-sufficiency, all that kept him unconscious of the great pulse that beats through the universe."

Do plants have a heart? Where exactly in the plant is it? Bose finds it by means of a sensitive galvanometer which he connects to various tissues. It shows him that the cells in the inner layer of the bark give the highest reading. Deeper inside the plant there is no reaction at all, nor in the outer part of the bark. But how can one determine that this electrical pulse actually indicates an activity in the plant corresponding to a heartbeat? Because it is subject to the exact same laws when exposed to pressure, stimuli and drugs. The channel transporting the sap may be regarded as an artery whose movements are its pulse. Plants have nervous tissue and vessels and beating hearts, ascertained with irrevocable certainty through measurement and irradiation. Do they also eat and sleep like us, one wonders?"

[…]

"Mysterious forces permeate the world; we see some of their effects, but their true nature and intent are unknown to us. It is surely futile to speculate about the endless possibilities, but if we call these obscure sources of energy 'the power inherent in things', we draw them right up close so that our imagination can survey them as if they were Ariel, a troll perhaps, popping out of its hut again and again. Any growth draws its capacity from this natural spring, the budding style is its child. One may argue that the artist's greatest, if not sole, task is to give concrete expression to the notion of 'the power inherent in things'. It contains all other motifs, for it is the origin of all suffering and all happiness."

[…]

"The history of ceramics begins with Robinson Crusoe who, in an unthinking moment, places an air-dried vessel too close to a fire and in his flurry spills salt onto it: glazes. It begins with Robinson, a cave, a fire and a faithful dog, for the reader to picture it all in their head, and ceramics' thousand-year-old epic is thus introduced. It is a little up and down with ceramics, mostly down, for it seems as though man, over the centuries, has lost his sense of simple and great effects in art. Moreover, every time a new technique creates a possibility for artistic expression, it very quickly reaches its full bloom; the rest is a retreat, repetition, deterioration. A thing has an appointed time, it rises, peaks and then sinks again, that is the law of all growth.

If a general mention of ceramics' development somewhat derails our subject, it may not be superfluous to attempt to position in an art-historical context the stoneware discussed in this book. Allow me to briefly indicate three different perceptions of the relationship between nature and art. They are linked to each their century, and the examples are taken from the history of The Royal Copenhagen Porcelain Manufactory.

The eighteenth century's perception of nature finds its most moving expression in the Flora Danica dinnerware. The decorations on this set are naturally coloured images of cut flowers, an old-fashioned herbarium served on voluptuous plates, lace-like, with scalloped gilded edges, like tongues of artificial nightingales. Man is the master of plants. Now they each attend the King's banquet, humbly giving their name in gold on the back of each plate, poor but honest relatives suddenly being noticed, Rousseau taking Fragonard by the hand.

The nineteenth century moves into Naturalism, schooled and sharpened by the art of photography. The perfect illusion becomes the goal, which must be the reason for the persistent popularity, in the 1880s, for under-glazed designs; that which resembles something will always possess an extraordinary power over ordinary minds, the joy of recognition is irresistible. It is not so much about how the flowers are as how they look. Pallid but life-like, realistic. Although technically brilliant, the genre is non-ceramic, and a great artist might at the time have led it onto a sensible path.

The twentieth century abandons Naturalism. The artist now seeks to look at the flower from within, sketch the principle of its structure, follow the plant right down into the seed, let its initial germ burst as he listens to the melody of the growth, in search of the essence of things. [...] His rendition of nature is no longer drawn from what he sees, but from what he knows or what he suspects. He is neither a romantic nor an individualist, but by lying in wait at the source of germination, like the hunter at the rat hole, he has a chance to understand the rhythm of the plant and thereby deliver something universal. His ornamentation becomes organic, means something. By thus melding the growth into his ceramics he works with a deliberate creative idea which leads him towards a style."

[...]

"It began in 1929 in Halier's studio, and today, twenty years later, I still passionately play ceramics' dreamy lottery. It is a matter of loving something and keeping on loving it. In ceramics this sentence has a definite meaning, and here the feeling is fiercely reciprocated: just as one eventually, by twisting and turning an ornament, establishes its correct proportions, one is often encouraged, indeed guided, by the kiln with its divine fortuitousness, which only a fool would spurn. Thus the ceramist becomes a romantic, and something essential is suggested as to the nature of ceramics and its limitations. I have been fond of potsherds since my boyhood years, and have longed in vain to participate in archaeological expeditions. Fragments with a little bit of landscape, or a snapped vine, rather broken than intact, thrived with me ever since they became mere cows standing in rows in their cigar-box stable; was my net a growing urge towards ceramics? Tureen fragments with purple herons, unearthed with a stick among the buttercup roots and rusty sardine tins under the spring sky on rubbish dumps in the banlieue, this was what I was crazy about. I even dared to defy the caretaker and his fierce dogs to get my finds out. While the other boys were scrapping, I, the little idiot, sneaked about with my spike, quiet as I was."

[...]

"The first decoration shown to me on a piece of ceramic was the fluted zigzag pattern, a primitive, timeless design, in which one's hand, when grabbing a stick, almost draws by itself. Its raison d'être on the glazed ceramic is obvious: in the kiln, as the temperature rises, the glaze trickles down the sides of the bowl. If a zigzag pattern is already engraved – or added in relief as on porcelain – the glaze will naturally run down along the grooves until it reaches the bend barring its way; here it condenses and continues as a broad stream with tributaries from two sides until it reaches the base. In this way, radiating out from the base, a star-shaped pattern occurs, which is entirely a ceramic result, and this is of vital importance. Another effect occurring during the firing is that the clay body, due to the altered tension in its mass provoked by the fluting, contracts unevenly, so that the bowls become either square or octagonal, depending on how many times the fluted lines meet. This obliterates the mechanical aspect and makes each bowl organic and individual. The budding style developed from the fluted style, which for the same reason is ceramically justified: the glaze runs around the proud areas which break through, repelling the glaze, so that the bare clay body is exposed. The glaze gets thicker or thinner, and the colour changes according to the thickness of the layers. Thereby the characteristic interaction between clay body and glaze appears dramatic, eruptive and naturalistic, which to me is the distinguishing quality of stoneware."

[...]

"Stoneware plays its own particular melody. The simple bowl or vase form is given life through adequate ornamentation, the tone at times gains a moving ring, embodying nature's horror and joy. But should one attempt a broader instrumentation it seems natural to try other angles: the poems and pictures in this book play with the same themes as the ceramics; they are based on the same observation of nature and sense of life, but probably in more richly nuanced syntheses. Nature sings with a hundred mouths. Is it possible to interpret a hundred voices in one bowl, the sensual world's desire and vanity's secret pain, an ambiguous, problematic world displayed on a piece of pottery? I turned my attention to the word, although I sensed this was not right. I probably just felt like writing, and so failed to appreciate the bowl, the only bowl, which is myself. I am holding it in my hand, the absolute redemption of the mind: by comparison, all expansiveness becomes nonsense, this is the right thing, but, well, I felt then the desire to take a long rest doing something different. My small piece of writing, *The Bird Cloud*, is a hymn to life's indomitable beauty, it describes the changing seasons, the hours of the day from morning until evening and from evening until dawn. The quiver of the sprouting style translated into words."

[...]

"The artist stands in the middle of life, gathering his material from all sides, but what moves one man leaves another cold; luckily life is multi-faceted and one should not come between man and his inspiration, it all depends on the exuberance of the mind. Creating art is a spiritual activity – with the mind being aided by a pair of strong hands, of course, let us not be too sentimental – but like Antaeus, the artist still has to renew his power through contact with the earth. Large and small are for him pure fiction, a world war seemingly passes without leaving a trace, whereas a blot of ink erects dragon fountains; flower or thunderstorm, the artist praises the creator in both.

We have seen how one ceramic style grows out of another. The simple fluted style becomes the budding style, culminating in a spherical vase, studded with little beads; a more ready-to-burst taut form within a regular repeated ornament is hard to imagine. I therefore tried to go beyond the budding form and arrived at the sprouting style that accentuates growth. That too evolves, leading to some extreme demonic pieces wherein are preserved both my joy at being in harmony with the creative spirit of spring and my fear of nature's fury. In these smouldering, gushing vases the stoneware bursts into song, and what else should clay be used for? For play when the heart swells and for comfort in affliction. For cheating time and creating life from the dead. Even a painful life is better than no life; from Actaeon sprouts the deer, he sinks. In his burning face, where clay and glaze embrace, the stoneware unfolds its true nature, becomes a truly unique art form with its own means and goals, the little sister of elder brothers. The sprouting style can only sprout from stoneware.

In the clay arisen from the depths."

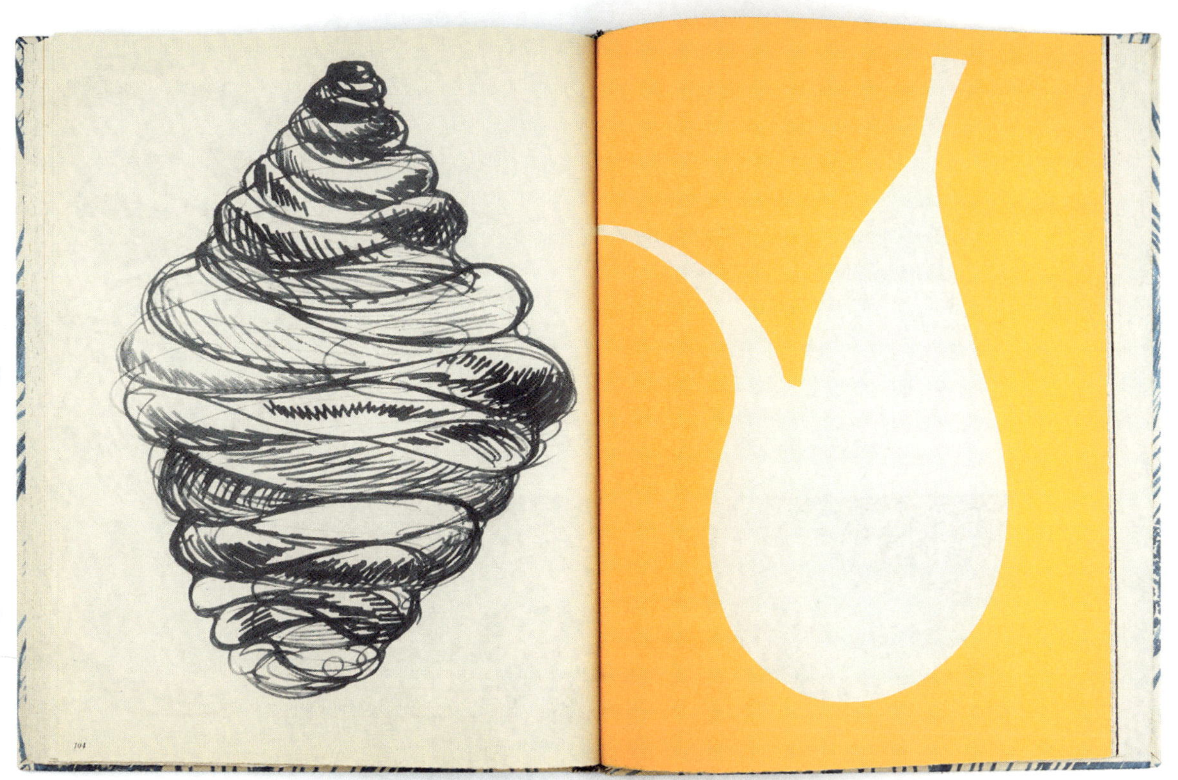

Spread from
Den spirende Stil, 1949

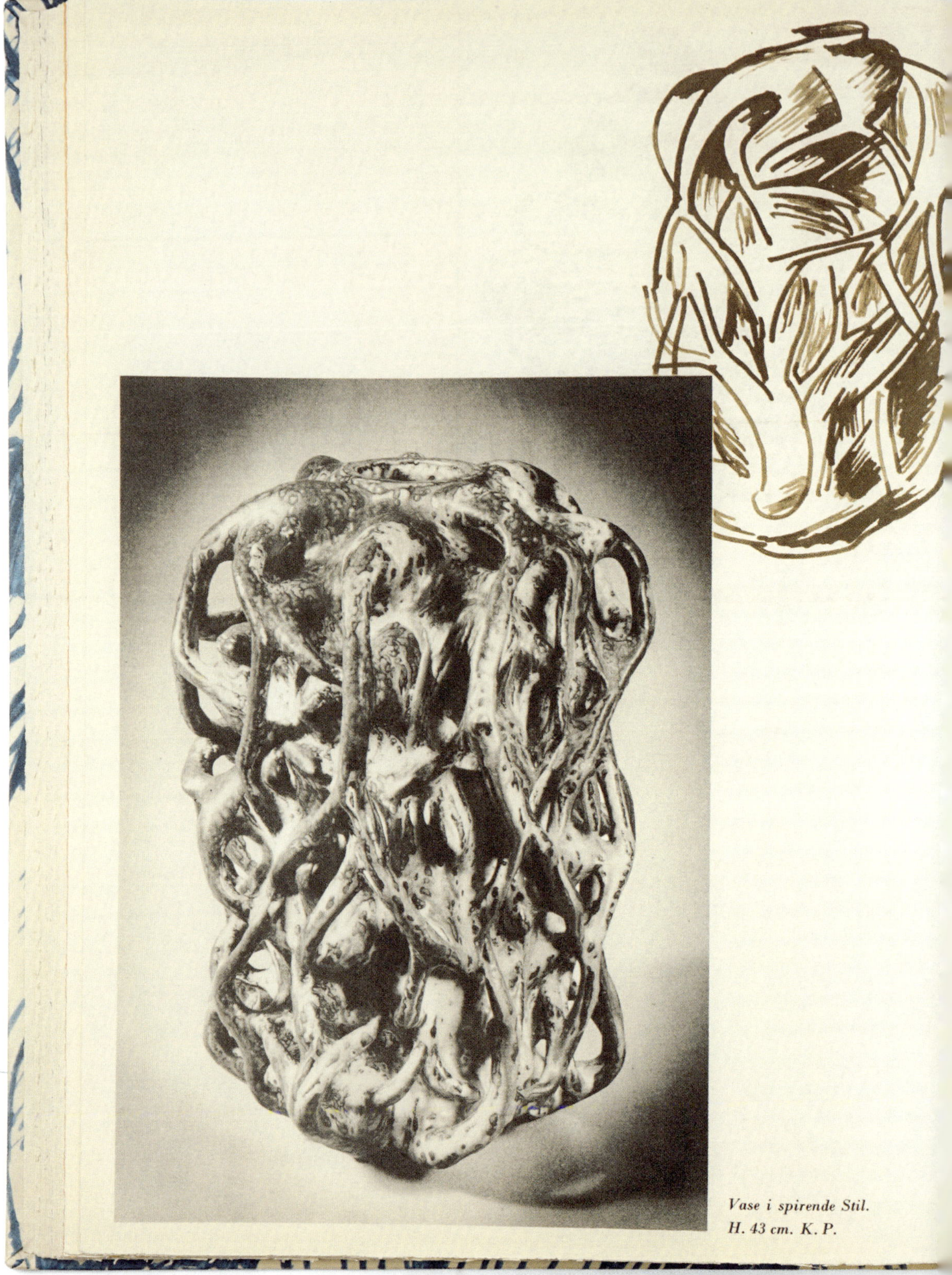

Vase i spirende Stil.
H. 43 cm. K. P.

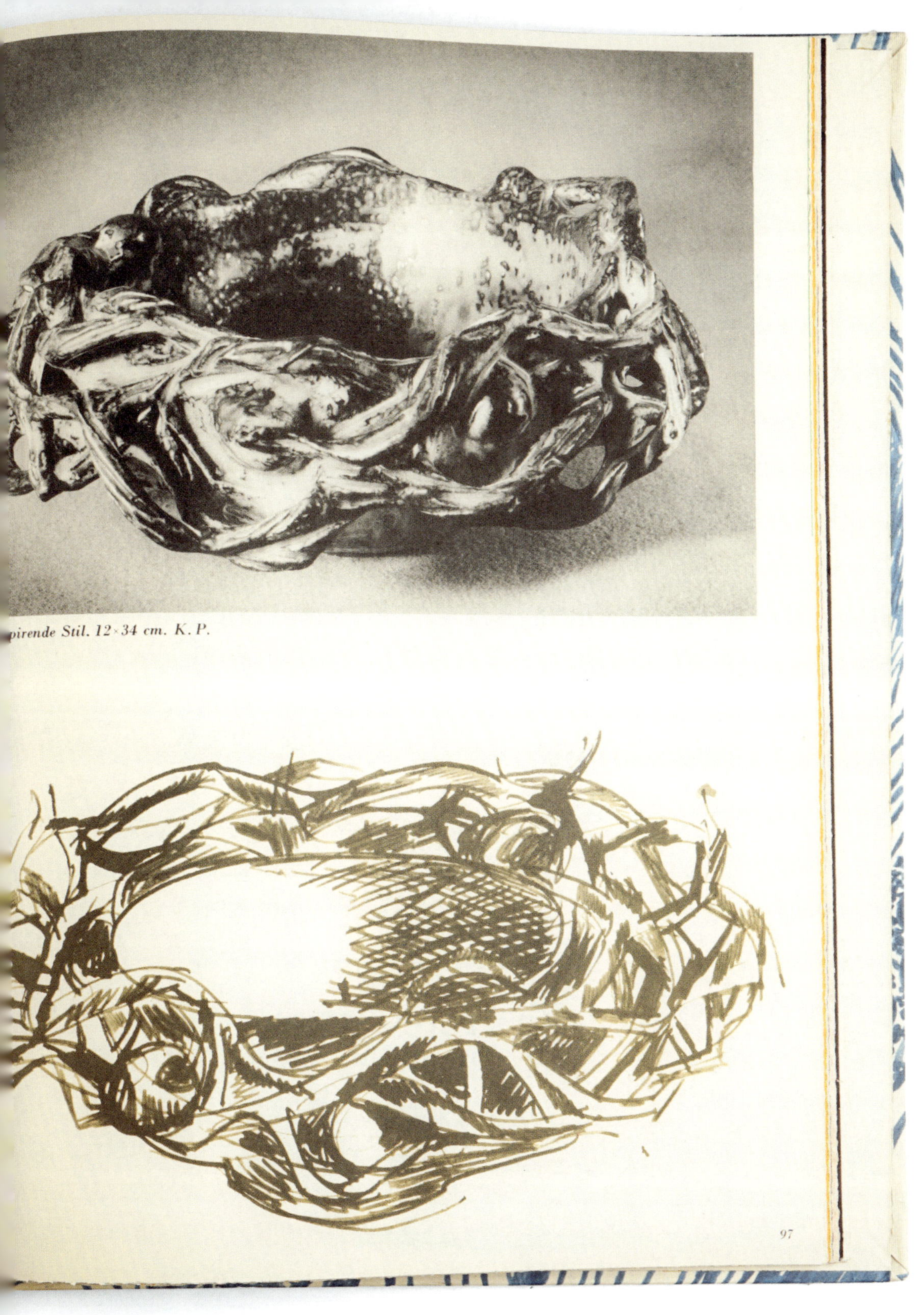

Spread from
Den spirende Stil, 1949

Small Things

De smaa Ting
Poem in *Fugleskyen*
Copenhagen 1935
Det Berlingske Bogtrykkeri

See p. 38

Small Things
(1935)

Behind curtains in your mind are all the real things,
all the ships plying your childhood's coast.
The bursting buds and the breathing leaves,
the ingenious form of the flower has a deeper meaning.
Talk to the sprouting seed that loves to grow,
trades a wise head for a burning heart.
In the twilight of the grass you will learn something important
about the caring or cruel connection of things.
The meadow, the forest and the long shore
are worthy of your attention, keepers of your joy,
whether you, by the green wheat field, let
your hand run along the ears' rows of seeds,
or you, in the glow of Indian summer, gather
the warm brown acorns to sketch from.
The nautilus spiral in the flagstones and the star of the fossilised
sea urchin speaks to you over the sea of time.
The conch's boiling mother-of-pearl mouth
exhales its salty breath into the clover wind.
The abiding, the eternal, you yourself are a seed in the sun,
sprouting, flowering, ripening, withering and sprouting again.
Let the timid mind soar like a kite
and put your ear to the ground, the small things are speaking.
Are you sad about the little things? Well! Then the
cloud will appear in his dark blue cloak.
With his beard on fire and a rumble on his tongue
he tips the watering can over you, and you are drenched to
the skin.

TING IKKE ORD

Af
AXEL SALTO

OM MINDESMÆRKER · HUSET PAA
PLÆNEN · VILHELM LUNDSTRØM
TALE I RADIOEN OM LUNDSTRØM
VOR UNGDOMS STIER · LEONARDO-
BØGERNE · TIL ELEVERNE PAA
AKADEMIET · KEND DIG SELV

FISCHER

The Paths of Our Youth, II

Vor ungdoms stier II
in *Ting ikke ord*
1951, Copenhagen
Fischers Forlag, 94 p.
Private collection

The essay *The Paths of Our Youth, II* forms part of two texts in which Salto reflects on his period in France, the Parisian art scene, and the growth and transformation of the landscapes of the south of France. Both essays can be found in *Ting ikke ord (Things, not Words)*, a collection of personal texts and works of criticism that engage with book design, the art milieu, and the academy of arts – and ends with the autobiographical text *Kend dig selv (Know Yourself)*.

The Paths of Our Youth, II
(1951)

Excerpts

"Why on earth did we leave? Because things at home had lost their meaning, everything had become obvious, nothing made us wonder, nothing demanded our ingenuity. Far from life's original trait of fight for survival your senses soon become idle, and as an artist you eventually become unable to say or do things of any real importance to people. Your imagination is perpetually confronted with itself, never with another reality. You turned a knob and the room was warm, how very innocuous. You looked up at the sky, oh, that narrow stretch over the dairy shop. How strangely wonderful the skies over Paris were in our youth, how different from what we were used to, because we were open to new experiences in this foreign world we saw a new context. And this is why we are rained in, in a cellarway in Vence, so that the familiar things can regain their original weight, and so, here we are. –

And then the sun came out in Vence! The Mistral has swept the sky clean, the countryside has soaked up all the rays. Alas, you are certainly sweet, my native country, but this you cannot match. Out there, to the east, the sun rises, like a red balloon sent aloft from Negresco's roof, and the whitish-blue morning sea. The luminous purple veil of mist in the valleys slowly dissipates as the sun becomes stronger, elves, what became of you, but the substance is constant, tomorrow you shall touch my mind again. The olive trees quiver in the aromatic morning breeze, the white undersides of their leaves blinking like a shoal of herring, twisting and turning, happily breathing. Life was indeed real, after all, the sun had not forgotten its chosen garden, now all is well. And the sun rises, sending sweet French kisses in equal amounts

"

to the living trees and the dead towns, as these towns, despite the sun, died, or are dying; but the trees are alive and well, these indomitable plants of the Riviera.

Take the orange tree, round like a ball, a picture of Earth's indefatigable ability to reproduce. At once, the dark green globe of leaves full of ripe oranges combines with the coming autumn's white orange blossom, and from the entire ball the new shoots explode as though the tree were clad in bright yellow blazing leaves."

[...]

"The night is here, the bright-eyed balmy spring night. Not a hot sleepless unpleasantness like later on, when frogs croak sonorously in the water tank, but a cool exhalation. Rest your ear against the stone balustrade and hear, through the silence, the springs purl and murmur, above ground and below ground, hear the meltwater from the mountains all around.

Alas, what peace, what relaxation this world has to offer, how sweet life could be. Soon I shall die, so let me die now, whilst the last joy, this wonderful night, comes to me in the glow of my senses' full light."

The Double Urn
(1935)

81

I have made a double urn,
so that we in death's dreamless
dawnless night
can be forever together.
Now give me your hand, my love,
and do not be afraid. We pass through the
fire together, resting ash against ash
until God opens all Urns.

The Double Urn

Dobbelurnen
Poem in *Fugleskyen*
1935, København
Det Berlingske Bogtrykkeri

See p. 38

BILLEDET — MAPPEN — BOGEN

AF AXEL SALTO

Vi maa glemme smag, stil og anden fordom og tage uceremonielt paa opgaven, siger maleren Axel Salto.

Det er sikkert nødvendigt at sprede Kendskab til de grafiske Processer, hvis man vil vente dybere Interesse for den grafiske Kunst som saadan og derigennem for Billedet, Mappen og den illustrerede Bog. Øget Sans for det bløde, fløjlsagtige Litografi, Fotomontagens Stofmodsætning, for Træsnittets summariske Sort og Hvidt og Raderingens Streg, der er plastisk som Blindeskrift, Sansen for dette skærper Vurderingsevnen og en virkelig Kærlighed til Grafik som særlig Kunstart bliver da først mulig. Der er Grund til at dyrke denne Kvalitetssans som Modvægt mod det overhaandtagende, kunstindustrielle Verdensprincip: billigt og daarligt; ikke mindst for Bogtrykkeren, for Haandværkeren er det af Betydning, at hans Modtagelighed for Farve- og Stofvirkninger er højt udviklet, da det ligger i hans Haand at realisere Fremtidens uomtvistelige Ideal: billigt og godt.

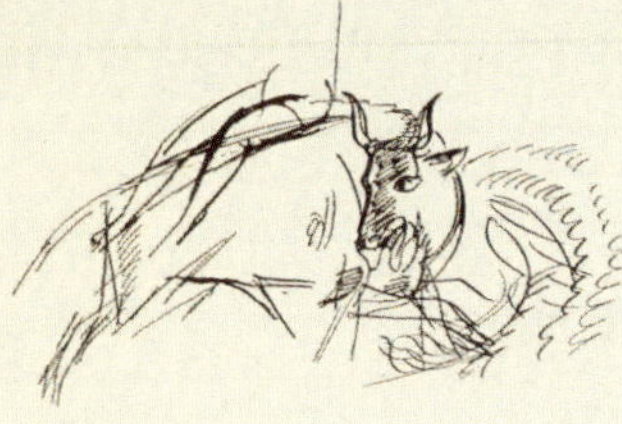

Maa jeg foreslaa følgende, som kan fremme Kendskaben til *La gravure*.

En Forening, inden for hvis Rammer et saadant grafisk Pionerarbejde naturligt falder, *Grafisk Kunstnersamfund* f. Eks., paatager sig at gennemføre en kunstnerisk og pædagogisk 3-Aarsplan, et Træsnitaar, et Raderingsaar og et litografisk Aar. I det første Aar afholder Foreningen en Udstilling af Træsnit, og til denne Udstilling knytter den Udgivelsen af en Bog, der behandler Emnet Træsnit udtømmende, historisk, teknisk og æstetisk. Som Illustrationsmateriale anvendes, foruden det historiske Stof, originale Klodser af Foreningens Medlemmer, derved spares Clichéudgift og en Række Kunstnere føres frem, forhaabentlig de talentfulde. Bogen gennemgaar instruktivt de forskellige Former for Træsnit og demonstrerer dem gennem Illustrationerne: Træsnit langs med og paa tværs af Fibrene, Xylografi, Camaïeux, Farvetræsnit, „au pochoir“-Teknik o. s. v. Træsnittene skaaret i den rigtige Størrelse med Bogen for Øje, et meget fest, helt overraskende Billedmateriale; blot at se et 5-farvet Træsnit i 5 Etaper arbejde sig hen mod sin Fuldtallighed er som en stigende Trommehvirvel.

Det næste Aar afholder Foreningen en Udstilling af Raderinger og udgiver 2det Bind af Bogværket, Bindet om Raderekunstens Historie og Teknik, med Illustrationer, dels originale Raderinger, dels Gengivelser efter Raderinger, der viser Prøver paa Stregætsning, vernis mou, Aquatinte, og hvad det altsammen hedder, ligeledes med Foreningens Medlemmer som naturlig Medarbejderstab. Endelig det 3die Aar kommer en litografisk Udstilling og 3die Del af Værket. Det kan se ud, som om jeg mister Interessen for Bogen, efterhaanden som den skrider frem, men det er ikke Tilfældet. Den bliver i Virkeligheden bedre og bedre, saa god at et spendabelt Fond maaske gerne vil hjælpe med til at realisere Planen. Vægten skal helt igennem lægges paa, hvad der er levende, har Spiren i sig til Vækst eller er i Pagt med Tidens Tempo og Teknik. Udover en naturlig historisk Placering skal f. Eks. en ukurant, overflødiggjort Kunst som Kobberstikket ingen Rolle spille, til Gengæld kan man saa faa et Kapitel om Fotomontage. Maaske er en helt anden Opdeling af Stoffet at foretrække og maaske er en anden Udgivelsesmaade bedre, det staar i hvert Fald fast, at Værket skal fremtræde i en festlig Dragt til dens Glæde, der tager det i Haanden. Kære Læser, ser du ikke Bogen for dig: *fra Blokbog til Hurtigpresse*, et Baal i sort og rødt og blaat.

Nu har vi skabt Kendskab til og forhaabentlig Interesse for det grafiske Blad; samtidig har vi

Image – Portfolio – Book (1934)

Billedet – Mappen – Bogen
Essay in *Bogvennen*
1934–37, Forening for Boghaandværk
Private collection

This article was published in the journal of the Danish Society of Bookbinders, Foreningen for Boghaandværk, and and makes clear Salto's preoccupation with the functions, art and craftsmanship of books. Among other collaborators, he worked with bookbinder August Sandgren on what they called Salsan papers, which were two-tone lithographic print patterns. These papers helped break the dominance of factory-made papers.

Image – Portfolio – Book
(1934)

Excerpt

"Alongside working with the book as an instrument of communication comes the equally pure cultivation of the book as an artwork, wherein all the possibilities of modern printing techniques can flourish. Belonging to this category is the book with photographic content, whose importance cannot be appreciated enough owing to the tremendous development of this technique and furthermore the book as, strictly speaking, an artistic thing in which text and decoration merge superbly. Therein lies to my mind book art's great possibility of renewal, using machines, photogravure-printing and colours. If the artist and the printer were to ignore tradition, as did Gutenberg when he invented the printing press, if they were to forget about taste, style and other prejudices, they have in today's reproduction technology such a rich instrument, that they could play the book right out of its old place, and that would be truly commendable, similar to Aldus' invention of the pocket-size format. In the wider world certain trends are emerging; may Denmark, true to its tradition, not hesitate too long. The book is learning about expressiveness from the poster where the text stands out and 'the coloured' becomes truly colourful. We must strive towards an unceremonious and humorous approach to the task, and then it will transpire that the line linking the twentieth-century colourful picture book with the fourteenth-century illuminated handwriting is intact, after all.

Duck the book and it shall rise from the rejuvenating bath in a brilliant new suit – life is so short."

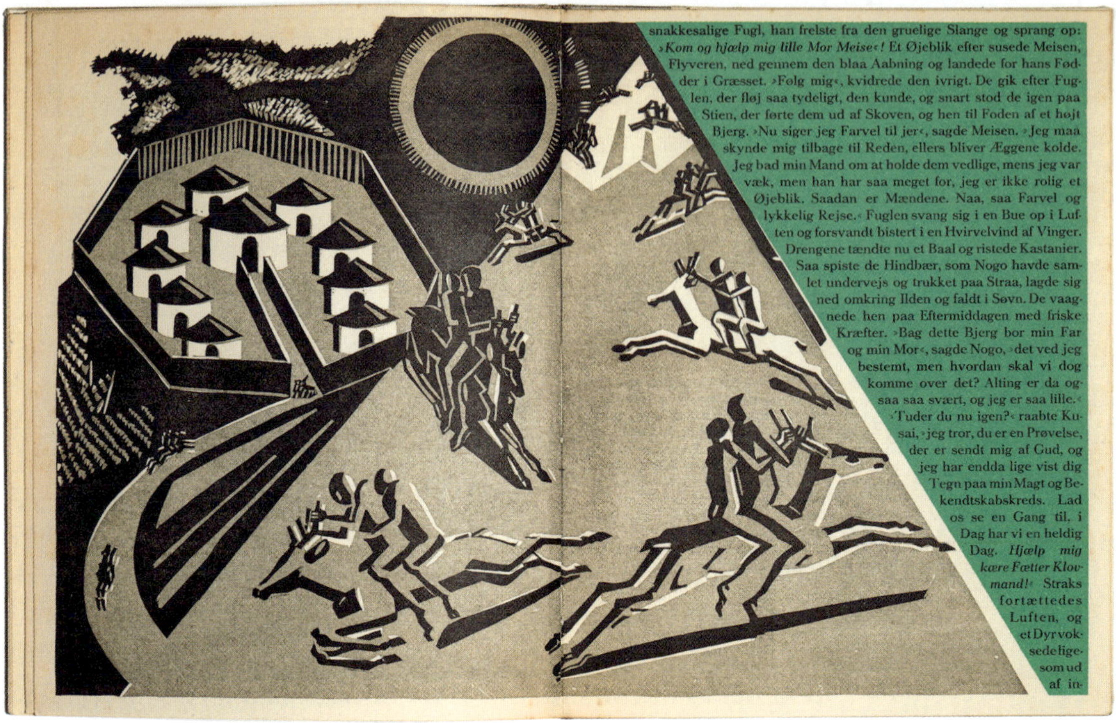

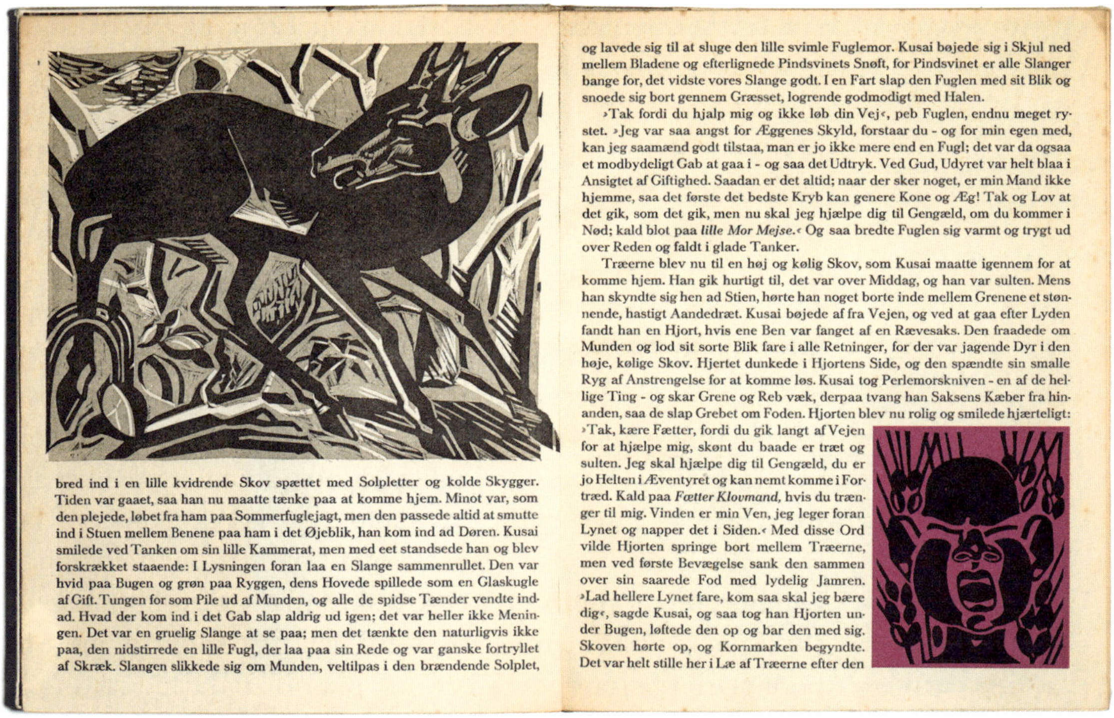

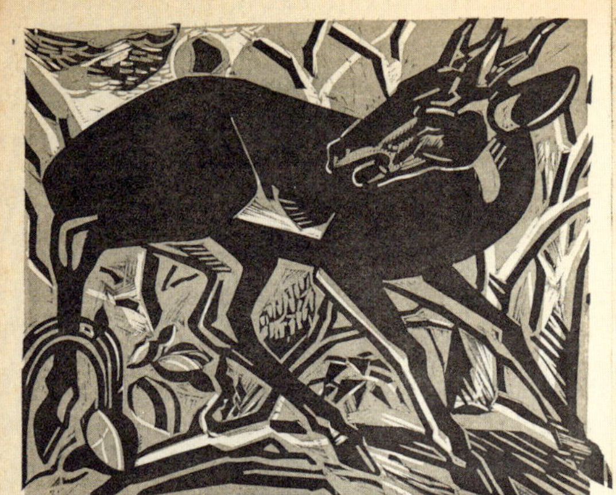

bred ind i en lille kvidrende Skov spættet med Solpletter og kolde Skygger.
Tiden var gaaet, saa han nu maatte tænke paa at komme hjem. Minot var, som
den plejede, løbet fra ham paa Sommerfuglejagt, men den passede altid at smutte
ind i Stuen mellem Benene paa ham i det Øjeblik, han kom ind ad Døren. Kusai
smilede ved Tanken om sin lille Kammerat, men med eet standsede han og blev
forskrækket staaende: I Lysningen foran laa en Slange sammenrullet. Den var
hvid paa Bugen og grøn paa Ryggen, dens Hovede spillede som en Glaskugle
af Gift. Tungen for som Pile ud af Munden, og alle de spidse Tænder vendte ind-
ad. Hvad der kom ind i det Gab slap aldrig ud igen; det var heller ikke Menin-
gen. Det var en gruelig Slange at se paa; men det tænkte den naturligvis ikke
paa, den nidstirrede en lille Fugl, der laa paa sin Rede og var ganske fortryllet
af Skræk. Slangen slikkede sig om Munden, veltilpas i den brændende Solplet,

og lavede sig til at sluge den lille svimle Fuglemor. Kusai bøjede sig i Skjul ned
mellem Bladene og efterlignede Pindsvinets Snøft, for Pindsvinet er alle Slanger
bange for, det vidste vores Slange godt. I en Fart slap den Fuglen med sit Blik og
snoede sig bort gennem Græsset, logrende godmodigt med Halen.

»Tak fordi du hjalp mig og ikke løb din Vej«, peb Fuglen, endnu meget ry-
stet. »Jeg var saa angst for Æggenes Skyld, forstaar du - og for min egen med,
kan jeg saamænd godt tilstaa, man er jo ikke mere end en Fugl; det var da ogsaa
et modbydeligt Gab at gaa i - og saa det Udtryk. Ved Gud, Udyret var helt blaa i
Ansigtet af Giftighed. Saadan er det altid; naar der sker noget, er min Mand ikke
hjemme, saa det første det bedste Kryb kan genere Kone og Æg! Tak og Lov at
det gik, som det gik, men nu skal jeg hjælpe dig til Gengæld, om du kommer i
Nød; kald blot paa lille Mor Mejse.« Og saa bredte Fuglen sig varmt og trygt ud
over Reden og faldt i glade Tanker.

Træerne blev nu til en høj og kølig Skov, som Kusai maatte igennem for at
komme hjem. Han gik hurtigt til, det var over Middag, og han var sulten. Mens
han skyndte sig hen ad Stien, hørte han noget borte inde mellem Grenene et støn-
nende, hastigt Aandedræt. Kusai bøjede af fra Vejen, og ved at gaa efter Lyden
fandt han en Hjort, hvis ene Ben var fanget af en Rævesaks. Den fraadede om
Munden og lod sit sorte Blik fare i alle Retninger, for der var jagende Dyr i den
høje, kølige Skov. Hjertet dunkede i Hjortens Side, og den spændte sin smalle
Ryg af Anstrengelse for at komme løs. Kusai tog Perlemorskniven - en af de hel-
lige Ting - og skar Grene og Reb væk, derpaa tvang han Saksens Kæber fra hin-
anden, saa de slap Grebet om Foden. Hjorten blev nu rolig og smilede hjærteligt:
»Tak, kære Fætter, fordi du gik langt af Vejen
for at hjælpe mig, skønt du baade er træt og
sulten. Jeg skal hjælpe dig til Gengæld, du er
jo Helten i Æventyret og kan nemt komme i For-
træd. Kald paa Fætter Klovmand, hvis du træn-
ger til mig. Vinden er min Ven, jeg leger foran
Lynet og napper det i Siden.« Med disse Ord
vilde Hjorten springe bort mellem Træerne,
men ved første Bevægelse sank den sammen
over sin saarede Fod med lydelig Jamren.
»Lad hellere Lynet fare, kom saa skal jeg bære
dig«, sagde Kusai, og saa tog han Hjorten under Bugen, løftede den op og bar den med sig.
Skoven hørte op, og Kornmarken begyndte.
Det var helt stille her i Læ af Træerne efter den

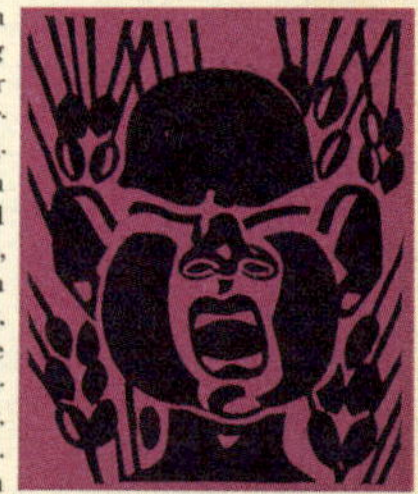

Spreads from Axel Salto's fairytale
Kusais Hændelser
1934, København
Berlingske Bogtrykkeri
Private collection

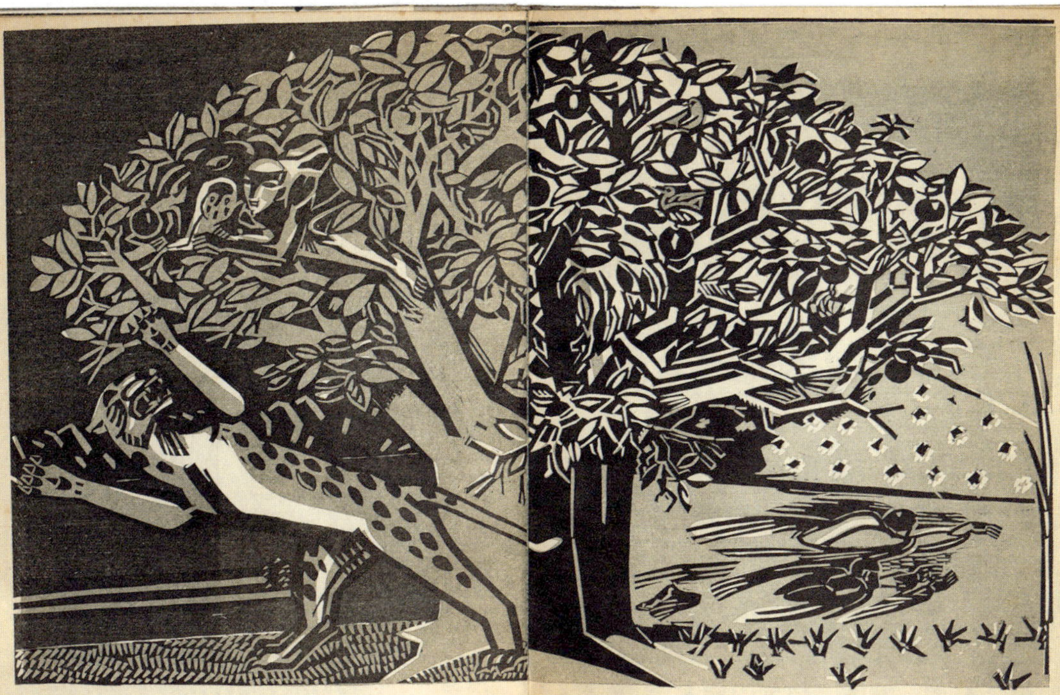

gammel og gigtsvag og maa bestemt være durkdreven; saa talte den tilmed born-
holmsk, det lød troværdigt. Lad os prøve: *Kom store Ben Horn og hjælp mig*!
Næppe havde han udtalt disse Ord, før Skildpadden stod foran ham og sagde
med Stemmen, der lød, som naar man spiller paa Redekam: ›Læg jer op paa
Toppen af mig‹, og saa svømmede den over Floden, saa Vandet brusede op om
det runde Skjold, og Flodhesten ærgerlig kneb Næsen til og gik tilbunds. ›Nu
skal I gaa den Vej dèr gennem Skoven, og Nogo skal lade være med at tude -

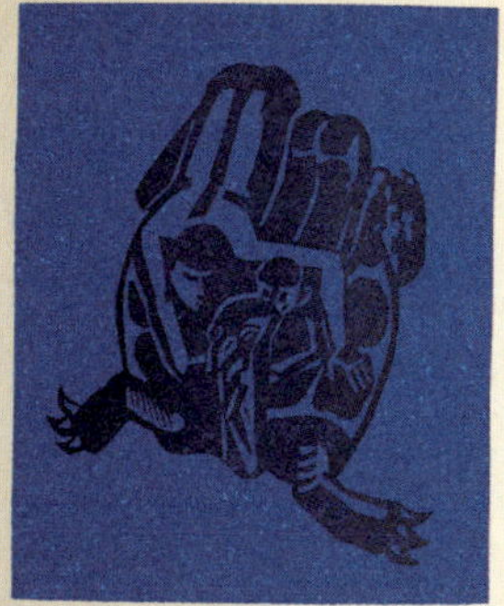

selv Flodhesten blev sgu bange for al den Væde.‹ Skildpadden op-slog en skralden-de Latter, saa Hovedet var nær ved at springe af. ›Deres Majestæt maa huske paa‹, sagde Kusai, ›at vi andre ikke som Spurve, eller om forladelse, som Engle, kan flyve i eet Spring hen-over en Natte-skov fuld af vilde Dyr og Leopar-der. Nogo er lidt anstrengt til For-middag, han er ellers en tapper Kriger.‹ ›Det for-nøjer mig‹, sagde store Ben Horn, ›at du synes, jeg ligner en Engel. Det er ikke alle, der ser det straks. Man kalder mig ogsaa Dyrenes Konge, fordi jeg er saa gammel og saa klog.‹ Med disse Ord for-svandt Skildpad-den, syngende i Luften som en Raket, bort over Trætoppene. - Nu kom igen Skov og atter Skov. Drageblodstræer skyggede for Solen som vældige Parasoller, og dybt nede i den grønne Dunkelhed kravlede Kusai og hans lille Ven om paa de knortede Rødder, til Stien blev helt borte mel-lem Fødderne paa dem. Kusai steg op i et højt Træ, der strakte sine yderste Grene op over de andre, men han saa kun Skovhavet bølge under sig, saa langt Synet rakte, og Solskinnet, der skar i Øjnene fra alle de knitrende Blade. De gik frem, og de gik tilbage, Perlemorskniven brækkede paa de haarde Slyngplanter, men det tabte Spor var og blev tabt. Omsider satte de sig trætte ned, og Nogo faldt i Søvn under et Palmetræ. Kusai tænkte sig om, vaagen som et Egern. Han saa mod Himlen, som skimtedes højt oppe mellem de mørke Grene, indrammet af en flimrende Krans af røde Drageblodsblade. Derved kom han i Tanke om den

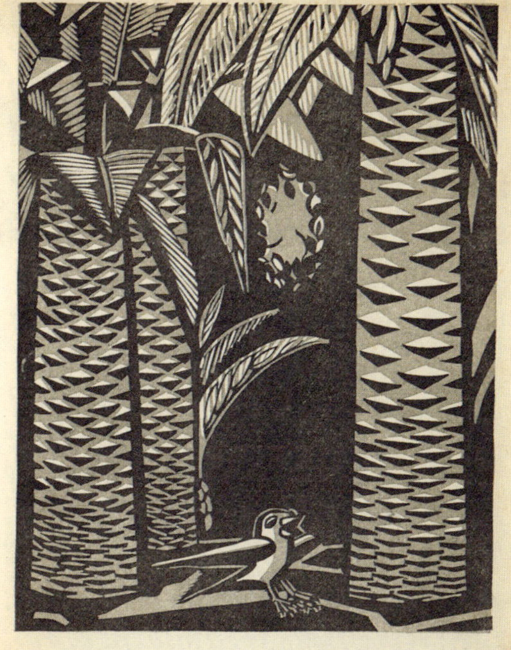

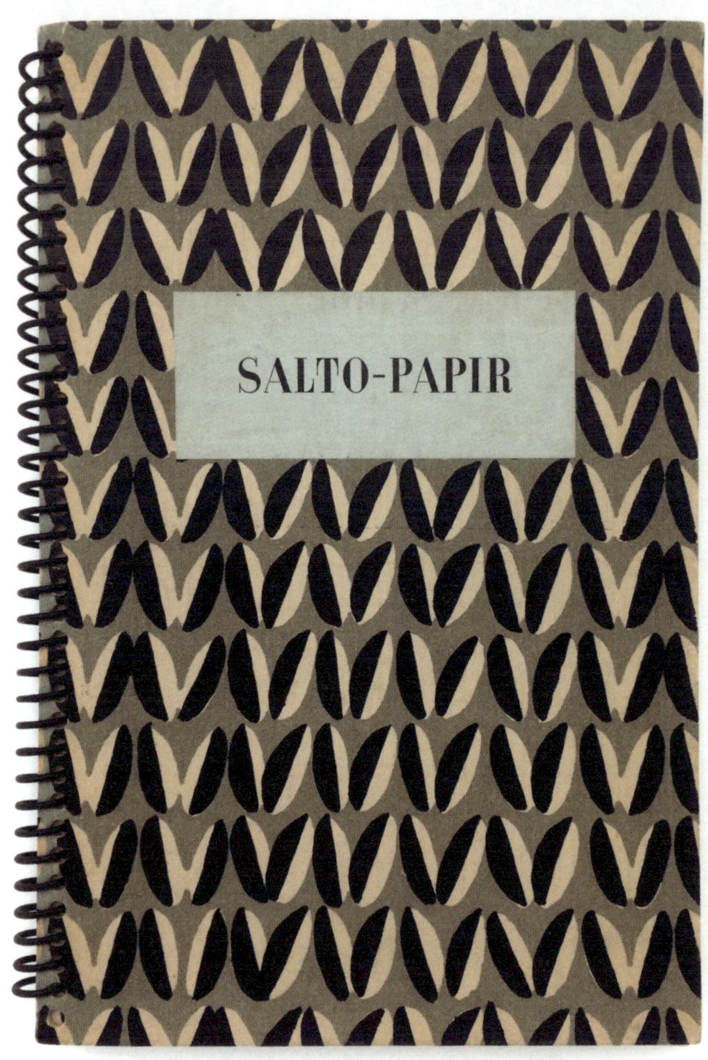

Salto-Paper

Salto-Papir
1943, Copenhagen
Fischers Forlag, 59 p.
Private collection

This book is a collection of Axel Salto's paper designs, for which there was high demand among bookbinders. Salto begins the book by providing an overview of his designs, and, against the backdrop of the Second World War, calls the colourful patterns a 'demonstration of optimism'. Several of the patterns were also available as home textiles through the wholesaler L.F. Foght. The Salto papers were also issued in a larger spiral-bound format featuring additional colour combinations.

Salto-Paper
(1943)

Excerpts

"For three hundred years every imaginable effect has been tried
out on bookbinding paper. These have moved from being pure
chance and shrewd craftsmanship to intentional and highly
sophisticated art. As endpaper, silk with hand-painted images
and fabric from the beloved's dress have been used. Pheasant
feathers, fish skin and snake skin have inspired the artist who,
furthermore, has received all kinds of ornamental impulses from
the microscope, from tissue structure to the microcosmos of a
water droplet.

The *Salto-Paper* designs that we send out are our attempt to
renew bookbinding paper at a time when this is much needed
– and, for that matter, all kinds of decorated paper for different
uses too, such as wallpaper, cartons, paper boards etc. – technically by a special lithography technique, artistically by a renewal
of the current ornamentation and by a more diverse colour range
than the usual one. They are a continuation of the old Salsan
Paper designs, launched by the renowned August Sandgren and
myself some years ago."

[...]

"The motifs used are quite simple, perhaps not all new, strictly
speaking, but then recovered, and they are hopefully varied and
colourful enough to be pleasing and enjoyable. With one excep-
tion they are all based on observations from nature, meaning
they are not direct nature imitations placed in a system side by

side; the motif of the ear is not actually an ear of wheat, yet the essence of the ear is preserved in the ceramic ornament which mimics nature in its way of organising itself. A simplification has taken place, an adaptation. Like a child drawing a face whose features are defined quite clearly with two dots and two lines, one vertical and one horizontal, so is the ear of wheat, just as easily understood, reduced to the essential, the actual grains in their typically diagonal position opposite each other. To further enhance the suggestion, these ears are rendered in mature soft colours so that everything in the best possible way may stimulate the mind kindly.

I imagine the books of Johannes V. Jensen bound in this luxuriant motif. Understanding the wheat ears as a bright motif, one must on the other hand realise that the paper nos. 20–25, for example, denote a very different mood. [...] No. 25, with its deep blue and blackish purple tones, would suit Othello, or Shelley's tragedy The Cenci. In my view, these books would gain an almost magically increased prominence if one were to give them an adequate cover. [...] In no. 11 something like a smouldering fire reminds one of Werther, or the poetry of Paul la Cour. There are sprouting bulbs of the light spring-like type, and heavy glowing pomegranates. Each pattern and colour combination speak their own language and belong each in their own place. Therefore we produce a great many variants, so that one may choose the paper that suits the mood of the book to be bound. The possibilities are of course far from exhausted with the present selection, but we hope to have introduced some useful and varied harmonies; could we start with them?"

[...]

"A binding should not only be practical and beautiful in its form and colour; the endpaper is not only mediation, a scaling down inwards towards the book. Choosing a motif in the gaily coloured world of paper to which we open the door, and singling out the colour combination that most closely embraces the spirit of the book and introduces its basic mood, allows one to give the book a huge increase in value: for me personally, having collaborated on the oeuvre, as it were, and therefore come closer to it, and for people in general, as the book only now is an indivisible whole thing, and therefore in every respect more valuable.

The Salto-Paper series is a demonstration of optimism, hence very useful, we believe, in these times of ours. It tells us that behind all misery lies the brilliant life that in the end will triumph."

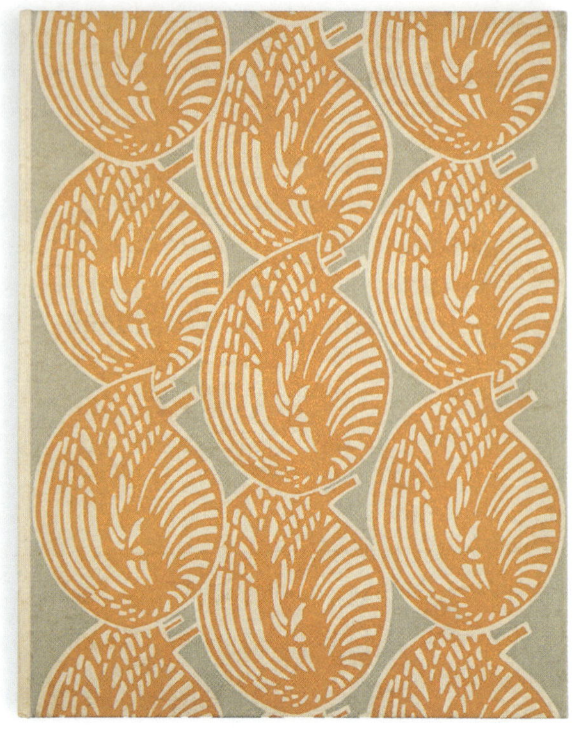
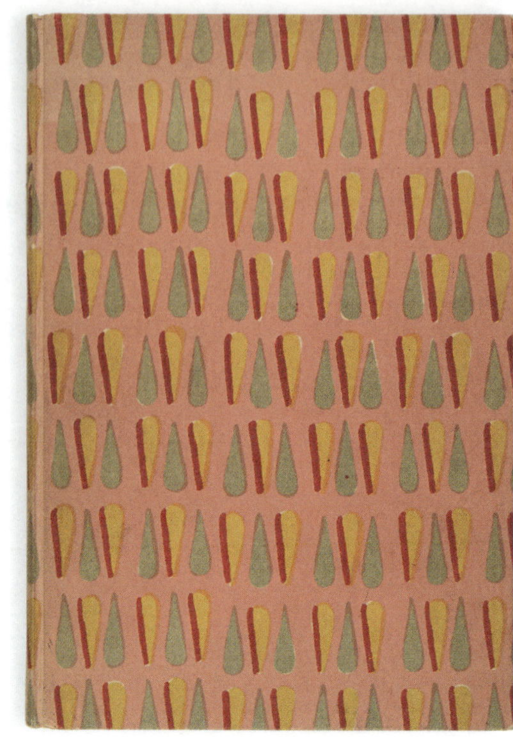
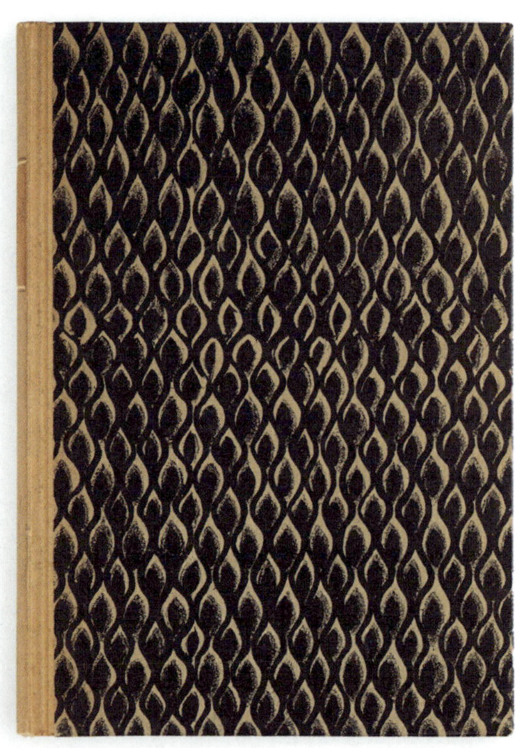

Various books bound in *Salto-Paper,* 1918–1961
Private collection

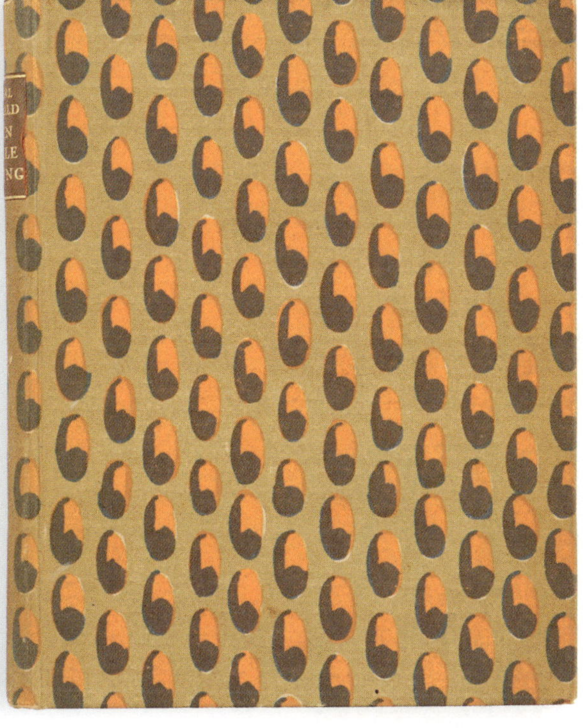

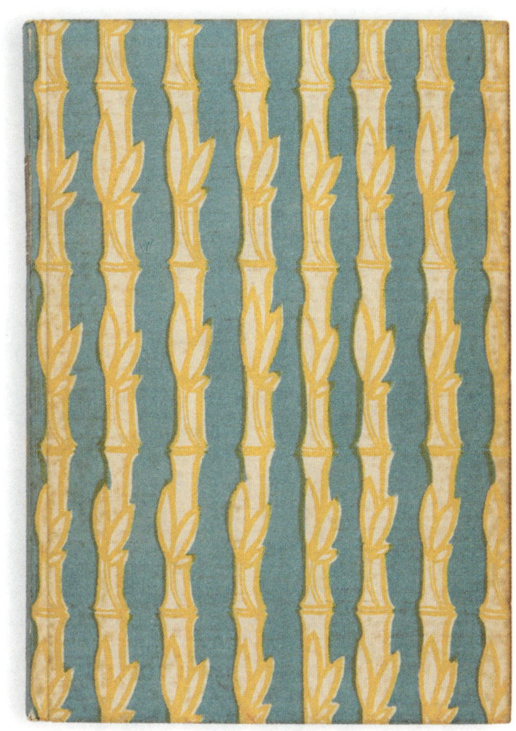

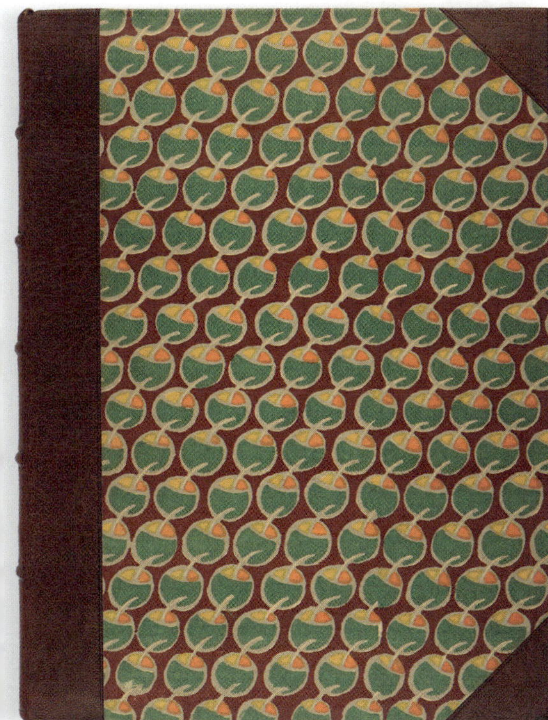

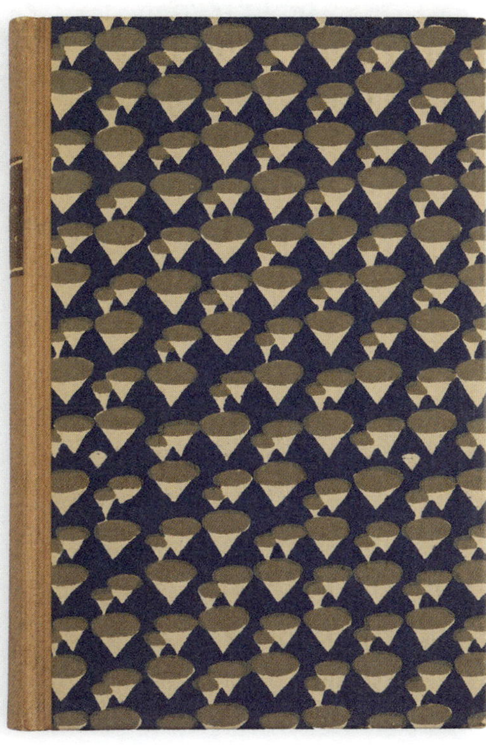

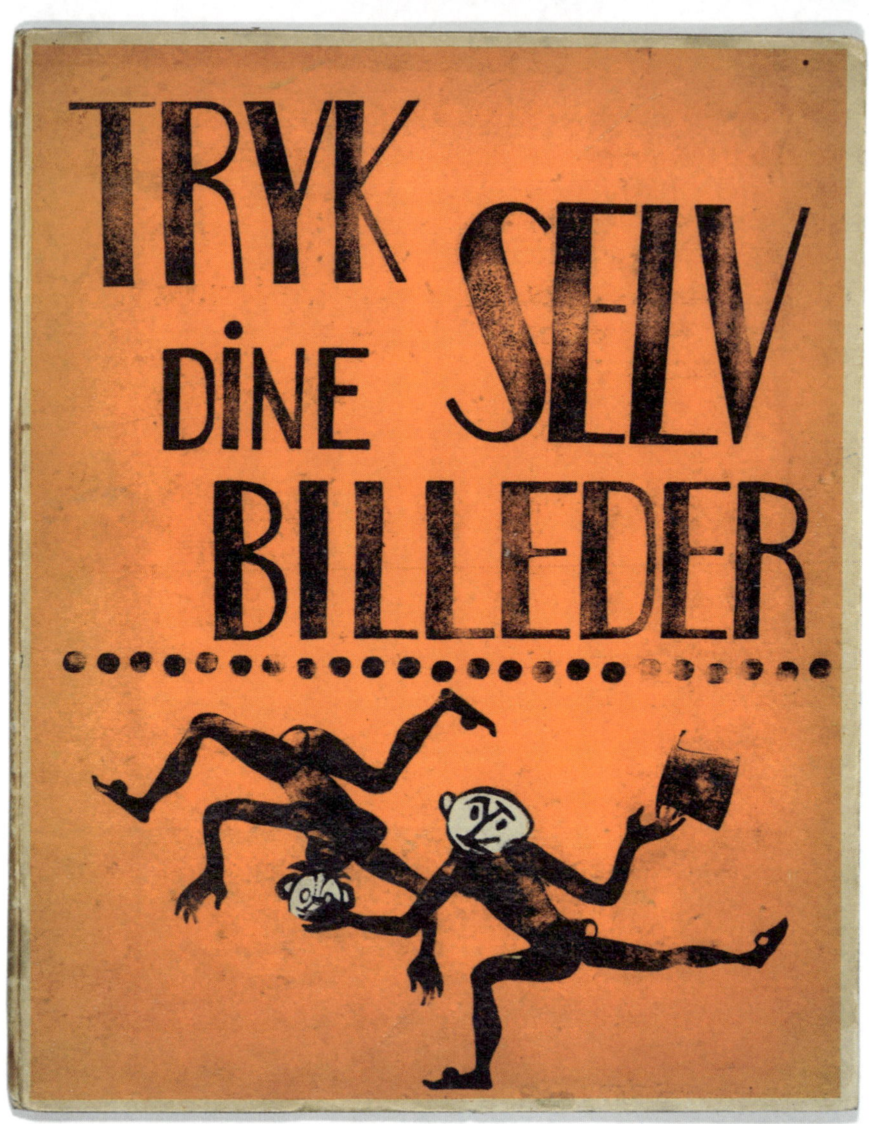

Print Your Own Pictures

Tryk selv dine Billeder
1943, Copenhagen
Fischers Forlag, 20 p.
Private collection

This is a practical book for children. Salto explains how to make linoleum stamps, discusses the motifs' endless variations and describes the possibilities to be found in the papers' different applications. In addition to this children's book he also wrote two fairy tales, *Kusais Hændelser* (1934) and *Galsindet Tyrk faar Klare Øjne* (1935), both examples of what are perhaps his most symbiotic book designs.

Print Your Own Pictures
(1943)

Excerpts

"With printing stamps one can make amusing, astonishing, indeed bewitching pictures. Once you begin to play with stamps, you give up on all other amusement, if you have the right kind of imagination, that is, but also if you are not overly imaginative, because when put to the paper, the stamps work entirely on their own: the imprint, which is not that interesting when printed only once, becomes more exciting the second time when you put a new impression next to the first one. This rule always applies for the stamps: *repetition is fun*. One man is no man, ten men are a choir. Inherent in these stamps are all kinds of toys, so to speak, ranging from fun to deep and serious matter. They may only mean some exciting play for a few days, but they can also be the introduction to a wide new world of ideas with infinite possibilities among which you take up permanent residence."

[...]

"When the printing stamp is evenly rolled with colour we are ready to make the imprint. If the paper is porous, nicely absorbent, and placed on a soft material, it will suffice, especially with small stamps, to press them firmly down onto the paper and then remove them; one then has a fine image, not uniformly black, but airy and light. If the paper is harder, and the underlying material not flexible enough, it can be necessary to give the woodblock a couple of light strokes with a hammer, to press it well down against the paper. Here, experience will tell one how hard the pressure needs to be."

"As I said at the beginning, it is repetition that produces the greatest effect when playing with printing stamps. Incidentally, this is an artistic principle that has been known since the dawn of time. "Bis repetita placent" was the Latin name, meaning repetition is pleasing. All ornamentation relies on it. So, this is what the stamps can be used for, *ornamentation*. A small figure, a flower, a snail shell repeated a hundred times in rows, next to each other, overlapping or interlocking, can be beautiful and fun. You can thus make paper for bookbinding, cover and flyleaf, use it yourself as covers for your own books, or offer it to a professional bookbinder."

[...]

"One can make cheerful pictures too with the printing stamps. You have no doubt visited Tivoli Gardens and may remember The Merry Kitchen, well, now you can make one yourself. Look how neatly the kitchen is arranged at first, everything is in its right place until you start throwing the balls, bang, here you can hit every time and smash whatever you like.

One can cut out a man in one piece and print him as he is, but one could also cut him up into smaller pieces, if I may put it that way. One stamp represents his body and head, a second one his leg, a third the other leg, etc. Thus you need five or six stamps printed closely together to get a picture of the whole man, but you may also let him gesticulate with his arms and legs and do a thousand tricks, like the worried little men in the back who find everything so difficult. You can endlessly combine their antics and invent unlikely positions, they will do whatever you want them to do. You may create the whole theatre audience too. A shirt-front, a top hat and a handsomely bearded face, and immediately you have the entire stalls before you. Promise to make it all as hilarious as possible. Who will make the best circus picture?

It is not only humorous pictures and manikins with moveable arms and legs and their hat down over their ears that it is worth your while printing on a rainy day. If you have read a good book, you could try to illustrate it; who knows, perhaps there is an artist hidden within you."

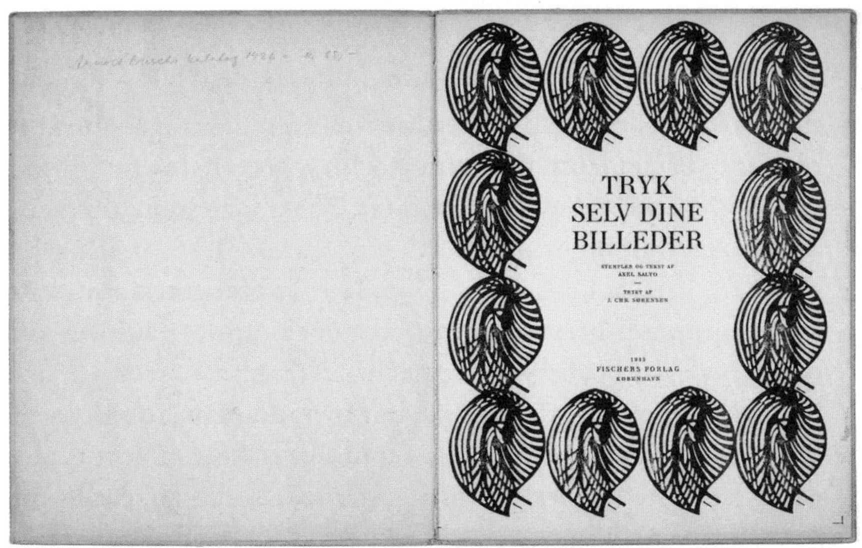

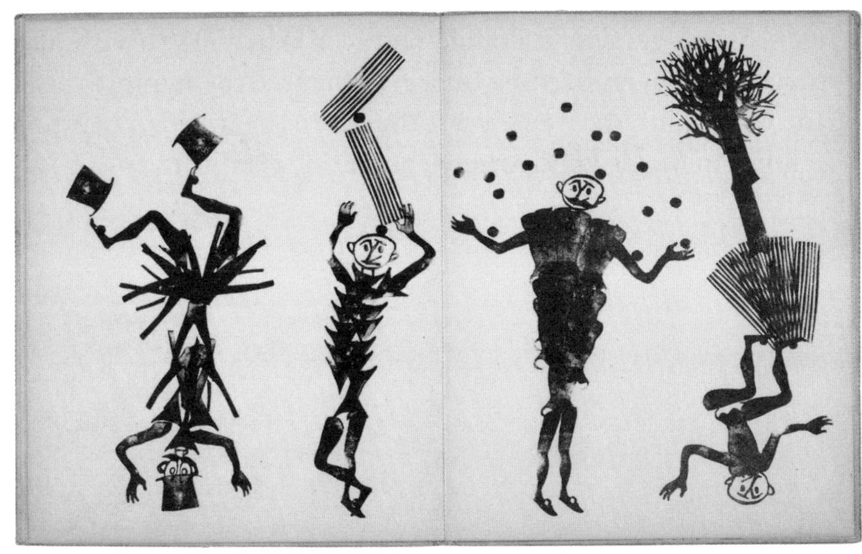

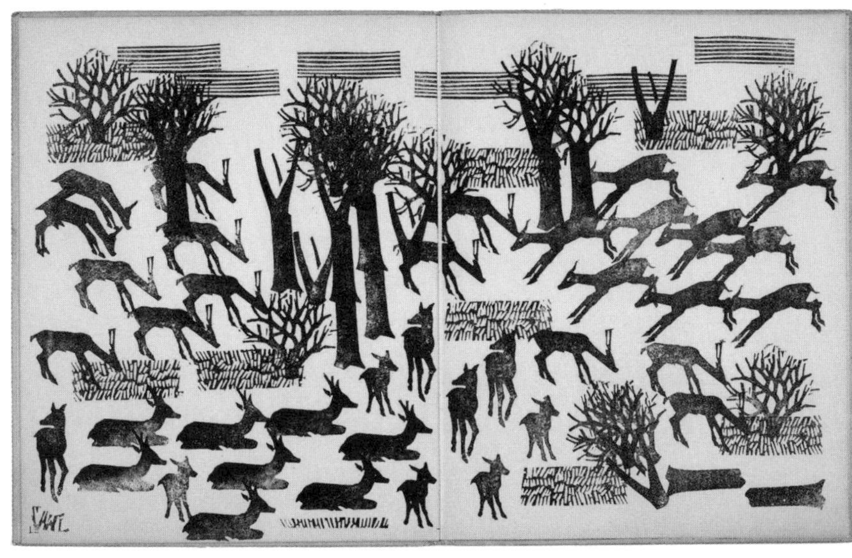

Spreads from
Tryk selv dine Billeder, 1943

"Finally, I would like to say a few words about the last picture in the book, I believe an explanation is required. It represents the old story of Actaeon, the hunter who was transformed into a deer and torn apart by his own dogs. The image shows Actaeon at the exact moment of his transformation, he is neither human nor deer, or he is both, if you like. Everything about him metamorphoses before our eyes, the deer's antlers, hooves and whole body erupt everywhere from within him. Actaeon, reaching boiling point, is dissolving, but in a moment he will settle down as an accomplished stag. I find this to be a subject that is easily replicated with the printing stamps as one can readily put a stag head on a human body, the knotted antlers can be printed bunch by bunch from the poor forehead, with the whole figure immediately gaining its double-nature. You may, if you wish, also transform a nymph into a tree, give the tree the nymph's head and the nymph the tree's head. You are in the world of printing stamps, in Magic Land, where you decide everything. –"

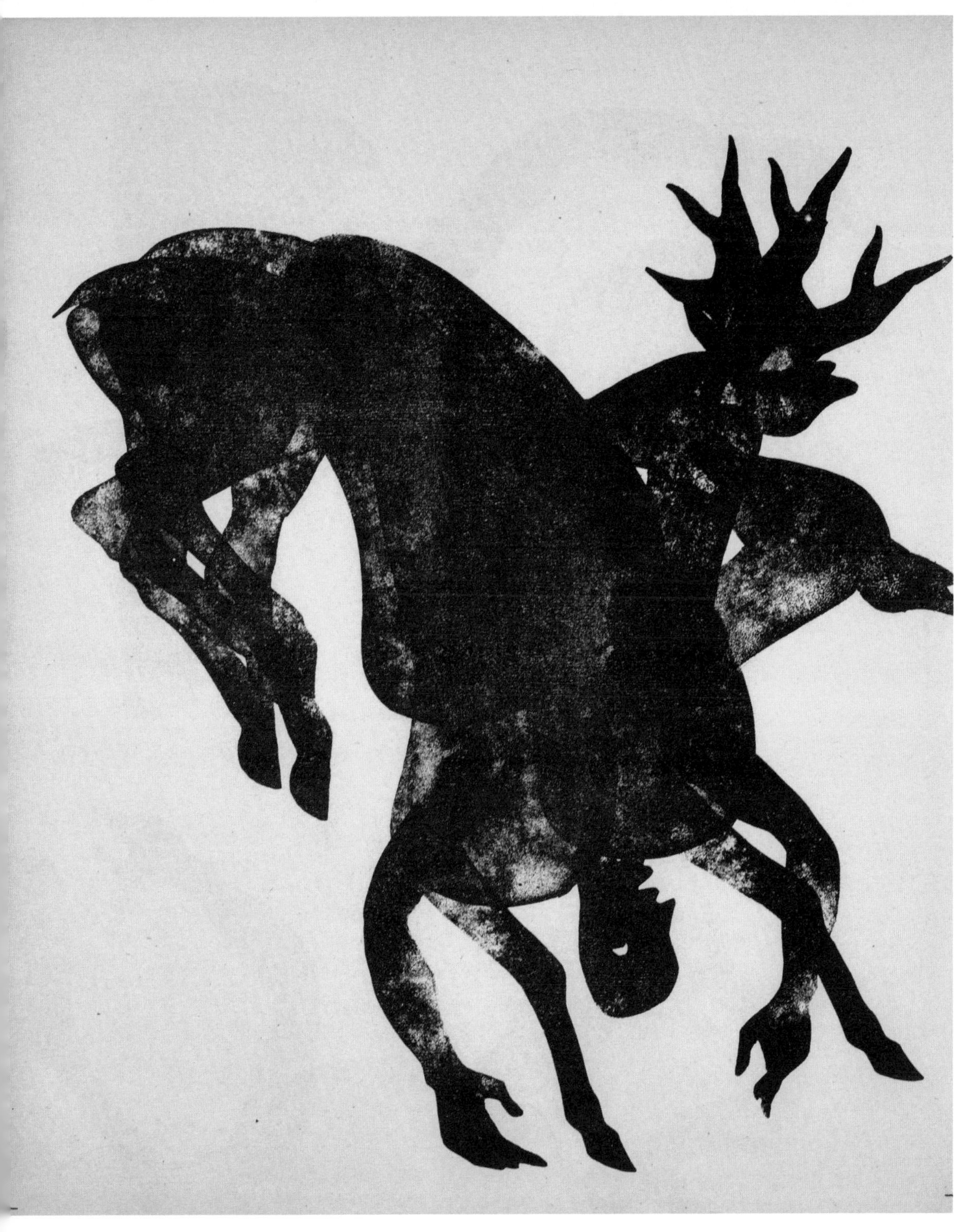

Illustration from
Tryk selv dine Billeder, 1943

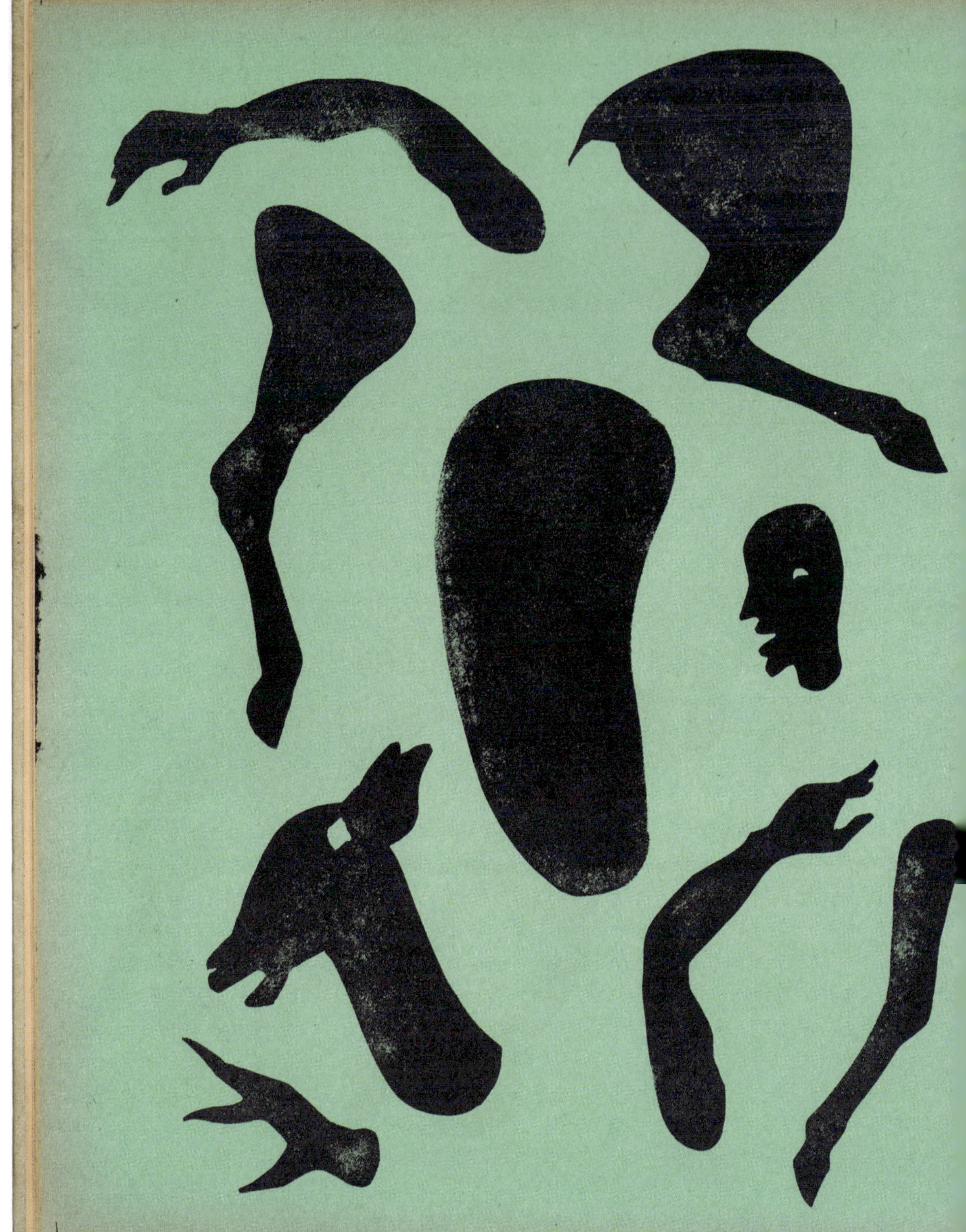

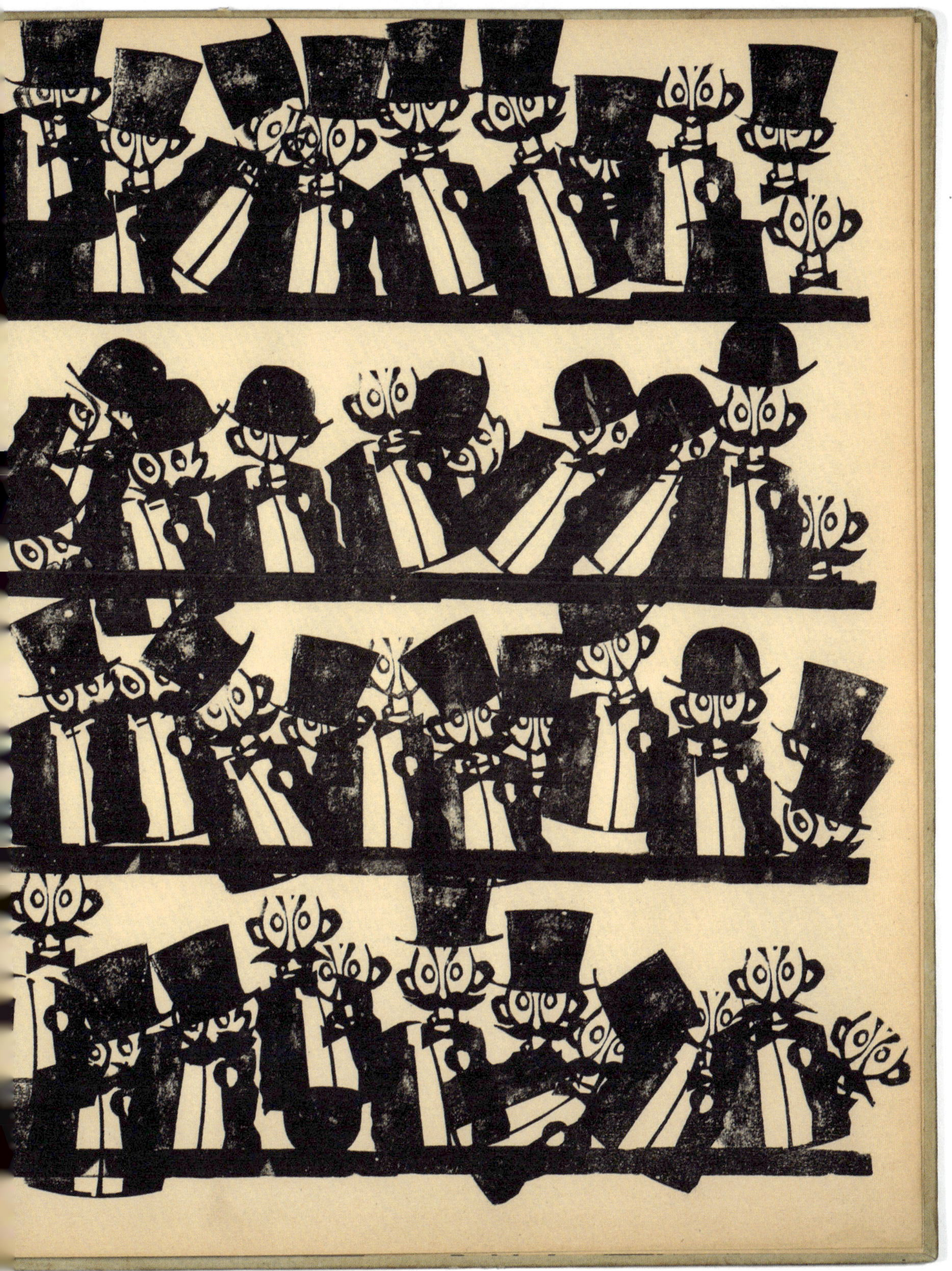

Spread from
Tryk selv dine Billeder, 1943

repeat,
revise,
return

Edmund de Waal

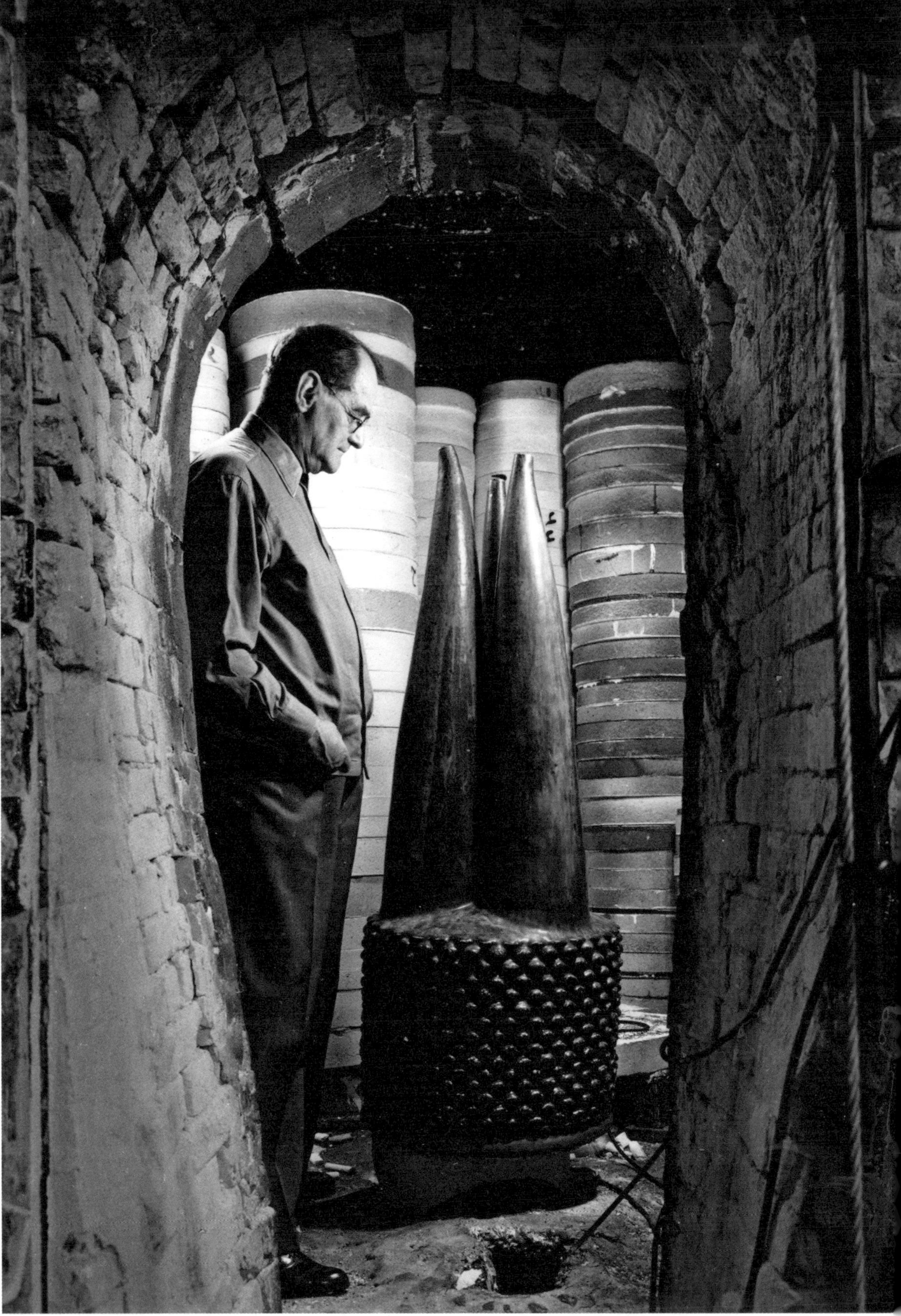

Nature repeats herself, or almost does:
repeat, repeat, repeat, revise, revise, revise

North Haven by Elisabeth Bishop

I

Looking closely at the photograph I realise that you must be tall. I know that slightly apologetic hunch, the way of accommodating objects on tables, a sketch pad, someone else smaller than you. You are in the kiln surrounded by the stacked saggars with that big, slightly sinister pot, *The Core of Power* standing on the ground in front of you. It reaches your chest and it seems to be looking back at you. We will get back to the subject of totems. Stay with me.

If we are going to get on I need to know how you pace the world. Your stride. So much of your work takes the form of a journey. You write a book for children about the adventures of Kusai who travels from his home on the beach, through low forest, high forest, across a river, towards a mountain, encountering magic animals until he finally returns home with parrot feathers for his mother's hat. It's a little dodgy in its colonial emphasis but the journeying itself is heartfelt. Your ballet is a quest too. There is one stoneware vessel that you created in 1939 which is a walk up to a hill town in France. It is summer and it is dusty. There are scuffles, a tail of a lizard over stones. The track winds through olive groves and orchards and the occasional rows of bean poles. Up

And up. The cypresses. And up.

And the town is folded into itself, one house into another, one window, a lintel, a doorstep, the bell-tower, a square that leads in three directions, steps. Everything is repeated, plural. And so the movements of this journeying up and round the hillside are a kind of stretching and pausing. A looking round.

"In the South of France we often walked from Cagnes to La Gaude. The road led up across a very hilly, sunlit mountain with forests, canyons, terraced olive plantations, roads, houses and paths, and I have attempted to put the memory of this lovely walk into a substance that not only *reproduces* but *is* itself the hard, sunburnt mountain. This is as close as you can get to your subject,…", [1] you write.

And then, because you should never waste a good idea, you take that feeling of a walk through a landscape and keep drawing it, inverting the hillside, doubling one hill on top of another, spinning it on its head, giving it a pedestal, taking that away. The path comes and goes, sometimes a line of intent, sometimes a proper road to the summit. I realise that you walk with your sketchpad in your hand. The "flight and perching of a bird" is how John Dewey described the being-in-the-moment and reflection-on-the-moment. In the Axel Salto archives in the museum there are thousands of drawings, returns, repeats, revisions. Your hands don't stay still.

We are going to get on.

(I like your name.
Axel and Salto balance)

We have to start somewhere so let's start at the mouth of the kiln.

Let's start.

More broken pots. More pots to break. It's Tuesday and early and no one else is in the studio, except the dog who has taken herself to her bed and is snoring already. My kiln is still too hot to be comfortable to reach into and extract the new black-glazed jars I've made. The temperature gauge of the vast green gas kiln shows 120 degrees but that doesn't mean much as the thick kiln shelves and the pots themselves will be much hotter. You don't open kilns, you *crack* them. This holds good even if it is several tons of steel, a heavy hinged door.

I crack the kiln. There is a black jar near the arch at the top of the kiln, eighteen inches inside, half-hidden behind a flotilla of small bowls. This black is my current favourite glaze, dense, river-stone dense, slightly metallic. I can see that the flame has worked up across the side, so that there is a run, a fluxing that you cannot control but hope to see. The jar looks beautiful in the shadows.

I'm wearing my heavy red heat-proof gauntlets but I manage to burn my wrist on the kiln shelf as I reach in to lift it out. It is the wrong weight. The glaze has run off the jar – I leave jagged porcelain on the shelf and bring out a jar with no base.

Two of the seven bowls have glaze that has run in the same way. They are *plucked*.

For a few hours after you take porcelain out, it sings. It settles into the world with high-pitched ticks.

I tally this firing. One extraordinary bowl, *donum dei*. Three pots for the hammer.

This is our territory.

You write in an early text in 1930 about the end of a firing, the wait for the pyrometric cones to bend that tell you how much heat-work has happened:

"With the 1280-degree cone down too, and the 1300-degree one beginning to wobble, it is time to stop feeding the fire and close the kiln, which is then left to cool down for a couple of days. And now! The long-awaited moment has come, the potter's romance, when the stoneware is brought out, scorching hot, creaking beneath the cooling glaze. The excitement, joy and disappointment of this moment are all worth the two months of preparatory work: right there are a hundred ceramic pieces!"[2]

I am going to steal "creaking" off you: I like that. Pots *creak* as they cool, as they change from one state to another, leave behind their infinite potentiality and cool into this particular thing in front of you. And then you continue and reflect that a "piece of porcelain is either successful or not; it only matters whether or not the vessel is crooked, if the material has a beautiful whiteness, if the decoration stands out nicely and clearly, that is, if the piece is technically good. When it comes to stoneware, a flaw or coincidence can be transformed into something beautiful and maybe point to new directions which will lead to new results. Thus the crackling, that was initially a mistake, contained possibilities for new ornamentation and effects in the material."[3]

And I can't allow you to be so pedestrian about porcelain – my beloved material – but I think it reflects all those conventions about porcelain *as* perfection, non-crookedness, niceness, clarity, the techniques in order. I wish you could read my book on this, the danger of obsession with whiteness, but I'm not sure we have the time. And here we are at the kiln-mouth – the place for vocalising – and you are unpacking the new vessels and examining them and are so absolutely right about flaw and coincidence, that generative spark which takes you off and away towards a denser mottled glaze (the fur of a faun, a weathered rock, the broken colours of a seashell), towards the folding and unfolding of a form.

All kinds of things can go wrong in a kiln.

I built my first kiln in Herefordshire in the lee of an old yew tree next to a damp barn. I had finished an apprenticeship and spent a summer working with silent potters in Japan. I had bought the kiln bricks from a Herefordshire potter who had gone bust. I had also bought his wheels, his ware-boards, an oak table for wedging clay, buckets and sieves, brushes, rock-hard bags of terracotta clay, jars of oxides, kiln shelves. I counted out £1000 and he looked relieved.

My first kiln looked like a very small chapel. I used a plan from Michael Cardew's *Pioneer Pottery*, a bible of self-reliance, full of tips on how to prospect for raw materials. The kiln was five feet long and four feet wide and I could crouch inside to load my stoneware casseroles, lidded soup bowls, teapots, teabowl, jugs and mugs onto the shelves. The arch above my head was a bit wobbly. My chimney wasn't particularly straight. I had to brick up the front each time I fired and little orange flames would find the gaps and lick.

Kilns work on the principle of directing heat evenly around all the pots, stacked on their heavy kiln shelves, and then out of the chimney. Kilns shouldn't leak, they should contain heat. I built mine so poorly that I found myself awake at three in the morning trying to coax the temperature higher, caulking the gaps between bricks, altering the dampers to see if I could get more pull of air through the kiln, praying.

Gaps in the kiln also meant that it cooled unevenly and damp Herefordshire air would sneak in. And the pots would *dunt*. They would crack. Sometimes you would discover this when you un-bricked the kiln. Sometimes days afterwards you would pick up a pot and tap it and it would sound dull, and as you ran your hands over it you would find the lattice work of fine cracks, and another batch were unsellable, unusable.

I tally forty-two firings over two and a half years at the Cwm Pottery, Rowlstone, Herefordshire. Twelve total failures. Twenty mostly wrong. Ten with enough celadon – green, oatmeal or tenmoku – black glazed pots to sell in the Herefordshire Guild of Craftsmen shop near the Cathedral, or pack in newspaper and hawk round my friends in London. Hundreds and hundreds of pots dunted. Dozens chucked over the hedge into the stream below the workshop. I broke several thousand.

Today, a Tuesday thirty-five years later, I pick up a hammer and reduce three pots to shards, fragments.

I think of your "excitement, joy and disappointment". And I know you knew how to break things up, how to start again with fragments.

V

Let us slow down here. We are by the kiln, we don't have to rush.

Indeed there are so many moments here to slow down and consider that I want to still our conversation.

I think of the photographer Eadweard Muybridge, those percussive stillings of a horse galloping, a man running. If these moments become gradually shorter can we find that exact frame of time when the vessel tilted in the kiln, the molten glaze gave up its hold on the clay body and spread? Can we go back further and further and find 'det brændende nu', the burning now. You thought about photography, thought about the recording of transformation, and then wrote about this now, drew it, made it happen.

There is a glorious lithograph you made in 1935:

> "I am working on a painting of cups falling off a tray. The picture is a representation of *The Burning Now*, the tense, uneasy yet strangely enchanted second between when the cups start to slide and then smash as they hit the ground. The falling, turning cups hover for a short moment in midair, like a bush that grows from the bottom cup that has already splintered upon contact with the floor, but whose shards still hang upright in the air, in reaction to the moment of the blasting."[4]

I love this.

Here is time standing still, the world, the body, the breath slowed to a breath-turn. There is nothing you can do to catch this cascade of cups as they fall. Your experience of this moment is both caught in the knowledge of what is happening and has happened, the slippage and the sound of breakage. And it runs backwards – "earlier and earlier, the unraised hand calm/The apple unbitten in the palm", as Philip Larkin wrote in his poem about a shied apple core missing the wastepaper basket.

Because the broken cups blossom back into the unbroken cups. The burning moment defies the banality of a present or a past tense or a future tense. Transformation is fissile. Objects hold their transformative, burning now in trust. If you can change, you can change again. The smashed cups talk to the clay in the potter's hand.

I remember writing about a Chinese bowl from the twelfth century "The bowl was made in Jingdezhen, thrown then moulded with a flower in a deep well, unglazed rim, green-grey with a slightly pooled glaze, some issues as the dealers would say, chips, marks, scuffs. It happens in the present tense and it is, itself, a continuous present of active, dynamic movements, judgements and decisions. It doesn't feel in the past, and it feels wrong to force it into one just to obey a critical orthodoxy. ... the act of reimagining it by picking it up is an act of remaking."[5]

Breaking, dropping, falling cups are an act of remaking too.

And breaking can be such fun. In 1943 you publish *Tryk selv dine Billeder*, Print Your Own Pictures, a book for children. It is an emphatically, gloriously funny exhortation to keep going. Repetition is the only rule, you write. Could there be anything more liberating?

I have your book in front of me as I write to you. It is big and orange and handsome with an impish-looking acrobat with a top hat in one hand holding another person in mid-air by the head, limbs dangling. Look at me, they are saying, join in. This is a manual for mucking about.

It involves stamps. Not postage stamps, but the kind you might have used in kindergarten, pressed into ink and then emphatically stamped onto coloured paper. It opens with a forest of trees and then three pages of your text. And then here is a green page with all the elements you will need. You are given some limbs for a person and some parts of a horse, four faces, a top hat and a cane, a bowl and a dish, the trunk of a palm tree, some foliage, some broken shapes and a thick black line. And a moustache. A glorious, bad-sort-in-silent-movies moustache.

And so here is a horse and here is a rider. And you are off, galloping, cantering, falling off, falling under, legs akimbo, forwards, backwards, breathless.

And here are four acrobats. One (highly moustached) is juggling balls. One is balancing objects precariously. Another is standing on their head and holding an ungainly tree high above them. And one sinister gentleman is balanced on the crown of their top hat, two spiky legs waving other hats high above him. Thump go the stamps down onto the page. More juggling balls. More legs. More hats. More is good.

And then here is the kitchen.

It starts in an orderly way. A shelf at the top of the page with fifteen cups. Two shelves mirror each other with bowls. Two shelves with stacks of bowls. A line of seven elegant vases – stamp, stamp, stamp.

And then down it comes. Bowls in mid-air and dishes clattering everywhere and the vases near the bottom of the page and the walking sticks are involved somehow and the air is full of things breaking apart, fragmenting, becoming shards. You see it. You hear it. You feel it.

One thing becoming something else, becoming other. A burning, breaking, glorious, noisy, *now*.

Imagine being given this as a child. Imagine this licence. You know what you are doing when you say *more is more*, when you say *again*, when you say *now*.

The final page is a deer and it is a falling man, one on top of another, one becoming another, "double-nature": "You are in the world of stamps, in wonderland, it is you who decides everything."[6]

"Art allows us to think the unthinkable, to posit one paradox after another in the hope of firming up wisps of our lives and feelings by transfiguring them, by giving them a shape, a design, a coherence, even if they are and will remain forever incoherent. Incoherence exists, which is why composition – art – exists", writes the novelist André Aciman. And he continues, "Grammarians called this unthinkable, imponderable, impalpable, fluid, transitory, incoherent zone the irrealis mood, a verbal mood to express what might never, couldn't, shouldn't, wouldn't possibly occur but that might just happen."[7]

Do you love this as much as I do?

"Unthinkable, imponderable, impalpable, fluid, transitory, incoherent" are such great words to have on the table as I pick up your drawings and books and poems and vessels and look at your textiles and the photographs of your exhibitions and think of how you created zones to experience so much feeling, so much contradictory, lyrical thinking-aloud.

It is also the kiln. Fluidity before stasis is probably the most cogent descriptor of a firing I have come across. The kiln is a zone of the transitory.

And it connects to your awareness of the earth under your feet: *Optegnelser fra en Rejse til Italien (1920)*, Notes from a Journey to Italy, published in the Danish art magazine *Klingen*, is where you describe how you and Lundstrøm are climbing Vesuvius, how you descend into the crater, the pumice stone under your feet, the moving, metallic lava, stone and fire.

A volcano and a kiln both hide and reveal a process of coming into being, an essential transformative inherence. Both are dangerous.

So I begin to look for this lean, this shifting, a deliquescence. It takes me to the heat of the kiln, the softening of the pyrometric cones. It takes me to the burning now.

The kiln is where unfired friable clay and glaze melt together. And sometimes vessels warp. They can move back to the state when you had just thrown them. If you throw a bowl on the potter's wheel and nudge it by mistake as you put it down on a board beside you, that slight movement will return later on. You will open the kiln and find that a perfect bowl will be ovalled. Clay finds you out. That nudge, the crack smoothed over by a thumb, the handle joined in a hurry, the clay slip that you hope will bodge and fudge an edge, a declivity: it all comes back.

And this brings me back to that first vessel in the kiln, your tripots, your great sculptures of three funnelling vessels held near each other on a textured plinth. The vessels reach up. They taper to the smallest of openings, a mouth. They feel like a reaching back into some history, some shared moment.

What do I call them? They are at the heart of what you do – vast and troubling, so public. You make *Kraftens Kerne* – The Core of Power – in 1956 for your exhibition in Paris that year. I want to ask who else is making anything of this ambition out of clay at this moment. The photograph of you standing next to one in the kiln endures. You and your work looking at each other.

You look implacable in this picture, but I am unsettled. I am anxious.

There is a moment in the mid-century when other kinds of sculpture seem to share this anxiety. In 1952 Herbert Read writes in his essay for the Venice Biennale "these new images belong to the iconography of despair, or of defiance … Here are images of flight, of ragged claws 'scuttling across the floors of silent seas', of excoriated flesh, frustrated sex, the geometry of fear." The primitive "religions of fear, terror, propitiation and retribution" corresponded to the existential anguish and unease of modern man. The ceramics of the 1950s show a profuse number of standing forms, totems, memorialized offerings, winged pots. Vessels have plinths to raise them up as if they had ritual use, or fragmentary attachments as if they had been recently unearthed. These pots aspire to the condition of grave goods.

And you are there before anyone else. You understand the deep metaphor of danger that lies in the transformation of clay to ceramic. You mine this metamorphosis of fluidity, possibility, the endless into frozen form.

You make totems. A totem is not "an archaic object", wrote Rosalind Krauss of the American sculptor David Smith; "Rather, it was a powerfully abbreviated expression of a complex of feelings and desires which he felt to be operative in himself and within society as a whole."

And these three tall thrown vessels that taper towards a small mouth, each slightly moving, leaning, are exactly that abbreviated expression. I feel unsettled by them as they seem to be so much more than the borrowed archaicisms of other sculptors of the time. Part of their effectiveness is that you develop a personal lexicon for how objects can carry meaning, working it out through texts and poetry and drawings and sculpture, your pots. I'm going to walk quite carefully with you now as I find your exploration of this compelling. Instead of reaching back into history to find precursors of objects of beauty for you to draw on, you write of *demonic things* in relation to the 'sprouting style' you developed in the 1940s:

"By this I understand objects which, beside the apparent, possess other, concealed properties which mark them off completely from their surroundings: things on which there is a curse or which have a special fate, which rub you the wrong way. The demonic can also rest in qualities in oneself which in a strange way blend with the object: things one remembers from an earlier existence, for example."[8]

You connect with those things that not only provoke anxiety, a somatic resonance of distress, but seem to speak to places of unresolved conflict in yourself. You seem to know them already: they hold you and you hold them.

And you give an example of a "newly found tiger from Chichen Itza in Mayaland … It is a primitive stone jaguar of extraordinary fierceness; its spots are inlaid jade and its flat back is the table on which the human sacrifices were placed when the heart was to be cut out of their living bodies; it still bears the traces of this." This leads you back to your own practice: "When I call the sprouting vase demonic it is because it regards me with the cruel unconcern of nature now I have shaped it. Quite unashamed it speaks of violence and assault, of trampling underfoot on the way to the lifeboat, and that men are wicked at bottom but must live. Some prickly vases tell of joy of growing, of quiet happiness. Not all are demonic, but this is, it is the devil's own vase."[9]

The beautiful stone jaguar with its brindled pelt of jade from a thousand years ago and this newly fired sprouting vase "regard me with…cruel unconcern." We will come back to cruel unconcern.

This belief that "qualities in oneself which in a strange way blend with the object" can lead you towards playfulness, to the quixotic, to solace – but can also lead to this whole body of work on the threshold of much more disturbing feelings. And one mood can lead to another.

Being at the factory in "high and playful spirits", you suddenly find yourself putting horns on a vase.

I'm pleased that you titled one of your books *Ting ikke ord*, Things not Words.

Actually, I am more than pleased. This is a title to get stuck into. And perhaps I could start with the poem *Not Ideas About the Thing but the Thing Itself* by Wallace Stevens:

> At the earliest ending of winter
> In March, a scrawny cry from outside
> Seemed like a sound in his mind.

The sun of late winter, surprising us out of what we felt we knew. The sun like a cry that seems to precede everything, a sound from far away. "It was like/A new knowledge of reality." The world of the senses precedes thoughts, the knowing through the body, tacit knowledge. And yet you reach for words because the shaping of words brings another iteration, takes sound back into the body again.

Rilke's *Das Ding Gedichte*, poem-things as much as poems about things, haunt the poetry of the early twentieth century. I once made a small installation and called it *Das Ding an Sich*, the Thing in Itself, a nod to Heidegger, a way of putting a very big title underneath a small shelf with some pots on it.

Words are things. They have weight and shape and texture.

Things is a good word to start an argument with. We have too many things. They clutter. We have too many words. They eddy and spill.

I look at your bibliography and you write poetry, essays, technical descriptions, newspaper articles, children's books, memoir. You edit magazines. And there are fairytales and laments and elegies. You are considered in descriptions of how to fire kilns, good on techniques. You are searching in the balancing of tone and speed in your writing. You love making books.

Your moods are fissile. You settle here and then you return to a subject, to a motif, an image.

You need to write just as you need to draw.

X

And you make new words. I have to tell you how much this pleases me. This compacting of words – sun-bush, water-full – shows you are alive to exigencies of language, of course, but it is also a fusing of them. They're indissoluble. *Ting ikke ord*: they have been fired together.

It suggests that you know the weight and texture of words: that words are things themselves.

And as you know, once something has been fired it cannot be changed back into its constituent parts. It can be fractured. That is why poems work on the page, creating a shape with jaggedness.

I look at your book on papers from 1943. It is a small book of samples, ring-bound, patterns repeated but each in five different colourways. I am unsure as to the purpose of this book. On one level it simply reveals that it is possible to have this pattern of bamboo in orange and green, the pomegranate in autumnal rust, or in alternatives of greater and greater vividness. On another it is joy, a book published in the middle of a world war that is "a demonstration of optimism and therefore we believe … useful in the present time. They say that life lies lustrously behind all sorrow and will triumph in the end."[10] And it is of course presenting your patterns to a world that uses them for the endpapers of books and the covers of notebooks and textiles and furnishing fabrics and advertisements. I admire your pragmatism.

But as you know how books work, how one image is held as a page turns and another is revealed, I remember that you enjoyed seeing your pots and cloth overlapping each other. I've been shown photographs of your exhibitions where vessels are placed in front of great falls of printed cloth where the pattern is made up of interlacings of sprouting pots. And you have designed this book so I go back and start again, pace myself through it.

Maybe this obsession with seeing how one pattern repeats itself is part of your fascination with the endlessness in nature that you talk of, write of, sketch, model, sample. You pick up one seed, one pine kernel, a shell with a particular whorl from a beach and draw it, think it through. And you found "sources of inspiration in photographic images taken with ultra-rapid exposures and in photographs of the scent of flowers. Figures under the microscope are just as suitable for the development of ornaments as affectionate observations of the flora and fauna of nature in natural size…. The woodcut of the sprouting bulbs was carved under the impression of slow-motion film, where a pod was seen to ripen, split and scatter its seed, or buds unfolded into flowers under one's eyes. In a few seconds, movements are shown which normally take days; thus here the long germinating process of the bulbs is concentrated in the moment of bursting forth."[11]

So both natural objects and the technology that allows photographs to document change allow you to think how, in the
words from Elisabeth Bishop's poem,

> "Nature repeats herself, or almost does:
>   repeat, repeat, repeat, revise, revise, revise."

With colour I have the feeling that once you started this set of
variations in the small book of paper, once you set this in motion,
then it might keep changing without you.

I woke up from a strange dream last night, thinking that I was
in some Danish house. This probably happens to many people.
There was poised furniture and clean floors and it was all very
mid-century. And the huge window had curtains of your fabric
of two deer under a tree, and the deer were moving.

Which brings us to Ovid.

"Now I am ready to tell how bodies are changed/Into different bodies" wrote Ted Hughes in his version of *The Metamorphoses*, and we need to think about bodies.

Creation starts with clay. You write that "the Persians venerated clay. The Prophet and his successors sanctified it with their bodies in the grave. All living things descend to the earth, become earth, and will rise again."[12] It ends with clay.

Gods make bodies out of clay, pinch a piece of earth into the shape of a person, bake them, breathe into them.

But more than this embodiment remember that pots have necks, feet, bellies. Bodies are vessels. And different kinds of clay are different clay *bodies*.

Italo Calvino writes of Ovid's *Metamorphoses* that it is "above all the poem of rapidity. Everything has to happen at high speed, strike the imagination; every image has to overlap another image, come into focus, and then vanish. This is the principle of the cinema: each line, like each frame, must be full of visual stimuli in motion. The abhorrence of the vacuum dominates both space and time. For page after page all verbs are in the present, so that everything is happening before our eyes; events pursue each other, and everything distant is rejected. When Ovid wishes to change pace, the first thing he does is to change. Not the tense of the verbs but the person."[13]

Which is brilliant.

Except that you don't change the person. For you it is above all Actaeon.

"On these transformation motifs I have formed several ceramic figures and cut many woodcuts; the myth of Actaeon especially has lived in me. Actaeon surprises Diana in her bath; he is punished by being turned into a stag and is torn to pieces by his own dogs. Actaeon is transformed into a stag; the animal rushes through him."[14]

This stops me before I have started. To write about Ovid is to write about one body living in the form of another. I list how Actaeon "has lived in me", how the animal has rushed through Actaeon's body and now rushes through the body of a Danish artist.

You make woodcuts and etchings of Actaeon, innumerable drawings of the moment of transformation, ceramic figures of heads with budding horns, sculptures of deer. "The ideas of transformation have lingered with me since boyhood. Walt Rosenberg translated Ovid into five-footed iambics and I illustrated them."[15] You write about the myth and it slides into and out of shadows in your poetry. The longer I spend in your company the more often I glimpse antlers eliding /into/ branches of trees in the pierced fretwork vessels you created. I feel the immanence of change in the way in which protuberances are starting to show; "the vase is like a living organism; the body buds, the buds develop, and sprouting, even prickly, vases are the result of this life."[16]

What drew you so intensely to Actaeon? Why this obsessive return? I've been re-reading Ovid and I had forgotten how violent these changes are, how much force, how dark the desire. To escape is impossible. There is no volition, there is no reciprocation, only a particular velocity to the becoming of your fate, a stumbling, a falling, a hurtling. You eat yourself to death, you are killed by a snakebite, you are torn apart by your own hounds. And each hound is named, as it is always personal. It is horror because once you have become a woodpecker or a constellation of stars, a bear, lion, stone, reeds by a riverside, a spring of water, a flower – narcissus or hyacinth or laurel or myrrh – you cannot change back. You become a seabird and your father becomes a sea eagle perpetually chasing you. Once you have changed gender or become hermaphrodite, or changed from stone to life, or from being alive to becoming stone, once you are Echo, your existence is caught: "nothing living is finished in its present form, all is movement, rising or falling" as you put it. That is to say you keep the transformation within you, latent. You *are* metamorphoses.

You slow down, allow yourself to refract, to move from one infinitesimal flickering moment to another, like the high-speed photographer, to consider what is happening with Actaeon: the motif must show the metamorphic moment itself, not before or after, but the very burning now. "The wonder happens in all its horror on the scene, like a machine that stands there with all its turning cogs … this is drama, not just an exterior action, a fable, but an inner development, which recreates the exterior form, which makes everything merge, makes the contours flicker, when, in a second, a hand will turn into a hoof."[17]

Unbidden I think of removing a spyhole into a kiln towards the end of a firing when the heat is at its greatest. If you are reducing the kiln – have the dampers across the chimney to reduce the oxygen flow to create particular glaze effects – the flames will lick out. You blow at them and peer into the red-orange, yellow-orange flames. They flicker, dance around the vessels, the pyrometric cones. Contours flicker.

Actaeon, cursed, racing through the woods, with his hounds, becomes other. "Let us imagine the transformation occurring in a moment," you write. "A human mind becomes animal, a miserable act being accomplished on the spot since the will of the goddess has the power and suddenness of lightning. Psychologically the reduction to animal is interesting, of an almost painful complexity."[18]

And this works for the artist as "the antlers burst forth from the confused brow, hands and feet wrap themselves in sharp cloven hooves, and the back curves into a bow. This play of forms in transition in the outline of the dual animal, mobile and stiffened into a statue at one and the same time, is extraordinarily rich for the imagination."[19]

So it allows you to trace the disappearing man and to trace the appearing antlers. And for you to bring out the alertness of the head of deer, its long back, its senses alive to danger, poised for flight, poised to disappear into the branches of the woodland, both immobile and flickering with potential movement, mobile.

And in doing so to understand "objects which, beside the apparent, possess other, concealed properties which mark them off completely from their surroundings: things on which there is a curse or which have a special fate, which rub you the wrong way." For Actaeon as story, as metamorphosis, is a demonic *thing*; "The demonic can also rest in qualities in oneself which in a strange way blend with the object: things one remembers from an earlier existence, for example."[20]

So this is why you choose Actaeon from amongst the cast that Ovid creates of heroes, gods of desire, priests, weavers, nymphs, huntresses, muses, daughters of kings, daughters of gods, goddesses of magic, and of war and of justice and of the hearth, centaurs, architects, nereids, fishermen, sculptors. All of them are subject to some unfolding story but you hold Actaeon's transgressions close.

Actaeon transgresses by trespassing on the privacy of Diana, Artemis. He transgresses by making sound when he should be silent. He unleashes the theatre of cruelty of creativity, how one thing becomes another through savage transformation: the "demonic can also rest in qualities in oneself".

You remind us that we hold this possibility within us, and that we cannot go back but can endlessly, iteratively, track the process of change.

I realise, belatedly, that Actaeon having transformed is then torn apart, breaks apart, becomes scraps, shards.

I do not know whether to pick this up. Some objects need respect, demand a wariness in approach.

Salto designed this vase in 1953. It is 38 centimetres high, too big for a hand to hold. It is heavy. The form is sprouting, budding. These vessels might be seeds or fruit. That is they contain a different future, one that will have to unfold. You wouldn't put flowers in it. It is a vessel that sits by itself.

Salto's glazes seem to be still molten. This glaze is sanguine.

I pick it up.

So I want to share this with you. It is Seamus Heaney thinking about creativity:

"Years ago Michael Longley wrote an essay on poets from Northern Ireland in which he made a distinction between igneous and sedimentary modes of poetic composition. In geology, igneous rocks are derived from magma or lava solidified below the Earth's surface whereas sedimentary ones are formed by the deposit and accumulation of mineral and organic materials, worked on, broken down and reconstituted by the action of water, ice and wind. The very sound of the words is suggestive of what is entailed in each case. Igneous is irruptive, unlooked-for and peremptory; sedimentary is steady-keeled, dwelt-upon, graduated.'[21]

I think of you when I think of magma. I think of your feeling for the instability of the world, the tremor of the currents deep in the earth, the pressure of the buds in spring, "bristling with potency." I see you amongst a cascade of paper, your hands moving as one sketch becomes another, another, the burning present a whirlwind like that of your sultan's "explosive rage."

Here you are in your kiln, in your suit, slightly stooped, regarding your finished work. A model of someone who is steadiness incarnate, a man of letters, creator of public works for the great institutions, revered, "steady-keeled, dwelt-upon, graduated."

And yet you are everything else too, irruptive, unlooked-for and peremptory. You write that,

"In these smouldering, these streaming vases the stoneware bursts into song, and what else should clay be used for? For play when the heart swells and for comfort in affliction. For advancing against time and creating life from the dead. Even painful life is better than no life. Out of Actaeon sprouts the stag; he sinks. In his burning face, where clay and glaze embrace each other, stoneware unfolds its true nature, becomes an art form of its own with its own media and aims, a little sister to big brothers. The sprouting style can only sprout in stoneware.

In the clay arisen from the depths."[22]

Axel Salto and Actaeon are about to take flight, about to change.

Got to go.

Pots to make of course and some scraps of writing to finish. I want to keep walking with you. I want to talk through some of your poems, and as I have gone down a side-track after reading Ted Hughes's *Metamorphoses*, I want to introduce you to his early poems in *Crow*. You would love them. They bristle with anxiety, flight.

My autumn notebook is full of questions and the winter one full of crossed-out pages and it is almost spring. I feel like we have spent a lot of time together.

Amongst other things I want to look at the markings under some of your vessels, *Salto* inscribed or raised, the elegant crown wrapped around Royal Copenhagen Denmark in pale olive, the three cobalt-blue waves, the pattern numbers in blue. Or are they year marks? It is part of an obsession I have about how to let things go. Markings and signings and namings and titling of the things we create are ways of pressing a final wish into the pocket at the last moment on the threshold. They might carry some tremor of intention with them, briefly. But we know they will not last.

I have enjoyed this time.

Notes

1
Axel Salto, "Epilog til
en Stentøjsproduktion
1929–1937", *Samleren,
Tidsskrift for Keramik,
Porcelæn og Glas*, vol. 14,
January 1937, p. 5.
See also pp. 212–213

2
Axel Salto, *Salto's
Keramik*, København,
Det Berlingske
Bogtrykkeri, 1930, n.p.

3
ibid.

4
Axel Salto, *Det brændende
Nu*, København, Grafisk
Cirkel, 1938, p. 8

5
Edmund de Waal,
The White Road, London,
Chatto & Windus, 2016,
p. 4–5

6
Axel Salto, *Tryk selv dine
Billeder*, København,
Fischers Forlag, 1943,
n.p.

7
André Aciman, *Homo
Irrealis*, Faber & Faber,
2021, p. 25

8
Axel Salto, *Den spirende
Stil*. København, Grafisk
Cirkel, 1949, p. 62

9
ibid.

10
Axel Salto, *Salto-Papir*,
København, Fischers
Forlag, 1943, n.p.

11
Axel Salto, *Den spirende
Stil*. København, Grafisk
Cirkel, 1949, p. 59

12
Axel Salto, *Den spirende
Stil*. København, Grafisk
Cirkel, 1949, p. 56

13
The Uses of Literature
(also published as *The
Literature Machine*), Italo
Calvino, 1980 or 1986.

14
Axel Salto, *Den spirende
Stil*. København, Grafisk
Cirkel, 1949, p. 63

15
ibid.

16
Axel Salto, *Den spirende
Stil*. København, Grafisk
Cirkel, 1949, p. 62

17
Axel Salto, *Det brændende
Nu*, København: Grafisk
Cirkel, 1938, p. 14

18
Axel Salto, *Den spirende
Stil*, København, Grafisk
Cirkel, 1949, p. 63

19
ibid.

20
Axel Salto, *Den spirende
Stil*, København, Grafisk
Cirkel, 1949, p. 62

21
Seamus Heaney,
'Lowell's Command',
published in *Salma-
gundi* No. 80 (Fall 1988),
p. 83

22
Axel Salto, *Den spirende
Stil*, København, Grafisk
Cirkel, 1949, p. 64

Edmund de Waal in his studio, 2023

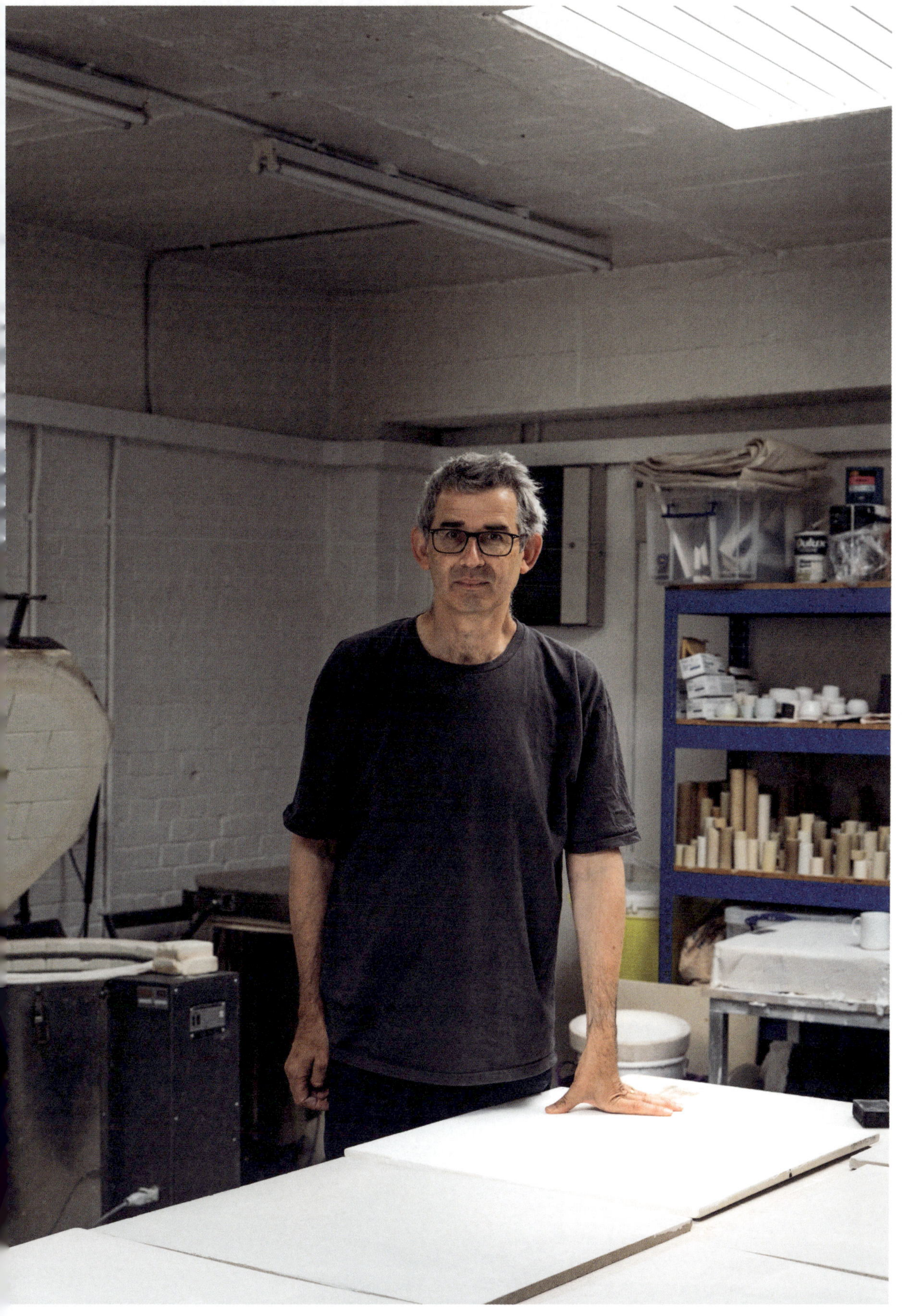

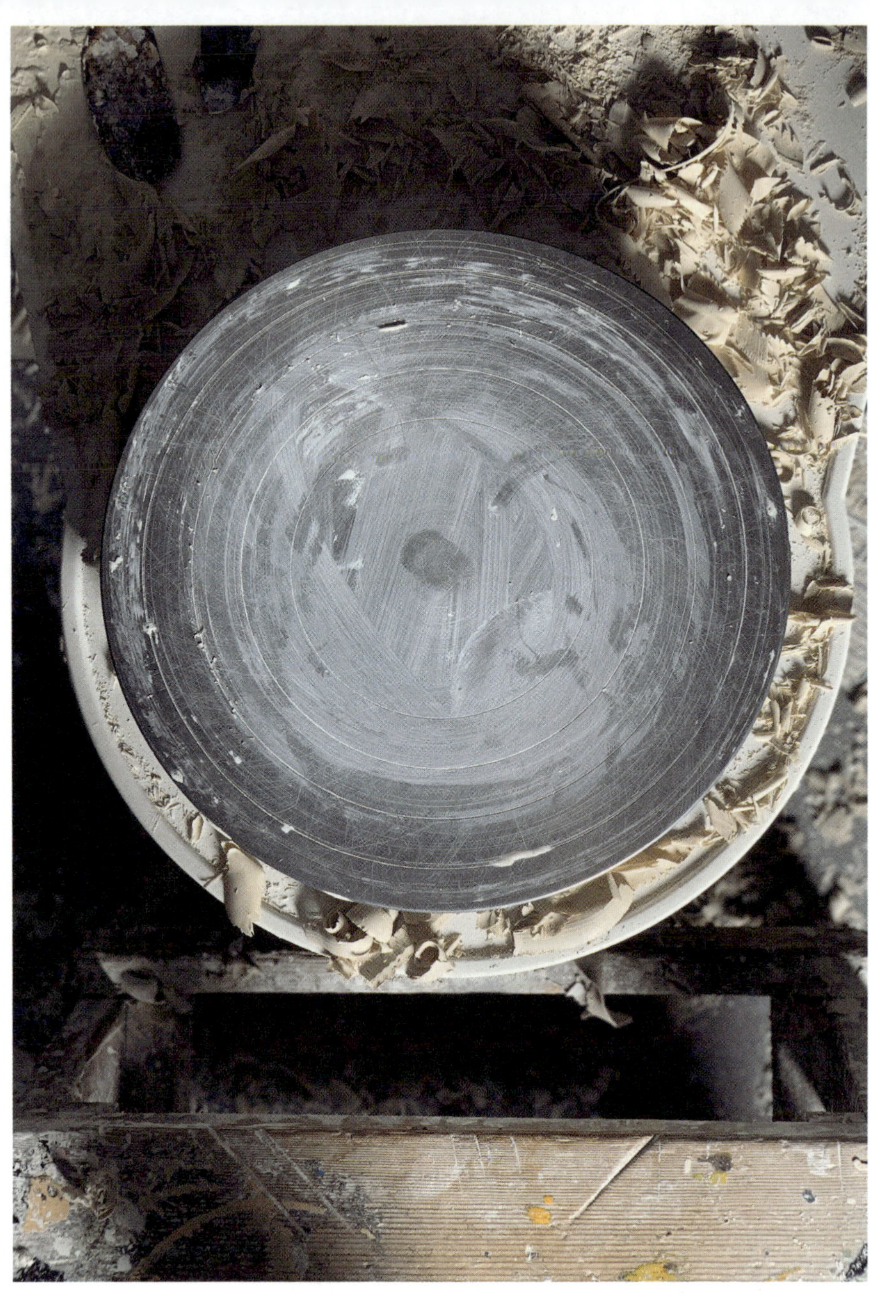

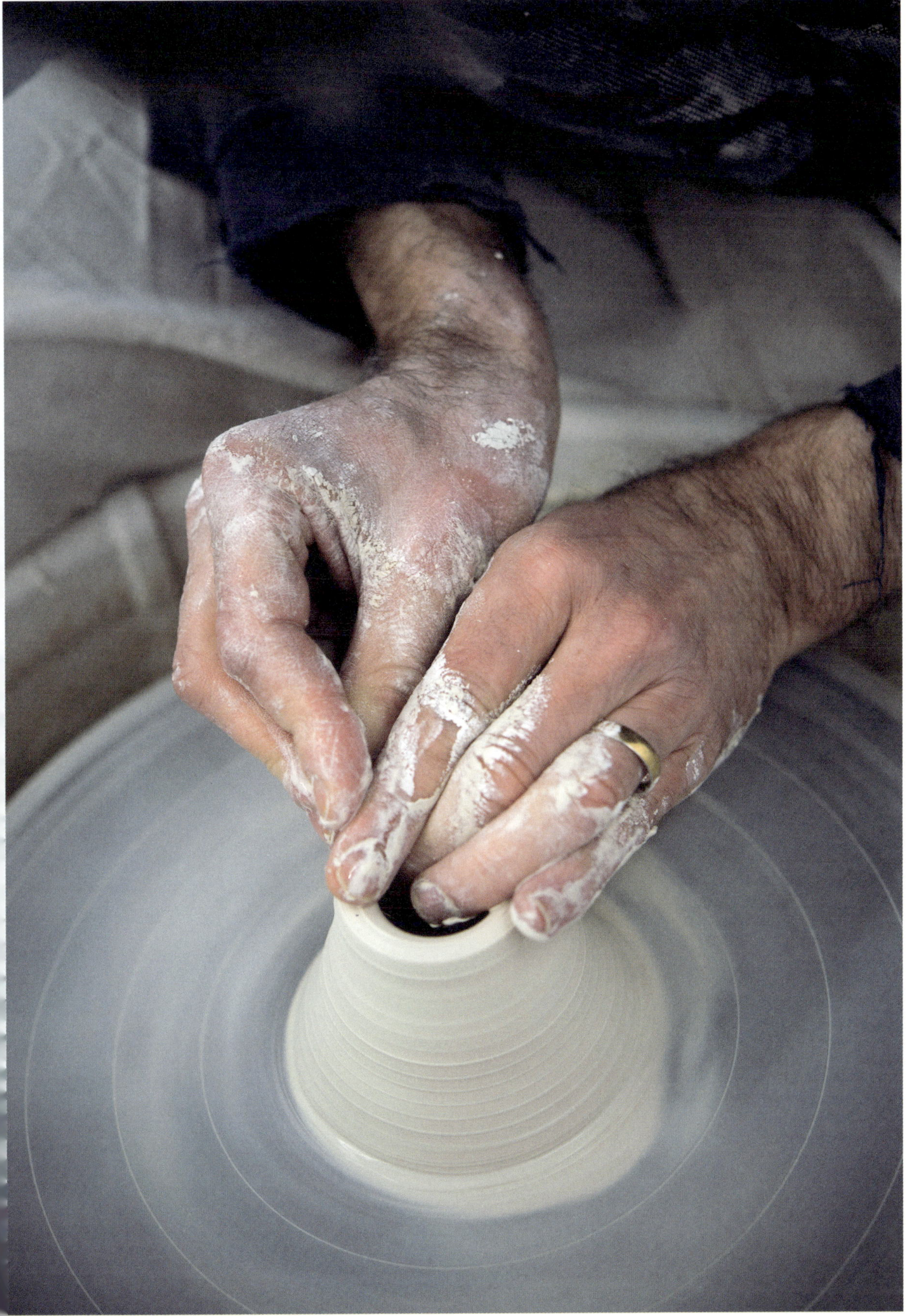

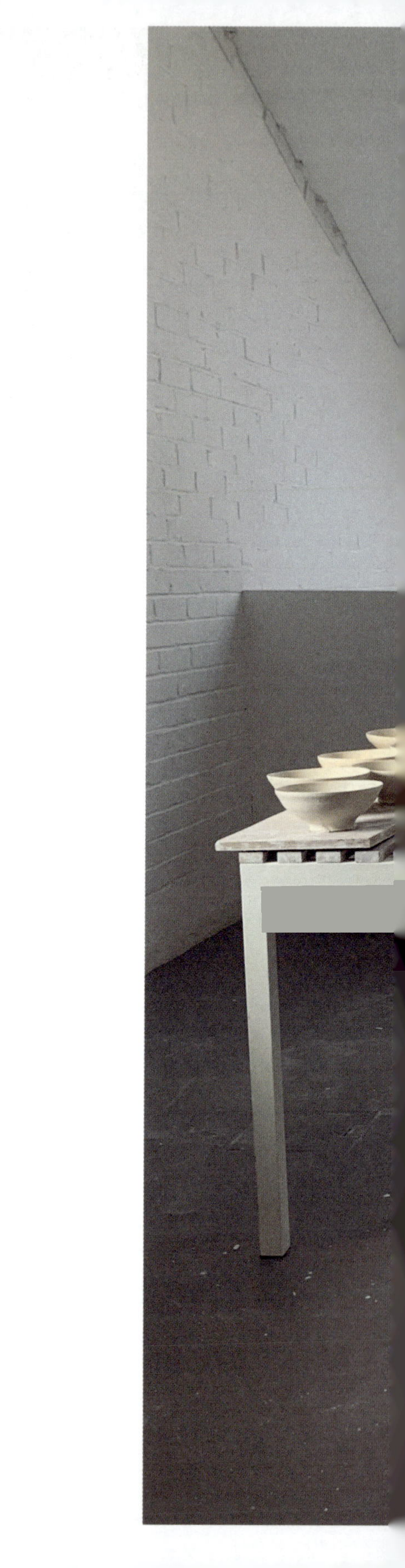

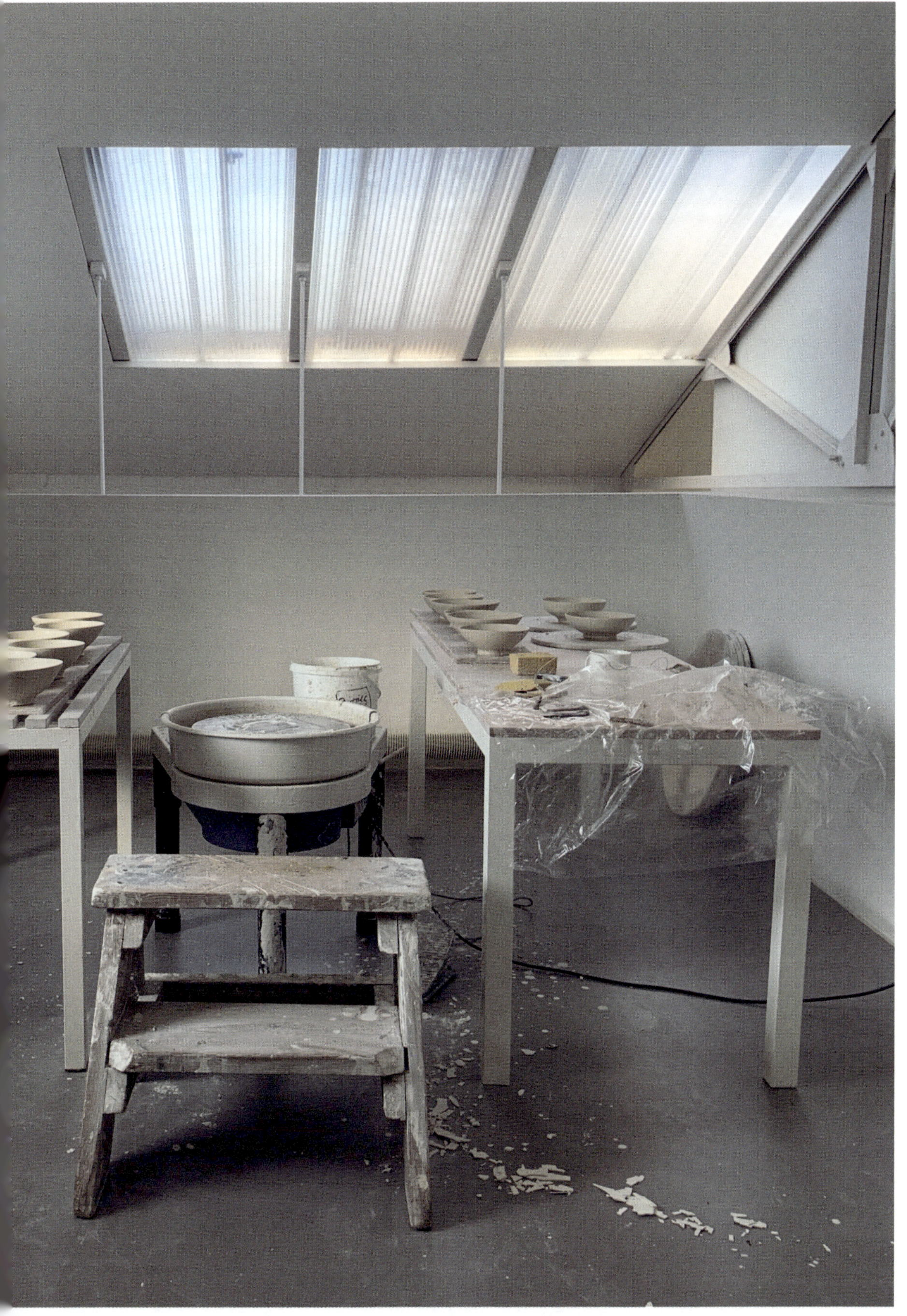

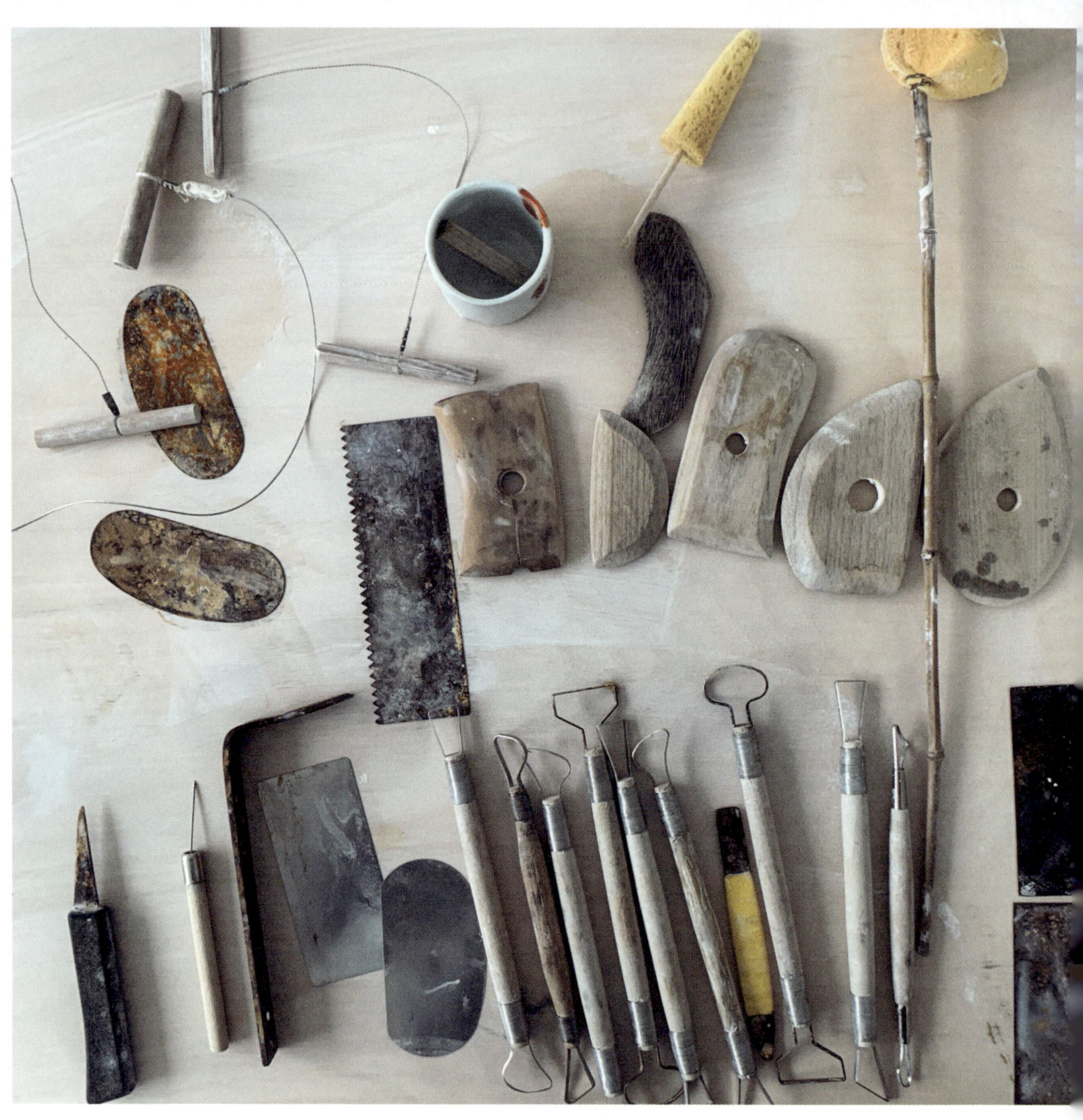

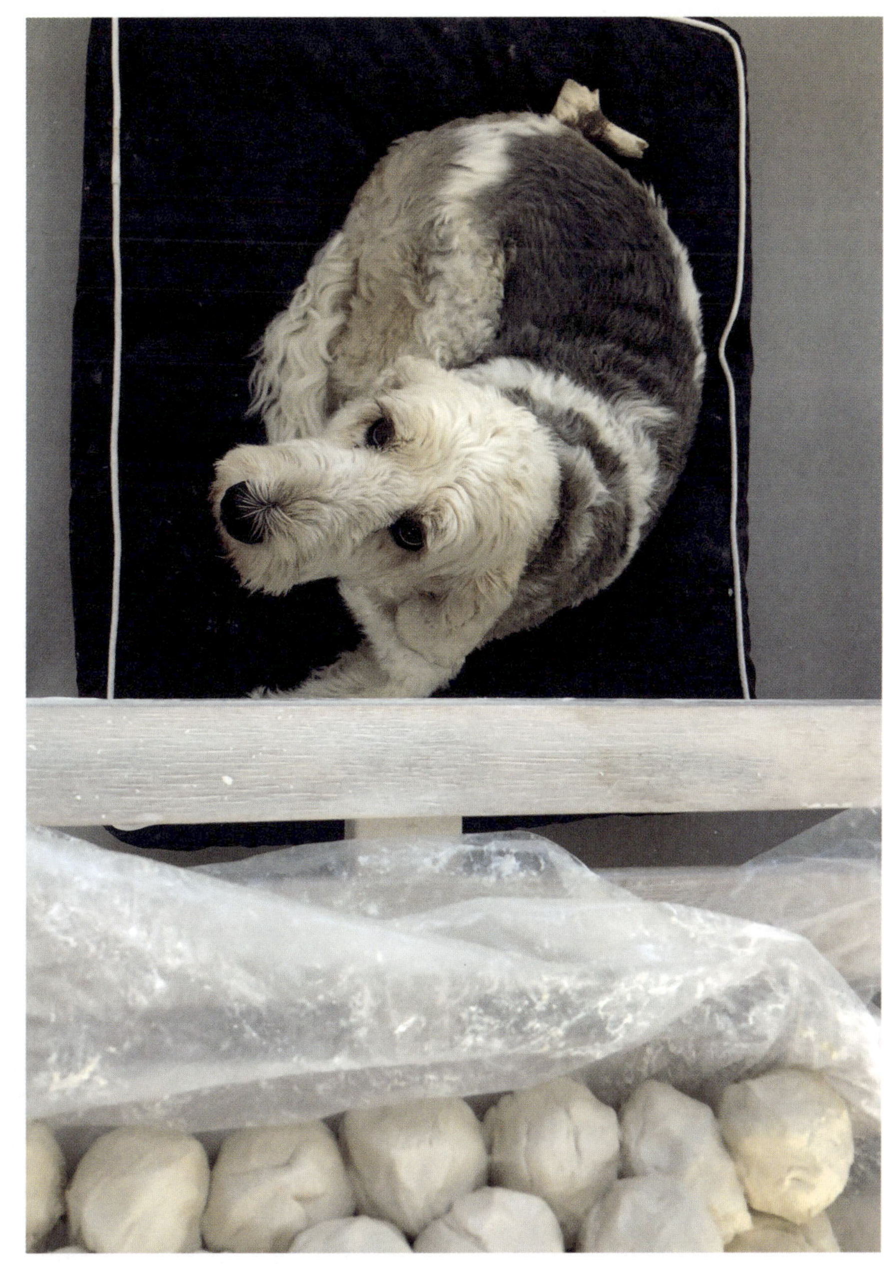

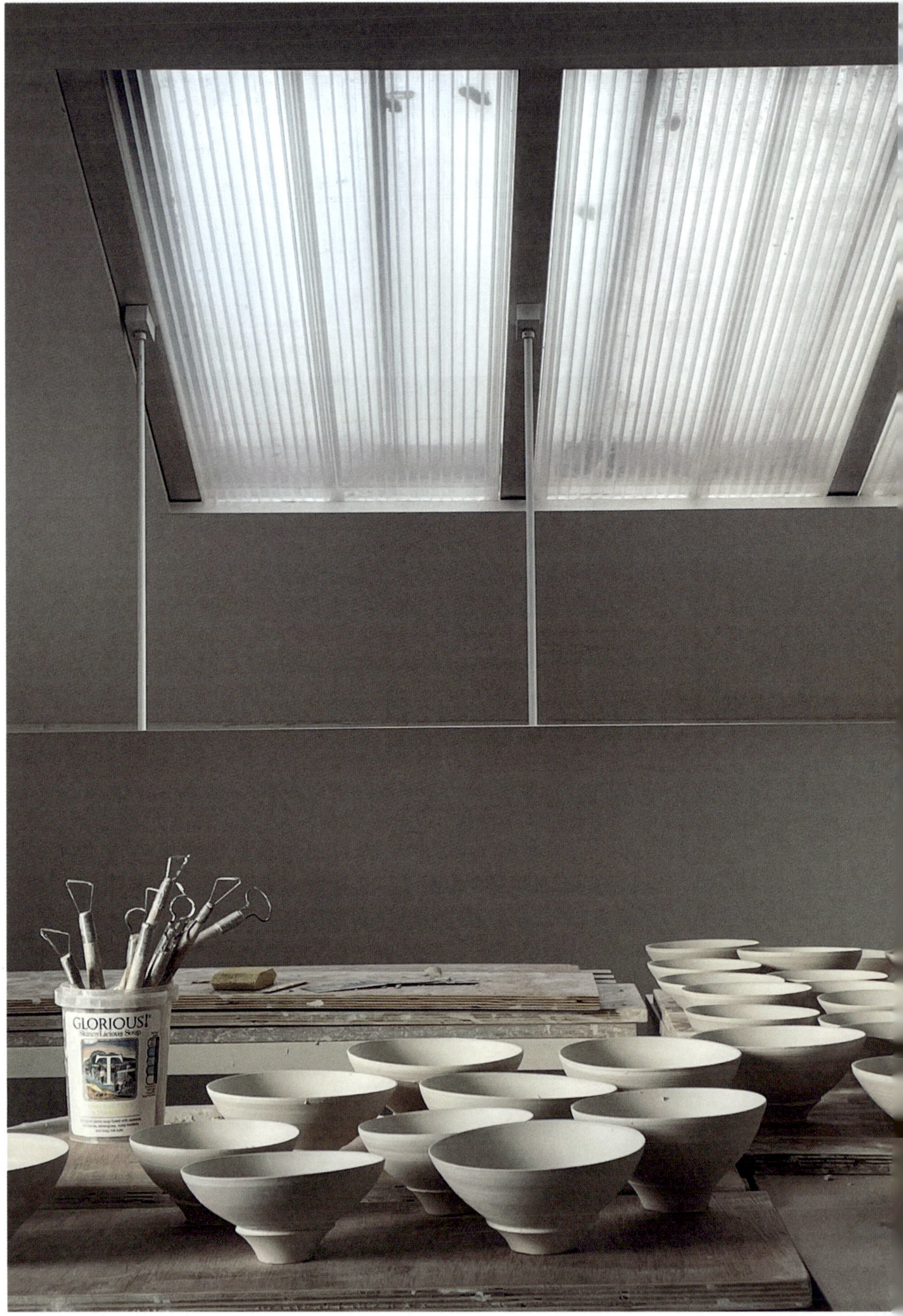

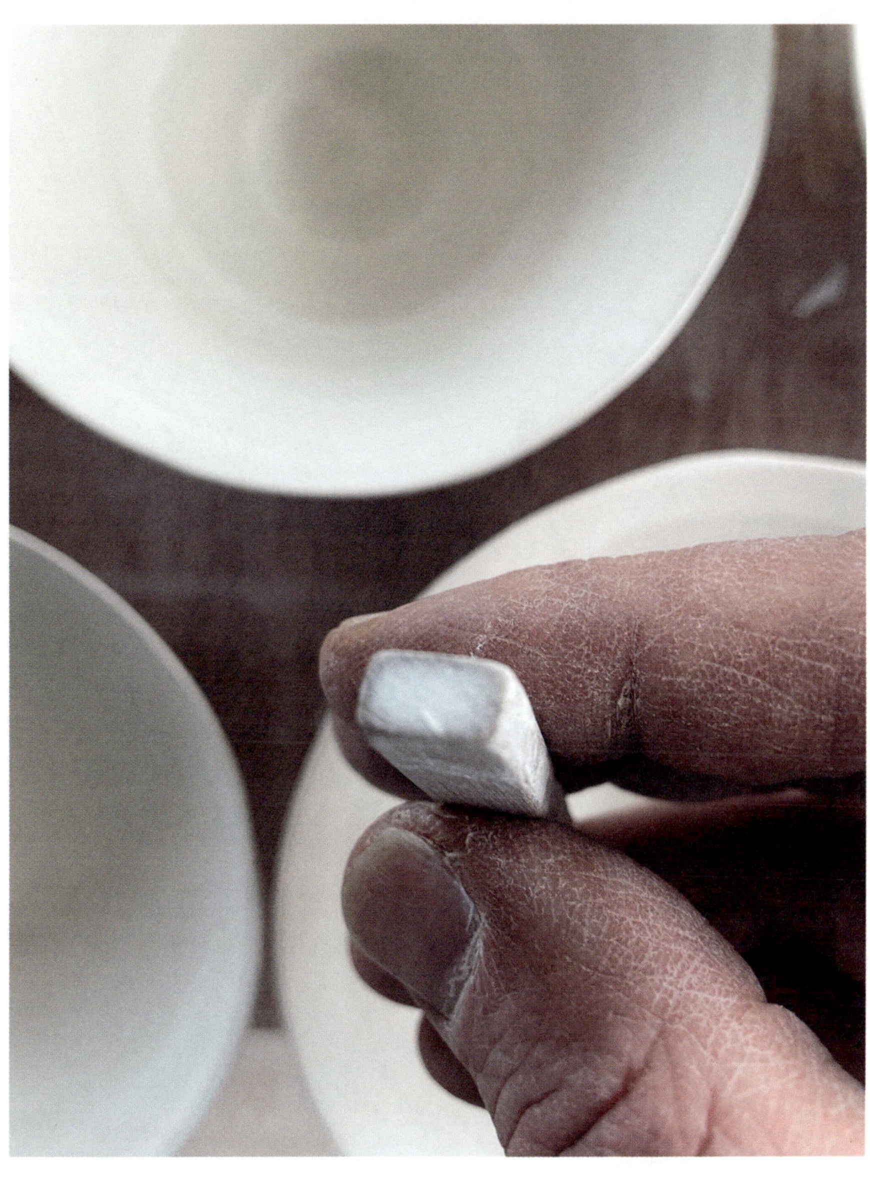

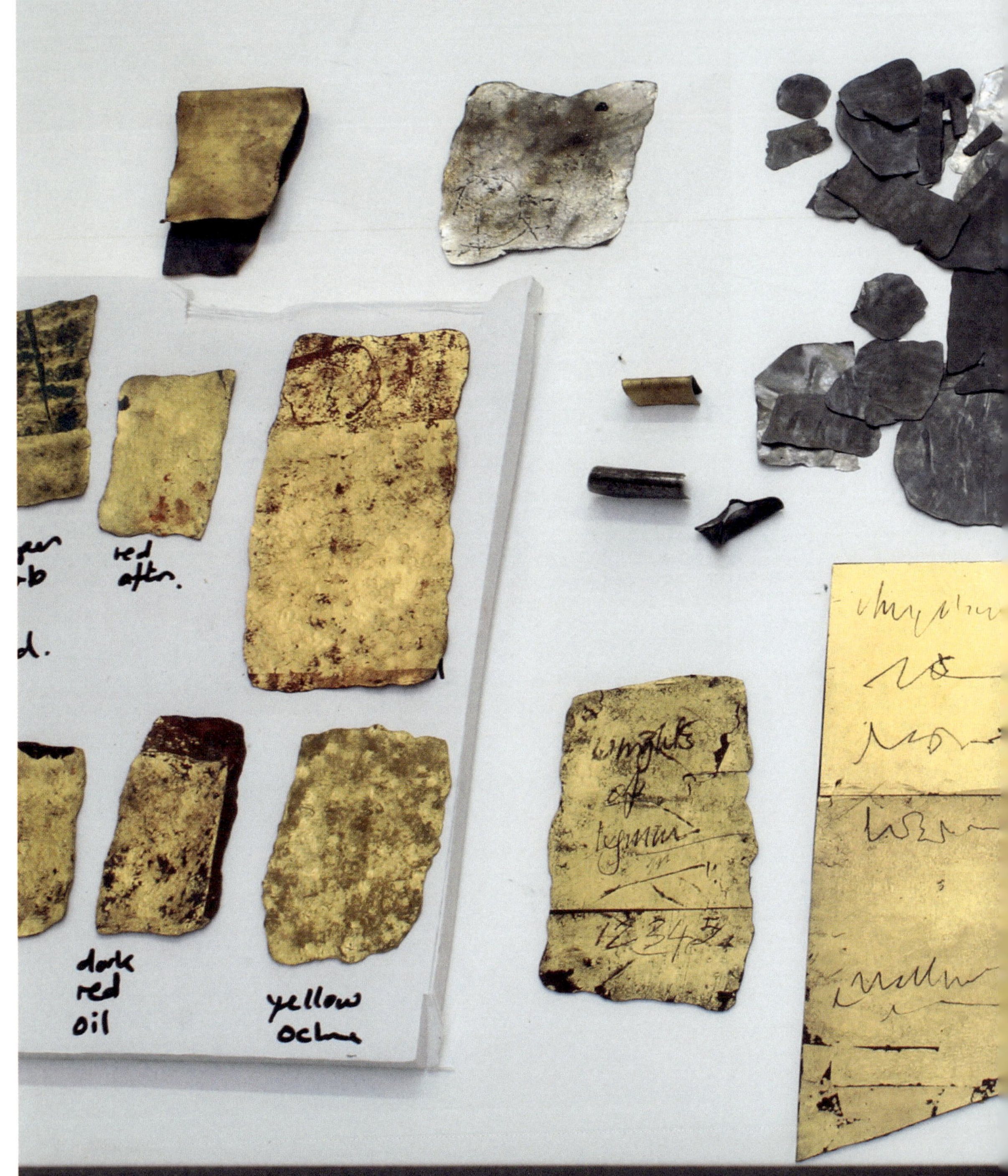

red
aftr.
dark
red
oil
yellow
ochre

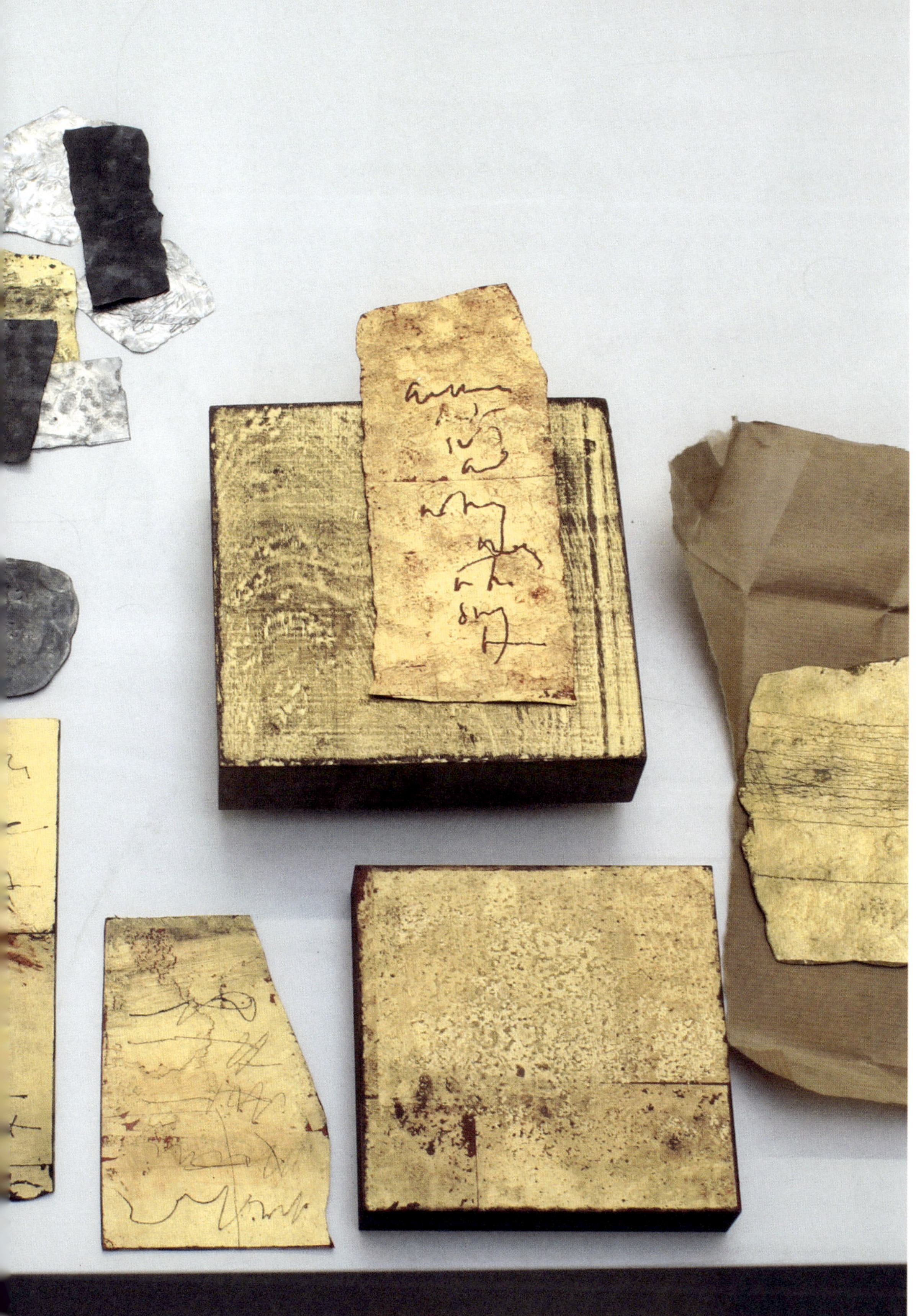

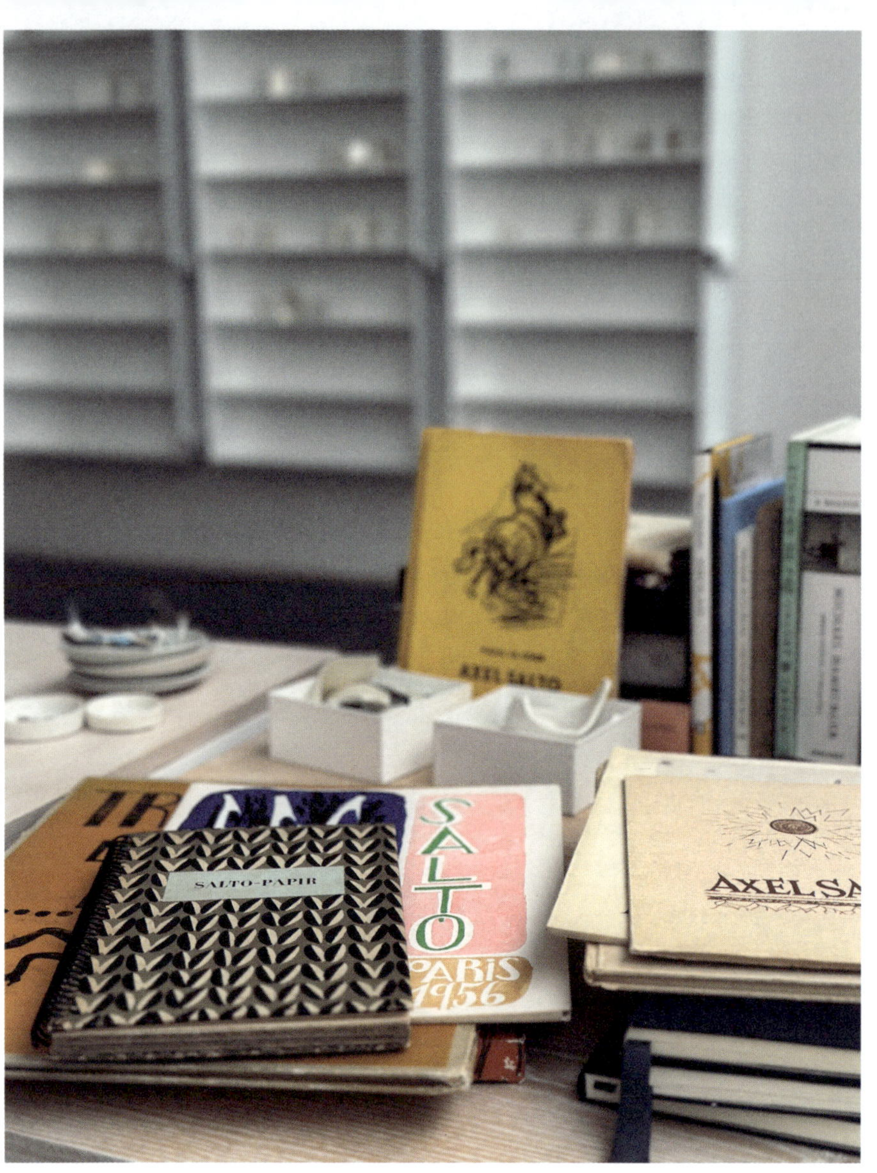

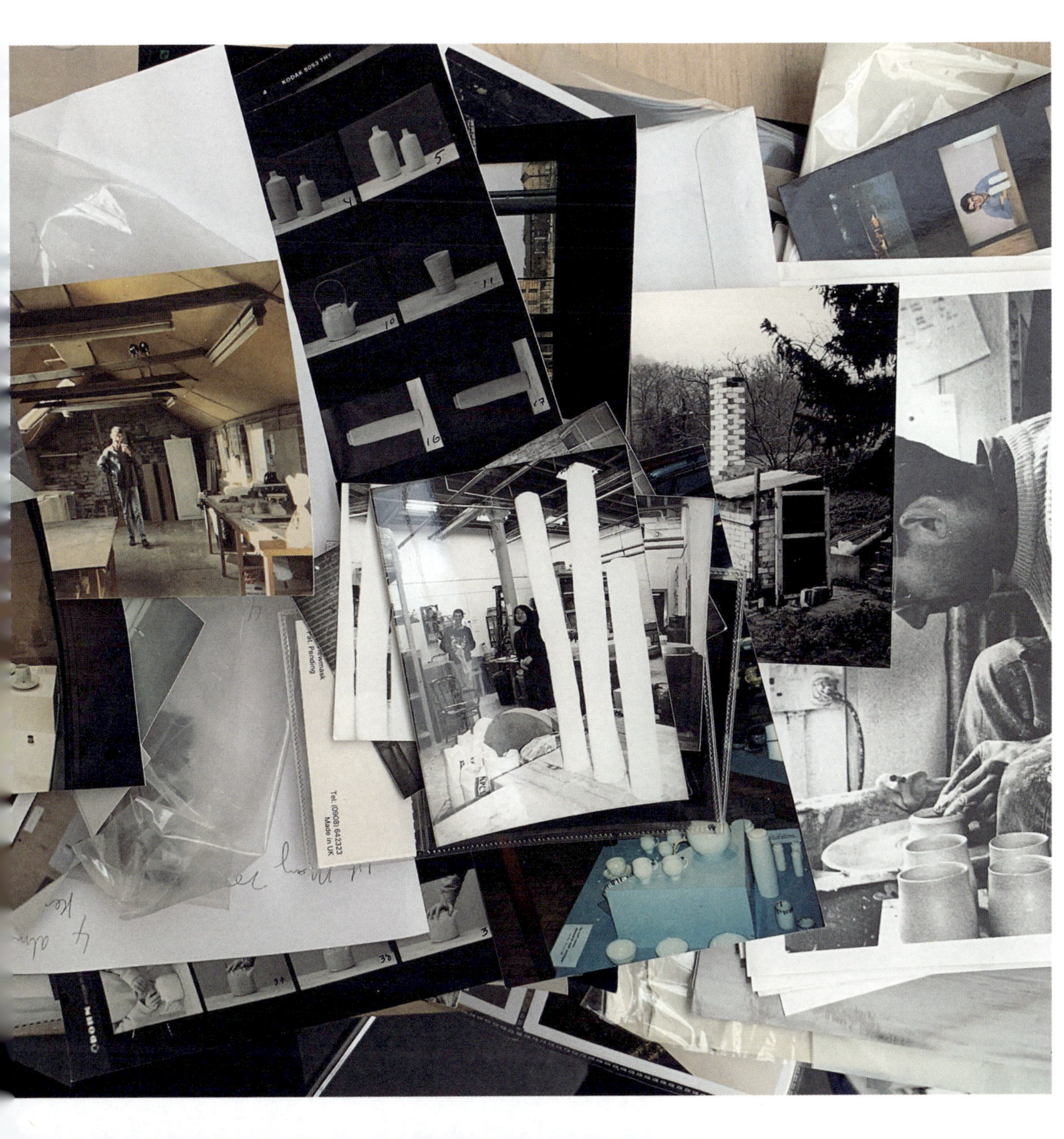

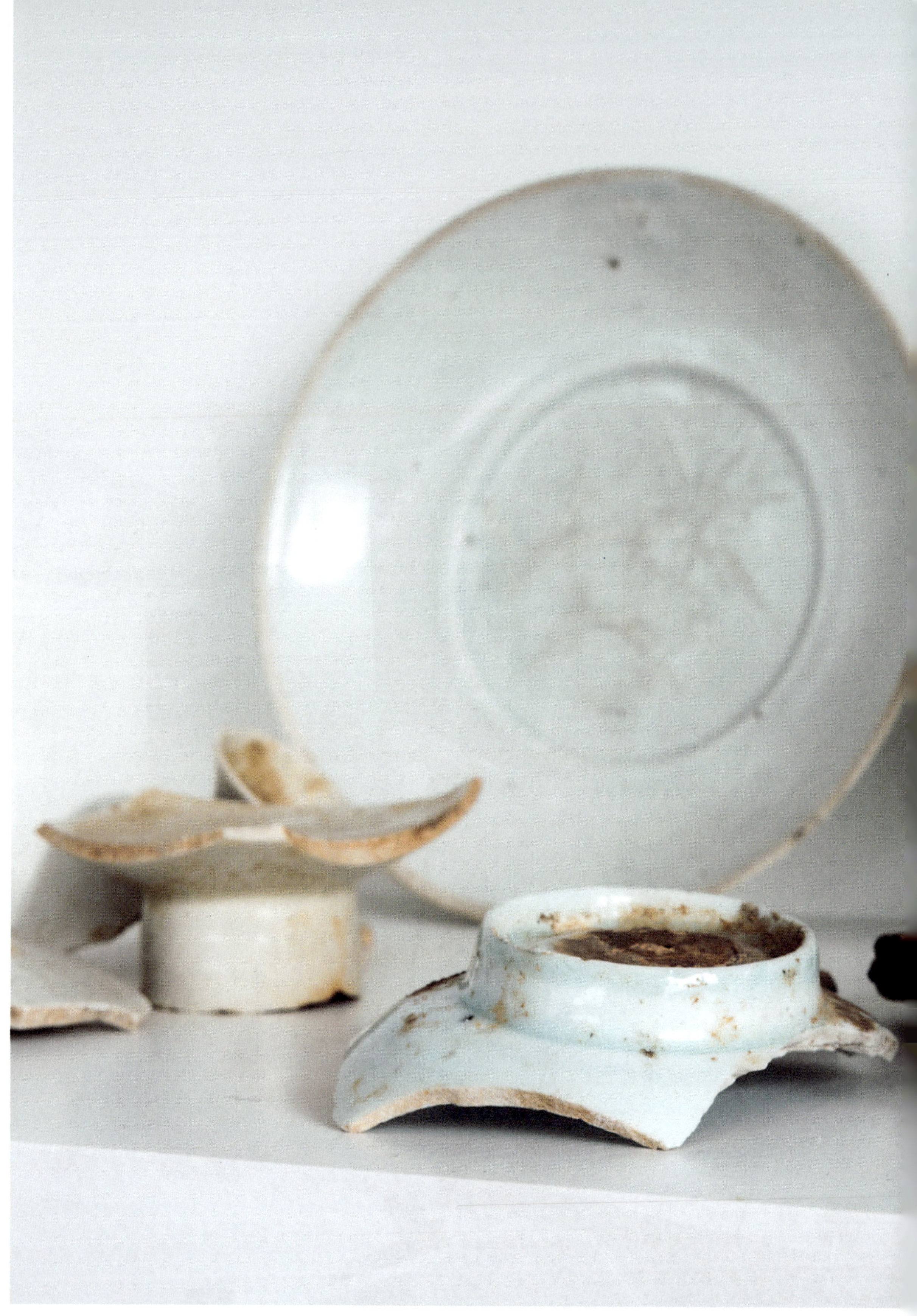

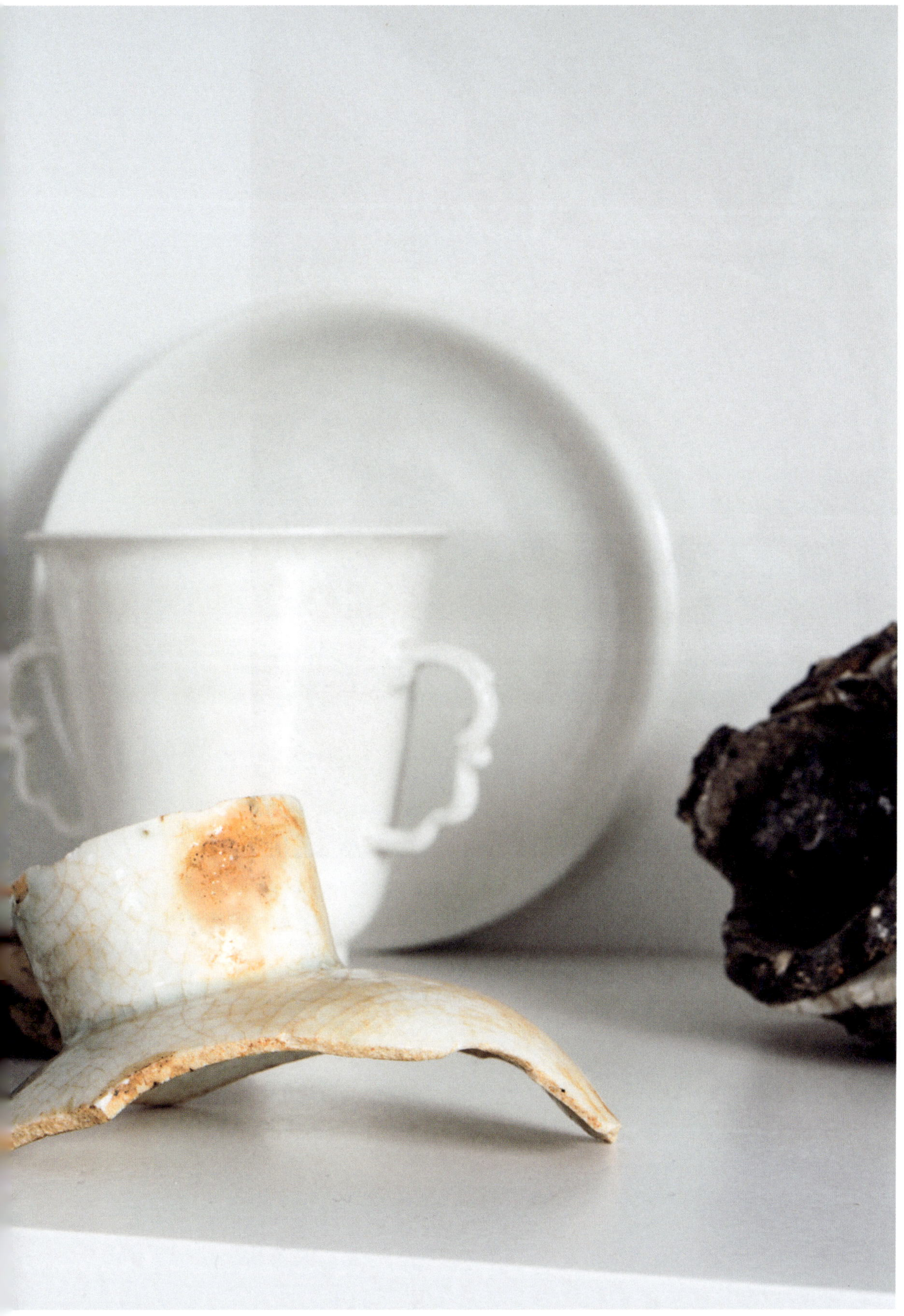

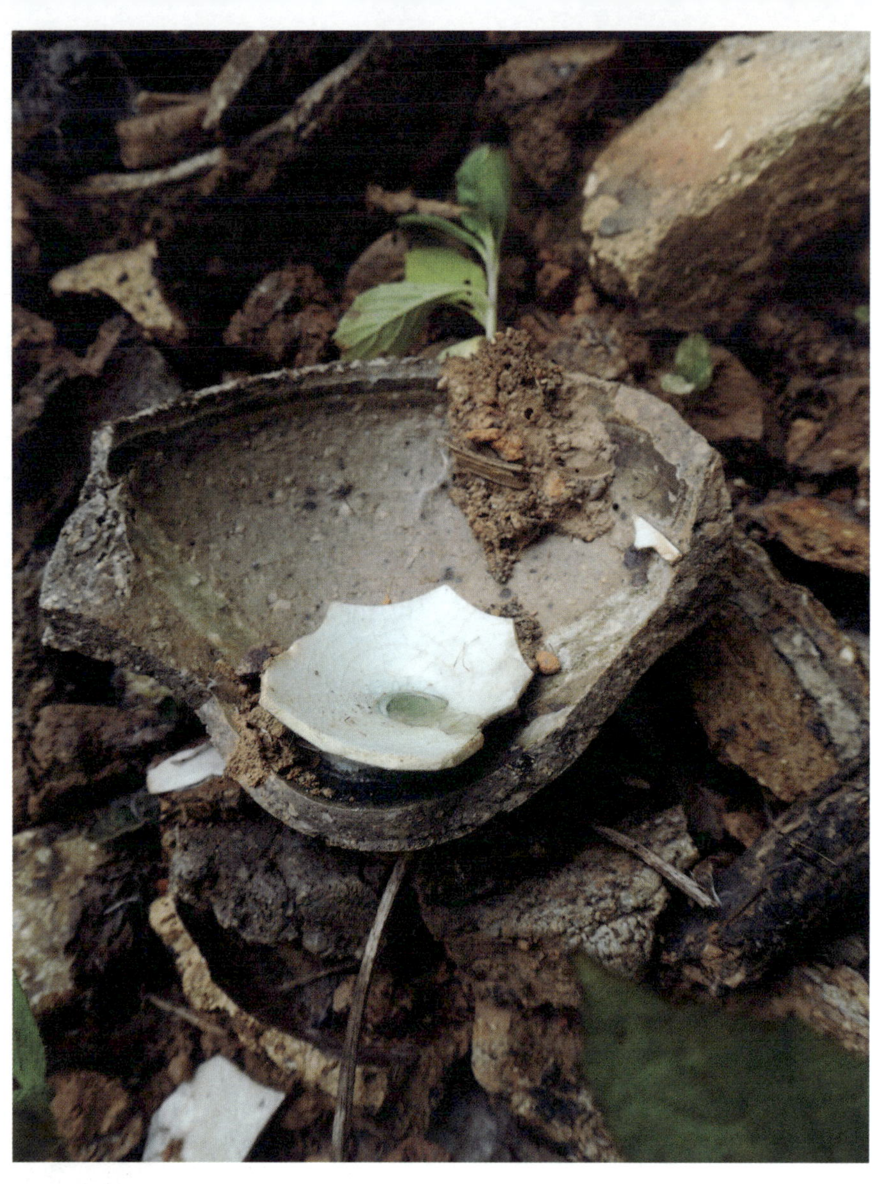

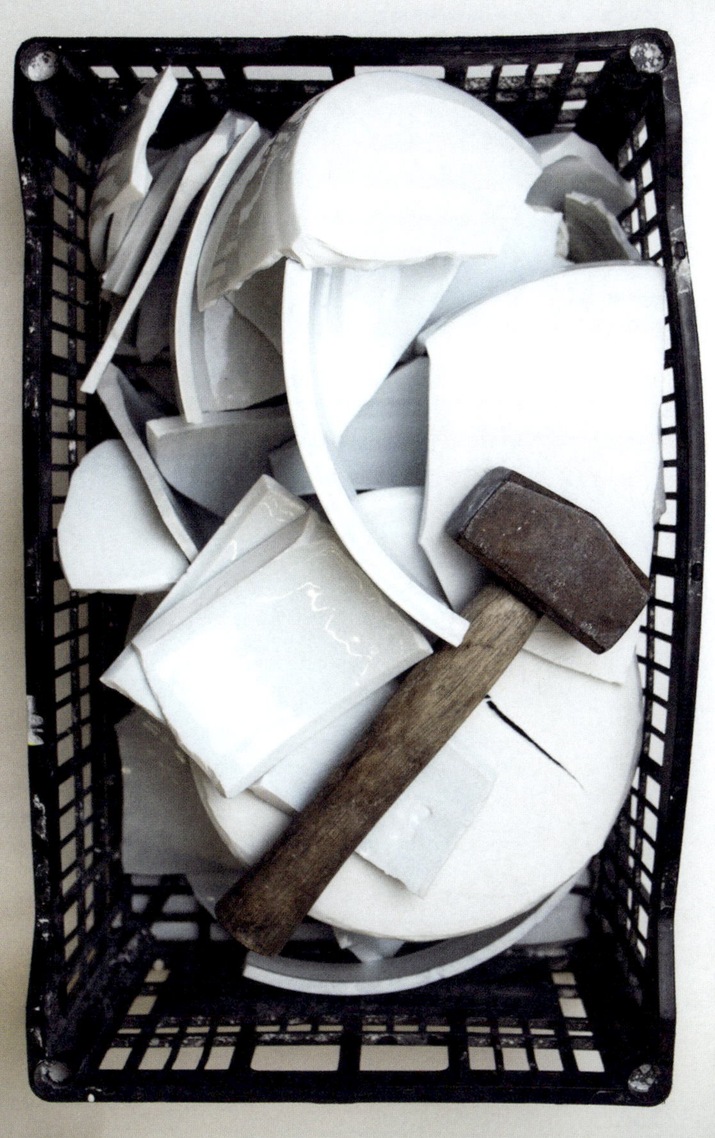

A
Conversation

This conversation between Edmund de Waal and Sanne
Flyvbjerg, curator at CLAY Museum of Ceramic Art Denmark,
took place in the artist's studio in South London in March
2023 with the sounds from his studio in the background.
It maps Edmund de Waal's encounter with Danish artist Axel
Salto and touches on vessels, words and journeys.

Tell me, when was your first encounter with Axel Salto?

My first encounter with Salto was in the decorative arts museum[1] in Copenhagen about thirty years ago. The museum was very crowded at that time and I remember coming across a display case of Salto's ceramics and being utterly flabbergasted, utterly taken by surprise. These vessels were unlike anything I had ever seen before, which is a strange thing to say because I have been looking at pots all my life. But they were utterly different and I was completely bewildered by these budding, sprouting vessels. I couldn't understand them. So my first encounter was actually feeling confused because I didn't think his vessels were beautiful. I thought they were strange. And the idea of seeing objects which were so considered and so strange made me realise that there was something going on there that I just had to get to grips with.

Did you know at that time how polymathic Salto's practice was?

No. It should be noted how little there was written about him in English thirty years ago. At that point there had not been any substantial international exhibitions of his work since the 1950s. I had no idea that he was this extraordinary multifaceted person, such an extraordinary writer, such an extraordinary designer and graphic artist. I had no idea at all. They were just vessels stuffed into in an old-fashioned display case in a museum in Copenhagen.

Axel Salto is speaking from the first part of the twentieth century. Does that historical gap affect your conversation?

No. The odd thing about a friendship with an artist of a different generation is that it does not matter if they died sixty years ago. It does not matter if they are a poet who died two hundred years ago. You can attempt to be a cultural historian and place them in Paris in the 1920s in Salto's case, or in postwar Scandinavia or as part of a design ethos in the middle century, but if you are walking alongside them and you are in conversation with them, cultural contexts sort of disappear. Because actually, in a very real sense, if someone matters to you as a poet or as an artist, your conversation with them is that of a contemporary. So Salto is not talking to me from deep in the last century, he is talking to me about things that I think are completely imperative now. He is talking to me now about feelings of anxiety, contingent ideas, the danger of beauty, where beauty sits in our lives, in a way as if he is talking across the table to me now like you are. I can't and don't want to talk about him as a really important artist of the 1950s. I want to talk to him about what I have just opened the kiln and found in my own life.

> *This is not the first time you've been walking with someone from the past. Conversations across time is something that runs through your practice. What kind of conversation is this?*

The really interesting relationships we have with poets or artists who have died, they put us on the spot. They continue to be interrogative. They continue to challenge. So it's not a safe relationship. The more I get to know and talk to Salto, the more complicated and challenging he becomes as an artist and as a questioner and as a person. There are some people who you might study or might be interested in and quite quickly, you feel like you know where they belong in your life. They have a place of safety in your life. They are a place of solace of some kind. I can think of people like for instance W. H. Auden or indeed Georgio Morandi, whom I've spent a lot of time thinking about and writing about. For both of those people, their practice or their paintings are places I go back to in order to feel restored, to feel calmer or to find beauty. But with Salto, he is fissile, he makes you uneasy, he is disturbing. He offers huge beauty, but huge complexity, and so we have a different relationship and perhaps we will continue to have a longer, lasting relationship. The conversation is just beginning. Stephen Greenblatt, the American literary critic, talks about solace and renewal, that artworks can have both, can give you a place of return to your sense of self, but also take you towards something new. And I think that's what Salto is doing for me.

> *How did you feel about taking him on as a conversational partner?*

Terrified. You know, rightly alarmed. Alarmed on lots of different levels. Alarmed, because I genuinely can't think of an artist apart from Picasso who has such an overflowing practice that finds articulation in every single craft and every single material that they come across. From language to painting, etchings, woodcuts, ceramics, metal, glass, fabric and paper. So in that sense alarmed because he challenges me by saying "What? You only write books and make pots? What do you do for the rest of the day?" But alarmed as well, because I think some of the central, core imagery he uses about time and about danger and metamorphosis are so profound that I am trying to work out quite where I stand in relation to them. So he challenges me very profoundly.

Getting to know Salto, what has changed since that first impression of him at the museum in Copenhagen?

Just delight. All the seriousness of Salto, his writings and his practice, those are one thing. But my God, I have fallen in love with his sense of play and pleasure. I am absolutely entranced by this conventional looking man, looking slightly professorial, who believes completely in play. That at the heart of creativity from infancy onwards, all the way into childhood, adolescence, student life and into adulthood, is his belief that things don't stay still. That you have to make a mess, that you have to pick things up and handle them and put them down and change them. And as soon as you have done one thing, you can look at it through a prism of colour and see how it is transformed into something else. That you can pick up stamps and make the percussive sound of stamping one thing onto another and see how an image changes. That you can, like Charlie Chaplin, enjoy the feeling of the world, of doors banging into your face and cups falling off trays, animals bolting through the forest. That at any moment, the world is capable of huge seriousness but also capable of pure, delightful playfulness. Why wouldn't you adore this man?

So the playfulness has been a surprise to you?

A huge surprise. I wrote about Salto for my book on twentieth-century ceramics which was about twenty years ago, when I knew only so much about him and quoted stuff about anxiety and put him amongst a group of artists dealing with postwar angst and the nuclear age. And now I realise that that was just me trying to locate him among those who I thought were his peers. Now I realise that I was mistaken.

But alongside the pleasure and sense of play, Salto's work is also in-
formed by great seriousness. He is intrigued by substantial questions
about growth and how closely creation and anxiety are connected.
Living in the nuclear age, that becomes even more evident. In 1949,
he writes about discoveries in nuclear science and says that he feels
affirmed that the "inherent power in things" is all that artists should
ever try to show.[2]

That makes a lot of sense to me. Because his inhabiting of the metaphor of change happens so early, and then to find that nuclear scientists are thinking how the world might look on an atomic level, that must have been an extraordinary moment for him.

Indeed. His urge to investigate the primary sources of things was
steadily inspired by discoveries in science and technology. How high-
speed photography could slow down movement and capture the
stages of a sprouting plant. How Indian scientist Jagadish Chan-
dra Bose could measure reactions inside metals and plants. Salto
celebrated what he calls the monumental detail.

I love that. And the monumental detail is also William Blake seeing everything in a grain of sand, isn't it? It's interesting, because he has that quality of looking at that profound tension of what is in front of him. The idea of any stone you pick up, any shell or seed is capable of profound attention and analysis. It is actually very rare, the ability to pay that kind of attention to the world.

Paying attention to the world is indeed something that you share.
Although your practices are visually very different, you seem to agree
on many things. Do you feel connected to him?

I feel profoundly connected to him. How am I not going to feel connected to him? How many people are there out there who care about pots and about poetry equally? Because I think he does.

So, there are things to talk about. Going into this conversation, do
you remember what you felt absolutely sure that you must talk to
him about?

I can't remember the beginnings of the absolute imperative, because very quickly I kind of fell into this free fall with him. Where do I begin? One of the first things that comes to mind is that I must talk to him about metamorphosis. I must talk to him about Ovid. I must talk to him about obsessive readings of

Ovid, because I feel convinced that it is as essential to him as it has been to me. I know that he illustrated Ovid's stories on several occasions, and their imagery is everywhere in his work. Ovid threads sculpture, painting, poetry, translation, drama and music for centuries. And there I find Actaeon in Salto's work and I want to ask him: Why this obsession with Actaeon? Do you have the same sense of horror that I have when I read Ovid? How can you bear to keep reading him, when it's so full of such terrible encounters? What is in the heart of all these endless stories of violent metamorphosis that draws you in? That's a real conversation I need to have with him and write about. That's one thing.

> *Ever since the beginning you have been fascinated with Salto's concept 'the burning now', introduced in his book from 1938. 'the burning now' is the very moment of metamorphosis, and he explains how he tries to capture that moment through three dramatic motifs: a tray with falling cups, a sprouting bulb, and the transformation of Actaeon. But 'the burning now' also works beautifully as a metaphor of the ceramic practice.*

Indeed. This moment of the transmogrification from one state into another. And for me that begins with the kiln. There is that extraordinary transition of putting vessels that I have made and glazed into my gas kiln and firing the burners. We did it early this morning, and in two hours' time we will be taking the brick out of the front of the kiln to look at how the flame is working inside the kiln, to see the saggar cones beginning to melt, which will tell us that at that moment the glazes have become liquid on the pots and are in this extraordinary moment of moving from one state to another. And then tomorrow morning, opening the kiln up, finding out what's happened and knowing that that cannot happen again. That is it. That process has ended. It's wonderful.

So for me it begins with the kiln. And of course 'the burning now' takes us to his ceramics, his budding, sprouting pots and his glazes in flux held at the edge of a vessel.

> *In 'the burning now', things change. They sprout, they transform and even break. Playing with boundaries was a big part of Salto's practice, and the chance of failure was part of his quest for imposing output. "I have always preferred burning mistakes to tepid accuracies,"[3] he wrote.*

How many burning mistakes do you want to look at? If you come into the studio kiln room you will see a huge bucket of broken pots. Recently I have tried to make large dishes out of porcelain which is very difficult and the glazing has not been possible. So we have many of these pieces that I have spent hours and hours making that have gone wrong. They are burning mistakes. So that is one literal way and that's part of the everyday life of being a potter. More interestingly than that is paying attention to the things which might indicate another, dynamic, sense of direction, like Salto says. Where you have done one thing – you thought you had control over a process, over an effect, over an idea – and then it has come out of this chemical moment, and you realise that it indicates a completely different direction to you. Your understanding of what you thought you were doing and what you are actually doing are at variance. It's that space of possibilities which is so exciting. It leads you off. Of course it does, and of course it should do.

And then you begin again. Making and remaking. Your work is full of repeated actions and similar vessels in large-scale installations. How is repetition connected to change?

In so many ways. Repetition of course is impossible. You repeat yourself, you make another vessel, you begin another text in order to understand why you can never make the same thing again. So what it does is that, temporarily and spatially, it articulates change. It sounds incredibly theoretical but it's not at all. It's straightforward. I sit at my wheel with ten bowls of clay, all of which are exactly the same size and I repeat myself, but of course each time I repeat the making of a vessel, I am a different person, my hands move sort of in the same way, my breathing has slightly changed and the ten vessels are going to be ever so slightly different. In that sense that is also a bit like Salto with his high-speed photography, saying: How do I look at gathering information on the moment of change, slowly? How do I look at the falling cups and see them here, here, here and on the floor? How do I see the person becoming the deer here, here, here and here? In the moment and in the repetition is a kind of slowing-down of the process of metamorphosis. It is extending 'the burning now' into your practice.

How do you see that in Salto's ceramics?

Freud talks about repetition as a way of delaying death, basically. It's very tough to think about the psychology of repetition. But I think repetition is about pleasure. When I think about Salto's ceramics, of course I think about the repetition in the pattern making on the surface of the vessels, the return to the pine cone or the sea urchin or the sprouting spikes, but I also think about repetition in terms of deciding to use one glaze, then another glaze and then another glaze. I see such intense pleasure on returning to first principles, returning, returning. And just seeing what's going to happen. It's very close to his idea of play. John Dewey talks about play in art being like the flight and perching of a bird. So, you are either, you are within flight, but then you pause and you see how far you have come, but you are on top of your telegraph pole and you know you have to fly again. So it is endless repetition of being within the experience and then that slight pause and then looking back. And absolutely, when I see the same ceramic vase or bowl that has been glazed in different ways, I get entirely that sense of him standing back and starting again.

As you say, repeating is also about slowing down that moment of metamorphosis and holding it. Salto tries to capture that vibrating moment in singular vessels or images. In your work, that movement often seems to take place between objects and framework?

In some senses the language that I use is absolutely about placement and displacement. By removing the vessels that I make out of the chaos and diaspora and flux of objects that exist in the world and putting them in vitrines or on shelves, what I am doing in some senses is creating a place or a pause. The piece in front of you there is called *a place made fast*,[4] which is a line from a Paul Celan poem, and what I am trying to do there is just simply pause words and phrases and pots for a bit. I think Salto was also very intrigued by that. I have seen enough images of Salto's work in context to be very intrigued by the relationship between objects. Here is someone who profoundly understood about how you put objects down in the world, and that the context in which you create them matters enormously for your understanding of them. When I look at photographs of his exhibitions from the

1950s, I see these wonderful dense room sets where he wants you to be fully immersed in the drama of his own work. I see him as a dramatist. His exhibitions are theatre sets in which you are invited to come and be the protagonist amongst the work. It is not a shop window that you pass by, it is a space to walk through and become totally involved. To hear his works surrounding you. Gesamtkunstwerk is the word hovering around us.

Salto always considered the total design of things. That is also very evident in his work with patterns, paper and book design. How would you describe his books?

A part of my walk with Salto is the idea of the presence of words in books. Of text as objects. That matters enormously to me. I absolutely feel that we are in conversation about that. I surround myself endlessly with books, trying to understand what it is to hold a text, to open, smell a book, feel it, not actually taste it, but feel the presence and the actuality of the words. Salto is a maker of books. And that's a wonderful thing to spend time with. He is so sensitive to paper. He is sensitive to scale. His printing book for children *Tryk selv dine Billeder*, which translates as *Print Your Own Pictures*,[5] is a complete joy. Isn't this the book you would have wanted as a child? It's breathtaking. This is one of the best pedagogical books that I have ever encountered. And hilarious. A joy, a delight. But part of it is his understanding of the need for a large-scale book. Imagine being a bit smaller than we are now and the joy of having this open in front of you. It indicates all kinds of possibilities for the hand. That's what I get endlessly with him, the different kinds of text and books he does indicate different kinds of reading or exploration. The scale and shape of the book is always connected to the content.

And then there are books which are much more for reading, but the idea of putting original art works within the books, that slows you down. There are all kinds of experimental things to do with his text which I find very exciting.

You are both writers. How is writing connected to working with clay?

It is a very fissile, uneasy and changing relationship. Obviously, there are parallels within what I make and I write. Parallels in terms of subject matter or mood, theme. But that's on the very basic level. That's on the most obvious level. I think the real answer is that on a Salto, molecular, atomic level, there is something much more interesting and complicated in the relationship between writing and making. Which is that they are both bodily actions.

And they represent something quite physical. Reading Salto, he seems to be building with words, shaping while writing. His texts are very descriptive, figuratively dense and full of neologisms. It almost seems as if writing sentences is like putting clay on top of clay.

I was so excited when you started to write to me about how he makes new words, clay on top of clay, that idea of compression of language or the breaking apart of language. The need to make new words and compounds. Fusing words together, that 'burning now' of language. But to me it makes perfect sense. Being a writer is not an intellectual exercise. Making pots and writing is part of the same thing. It's not divided into making something with your hands and then something with your head. They are both about making. It's tacit. It's in the hands. My writing is an accumulation. I build in the same way that I think Salto does. I can't read Danish, but I can read you reading Salto. And I feel that. And building books is part of that. Not just texts spinning off into the world, but books.

So, language and vessels are profoundly connected. But what do Salto's vessels say? What do they tell you?

One thing they say is that there are an infinite number of ways of taking up space in the world. I am thinking aurally here. Vessels have very profound sound qualities for me. So, some of his vessels are murmurs and some are elegies. Some are epic, some are lullabies. They all have different cymatic invitations. Some vessels take up a lot of aural space, some are more quiet. Some of them invite just the end of a fingertip to trace a line or to feel the point of an extrusion, to feel a clay body. Some invite part of a cupped hand and to be lifted and feel the weight. Some invite two hands and some of his big works invite an embrace, almost to be leaned against. Some vessels are to be lived with in intense proximity, to be moved around, to sit close to your everyday life. Some are to stand sentinel, almost like grave markers far away from you but as objects that need gravitas and to be away from you. When I listen, I can actually hear all these vessels, and their sound is not necessarily benign. His lovely, big tripots,[6] those seem to me completely Orpheus-like. Seeing those or hearing them, they go back to the beginnings of poetry and music, and for me they are about a song happening at the moment of destruction.

> *So, we move from anxiety to play to pleasure and back to anxiety and even destruction. Salto knows that these states are deeply connected. A sprouting vessel may very quickly turn into a demonic one, just like Actaeon may soon transform into animal. And his own artistic quest is an ongoing journey into those unpredictable moments.*

It seems to me that one of the reasons why Salto is so compelling is that he is unflinching about anxiety. About the central place of anxiety within his own work, and by extension within the creative process more widely. It speaks a truth to me which is that trying to create art of any kind is inherently going to fail, is going to fall short of aspiration and expectation. You are going to feel anxious that you have not been attentive enough to what is going on or unable to find a language that is sensitive and subtle enough to express what you need to express. At the same time, you are anxious because you know that you are not going to stop. That each failure to achieve what you had hoped to achieve indicates a lacuna or makes a space to which you have to return in order to start again. So, it seems that Salto understands that iterative process of failing in order to achieve something and needing to come back to it. Why wouldn't you want to hang out with a man who understood that?

There are artists whose emotional bandwidth is quite limited. They do lyrical or they do angry, and I suppose I feel with Salto that his emotional bandwidth is very, very substantial. That he moves between different feelings constantly.

> *Great things may come from difference and contrast. Which brings me back to your encounter with Salto. Thinking of your porcelain vessels in relation to Salto's stoneware, there is quite the visual contrast. Your vessels represent two very different voices. In Salto's work,*

Absolutely. It is, on the very simplest level. There is Salto with his, as you say, operatic glazes and colour, the viscous, liquid and glorious sense of pattern and pooling and iridescence and indeed that extraordinary eruption from the inside. So, what I am doing with these empty vessels? It's a pretty substantial visual contrast. But of course what I am doing with my vessels is to try and investigate and articulate spaces between objects as much as within a single object like Salto does. Whereas Salto can create dense patterns on a single vessel, I am creating patterns within multiples. So there is that element of repetition again. It is just happening in an extended way within my vessels, but it's in a very compacted way within his.

And vessels mean something to both of you. Salto saw his own life in a bowl. He saw the bowl as a witness, as something that would outlive him, an existential thing. What do vessels hold for you?

I am almost sixty. Next year it will be fifty-five years of making vessels out of sixty. So they have held multiple meanings, as I have been growing in my life, multiple experiences. For me, a vessel is the simplest image I have got for a held breath. That's what my vessels are. They contain a series of movements that I have made with the most basic of all materials in the world, which is the earth. And by doing that I am just holding a small part of the world and containing it. In the real knowledge, because I don't think things continue, that it will become broken at some point. So for me the existential element of the vessel is its eventual breaking. Its holding of something in a temporary and contingent way and its eventual breaking. And that's fine with me. That's what it's all about. And the breaking is of course a return to the earth. It's a cyclical thing.

Salto does not talk directly about history in relation to his own art. But history is embedded in his art. The feeling during a time of war, between the wars and post-war. How do your vessels talk to history?

They talk to history on several levels. My choice of material is profoundly inflected by history. By using porcelain I am already within history, I am embedded within a very long, complicated, difficult history of making which I think about a lot. All the people who have made things out of this material before me for all those different reasons.

And then simply because of the last twenty-five years of my life writing about loss and about how objects have been inherited, given, bartered, sold, looted, stolen, restituted, mended, passed on, passed over, forgotten, recovered. I feel like the presence of objects as witness is something that I cannot escape. And they cannot escape. There is no neutrality for me around objects.

I think Salto would agree. Objects relate to each other – and to people. They are part of a larger story and touched by many hands. Even on a very pragmatic level, that was how he understood his ce-ramic art. He always talked about the potters and technicians who enabled his objects. "If anyone applauds me," he says, "I will point at my friends and ask them to share the commotion."[7]

You begin by knowing and recognising how profoundly you depend on and value the people you work with. The levels of conversation, of skill, of sensitivity built up over decades. Some people in my studio have been working alongside me now for twenty years. As much as Salto, in his proper humanist and dem-ocratic way speaks to the collective skills and knowledge of the people he works with, I recognise that completely. In a world where people are only interested in the autograph work; you are the singular begetter of this thing, well no. There is absolutely the existential moment of making a pot by yourself or making a text, but then there is the whole collective endeavour that al-lows it all to happen. While we have been talking, we have been listening to the studio. I have been hearing vitrines being put up on walls, silver being beaten. The firing of the kiln in the studio. All these things have been going on while we have been sitting here talking about 'the burning now'.

There seems to be many profound concurrencies between the two of you. But in every conversation there are things to debate and question. Is there something about him that you don't understand?

A beginning of a response to that is that I wouldn't dream of thinking I understood him. I think that would be arrogance beyond any measure. I am trying to think of all the things I do want to ask him and understand. But thinking about the pacing of his work, I suppose one thing I genuinely would love to know more about is him and music. It would be fascinating to ask him about that. Because I feel like his work is so inflected with music. I hear music. And I just want to know who he is listening to. And I suppose, because I am slightly synaesthetic, I would love to know whether he hears music in his work. When I look at his sketchbooks and the rapidity of his sketches, I think there is someone who is hearing things as his hand is moving.

Salto is exploring, journeying with his line. I know that you like to describe this conversation as taking a walk with Salto. Why do you see it that way?

Journeying and exploring was such an important part of Salto's practice and life. But I guess the first thing to say is: Why wouldn't you go for a walk with this man? You want to see what he is seeing. You want to walk alongside him. You want to feel his pace, to see how fast he walks, how slowly he walks, where he stops and what he picks up. That's the image of it. But the reality is, of course, that all the best conversations happen when you're not holding on to the conversation. When it's drifting past you in the world over your shoulder. And so I feel like I have been walking alongside him, sometimes leaning in to listen to him. Sometimes looking at the same things in the landscape. Sometimes comparing notes. Just trying to understand his pacing of the world.

Notes

1
Designmuseum
Denmark, previously
Kunstindustrimuseet,
Copenhagen.

2
Axel Salto: *Den spiren-
de Stil*, Grafisk Cirkel,
København, p. 18.
A retrospective book on
the occasion of Salto's
sixtieth birthday.
See pp. 64–75

3
Axel Salto: *Salto's Træsnit*,
Det Hoffenbergske
Etablissement, Køben-
havn, 1940, p. 38

4
Edmund de Waal:
a place made fast, 2014.
Porcelain, wood,
aluminium, glass
230 × 300 × 11 cm.

5
Axel Salto: *Tryk selv
dine Billeder*, Fischers
Forlag, København, 1943.
This book encourages
children to play with
stamps and repetition.
See pp. 92–99

6
Axel Salto made several
of these sculptures in
two different sizes and
different glazes. They
were all called *Kraftens
Kerne*, which translates
as *The Core of Power*.

7
Axel Salto: *Ting ikke Ord*,
Berlingske Aftenavis,
1949. Newspaper feature
on his sixtieth birthday
and connected to a ma-
jor retrospective exhibi-
tion at Charlottenborg
in Copenhagen.

Edmund de Waal
the burning now, (external walls), (detail)
2023
porcelain, graphite, gold

Ovid

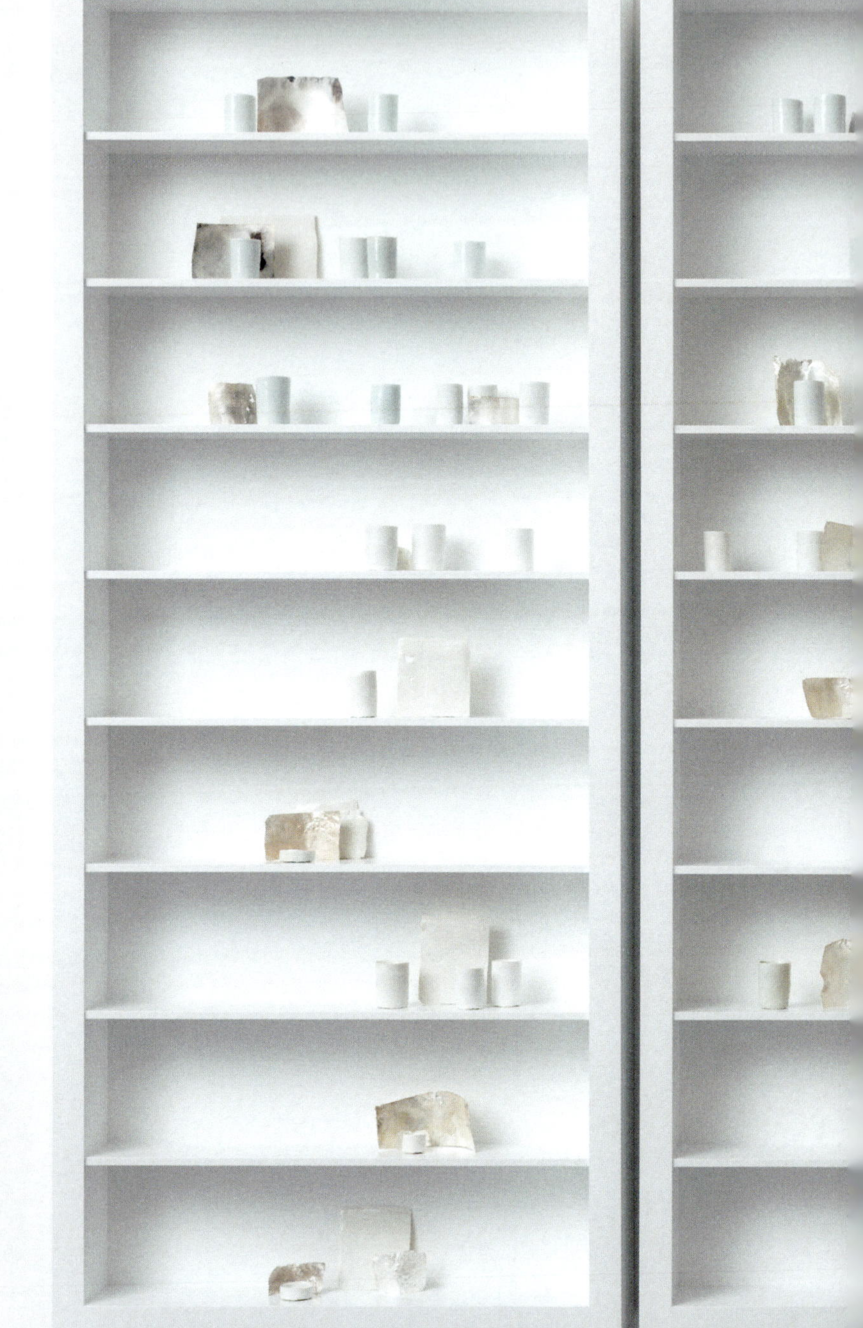

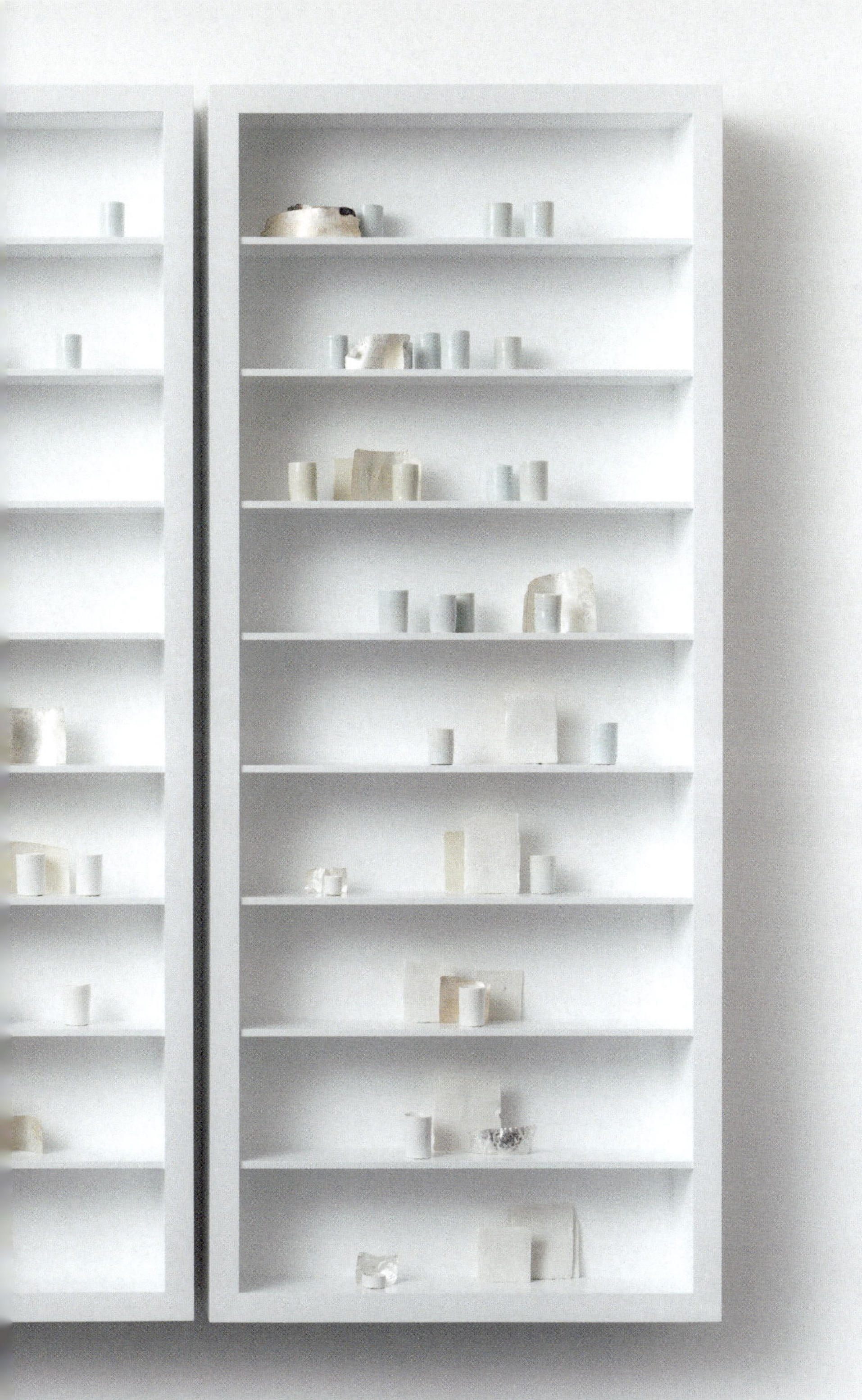

Edmund de Waal
the burning now
2023
Porcelain, silver, aluminium and glass
220 × 276 × 20 cm

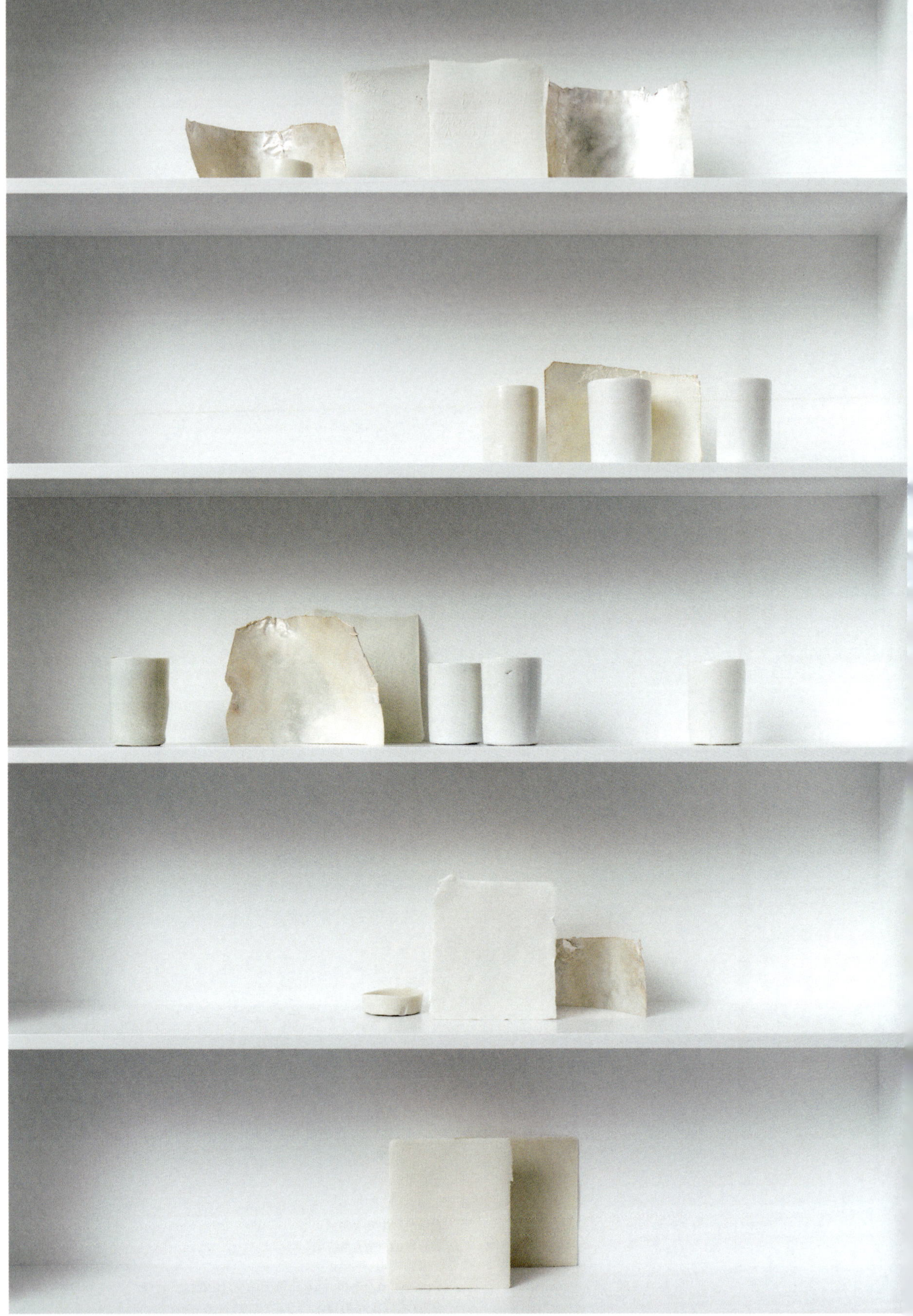

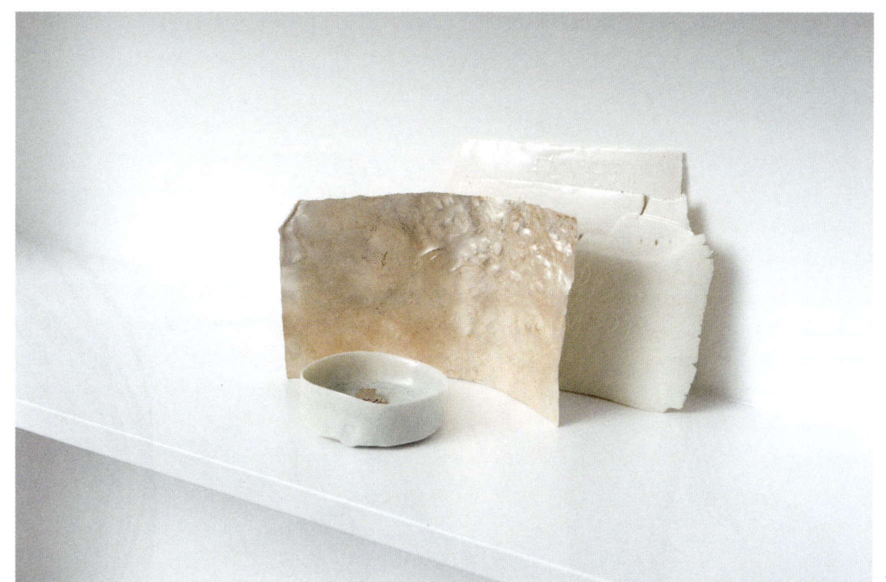

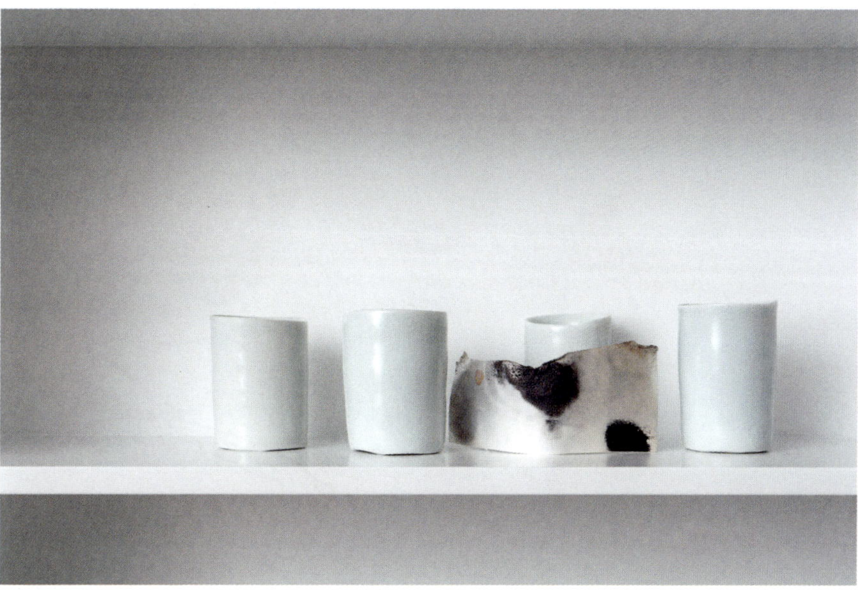

Edmund de Waal
the burning now (detail)
2023

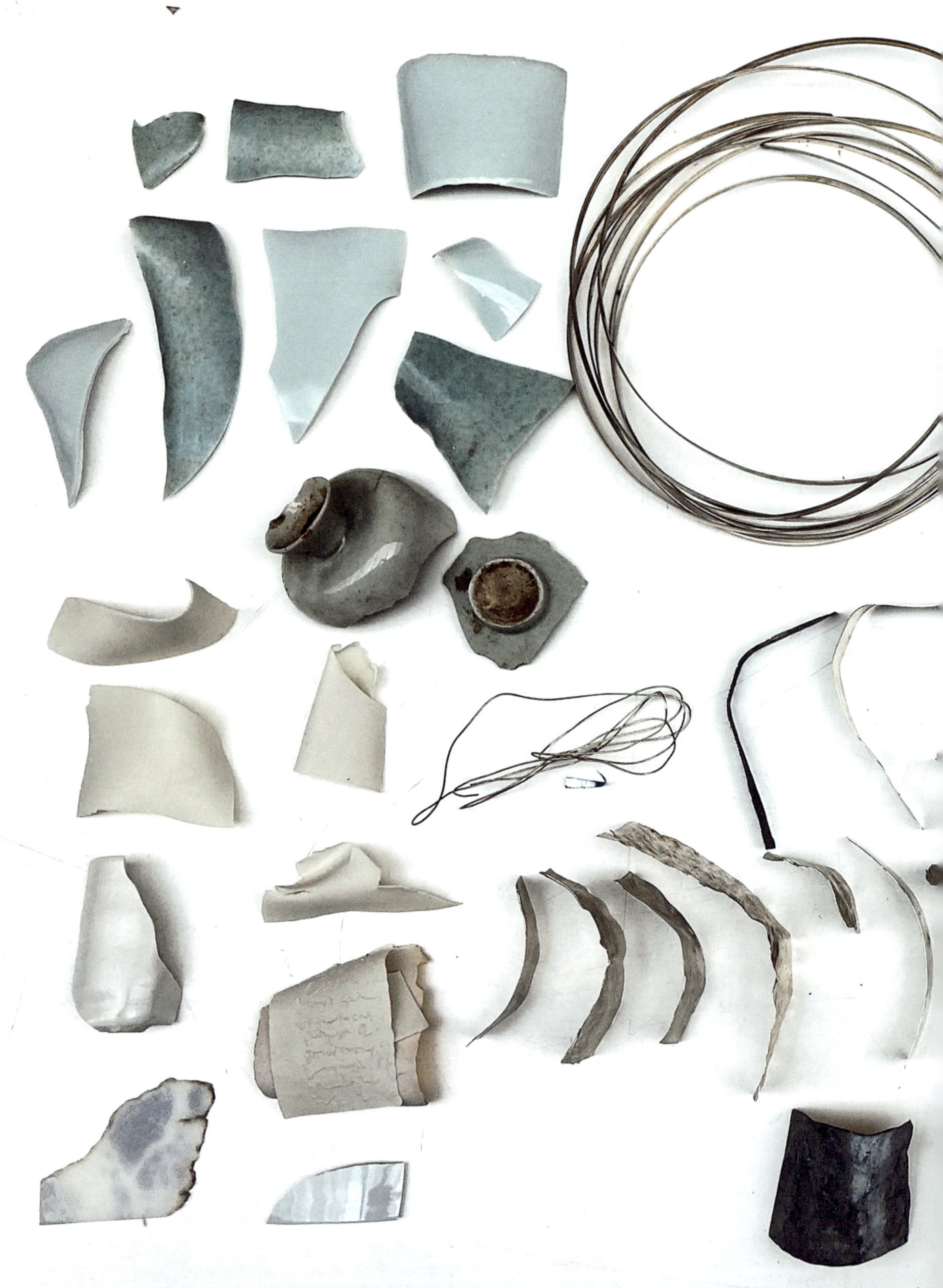

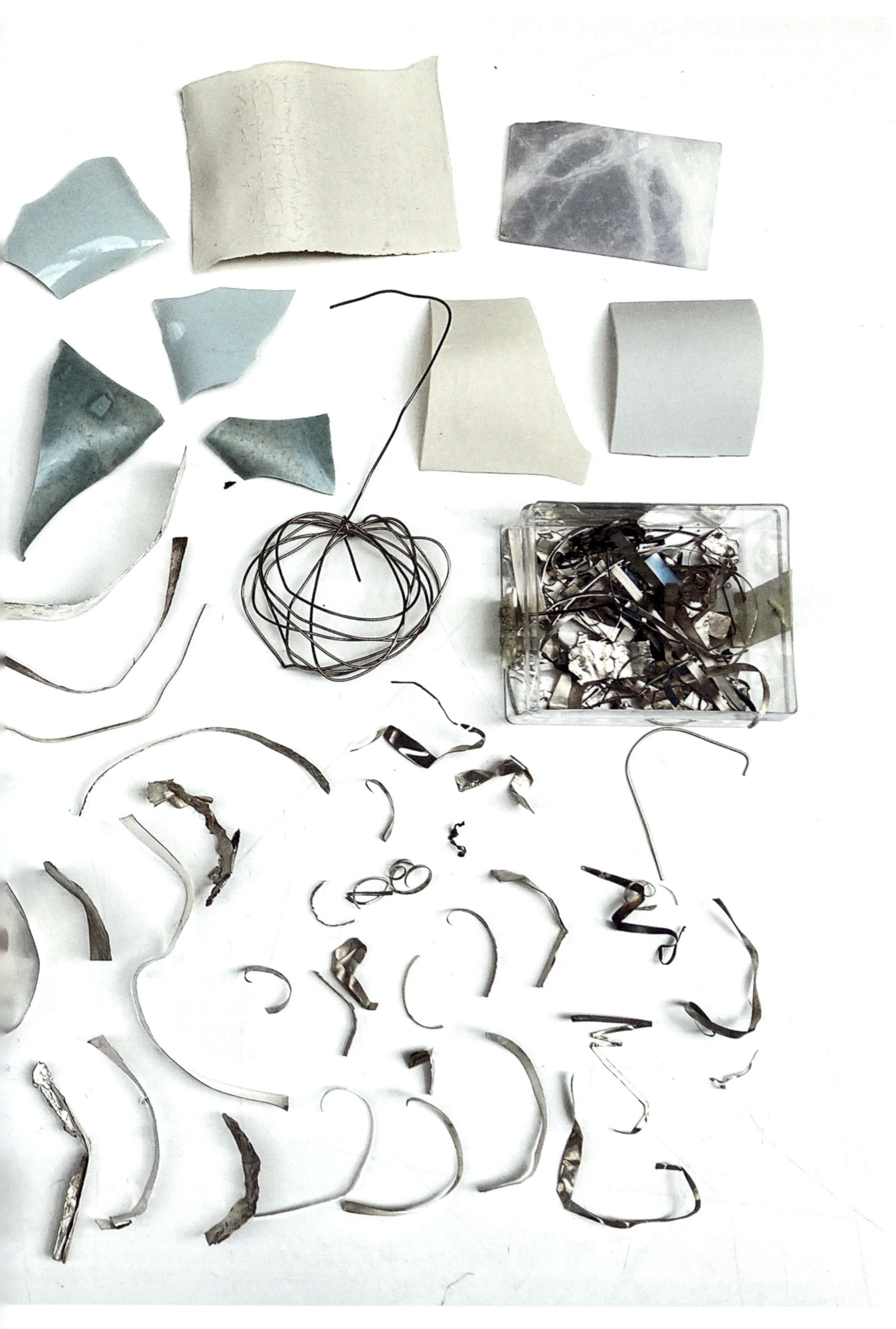

Edmund de Waal
the burning now (external walls, detail)
2023
porcelain, graphite, gold

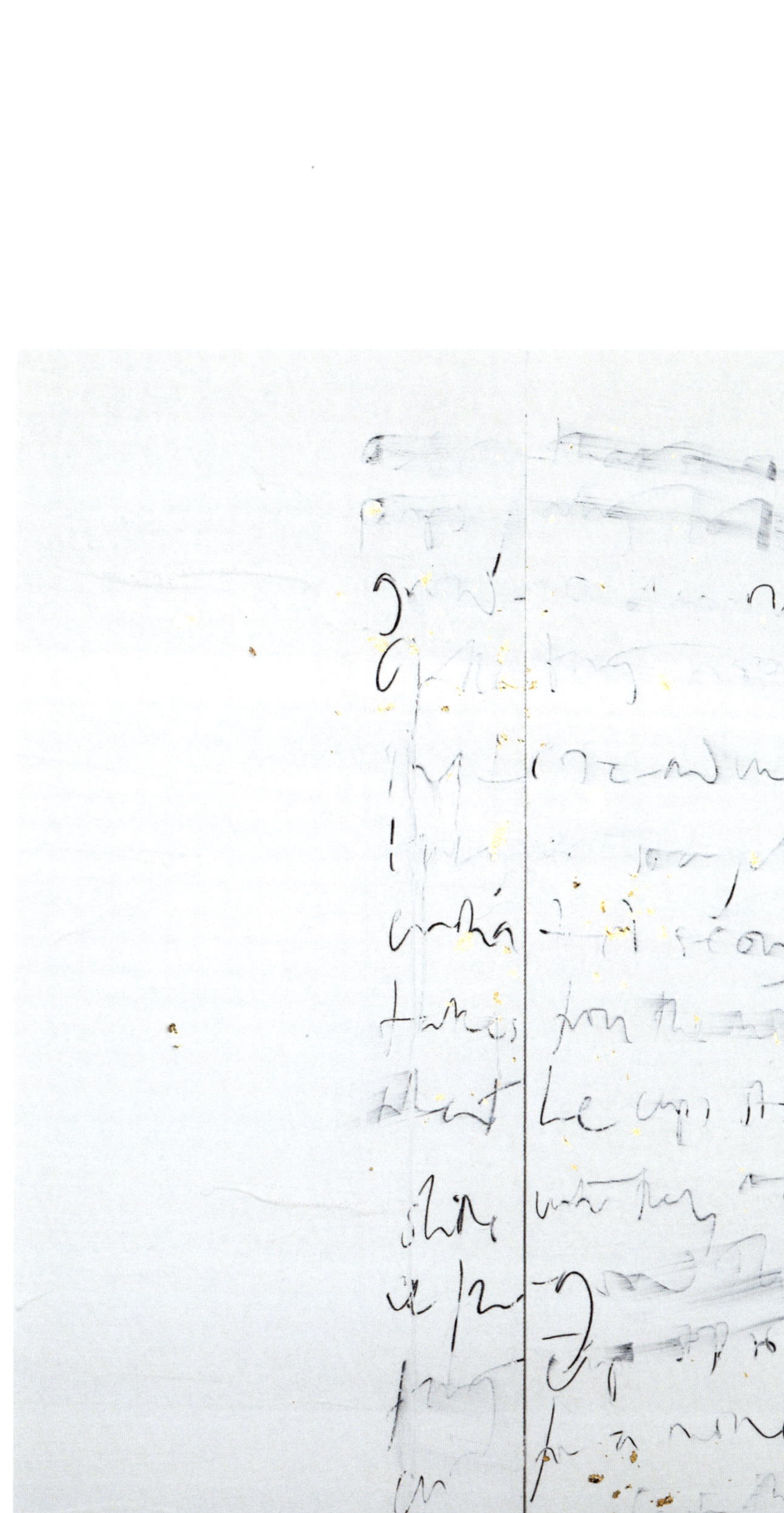

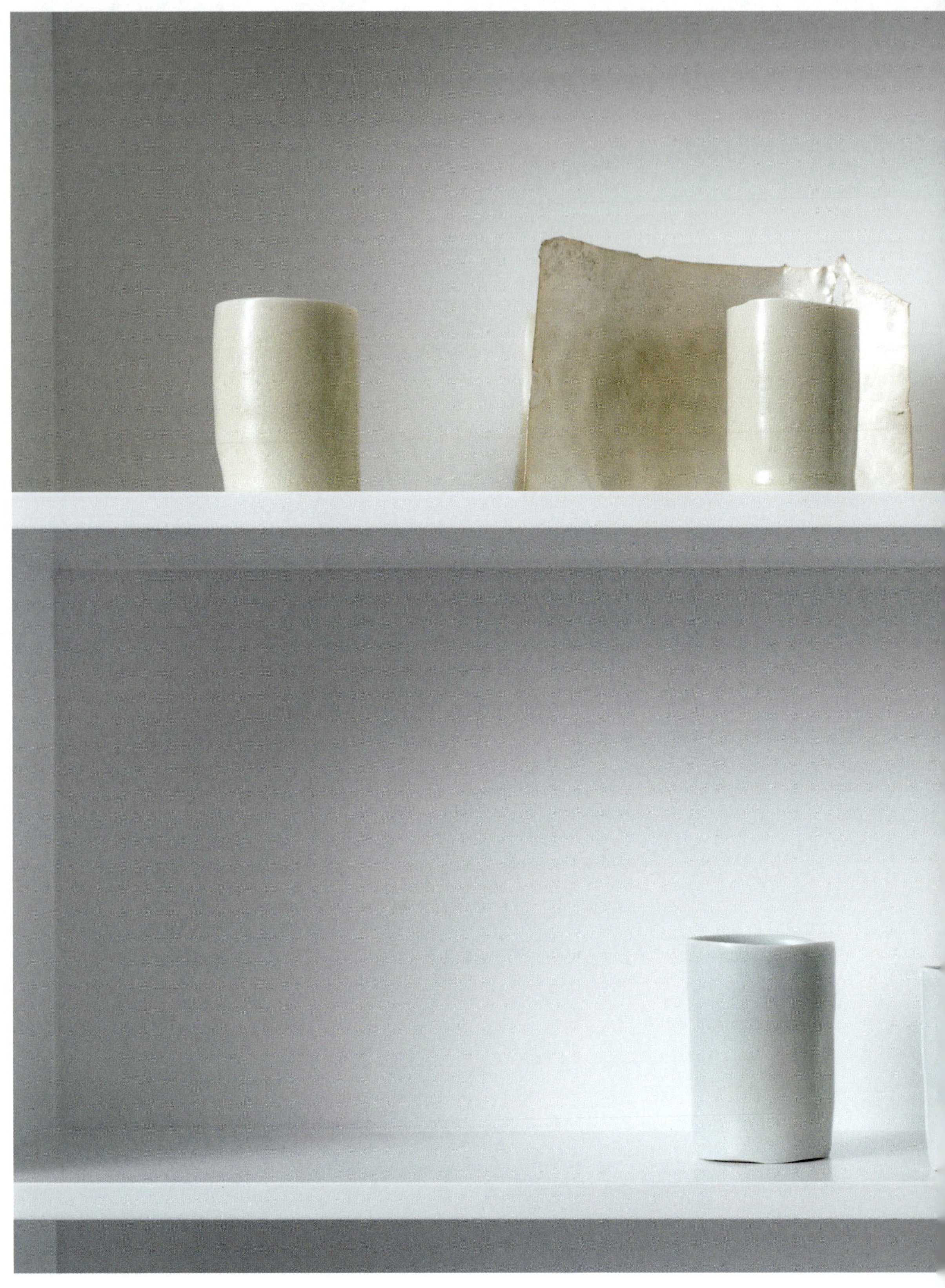

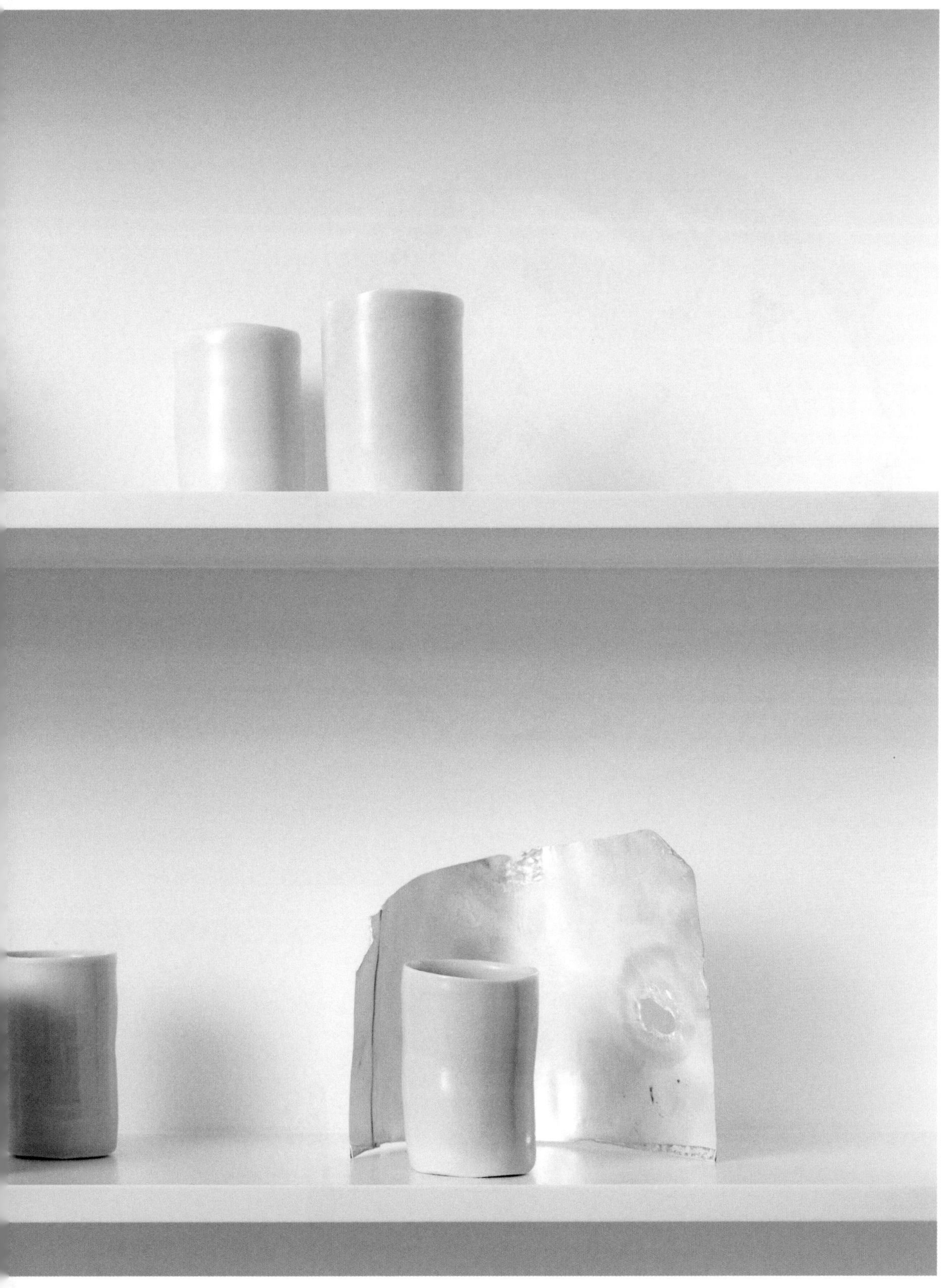

Edmund de Waal
the burning now (detail)
2023

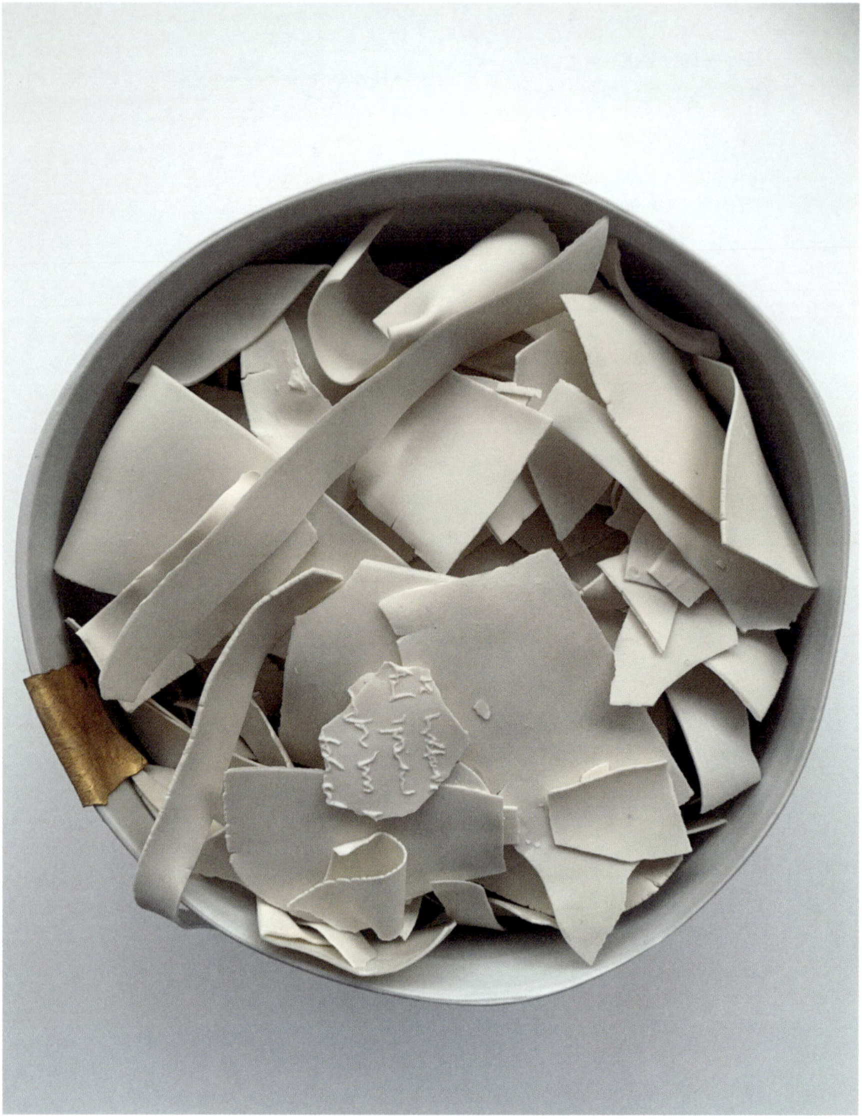

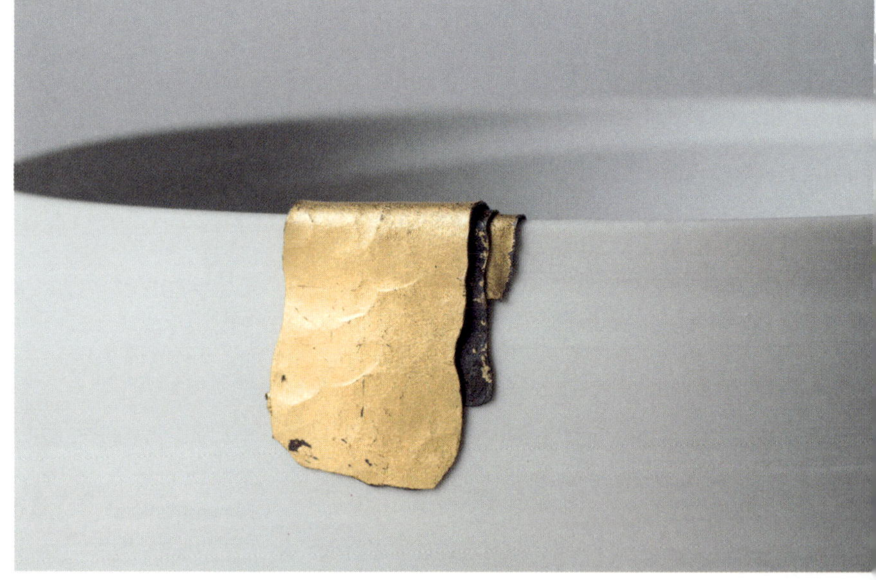

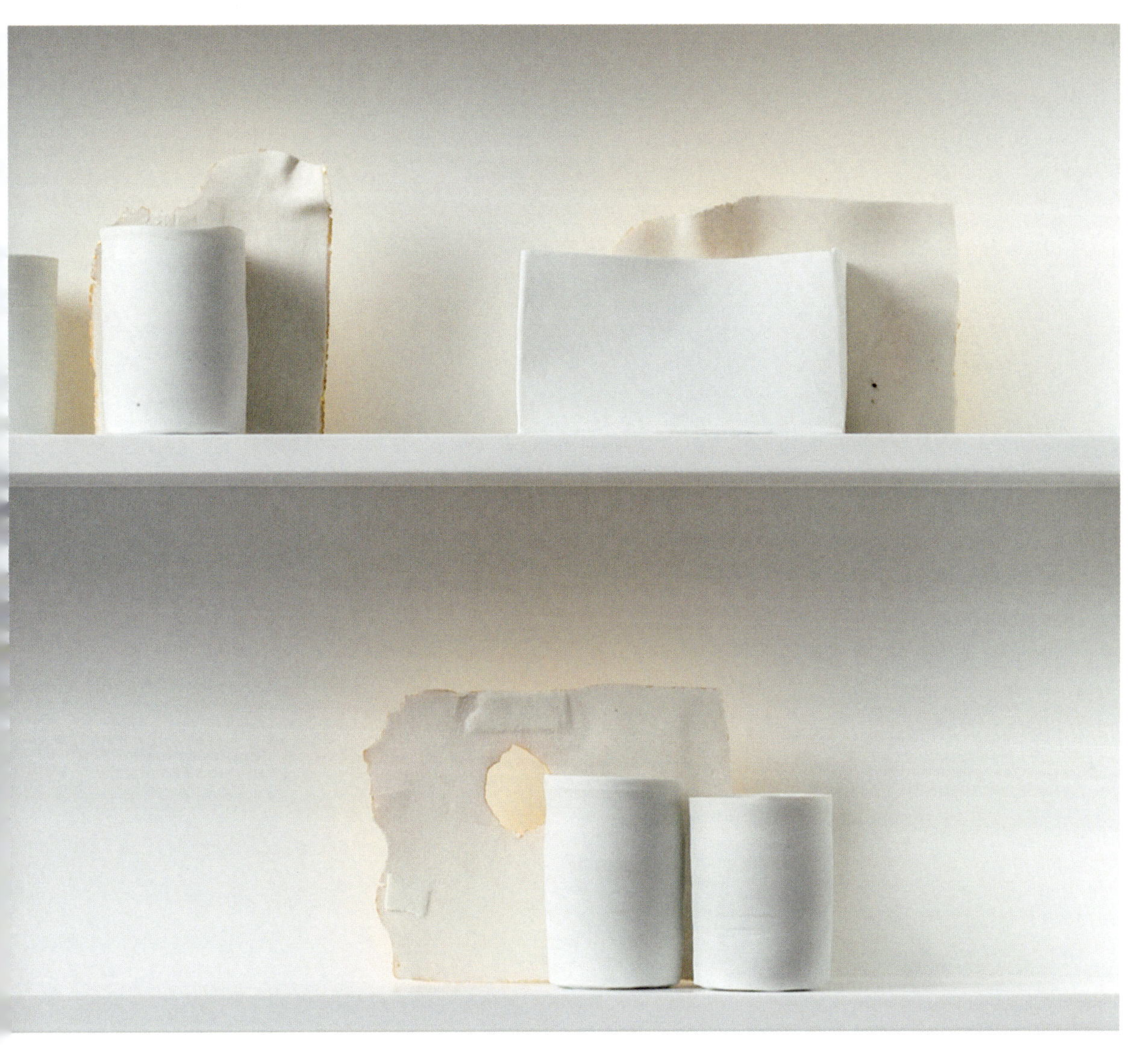

Edmund de Waal
details of work in progress in the studio

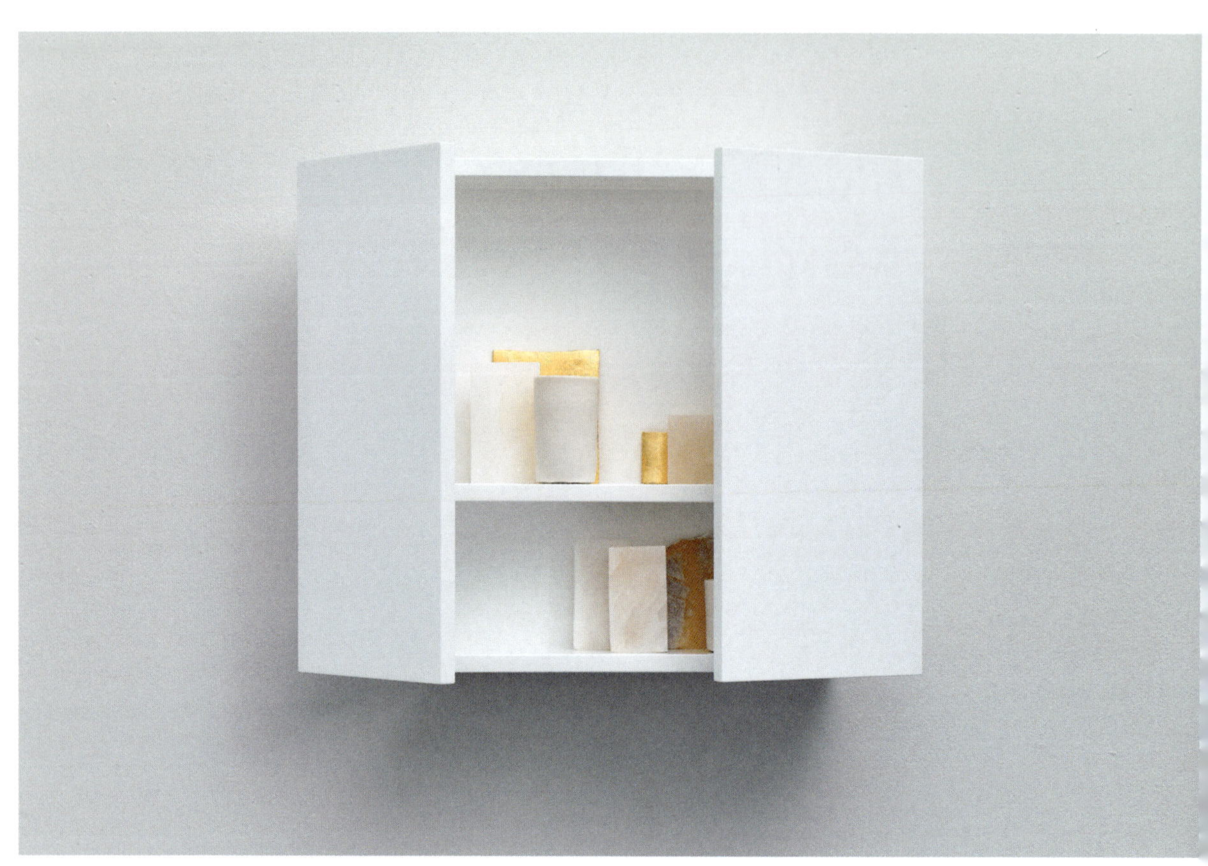

Edmund de Waal
out of this same light, III, 2021
Porcelain, alabaster, gold and wood
43.6 × 38 × 16 cm

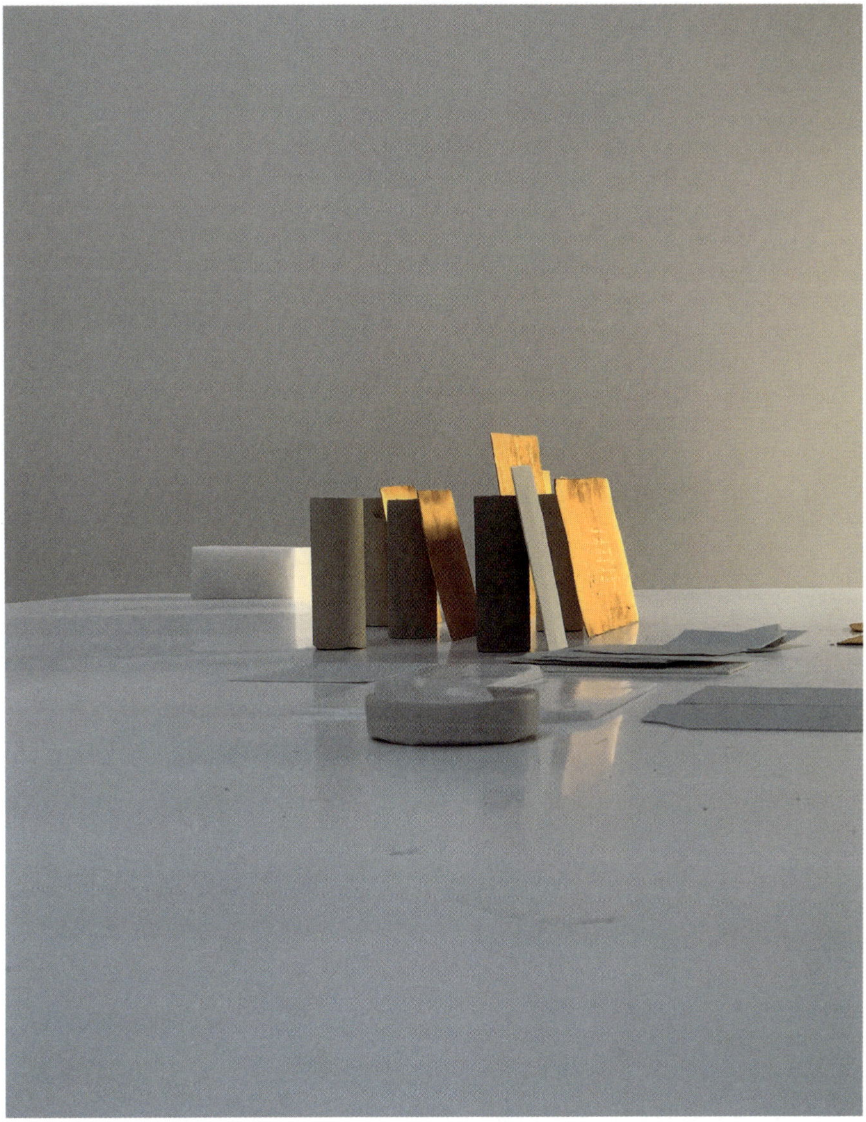

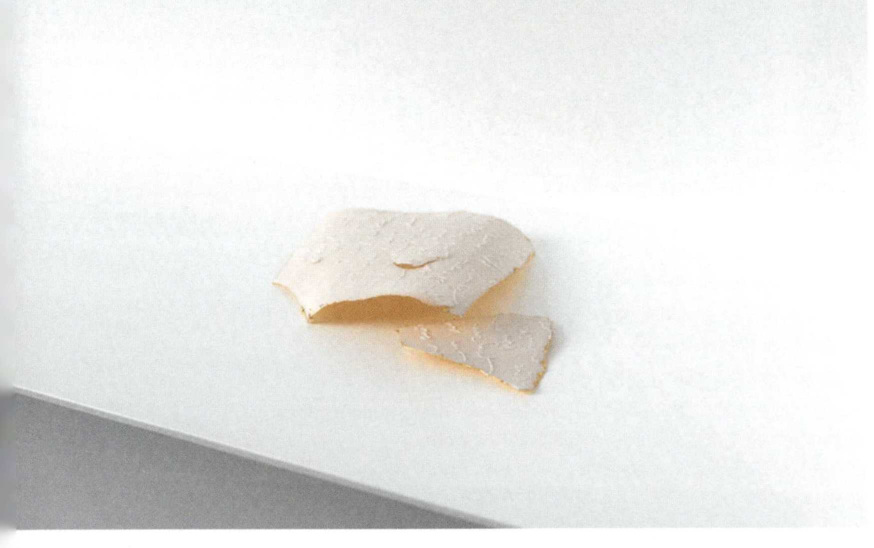

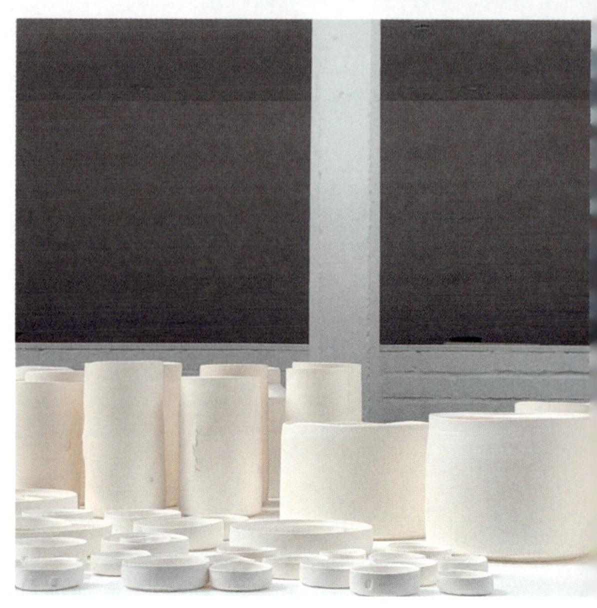

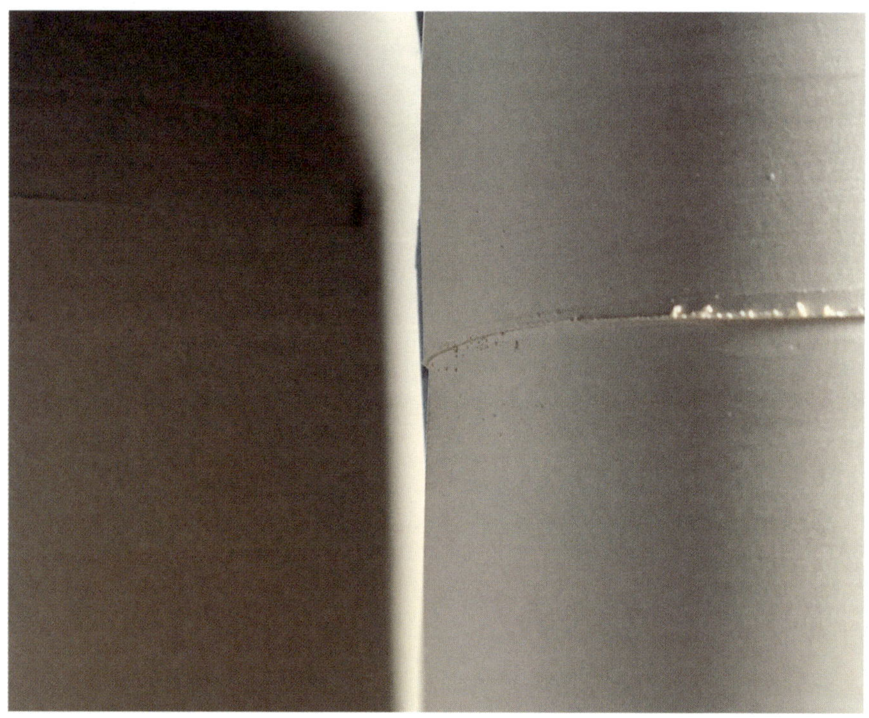

Right
Edmund de Waal
a place made fast, 2014
Porcelain, wood, aluminium, glass
230 × 300 × 11cm

Agnes Martin
On a Clear Day, 1973

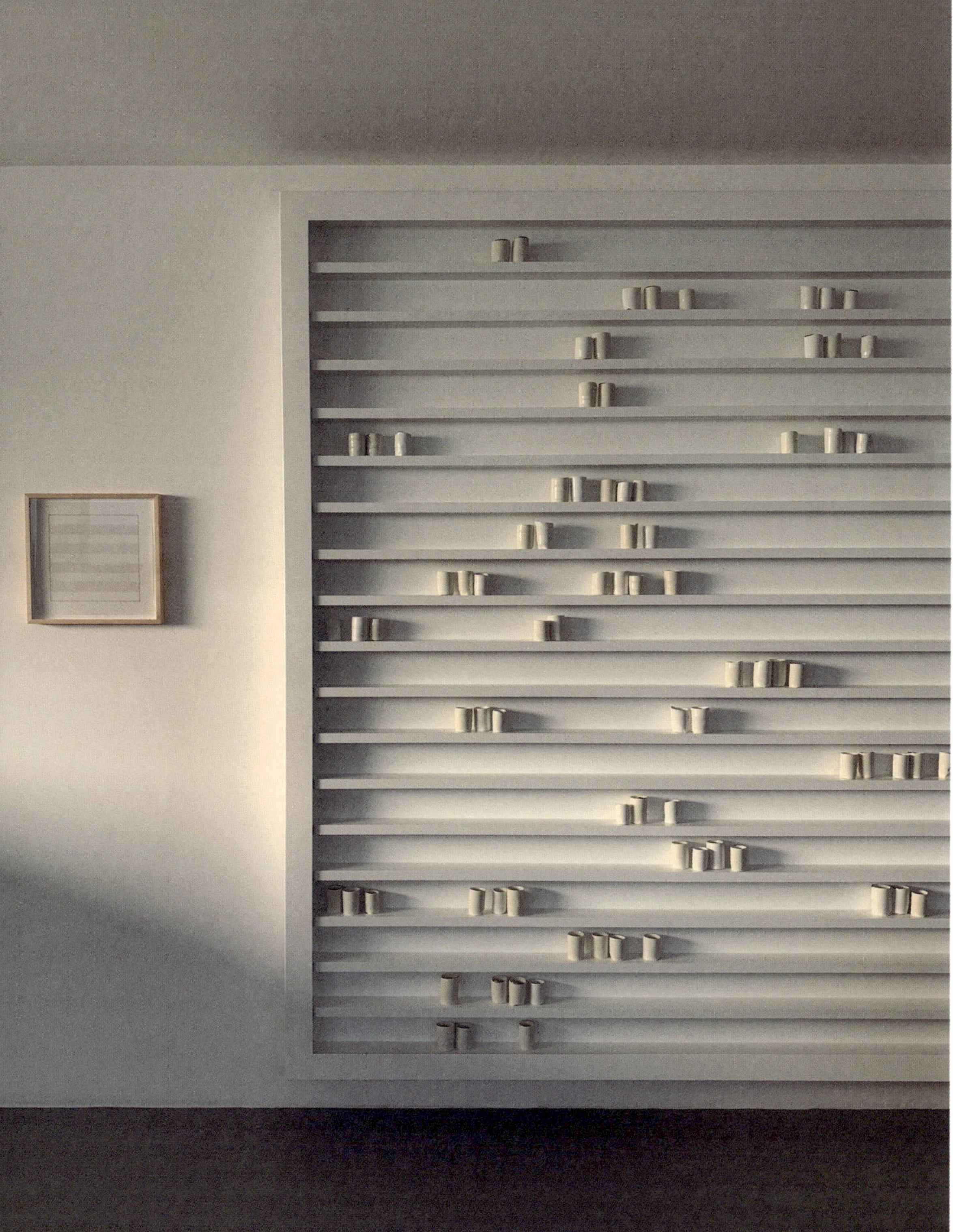

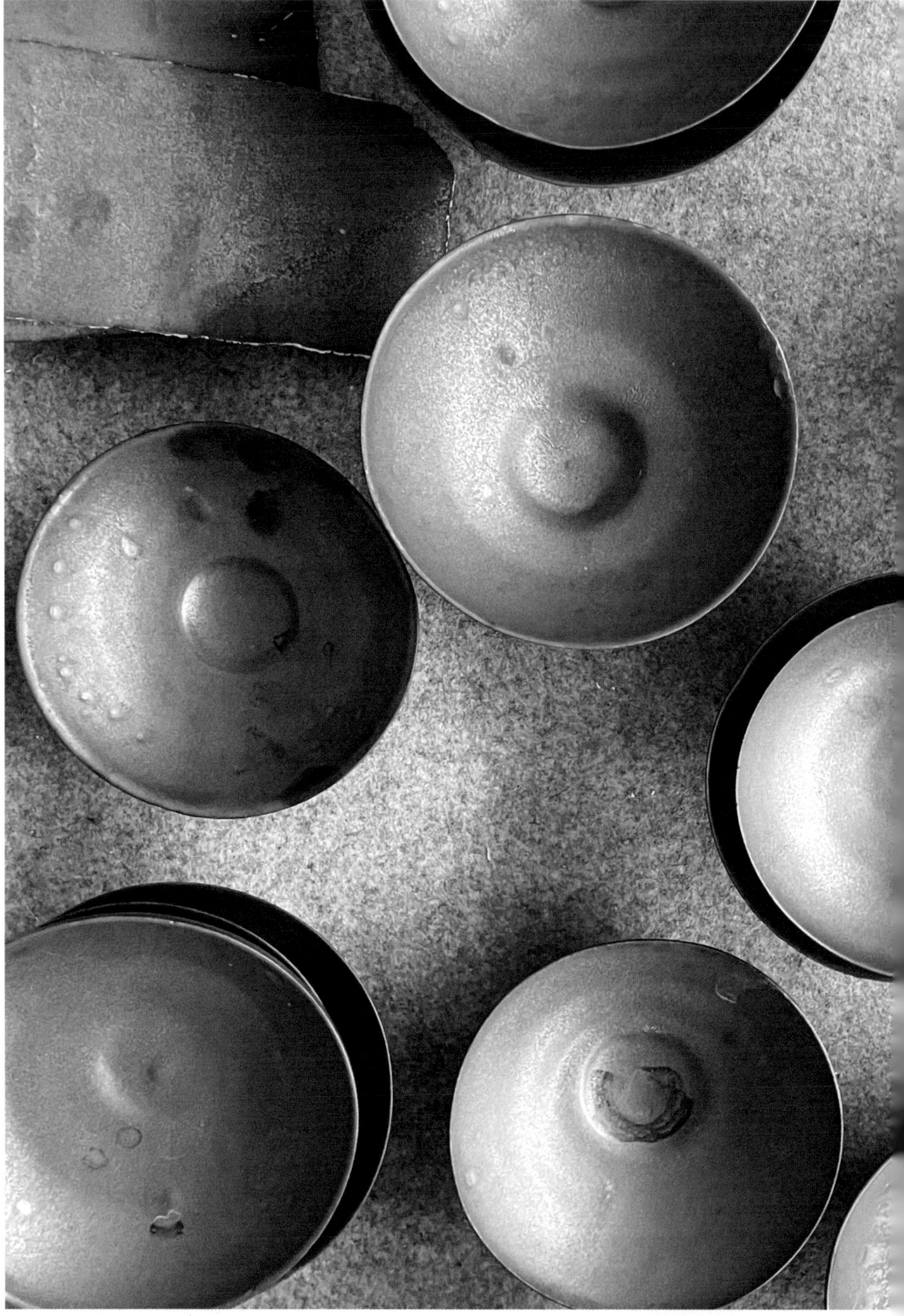

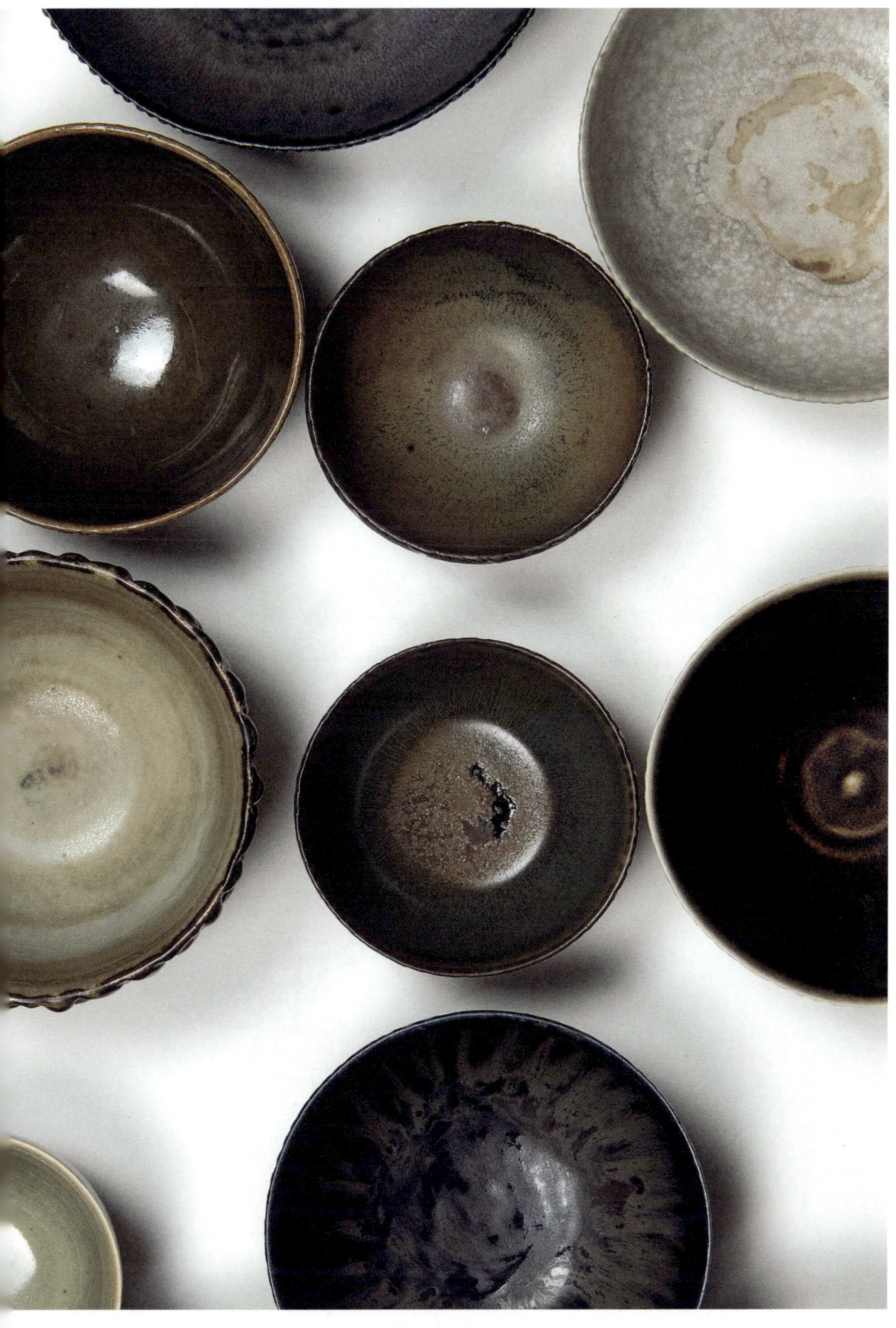

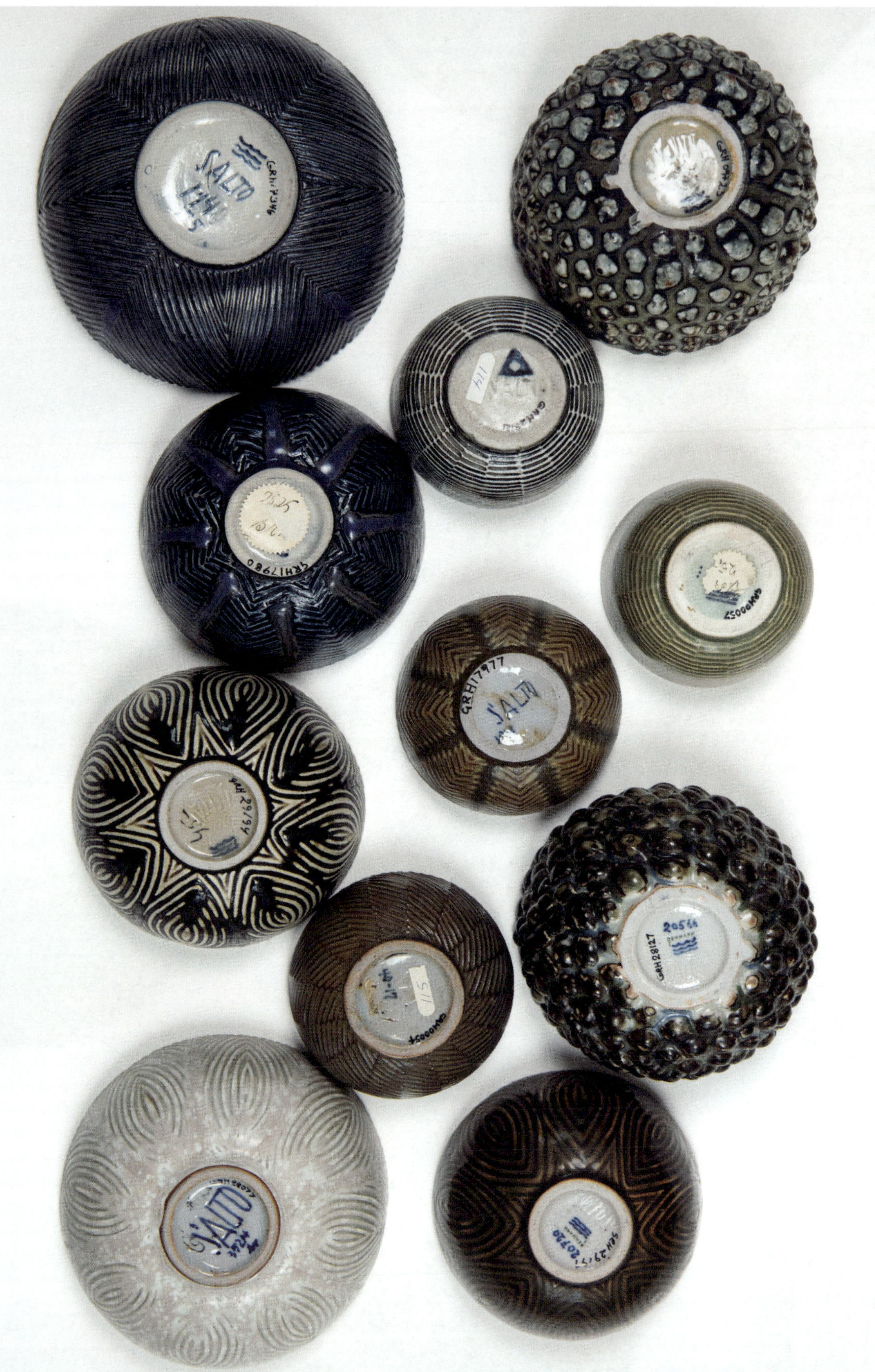

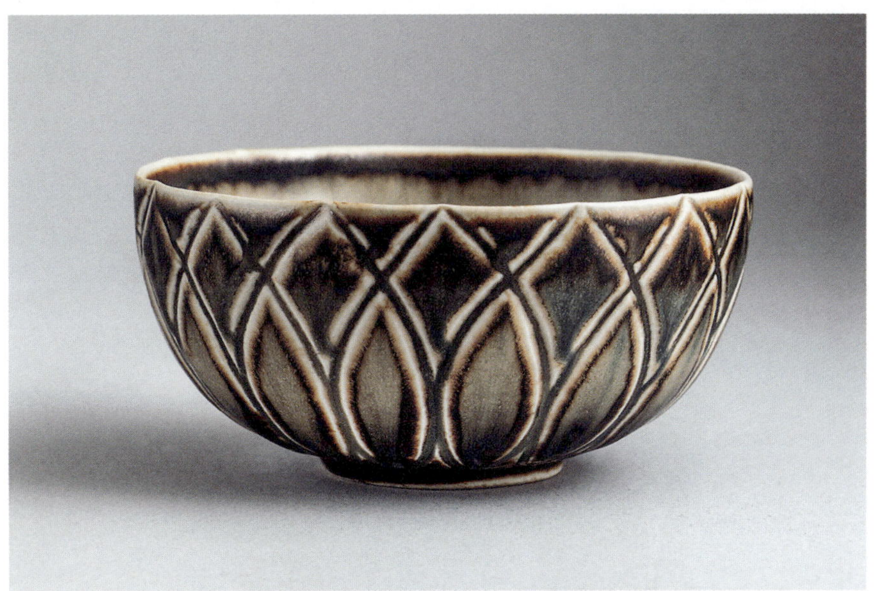

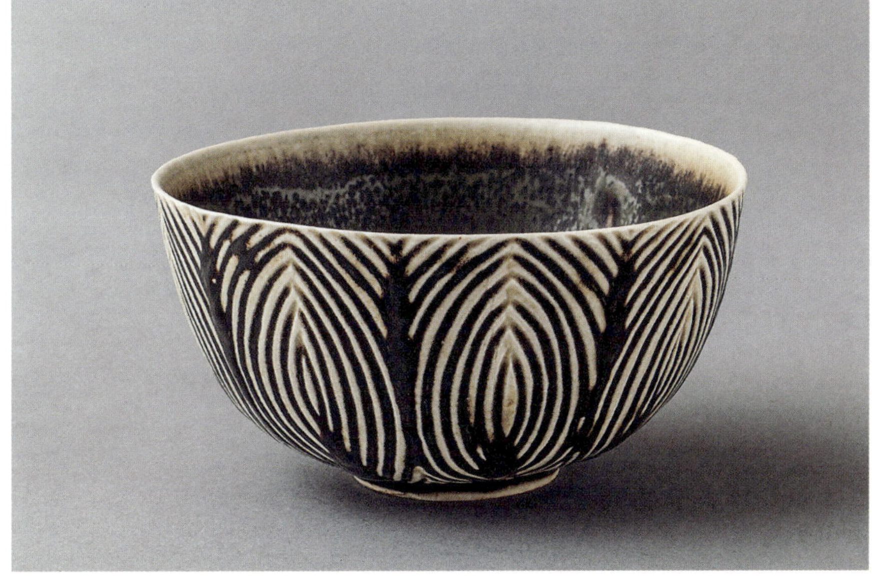

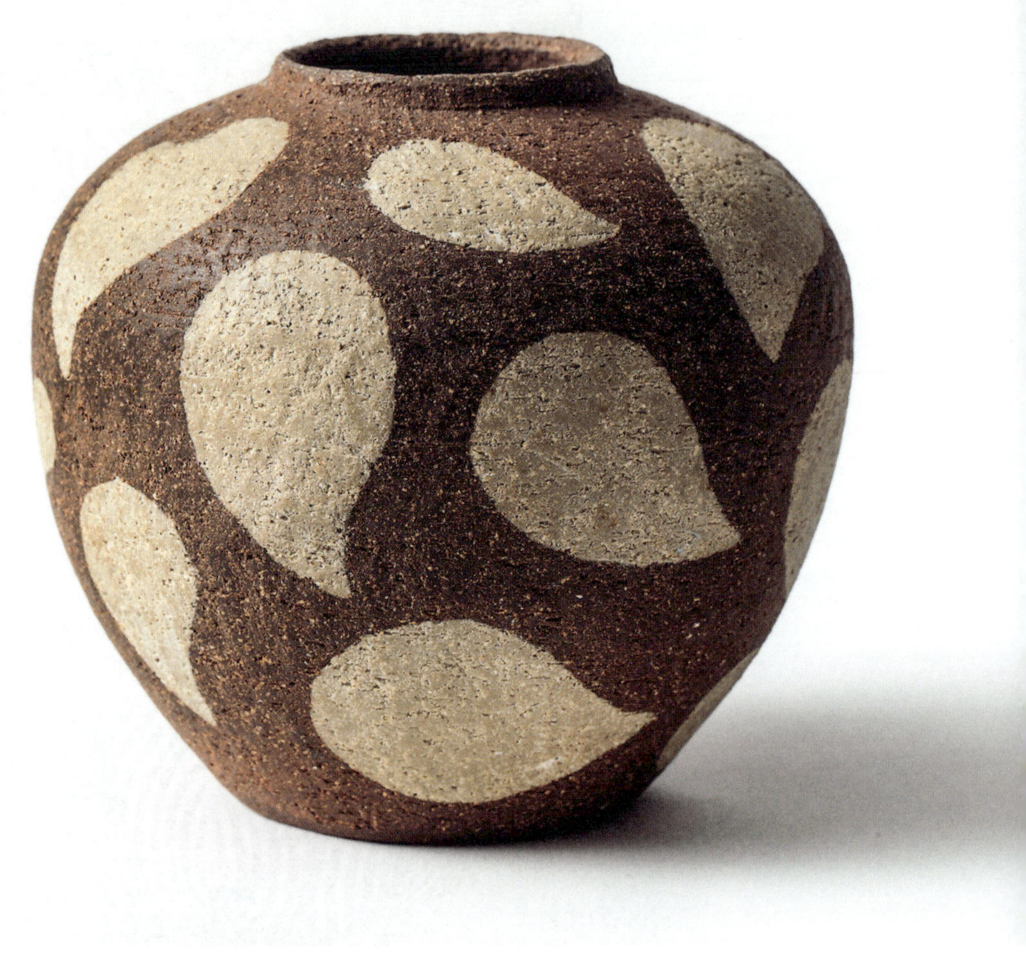

Axel Salto
Vase, n.d.
Unglazed stoneware, H: 10 cm
CLAY/The Royal Copenhagen Collection

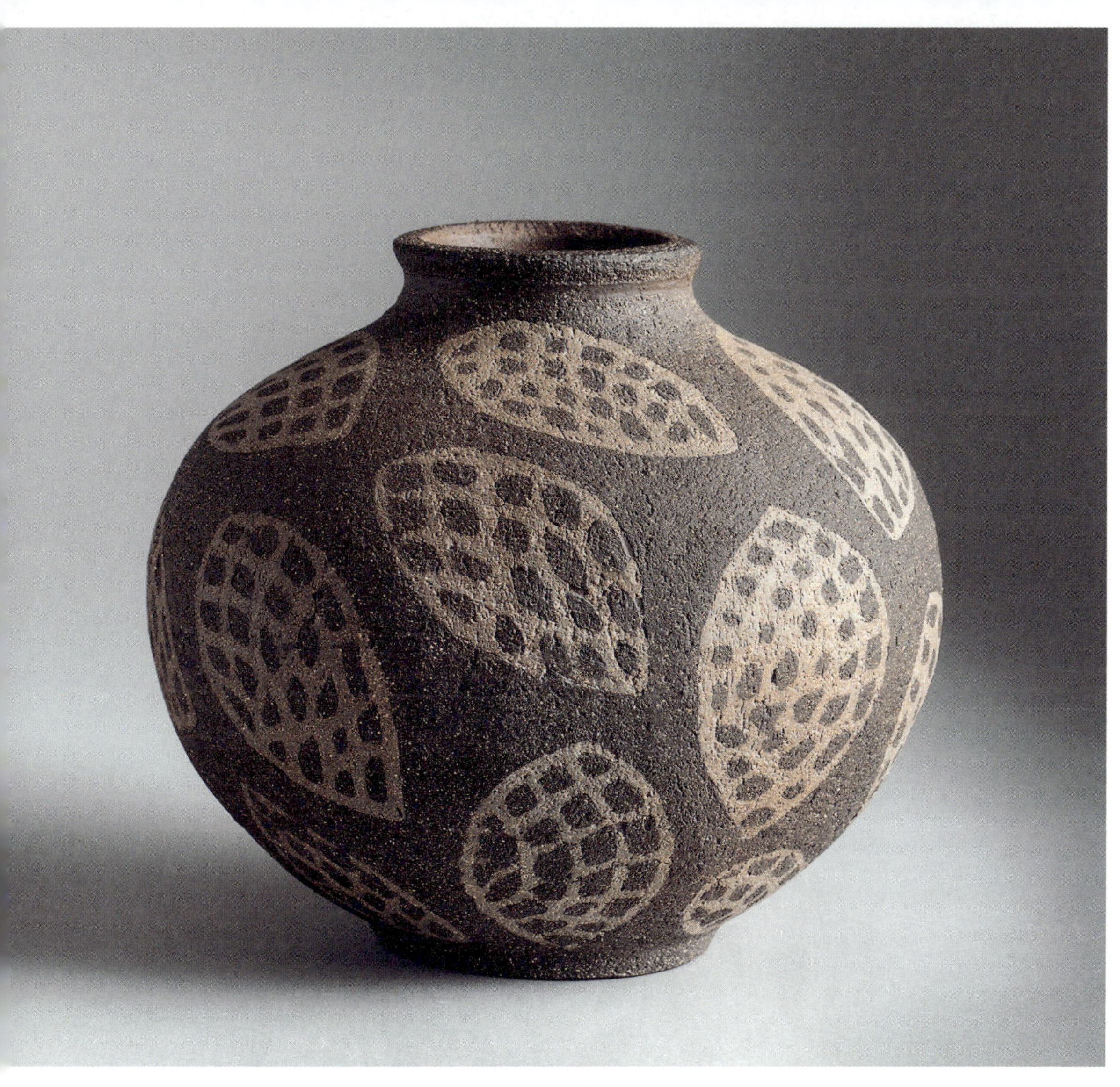

Axel Salto
Vase, 1940's
Unglazed stoneware, H: 18 cm
CLAY/The Royal Copenhagen Collection

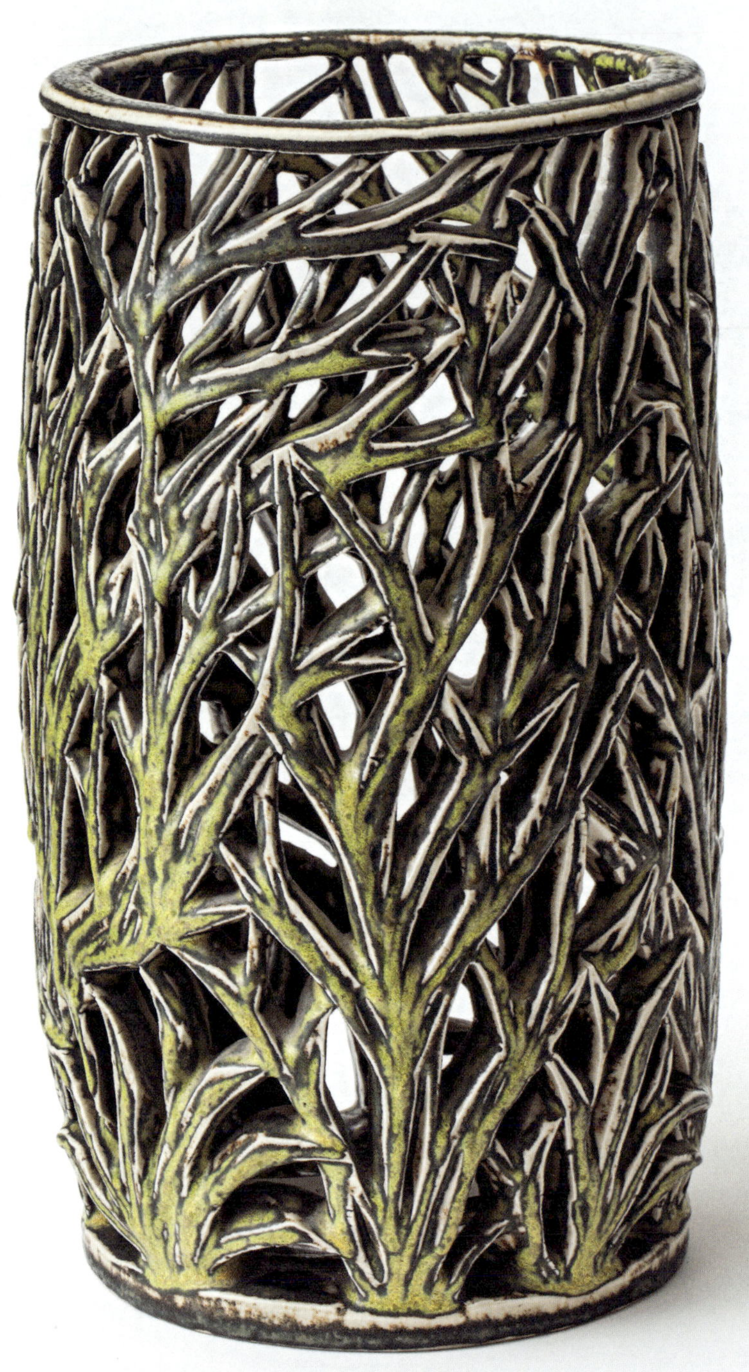

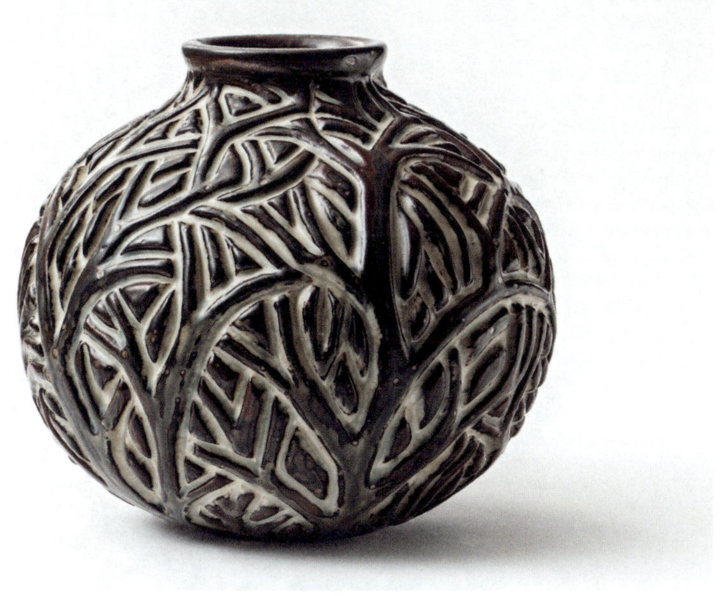

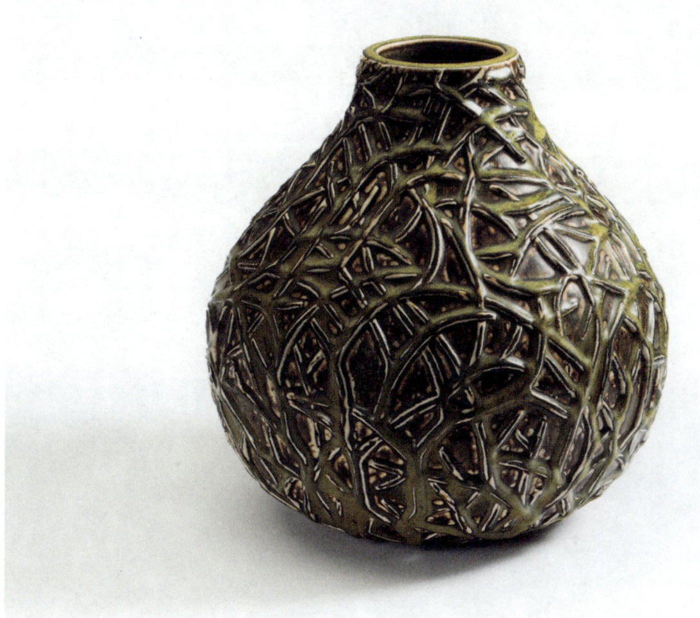

Top
Axel Salto
Vase, 1969–74
Stoneware with Sung glaze, H: 19,5 cm
CLAY/The Royal Copenhagen Collection

Left
Axel Salto
Vase, 1930's
Stoneware in Solfatara glaze, H: 30,5
CLAY/The Royal Copenhagen Collection

Bottom
Axel Salto
Vase, 1949
Stoneware with Solfatara glaze, H: 32 cm
The Tangen Collection/Kunstsilo

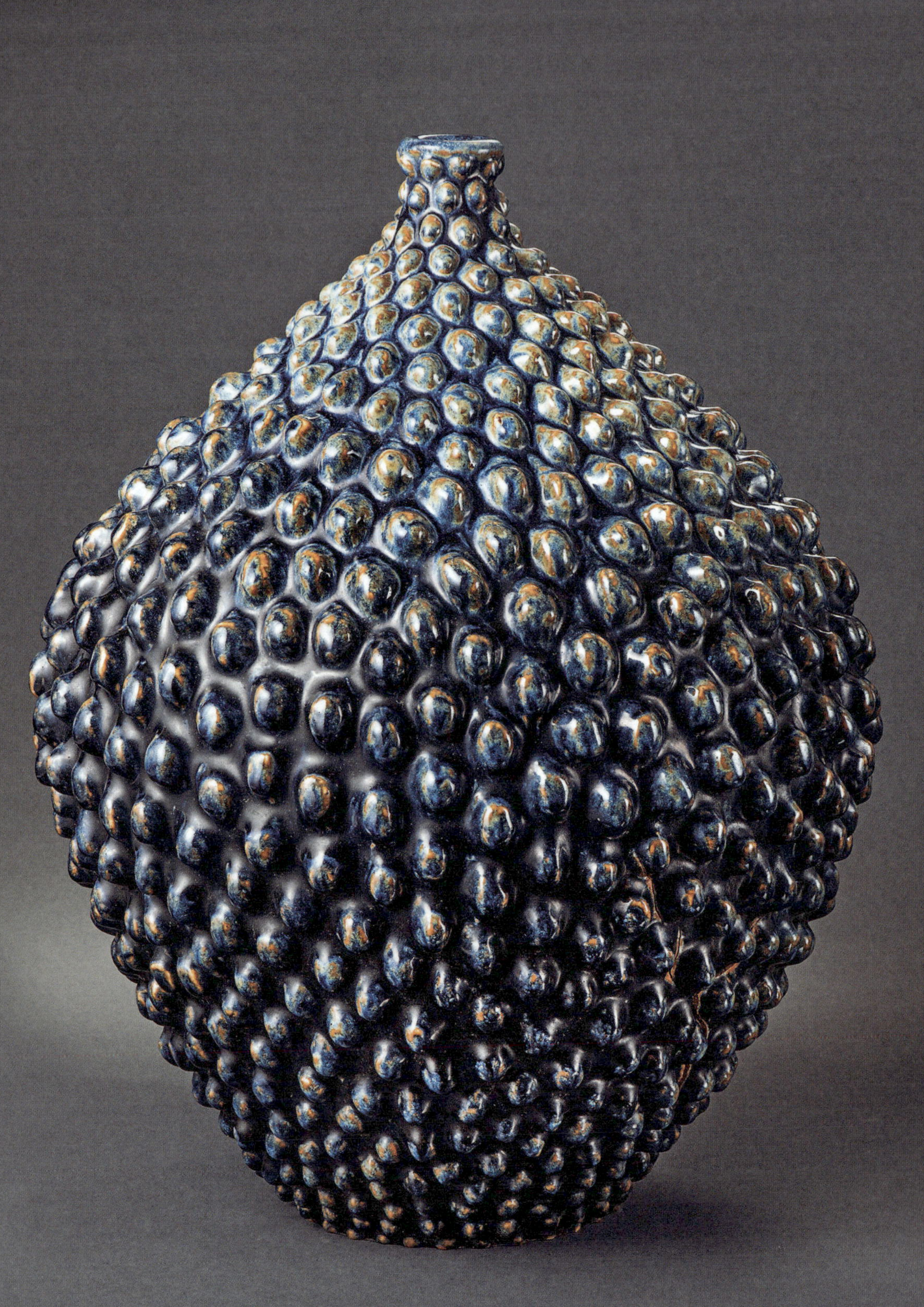

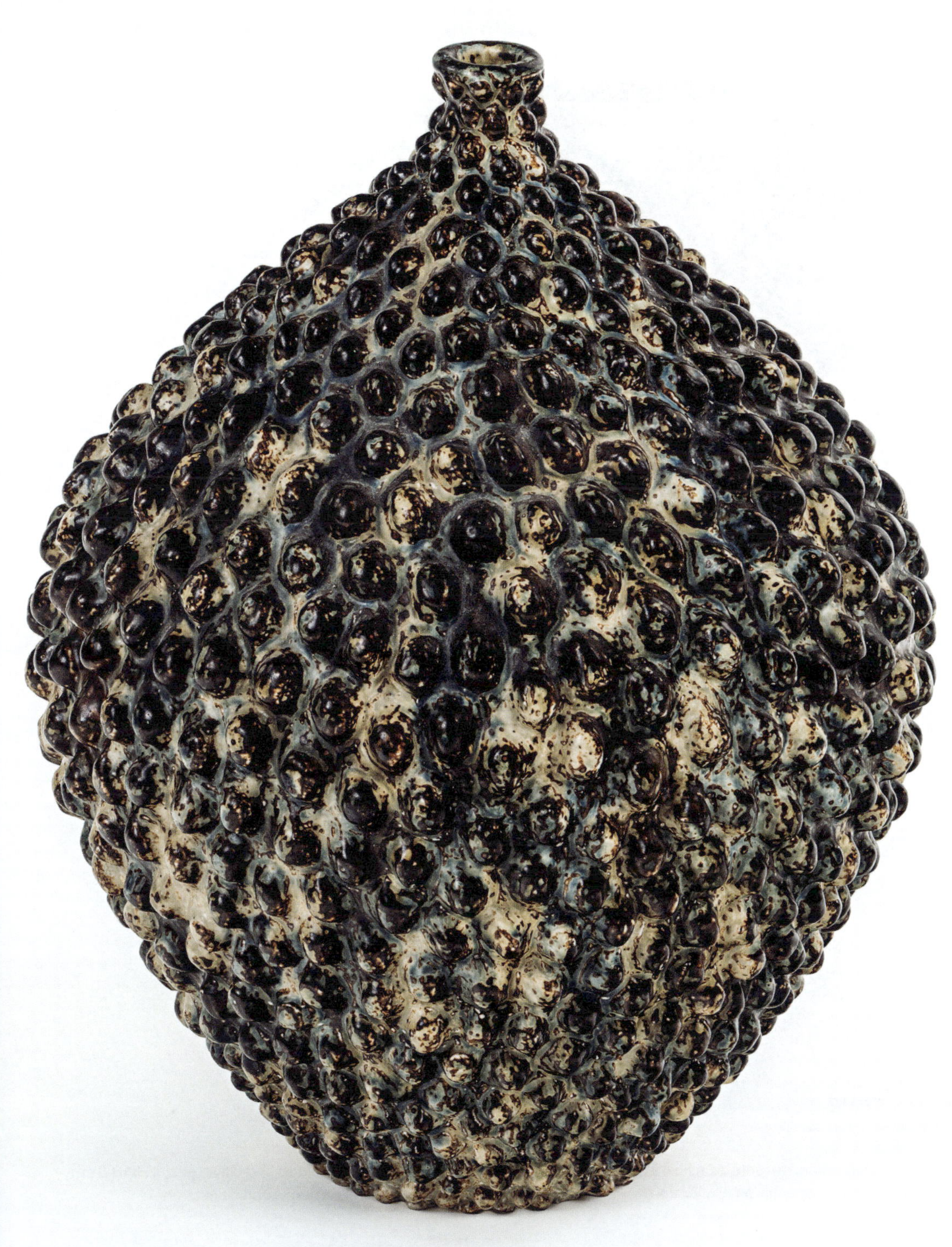

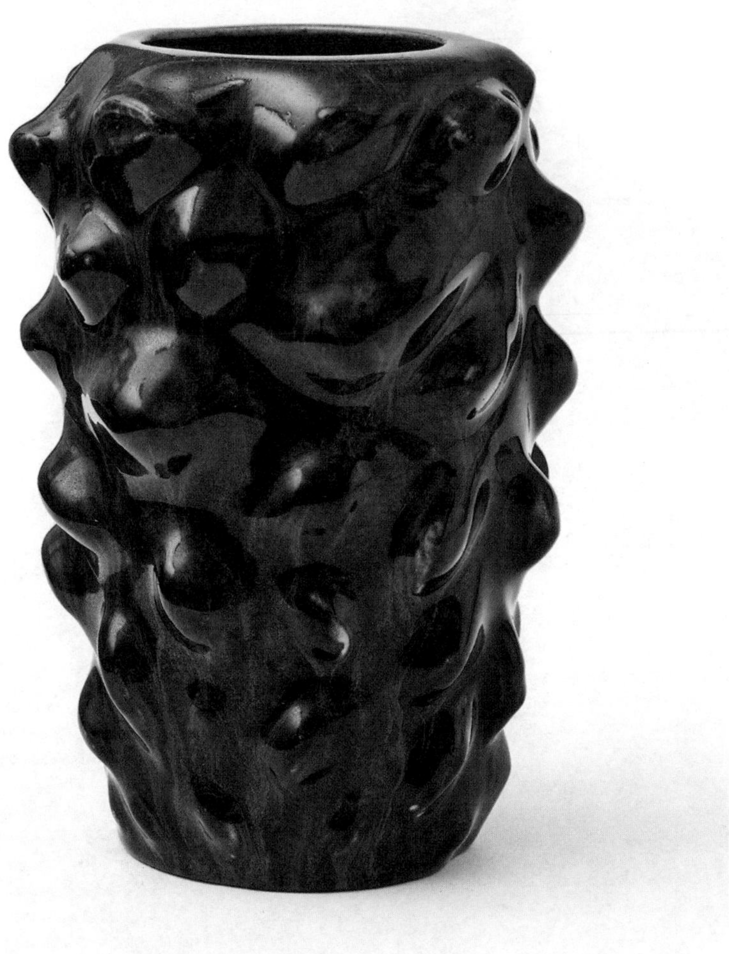

Previous spread, left
Axel Salto
Vase, 1956
Stoneware with Blue Mussel glaze, H: 49 cm
CLAY/The Royal Copenhagen Collection

Previous spread, right
Axel Salto
Vase, n.d.
Stoneware with Sung glaze, H: 50 cm
The Tangen Collection/Kunstsilo

Above
Axel Salto
Vase, 1969–74
Stoneware with Ox-blood and Olivin glaze, H: 18,8 cm
CLAY/The Royal Copenhagen Collection

Right
Axel Salto
Vase, n.d.
Stoneware with Celadon glaze, H: 19 cm
CLAY/The Royal Copenhagen Collection

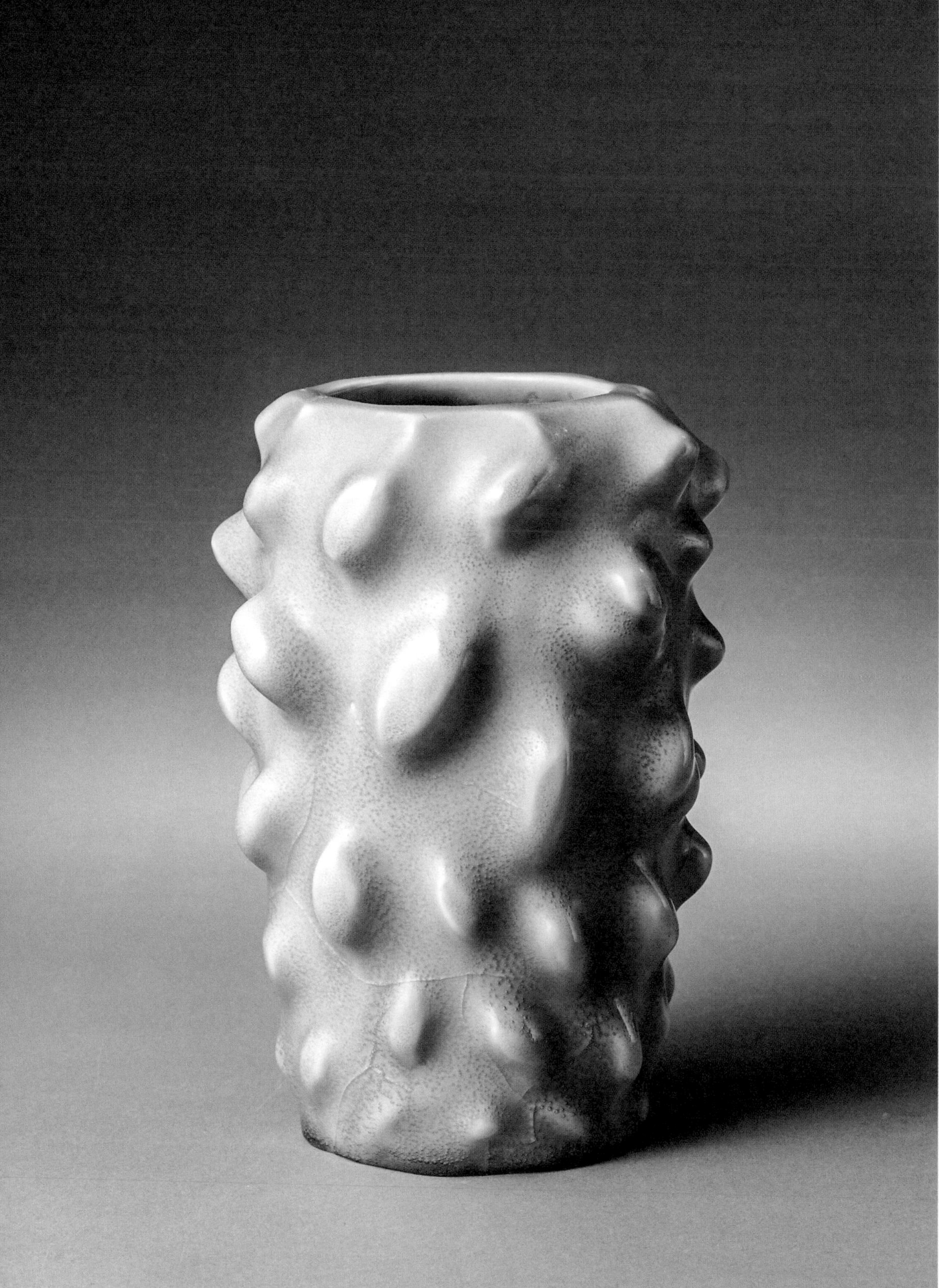

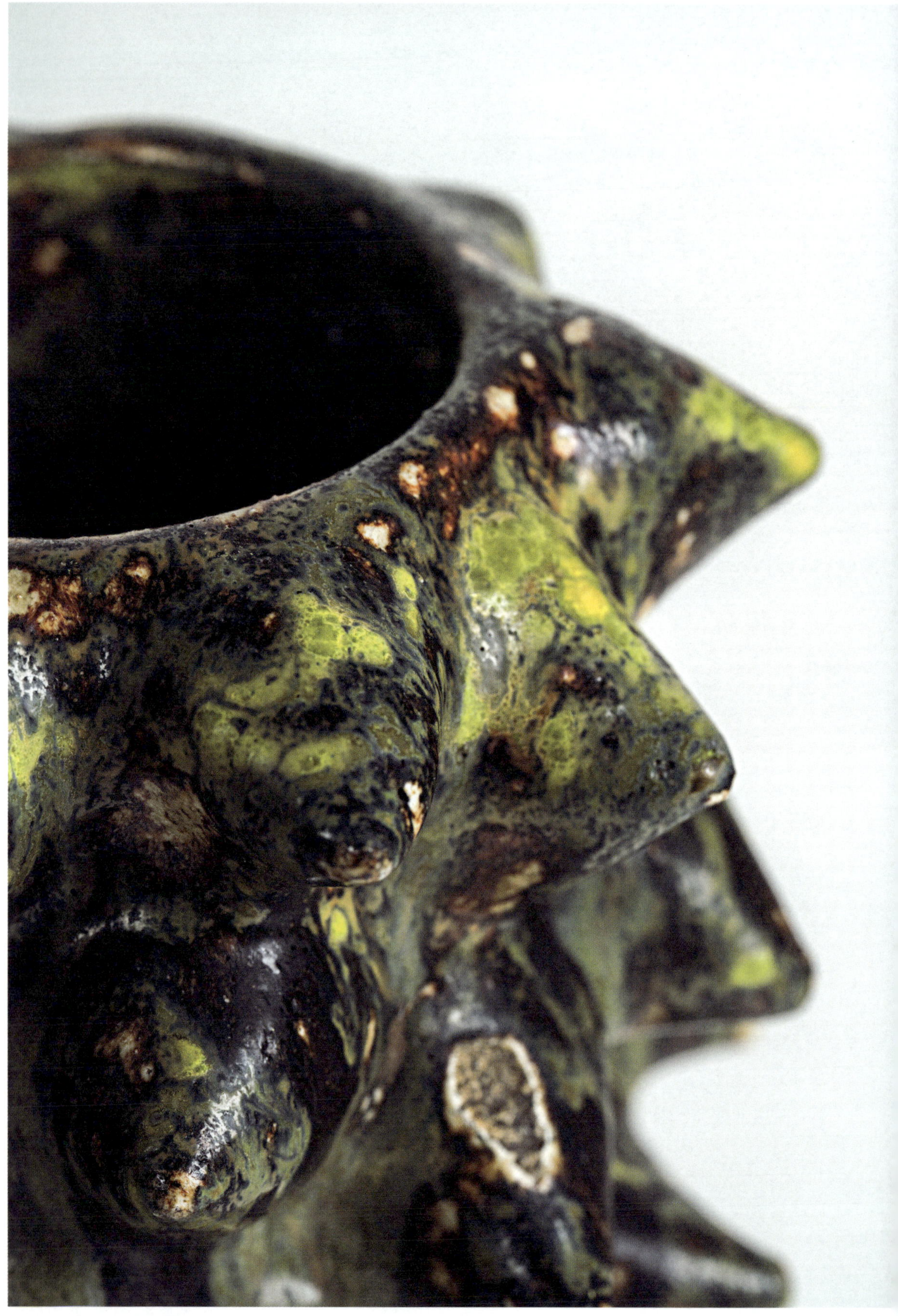

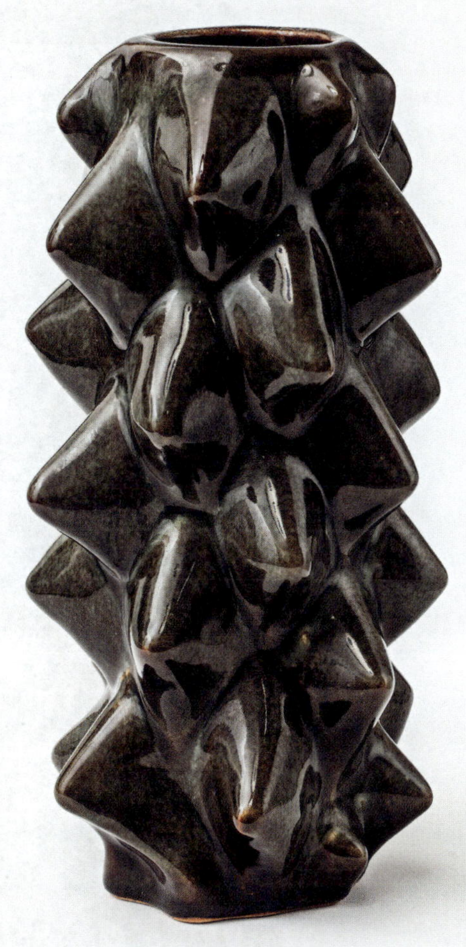

Axel Salto
Vase, detail, 1940's
Stoneware with Solfatara glaze, H: 26,5 cm
The Tangen Collection/Kunstsilo

Axel Salto
Vase, 1975–79
Stoneware with green Olivin glaze, H: 31 cm
CLAY/The Royal Copenhagen Collection

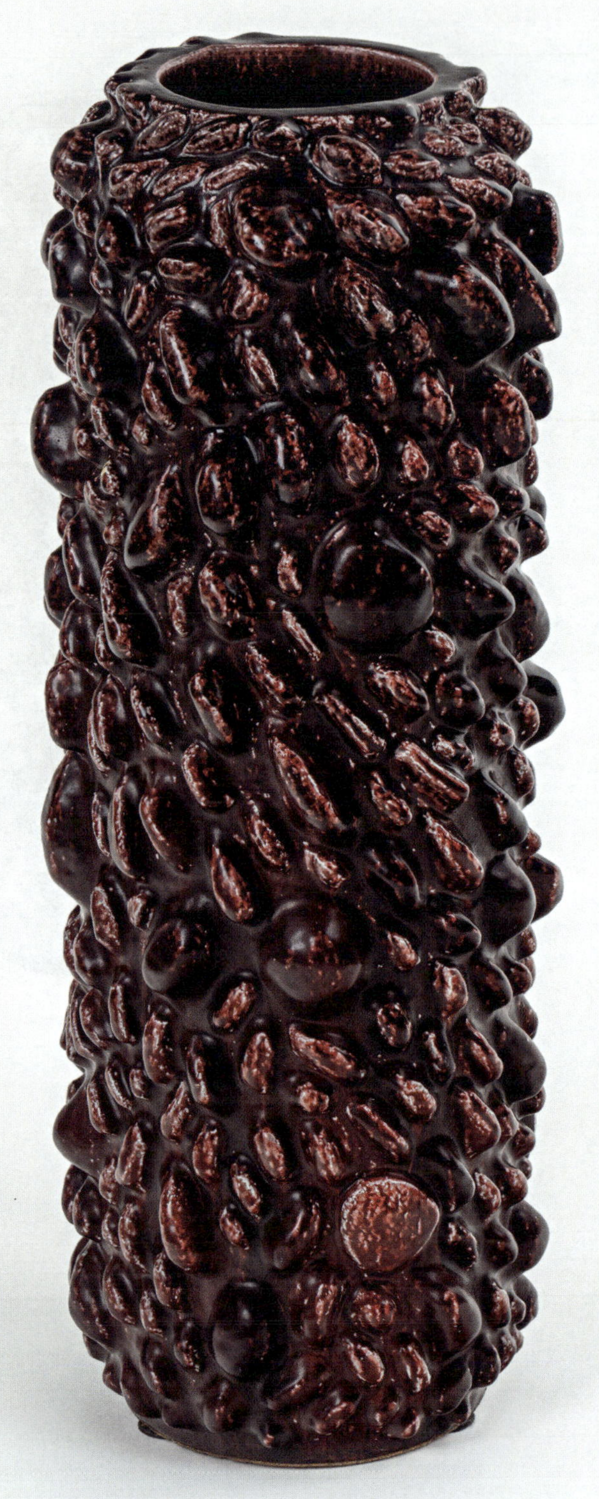

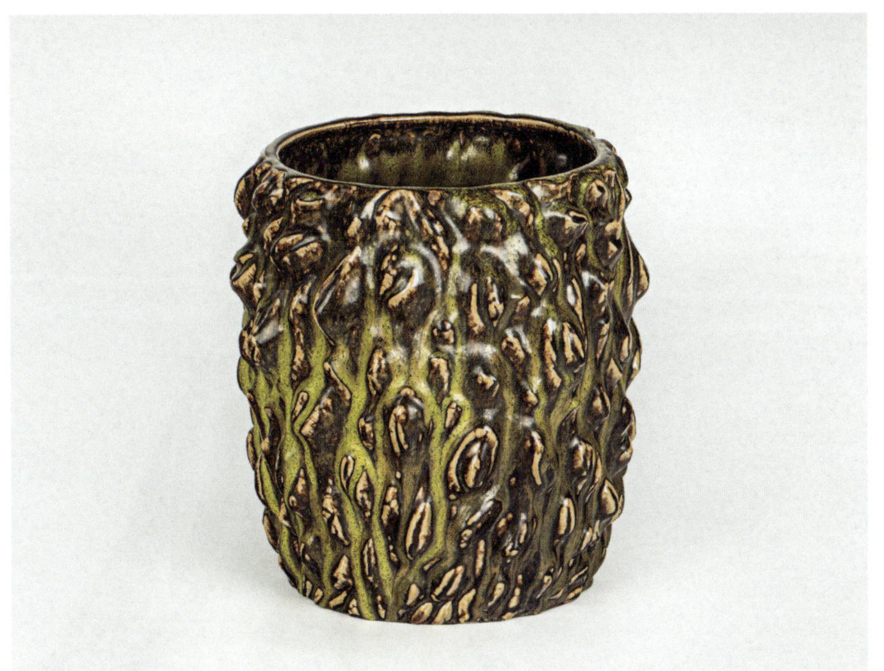

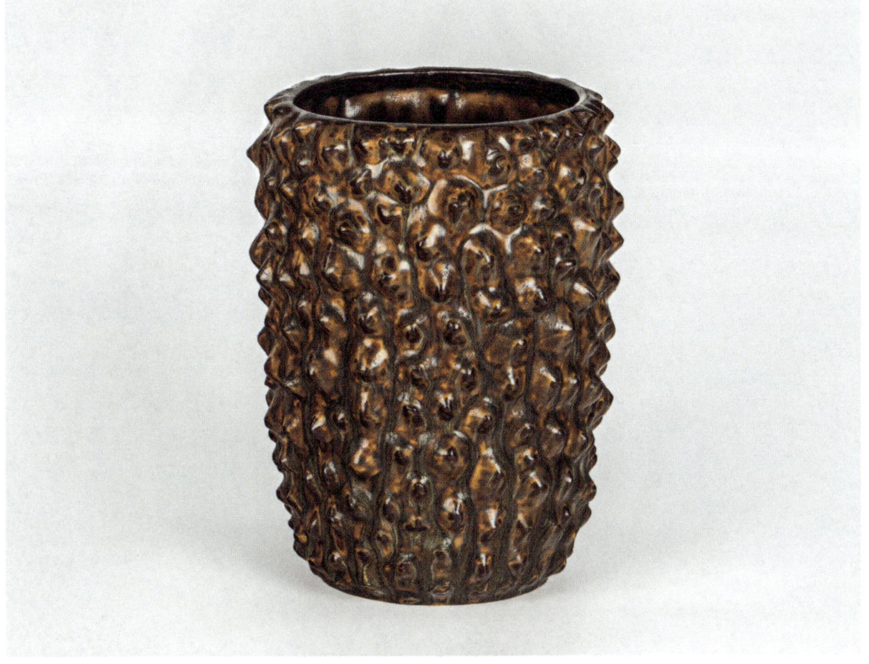

<table>
<tr><td>

Left
Axel Salto
Vase Kameleon, 1960
Stoneware with Ox-blood glaze, H: 69 cm
The Tangen Collection/Kunstsilo

Top
Axel Salto
Vase, n.d.
Stoneware with Solfatara Glaze, H: 29,5 cm
The Tangen Collection/Kunstsilo

</td><td>

Bottom
Axel Salto
Vase, n.d.
Stoneware with brown glaze, H: 25,5 cm
The Tangen Collection/Kunstsilo

Next page
Axel Salto
Vase, 1946
Stoneware with Solfatara glaze, H: 38 cm
CLAY/The Royal Copenhagen Collection

</td></tr>
</table>

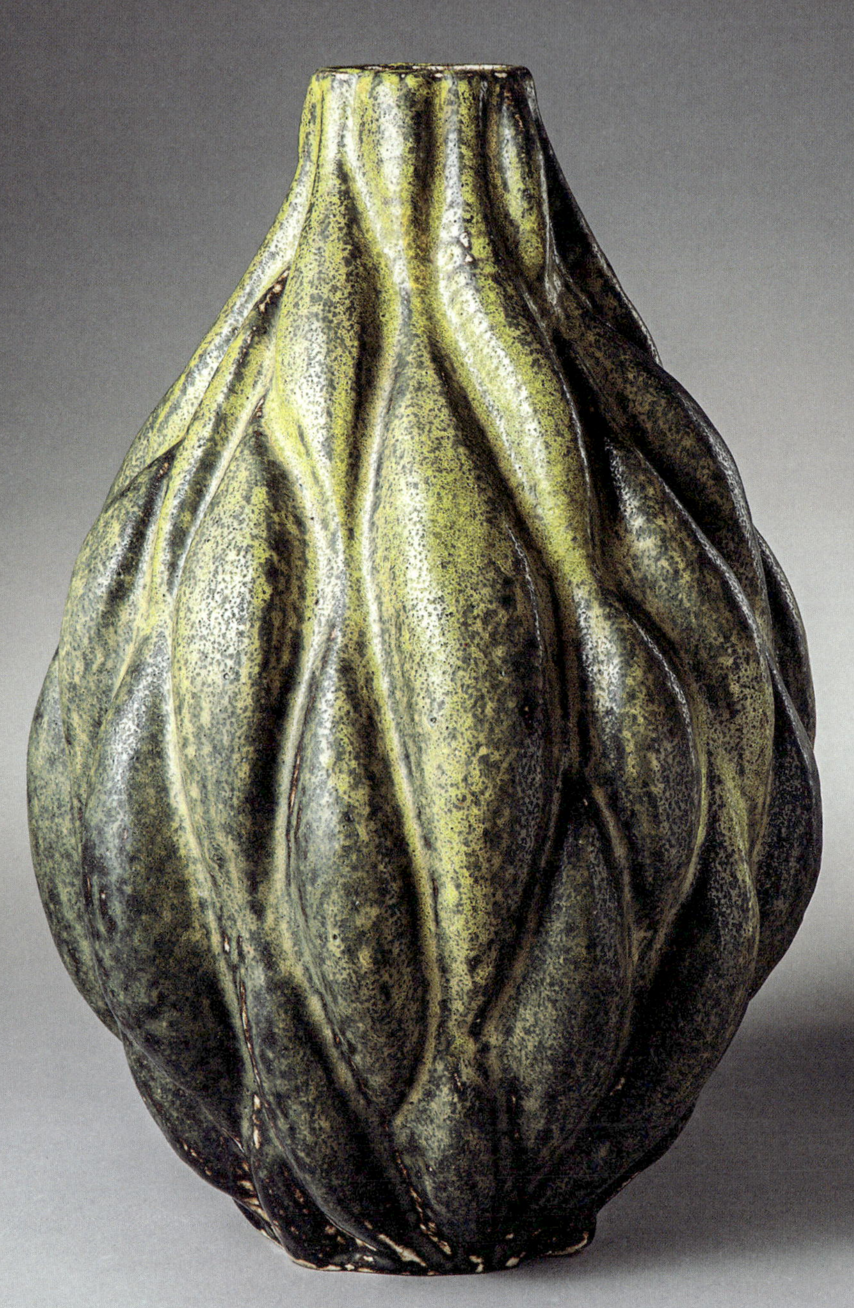

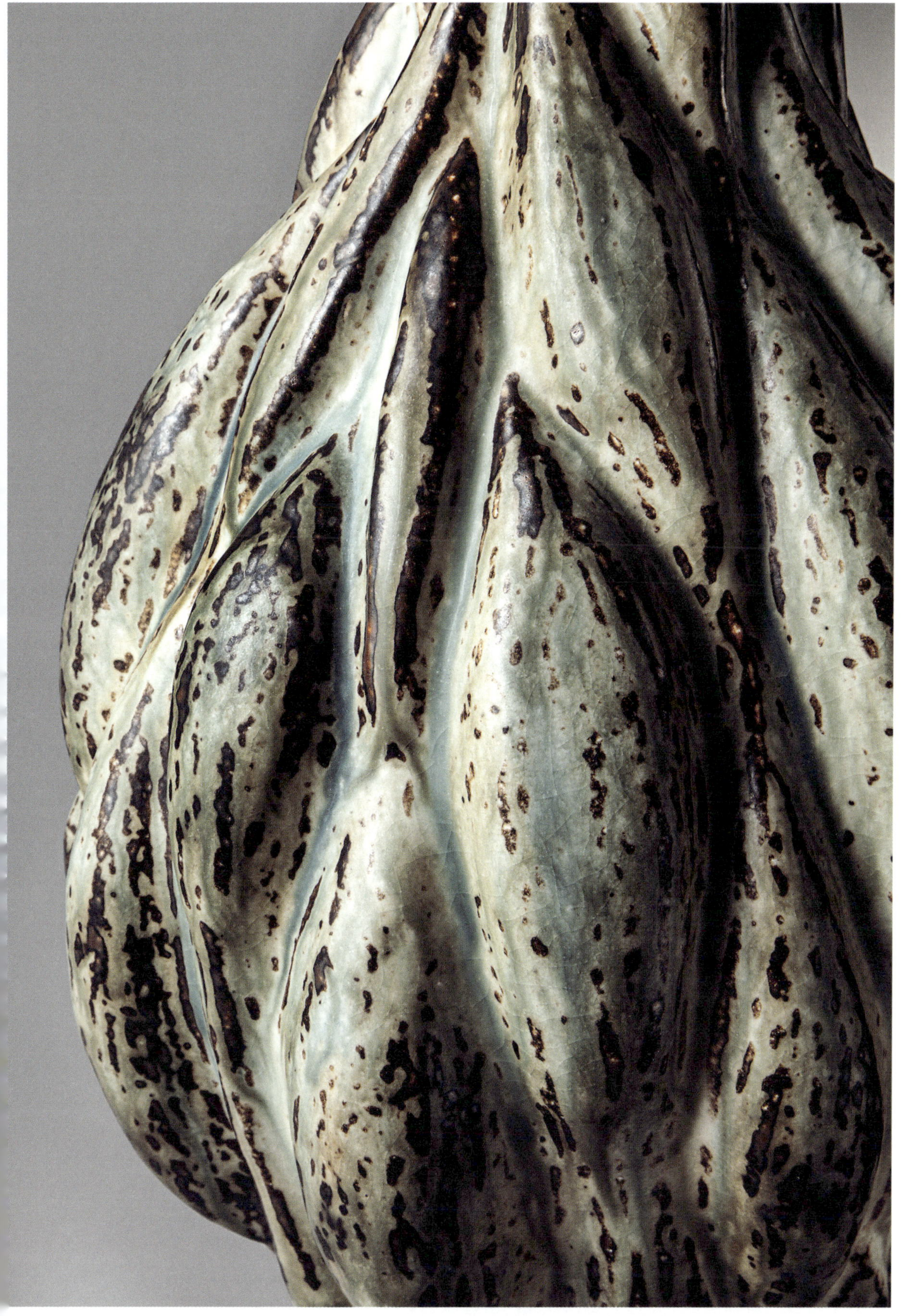

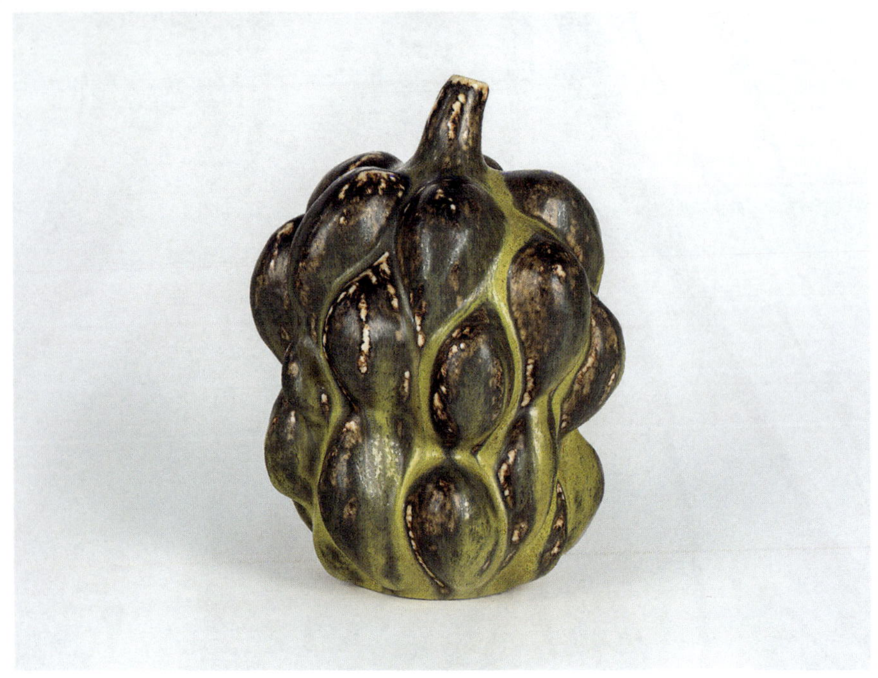

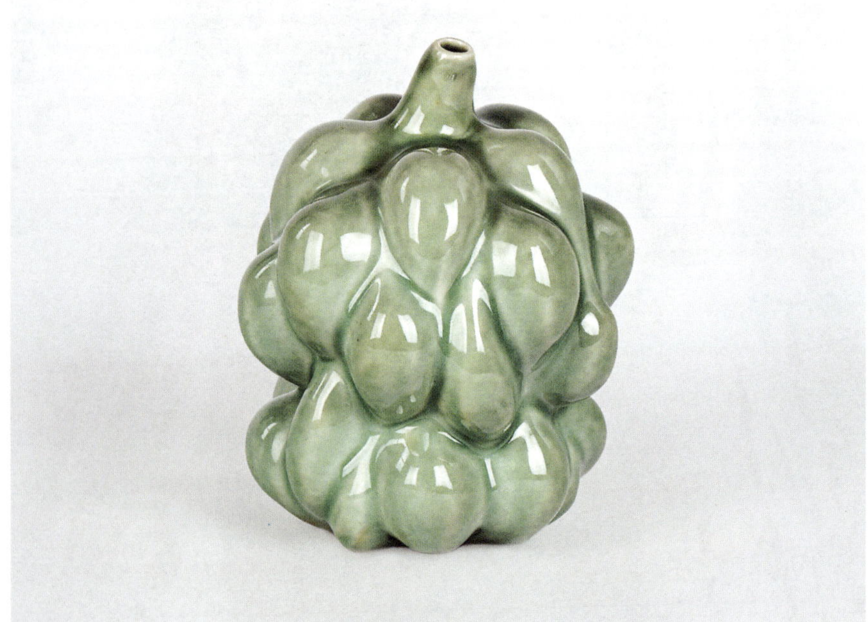

Previous page
Axel Salto
Vase, detail, 1975–79
Stoneware with Sung glaze, H: 37,5 cm
CLAY/The Royal Copenhagen Collection

Top
Axel Salto
Vase, 1946
Stoneware with Solfatara glaze, H: 22,5 cm
The Tangen Collection/Kunstsilo

Bottom
Axel Salto
Vase, 1969–74
Stoneware with Celadon glaze, H: 22 cm
The Tangen Collection/Kunstsilo

Right
Axel Salto
Vase, 1946
Stoneware with Sung glaze, H: 22,5 cm
CLAY/The Royal Copenhagen Collection

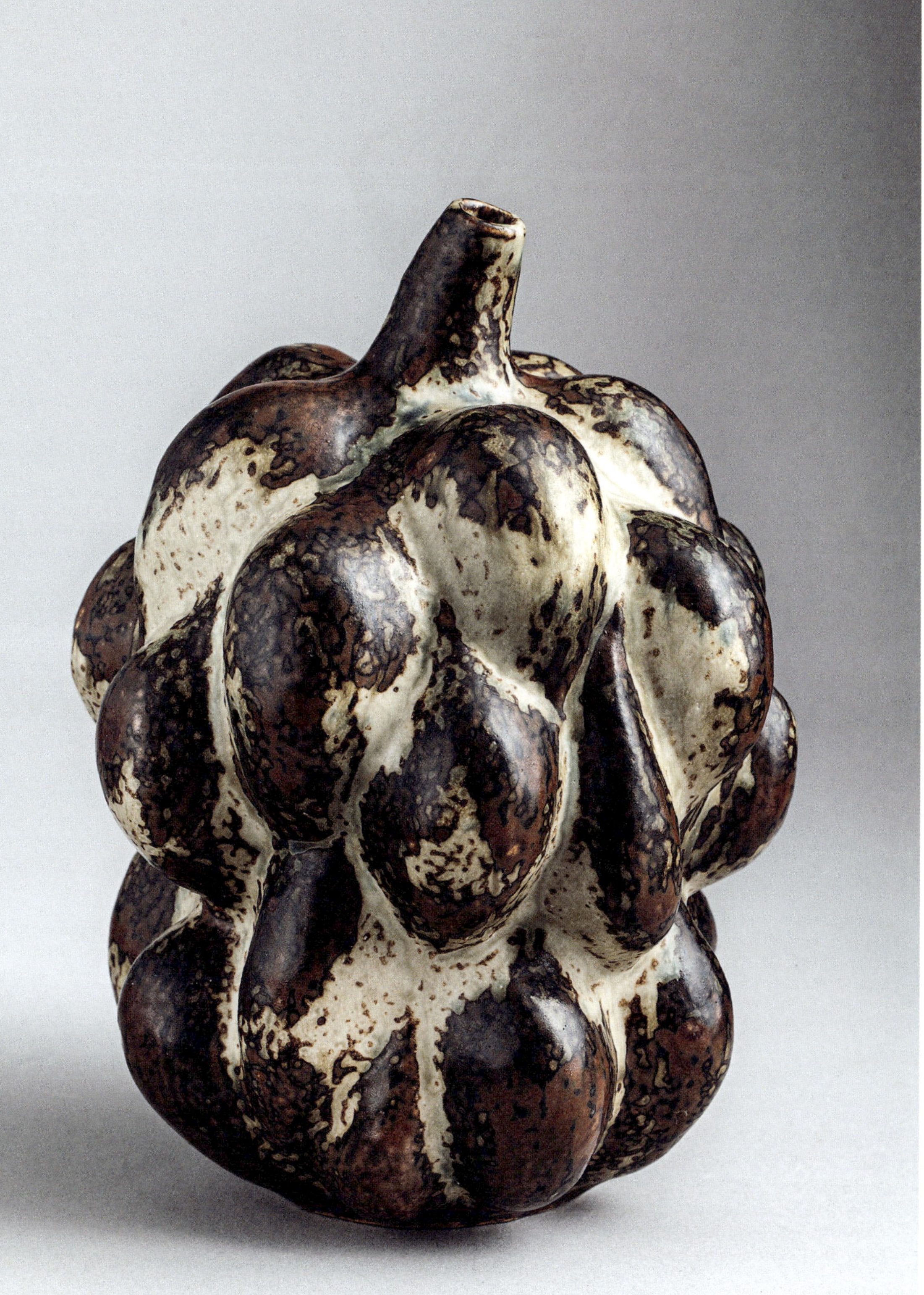

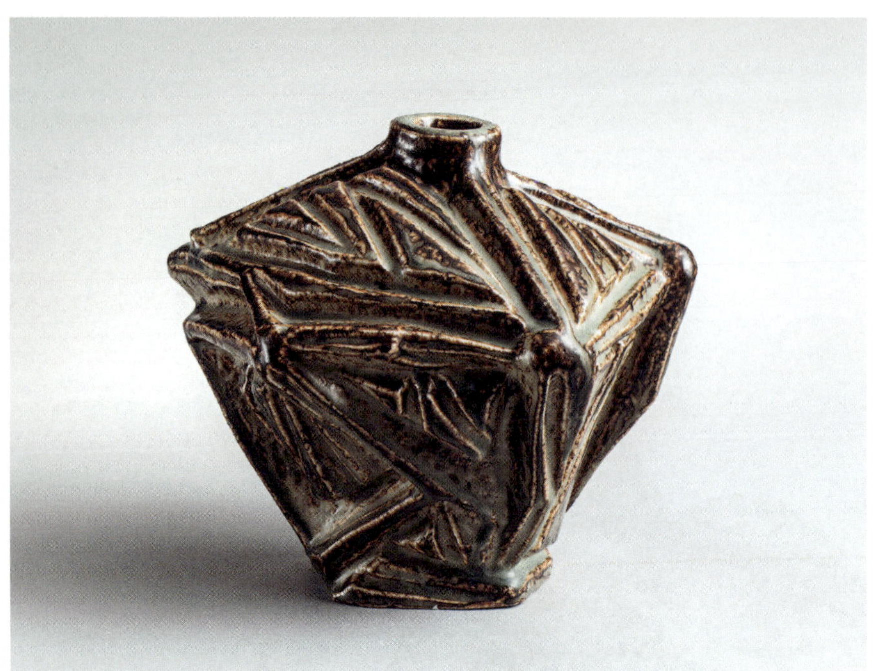

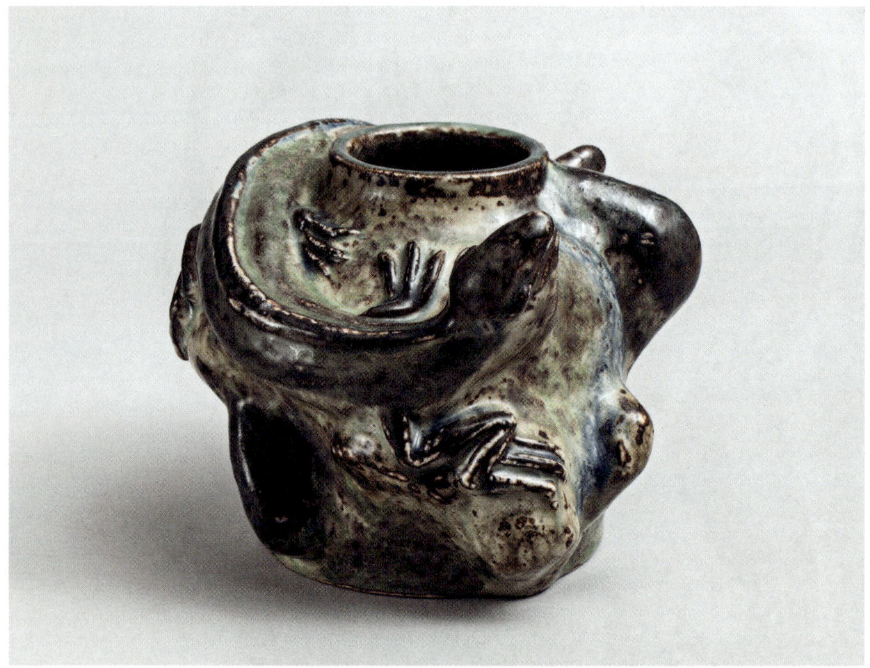

Top
Axel Salto
Vase, 1949
Stoneware with Sung glaze, H: 23,5 cm
CLAY/The Royal Copenhagen Collection

Bottom
Axel Salto
Vase with lizard, 1959
Stoneware with Sung glaze, H: 15 cm
CLAY/The Erik Veistrup Collection

Right
Axel Salto
Sommervase, detail, 1975–79
Stoneware with Sung glaze, H: 32,5 cm
CLAY/The Royal Copenhagen Collection

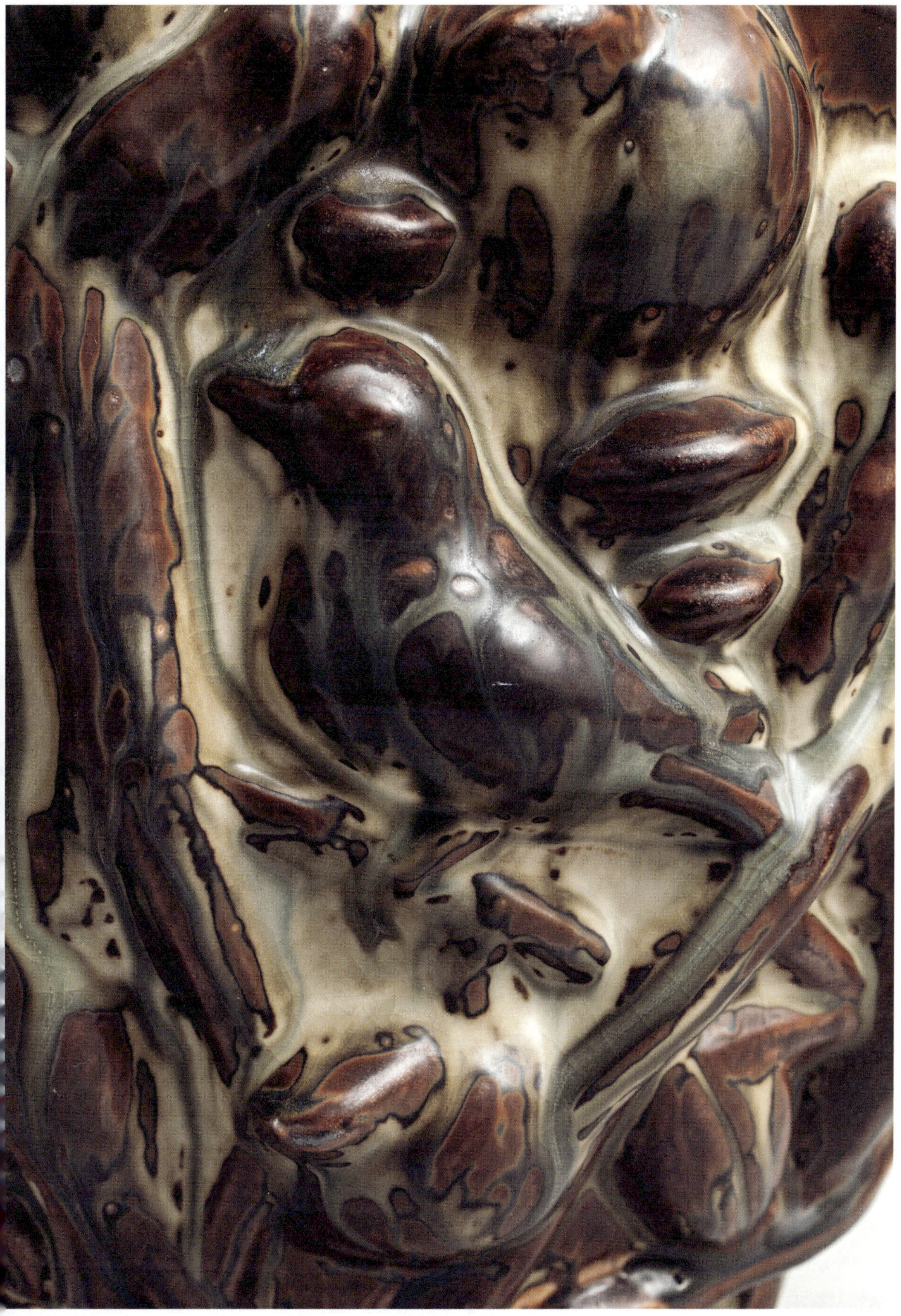

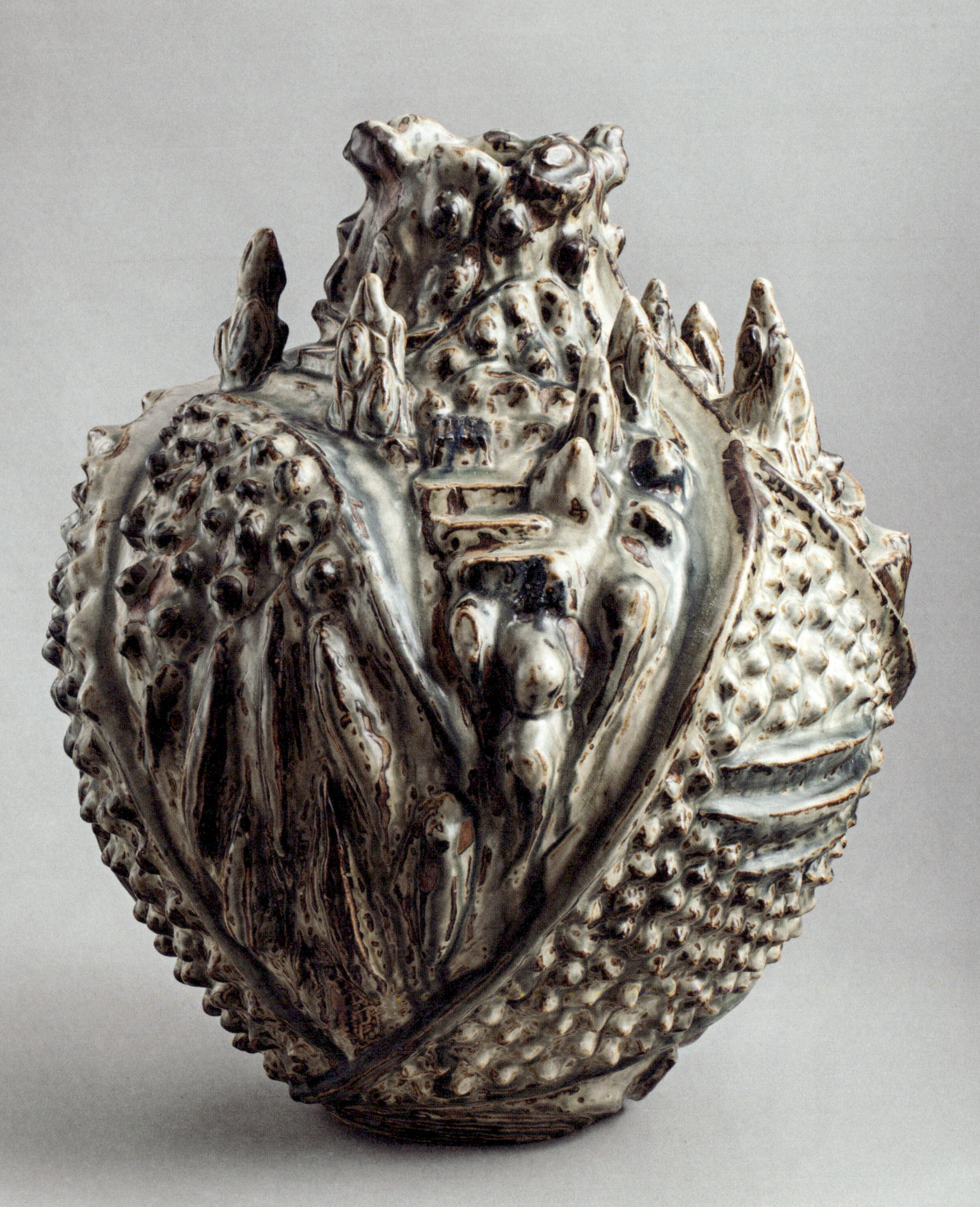

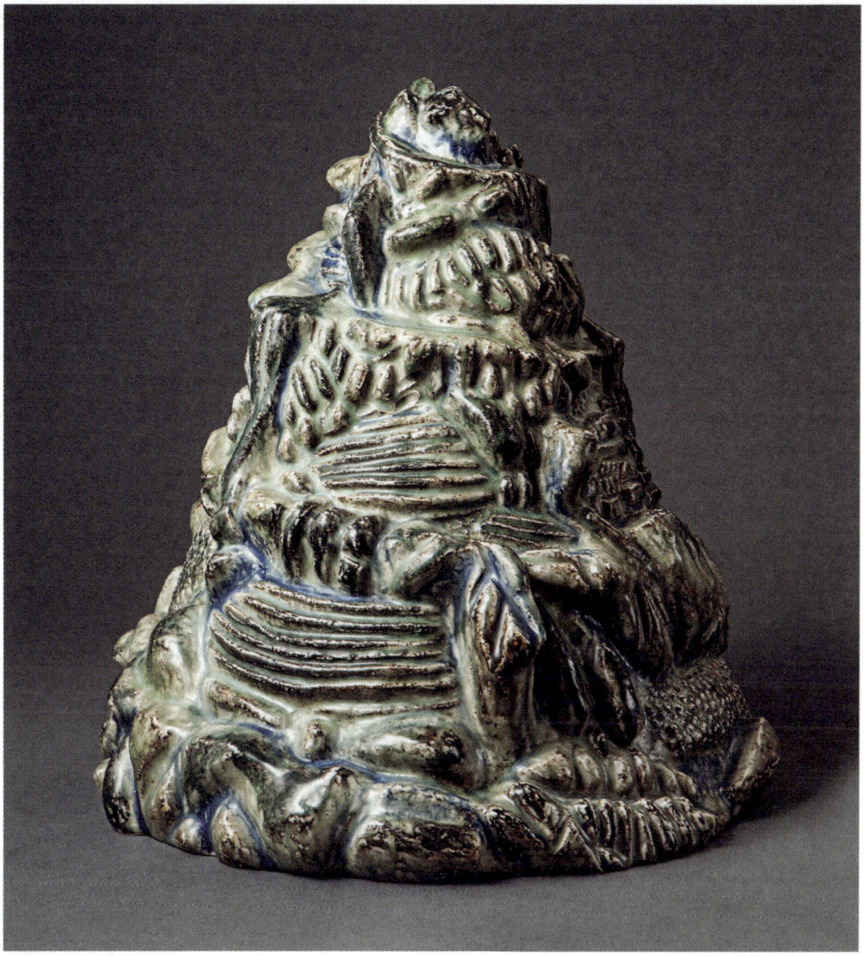

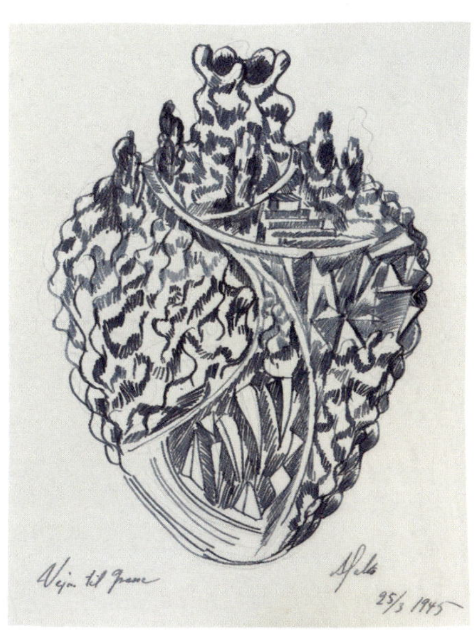

Top
Axel Salto
The Road to La Gaude, 1939
Stoneware with Sung glaze, H: 40 cm
CLAY/The Royal Copenhagen Collection

Bottom
Axel Salto
Sketch *The Road to Grasse*, 1945
Graphite and ink on paper, 240 × 182 mm
CLAY Museum of Ceramic Art

Left
Axel Salto
The Road to Grasse, 1936
Stoneware with Sung glaze, H: 46 cm
CLAY/The Royal Copenhagen Collection

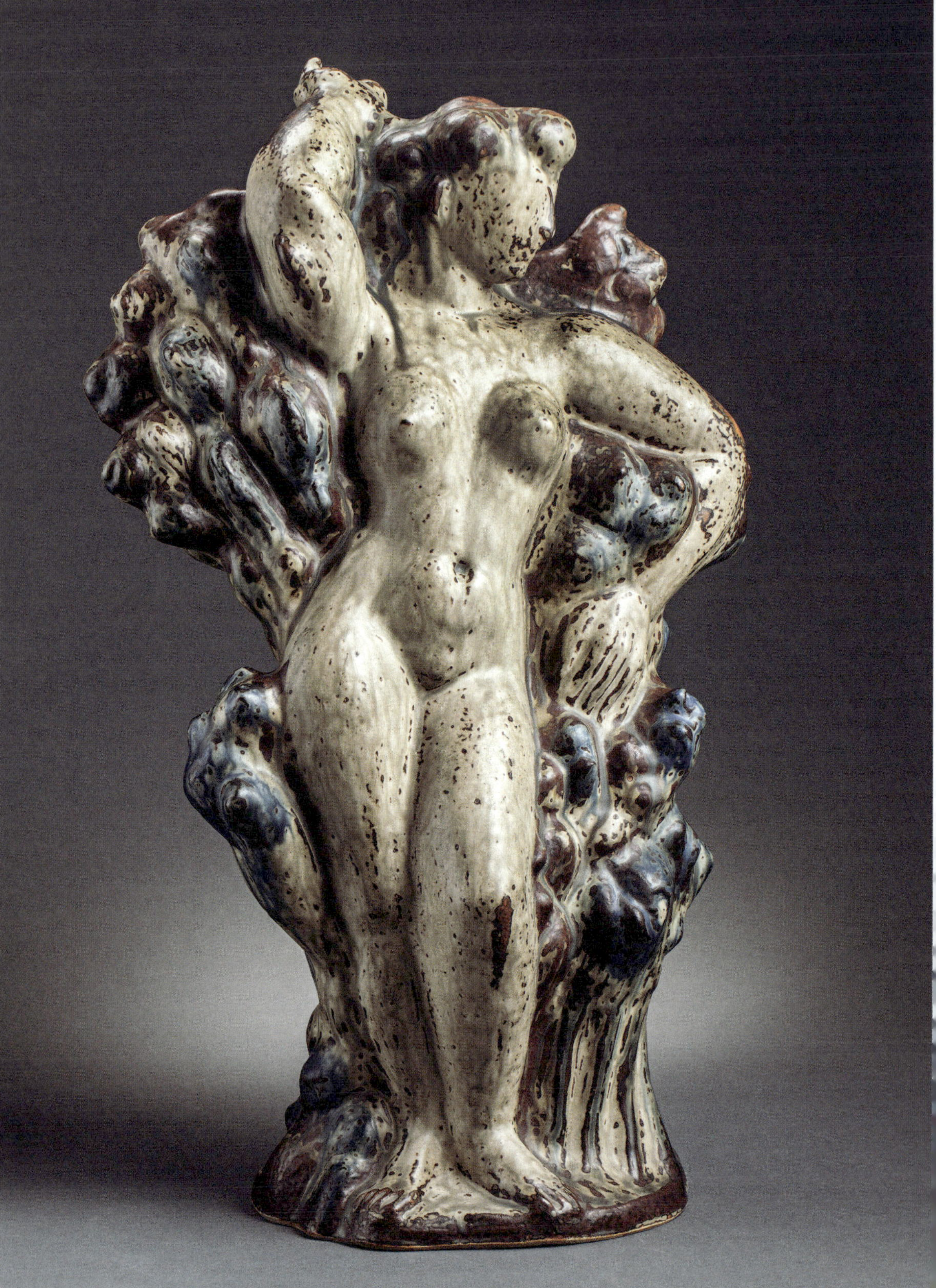

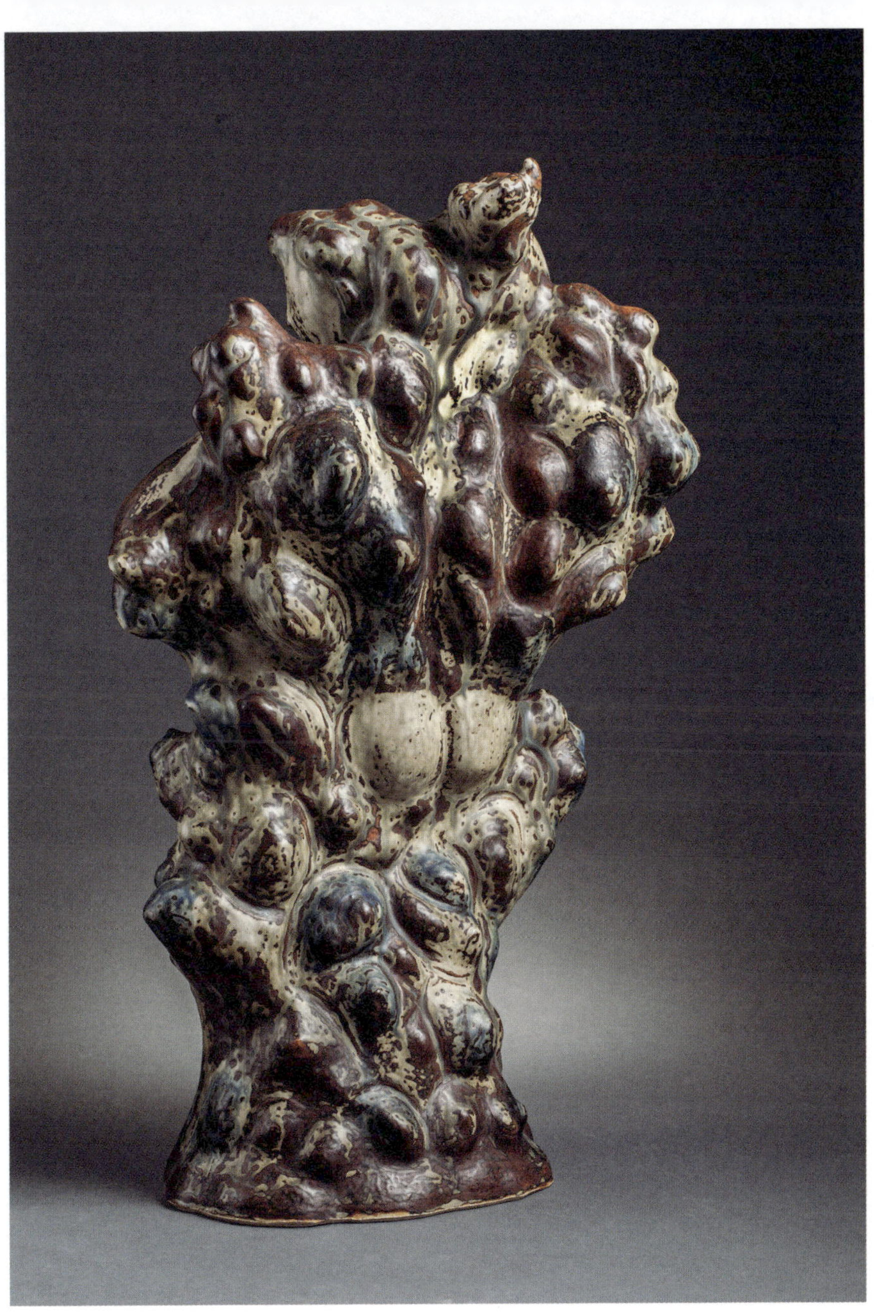

Axel Salto
Daphne, 1942
Stoneware with Sung glaze, H: 58,5 cm
CLAY/The Royal Copenhagen Collection

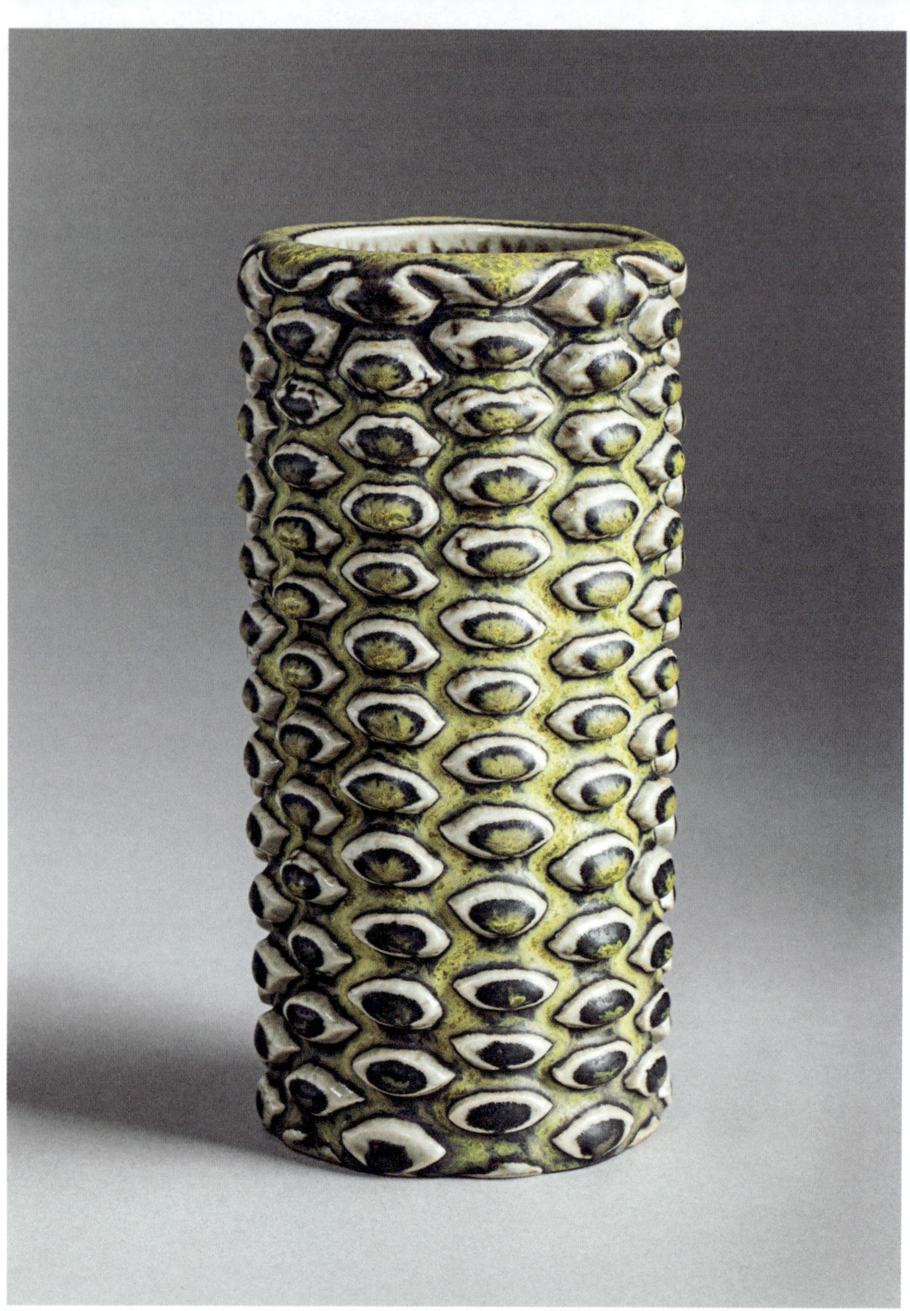

Above
Axel Salto
Vase, n.d.
Stoneware with Solfatara glaze, H: 15 cm
CLAY/The Royal Copenhagen Collection

Right
Axel Salto
Vase, 1953
Stoneware with Sung glaze, H: 43 cm
The Tangen Collection/Kunstsilo

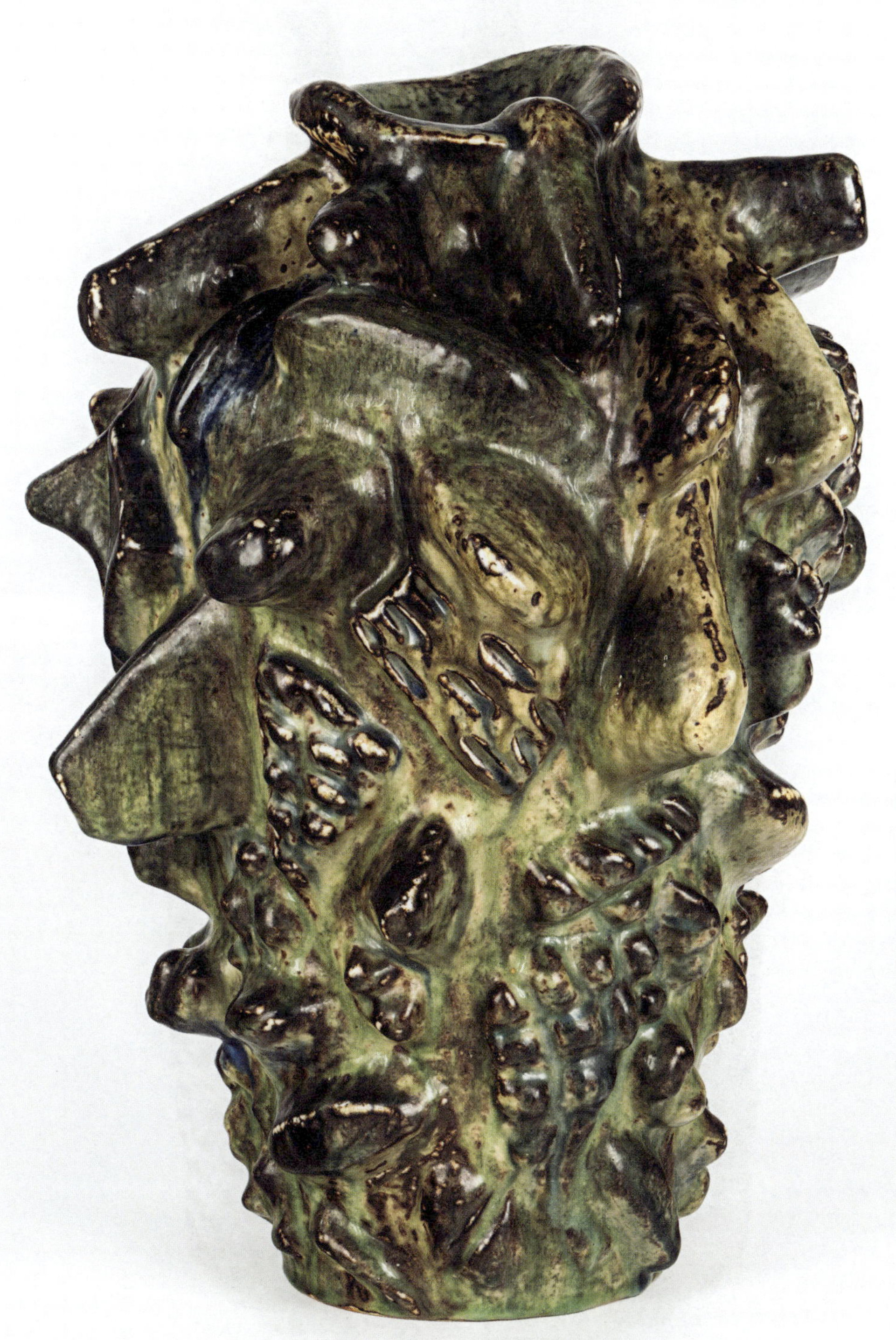

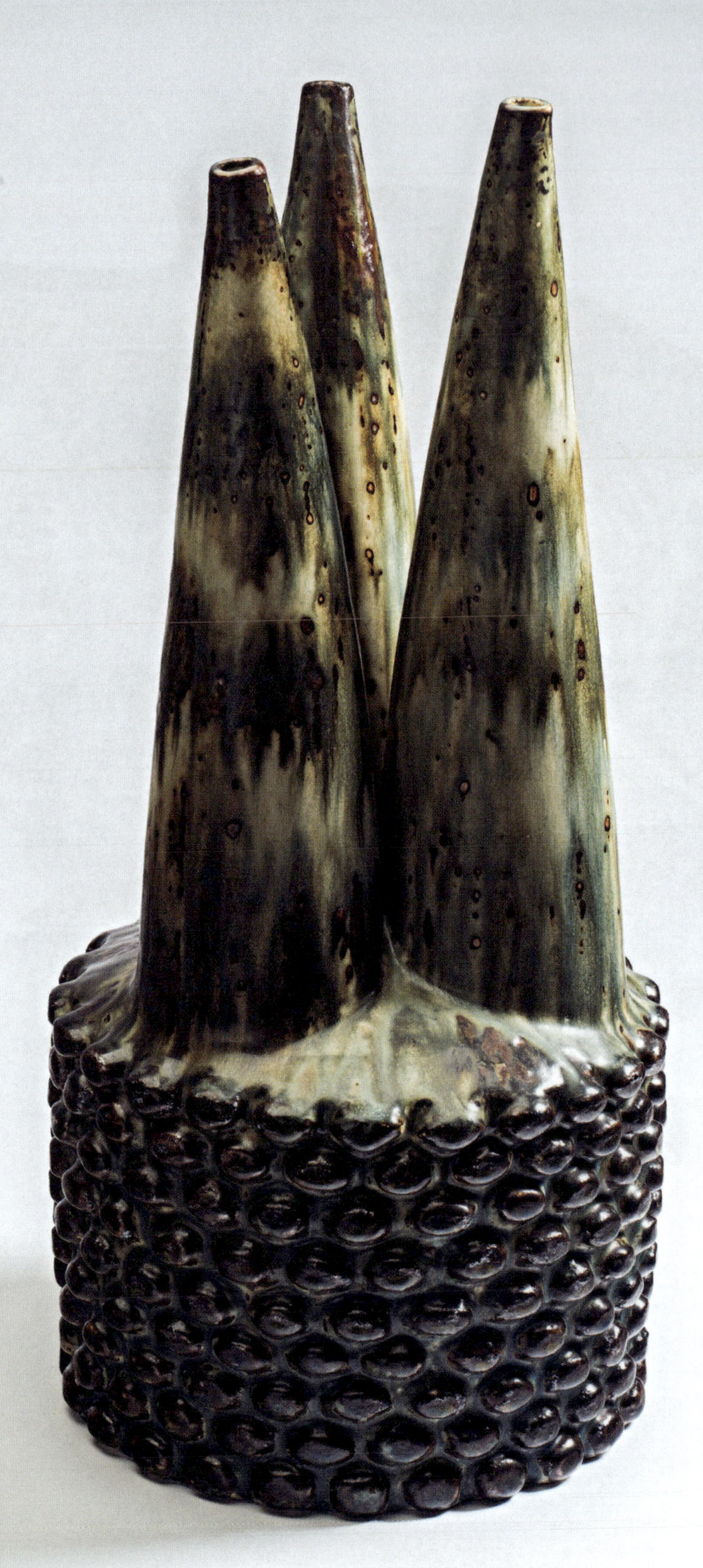

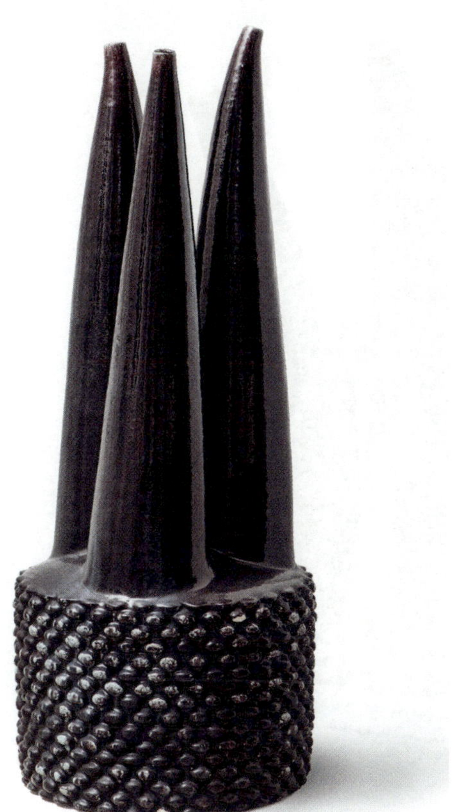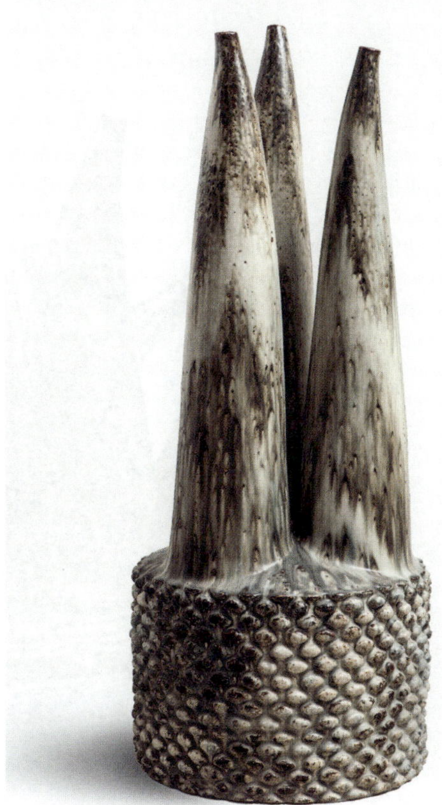

Above, left
Axel Salto
The Core of Power, 1956
Stoneware with Ox-blood glaze, H: 132 cm
CLAY/The Royal Copenhagen Collection

Above, right
Axel Salto
The Core of Power, 1965
Stoneware with Sung glaze, H: 53,5 cm
CLAY/The Royal Copenhagen Collection

Left
Axel Salto
The Core of Power, 1969–74
Stoneware with Sung glaze, H: 54 cm
The Tangen Collection/Kunstsilo

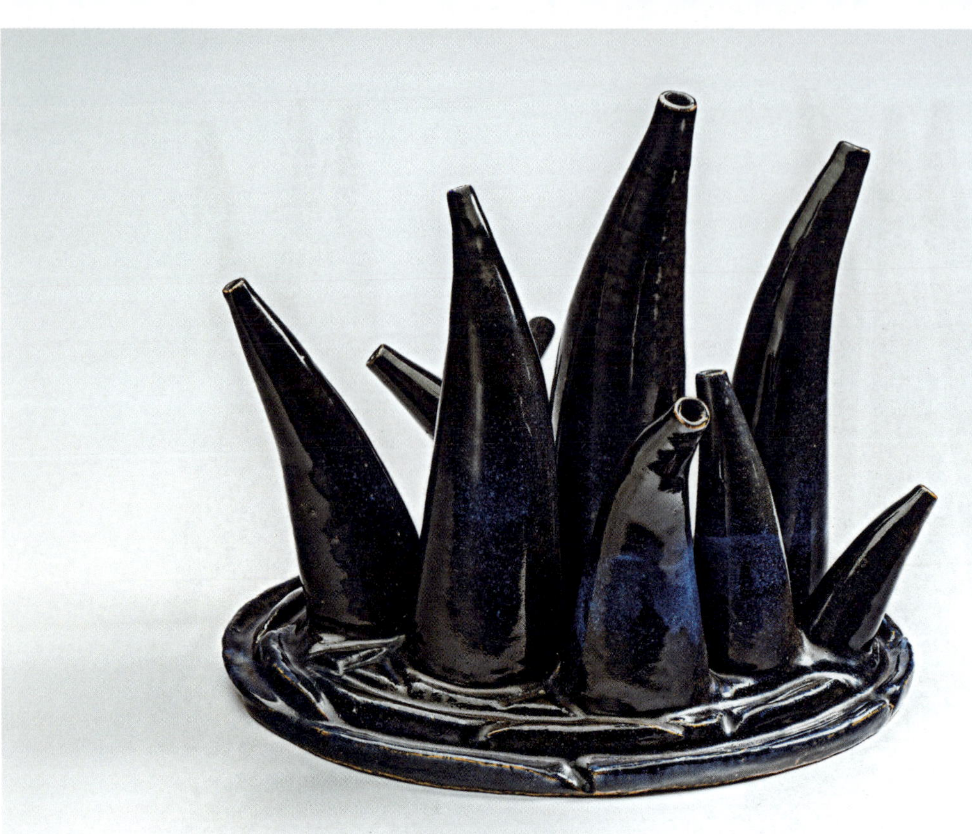

Above
Axel Salto
Object, 1956
Stoneware with Blue Mussel glaze, H: 33 cm
The Tangen Collection/Kunstsilo

Right
Axel Salto
Vase, 1950's
Stoneware with Blue Mussel glaze, H: 28 cm
The Tangen Collection/Kunstsilo

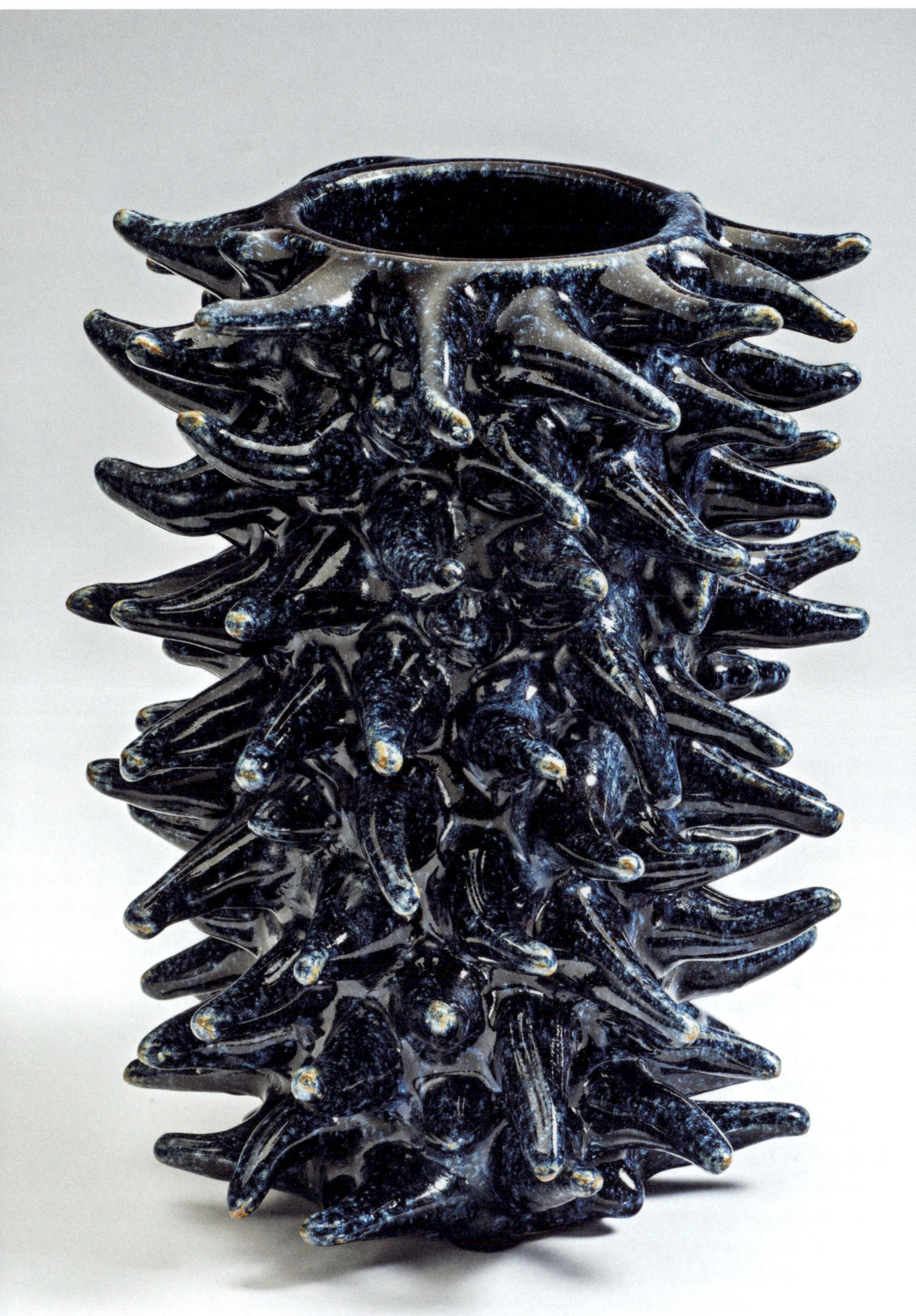

A singing world, a place of fire

Sanne Flyvbjerg

'As scientific knowledge tends towards a definition of all matter as frequency, the underlying principle of movement must impose itself as artistic leitmotif, forces flowing, the transition from one form to another, transformation.'

Axel Salto, *The Sprouting Style*, 1949

Sitting at the piano and pressing down the sustain pedal removes the overall dampening of the strings, which are now left open and sensitive. Should we then call out or sing, the strings respond with overtones and undertones according to the timbre of the voice. There is resonance. Rather than an echo, resonance is a response that is both slightly deferred and stands in relation to this call. Resonance is synonymous with sonority. Sympathy. Connection or understanding, a kind of sympathetic oscillation. We do not see it, but we feel and hear it when energies collide. Sometimes these oscillations are dampened. Round smokestacks are clad in spirals so that the resonance generated by the wind does not weaken their structure. We moderate the wind's movement, disturbing its whorls or bringing them under control. But regardless, there's always resonance in the world, always motion, always exchanges of energy. And there's nothing extraordinary about that. It is pure physics. And yet it is utterly enchanting. There is always the potential of a call and a response. We inhabit a sonorous world.

To listen to the world

The conversation between Edmund de Waal and Axel Salto begins here, with this primal experience of the world. For both artists, listening attentively to the world constitutes the core of the artistic act – listening to the world and exploring its matter through language and material. Let us leave behind the superfluous fact that the two artists are not alike; what is more important is that they have something to say to one another – that behind the immediate difference between Salto's expressive eruptive stoneware and de Waal's quiet installations of white porcelain are two voices that both speak of the caprices of fire and the gift of that which cannot be controlled.

In the modern world we often turn away from that which we do not understand and cannot control. We seek to constrain, or we remain on the surface, watching from a distance. But these two artists venture into the world's underlying currents, its wild and unforeseeable narratives. Both are practising, pragmatic artists, but also sensitive souls who seek a deeper understanding of the stories hidden beneath the surface. Through their writing we gain access to their thoughts and are able to follow them into the existential layers that underlie their art. They write about their relation to touch, to landscapes, journeys, materials and objects. Writing is a drawing tool, a companion and a quivering sphere of human experience. And they proceed with feeling, with joy and playfulness, with excitement and unease, but most of all they are driven by a compelling need to connect with the world and to embed this very experience of the world into their art. They slow down. They chance upon things, turn them over and look at them: a seashell, a tiny Japanese figurine, or a potsherd found in the ground. It starts with something in the hand – and with being able to feel it. The German sociologist Hartmut Rosa calls this basic conversation with the world a 'resonant' relationship.[1] Resonant relationships give meaning to our lives, Rosa writes, and they arise when the 'strings' between us and the world suddenly vibrate to such a degree that we are moved. This is partially intangible. As, by definition, is resonance. Resonance is sound we cannot grasp, but at the same time an energy we feel. Both Salto and de Waal explore this deep connection with our surroundings and the meeting between the two artists is thus one about sensory perception and feeling. It's about drawing close to something. About listening to the world. The creative act becomes a response to the sound, the call of the world.

It comes from the earth

We are among the small things, Salto writes.[2] He collects shells, buds about to burst, stones and pebbles. Natural concentrates, as he calls them. He peers at the surface of sea urchins and pinecones and reproduces their beautiful structures in his art, but is soon preoccupied by the forces in nature creating them. He discovers that behind the small things are large, slow, yet constant movements. All this, he finds, stems from the pulse of the world, which is continually creating patterns and forms in nature. Metamorphic activity. Limestone transforming into marble as it is exposed to millions of years of heat and pressure. Lava flows, solidifying and becoming fertile soil for plant life. Seeds germinating. Branches budding, growing leaves and fruit. Fruit dropping and lying on the ground for a while. Some fruit decomposing and becoming humus. Other fruit splitting open, sprouting again and sending roots down into the earth. There is an inherent force in things, Salto writes, and the artist's greatest – and only – task is to give concrete expression to this force. His vases thus bud and sprout, and he shapes them so they resemble sprouting plants or the bubbling surface of water, bulging just before the geyser leaps skywards. He receives a plain vase from a potter and then sculpts its surface so as to lend motion to its fundamental form. The vase grows towards an undefined outer contour, in the process of becoming.

Over the course of his life, Salto delves deeper and deeper into the matter. From focusing on the surface, he works towards a kind of sintering ideal in which he seeks to show that form and content not only affect each other but are already deeply linked, as are the forces in nature. The patterns on the surface are not mere decorations, they demonstrate the motion that gave rise to them. The motifs are not applied onto the ceramic object, it is matter itself that grows from the sides of the bowl. Salto seeks to show the inherent force in things, not least the motions in nature, and hence his glazes run down and along the vases' protrusions like a landscape of yellow rivers, of bubbling lava or green roots branching out in search of water. There is uncertainty as to whether these are plants or landscapes, and it is does not matter. What does matter is the motion. These things are in motion, from one stage to another, or quite simply on their way to becoming.

Salto writes about the Indian scientist Sir Jagadish Chandra Bose, who measured the reaction of plants, stone and metal to pressure and heat.[3] Bose concluded that reaction – perhaps even feeling – is everywhere. There is activity and transformation in even the hardest materials – in stone, in metal, in us. Slow, fundamental movements that lead to significant change. There is sound. And for Salto, listening to the world, and responding to it, is always important. He senses an obligation. It is a settling of accounts, he writes, between the ceramist and the fluted seashell on the shoreline. The pleasure of finding this object obliges him "to return the discovery in the form of a bowl".[4] This was his way of immortalising a good moment of resonance and fixing it in a ceramic form.

Bose's discoveries inspire Salto's motif *The Living Stone*, which he draws, prints on paper and textiles, and scores into his ceramics. Shaped like a teardrop, a streak of energy winds around it before finally shooting out beyond the stone's edge. He remains inspired by science and technology throughout his life since this gives him access to motifs demonstrating the inherent power in things. But it is man himself who is the most delicate of all devices. "Science is yet to give us a finer instrument than the human instinct",[5] he writes. Salto understands that our relationship to the world is one of resonance and that art, too, is a sonic experience. The glaze catalogue of the Royal Copenhagen Porcelain Manufactory is an instrument to be played. His finished bowls and vases play a variety of tones, creating moving sounds that evoke the delight and despair in nature. A multicoloured woodcut is flute music created by the meeting and divergence of the printing plates' various voices. The more numerous the media, the broader the instrumentation, Salto writes. Responding to nature, art thus rings out with disparate sounds as it "sings from a hundred mouths".[6]

It begins with the clay

A sonorous world is also a world that moves us. A world of touch. Edmund de Waal begins every day with a lump of clay. He places it on the wheel and throws a small porcelain cylinder. There is sound from the clay and from the rotation of the wheel. His studio is filled with music and noises from the kiln. He throws another small porcelain cylinder, repeating the act again and again. He makes small vessels for the hands, variations from the same beginnings. The porcelain clay is difficult to work with, but the unruly material brings him indescribable joy. It's like getting to know a friend, he says, it demands tranquillity and attention.[7] The porcelain is so alive and so complex that it forces him to slow down. Promptly, the clay responds. The slightest pressure changes everything. The material "records every movement of thinking, every change of thought".[8] The music helps just enough to loosen the control and follow the material. He probes the clay, pulls at it, explores the porcelain's limits, just as Salto did with his stoneware. He extends the vessels upwards as far as he can. He pulls the soft mass outwards and releases his grip. And as the sides of the pot are being pulled upwards, the clay responds and "the volume changes like an exhalation, something being said".[9] The little vessel seems to absorb the resonance, and as he cuts the pot from the wheel and sets it aside, its mouth quivers for a moment before it finds its composure.

A clay pot is a body. It may have shoulders, a foot, waist, lip and mouth. Edmund de Waal's cylindrical vessels are simple bodies with mouths forming an 'o'. Every little vessel is a breath, a rotation of time. And time moves ever onwards. The pots dry; thereafter he works them over again, paring off, smoothing out, perhaps pressing a slight unevenness into the side of the soft little body. Then firing, glazing, firing. Some break in the making, but at length there is a collection of small pots, thousands of small pots to be put out into the world in various groupings. There are also slices of porcelain, tiles, and sometimes plates. The objects are put together and ordered in clusters or runs, then framed. The frame may be a building – a museum, a house, a mansion. It may be a crack in the floor, a vitrine on the wall, or a place near the ceiling. The vessels are distributed, some closely together, others a little apart, but always in conversation with each other, in consonance. The vessels do not say much, but they do resound. They borrow from each other's voices, leaning upon one another and the stories in those rooms where they have been placed. Some are placed in wall-mounted vitrines looking like lined paper. Here the little vessels are distributed like words, notes, breaths of air, or rhythms. One pot nudges up against the next, like words in a sentence or musical notes. "A stack of bowls is a chord",[10] de Waal writes. But it could also be a poem. Words and ceramics are deeply connected.

Look closely. These are not just white pots. These are pots in shades of white, cream, blue and green. Pots of no fixed significance, yet with a wealth of signification, open questions through which we might see the world. They call for care, for enhancing a fine detail, for spending time. And they invite us to connect with things we cannot attain and perhaps cannot understand. Things behind glass. Things up there beneath the ceiling. Tucked away, perhaps to indicate that an active effort is required in order to hear what the objects are telling us. Objects carry meaning, and some seem to "retain the pulse they had when being created".[11] This is important. Objects are bearers of history. They bear the movements of the hands that created them. They remember the material that was extracted or worked so that the object could be produced. Objects are bearers of historical events while simultaneously becoming part of history. Handled. Collected. Repaired, restored, bought, melted down. The object is imbued with a voice and memory that deeply interests de Waal – the pulse within things which we hold in our hands and for which we are responsible. Whereas Salto seeks to draw out of the vase the inherent power contained with it so as to confront us with the intense moment of transformation, de Waal draws the story into his vessels, and into the spaces between them, so that we have to actively approach them with our sensory apparatus. Perception is a spiral, slowly unfolding, slowly transforming us. And so let us linger a while.

Smouldering, burning
Clay cannot be hurried. Firing cannot be hurried. They impose a natural relationship with time. This seems more important than ever. Hartmut Rosa talks about burnt-out modern human beings, unhappy in a high-speed society where the pace is continually increasing. The goal of modern society is to grow at the same time

as it becomes more efficient. The relentlessly high tempo leads to a sense of alienation, of losing a sense of ourselves, and that the world is muted. Resonance is absent. "Alienation designates a *relation of relationlessness* in which subject and world confront each other with indifference or hostility, if not repulsion, and thus without any inner connection",[12] Rosa writes.

It is not the runaway energy of the high-speed society that might connect us with the world and give us the perception of resonance. It is slow movement, in tune with the body, which brings us and the world together in a mutual relationship. This is the very spirit of Salto and de Waal's art, which they convey each in their own way. It requires time with the seashells on the shoreline. It requires the investigation of form and material. Experimentation. Mistakes. Expeditions into the landscape, into things. Into the expanse of a moment.

Salto writes about 'the burning now'. He takes inspiration from high-speed photography. This reveals to him the very moment of metamorphosis: the burning now. With this technique time can be sequenced, so to speak, and the forms that 'hide' within the movement seen. Now he is able to dwell in the moment of transformation, investigating this ambiguous glimpse of a water jet twisting and turning or the surface of a bulb splitting open as its shoot begins to sprout. 'The burning now' is the moment in which something is in between stages. It opens up new motifs in his art. He writes about capturing the moment a collection of cups slide off a tray, splintering on the floor like a flower unfolding. He writes about Ovid's *Metamorphoses*, which had fascinated him since his schooldays. These tales are breathlessly transformative sequences in which everything can alter its form, meet destruction, and then be constructed anew. He is particularly fixated on the myth of Actaeon, in which man is transformed into beast. It is a metaphor for the uncontrollable duality of matter he encounters again and again when exploring nature. The lurking of the demonic in the moment of creation. The bad bacteria consuming the good, but which is life all the same. Actaeon secretly watches Diana bathing and is punished by being transformed into a stag torn apart by his own hounds, who no longer recognise him. Life becomes death becomes food and nourishment. He is absorbed into their system, which continues in the world. "No living thing is complete in itself",[13] Salto writes. The myth of Actaeon is a tale of the great forces in the world and of how all life belongs to an extended process. The human too. He is consumed by the beast and then by the earth. From earth we extract clay. And Salto forms Actaeon from clay.

How is anything altered from one form to another? Transformations are life-affirming and unpredictable and alluring like fire. It is a fundamental question, and a vital one in the conversation between de Waal and Salto. Transformation is not merely something incredible that occurs in mythological tales, it can be found there in the material being held in one's hands. And all of a sudden we seem to have "gained access to an irrational world, or rather, we seem to have abandoned a fictional idea and be on the way towards grasping a real idea".[14] The world is moving in a real yet magical way all at once.

A burning now

The pots are placed in the kiln. Now it is up to the conversation between fire and clay whether the forms shatter or sustain. The fire is movement; the fire alters the material, the form. The fire is in direct contact with the material, touching, pushing, melding it, cracking and hardening it. Once inside, the object is on its own, given over to the fire. And through the kiln's peephole the clay can be observed glowing and changing colour. "Contours flicker",[15] de Waal writes. In the kiln, the vessels are in between stages. They burn and sing, resonate with sound from the heat and pressure. A flame is merely the visible combustion of gas. A glaze firing is a series of chemical processes, melding minerals and oxides together. But it is also a poetic synthesis pointing towards the wild forces of nature. The kiln is a magical furnace wherein glazes acquire colour and run into each other, where the ceramic is impressed with the resonance of this red-hot room.

We face the uncontrollable. This may be the finest way to

approach the world. Things die under total control. The world becomes mute, as Rosa writes. We must probe our way to a vivid conversation with the world and with each other. Porcelain is wonderfully obstinate, "it doesn't want to move the way you want it to move",[16] and it is unruly. This is why perfect porcelain objects are uninteresting to de Waal, because they do not tell the material's tale. He strives to make beautifully imperfect vessels that you want to hold in your hands, that speak of porcelain's complex nature. And Salto, too, is fascinated by chance and uncertainty; a coloured woodcut, for example, may show a slight shift between the lines or the layers of ink. He deliberately creates grooves and ridges on the surface of his pots for the glaze to run around, and the unpredictability of the way the glaze runs and the interplay of the colours is where he derives most of his pleasure in making ceramics. He controls the process only to a limited degree. The rest is left to forces beyond him. And no one is able to predict what the firing will produce. But flaws and unforeseeable crazing in the glaze can "become beauty and perhaps suggest new directions which may lead to [...] new ornamentation, new textures".[17] Uncertainty is a magical ally. Mishaps have transformative potential. When a bowl collapses on the wheel, it is both "a pot gone wrong, but it is simultaneously this extraordinary sculptural object". Any unsuccessful thing is always on "the metamorphic, poetic edge of lots of other things",[18] de Waal explains.

Play is important to both artists. While playing, things take on new forms and new meanings. Things break and change shape. One thing can be two things simultaneously. Play, too, is resonance. Play takes us to new and unforeseen places. Good games always get played again. They are played again because of the sense they give that something important is at stake, something magical and free – something unpredictable. A relationship of resonance is inherently uncontrollable, Rosa writes. We enter into an unpredictable relationship which transforms us. But the transformation cannot be controlled and "there is no method, no seven or nine-step guide that can guarantee that we will be able to resonate with people or things".[19] Nor can we control how an encounter or a conversation will influence us. But sometimes, by persevering, living dazzling pieces of pottery can emerge from the kiln. Until that time comes, all that there is to do is peer into the kiln's fire where contours flicker and worship the wonderful privilege of being in a world of ambiguity, and sensing it, intensely and continually. "The point", writes Salto, "is to love something and to keep loving it".[20]

Mountains of clay

And to write about it, to take pleasure in stringing words together into sentences, because that too is an exploratory journey into the material and the experience of the world. Salto originally trained as a painter, yet painting is not a presence in his books, but rather the different media and techniques with which he is becoming acquainted, the unfamiliar. He writes his way into the material, connects with it, somehow listens to it, as though trying to catch all the overtones, undertones and timbres of the subject. His language is sensual, saturated and physical, he builds with the language, plays with it, sticks words together as though they were clay. He writes about ceramics, about his process with the clay and about what he learned from fellow ceramists with whom he worked. He writes about the history of the woodcut, its tools and methods. He expresses his ideas about being creative. He produces a book about printing for children which describes in detail how to make and use stamps. He writes about the joy of repetition and of stamping pictures into life, pictures in which things can grow, balance and fall apart freely. He writes about his pattern and paper designs and produces several books with carefully considered designs in which form and content come together in greater unity, vitrifying like body and glaze in a fine piece of stoneware.

Yet Salto knew that any form of mastery is but a paradoxical nook of a greater organism. An artist has to be thorough and become proficient, but, as with everything else, "be moveable within the moveable".[21] Mastery is also 'becoming'. Art is a process in which we seize upon the world and continually convey our experiences. Perhaps this is why his writings are somewhat palimpsestic: he writes new texts but also reuses his older ones, editing them together in new ways, refining them a little, just as he repeats the form of a pot but with a new glaze. He backtracks, learns, repeats a sentence, changes a word. He returns to the paths he wandered as a young man in the south of France and writes about his walk up the mountain towards La Gaude. He describes its slopes, its daffodils and mimosas, and inserts the sad transformation of the town into his mention of the fertile landscape he once sculpted as a stoneware mountain.

In Jingdezhen there are mountains of porcelain. Edmund de Waal travels to China to map out the material he has held in his hands and shaped into thousands of vessels. Tens of thousands, if one counts the unsuccessful ones. And now he stands on top of a mountain of porcelain shards, "a tumbling landscape of brokenness, a lexicon of all the ways pots can go wrong".[22] All these failed attempts with an unpredictable material. He discovers a powerful history of how porcelain has been extracted, refined, smuggled and sanctified, and he traces in detail this "pilgrimage of sorts" through writing about it. In *The White Road* he journeys into the material, and his writing becomes a sensory perception of and a reflection on porcelain, but at the same time a materialisation of the artist's dialogue with the fabric of the world. The reader does not merely join de Waal in his journey of discovery but is also transported into his own experience of resonance and transformation along the way. This occurs through language and attention to the material and its tactility, through his description of the emotional sensation as well as the author's pursuit of understanding. By the end of the book, porcelain is no longer a mute designation of something the majority of us associate with dinner sets. It has become vivid and harmonic; it has become landscape, experiment, intrigue, power-symbol and testimony. The road has become white. It has become our history. Our relationship to porcelain is re-enchanted through language. In *The Hare with the Amber Eyes*, de Waal explores his ancestry

through a collection of netsuke he has inherited. The memoir is
told through the journey of the netsuke from one address to the
next, but it is told just as much through the author's perception
of the life of these objects. Again, our relationship to objects is
re-enchanted through his "love affair with tactility and touch".[23]
Suddenly objects are not just objects but wandering things with
numerous tales of sorrow and joy, loss and reunion. The world
around us is a fragile place of relationships and objects that we
seize and hold on to. Precisely like the netsuke de Waal carries
in his pocket throughout his journey, and which he returns to
and touches, as a repetition and a new beginning.

Open strings

And so, to love something and to keep loving it, even when the
love affair does not perhaps evolve exactly as one had imagined.
The netsuke led de Waal to places he had not envisaged, on de-
tours, diversions and along circuitous routes. Salto suddenly
adds horns to a vase he thought of as a sprouting plant. The
uncontrollable is a gift and a threat; it is the very life force of
nature, and it is unpredictable growths or the coming of death, as
depicted in Ovid's *Metamorphoses*. This meeting of Axel Salto and
Edmund de Waal is not about being alike but about seeing the
beauty of contrast and risk. Both artists have a deep love for the
ambiguity consistent with their explorative urge to create. But
it is also consistent with the way our world is constructed, where
different life forms arise as experiments of nature, imperfect but
full of life. The aim is to create quivering moments, to convey the
wonderful, playful, delicate, disturbing and powerful matter of
which the world is made. Sound emanates from the world, and
we stand amidst a web of sine waves flowing through it.

Categories no longer seem so important. Porcelain is a piece of
paper. The journey is writing, the language is clay. Ceramics is a
poem, vitrines scenography. It all points to one thing: intimacy
between people and the world. Salto exhibited whole forests of
budding vases and smouldering glazes against a background

of his colourful textiles, prints and paintings. De Waal makes installations and simple vitrines full of space, air and suggestion. But both methods point towards the same thing: the evoking of a new resonance in art. And, as Rosa writes, art is perhaps the most essential field of resonance for the modern human being, because here one may connect with the world through art and create meaning.[24] But Salto and de Waal are concerned with more than creating meaning and achieving personal resonance. Their work is also about exploring the very energy in nature, the life of objects, and how we are part of a wonderful place wherein everything acts on everything else. Their work conveys the very experience of resonance and establishes a personal dialogue with the world through art – pointing out the plant in the earth or the object in our hand, using the space of art to accentuate the transformation in the interim, even beyond the space of art. Becoming a sounding board. Revealing the world in flux, but also to freeze this movement in a moment of intensity, in a burning Solfatara glaze or the hint of tinges in white porcelain. It is about the burning now. It is "about slowing you down and making you look, and think, and walk around objects", de Waal explains. That's all. "And that's not a bad thing to want to do".[25]

Listen. This is a conversation about the earth, about the clay beneath us, dug up and shaped into vessels by our hands. It is a conversation about creating object after object and feeling that the repeated act is of huge significance. It is a conversation about speaking through clay and sculpting with language, about sketching one's way into the drama of metamorphosis. The moment when a butterfly emerges from its chrysalis. The moment when the fire flares up. The moment when the clay body and glaze meld together. The sintering where two things become one. The moment where man becomes beast. The moment when an object changes hands. It is a conversation about feelings, unease, care and attention. About shaping things, seeing them shatter, and keeping going. About shaping that piece of the world being held in one's hands, and then giving it over to chance, placing it back into the world, where things wander. Where things go wrong. Where the firing may fail, where the pot may crack, where the ink may shift, or where words are not enough. Or where words perhaps go too far. And then trying again. Putting new words together with old ones, juxtaposing old with new. Sitting down and trying afresh, the clay on the wheel, all over again. Shaping another lump of clay. Pulling the clay, hoping to be able to stop, not immediately before but precisely at the point of breaking. Lifting the damper from the open strings and letting the sound linger in the air.

Notes

1
Hartmut Rosa, *Resonans*, København, Eksistensen, 2016 og *Det ukontrollerbare*, København, Eksistensen, 2022

2
Axel Salto, *Den spirende Stil*, København, Grafisk Cirkel, 1949, p. 43

3
Axel Salto, *Den spirende Stil*, København, Grafisk Cirkel, 1949, p. 14 ff.

4
Axel Salto, *Salto's Keramik*, København, Det Berlingske Bogtrykkeri, 1930, n.p.

5
Axel Salto, *Den spirende Stil*, København, Grafisk Cirkel, 1949, p. 45

6
Axel Salto, *Den spirende Stil*, København, Grafisk Cirkel, 1949, pp. 49–51

7
Sam Anderson, *Edmund de Waal and the Strange Alchemy of Porcelain*, Feature, The New York Times, 2015

8
Edmund de Waal, *The White Road - A Journey into Obsession*, London, Vintage, 2016, p. 5

9
Edmund de Waal, *The White Road – A Journey into Obsession*, London, Vintage, 2016, p. 4

10
Edmund de Waal, *The White Road – A Journey into Obsession*, London, Vintage, 2016, p. 72

11
Edmund de Waal, *Haren med de ravgule øjne*, København, Hr. Ferdinand, 2013, p. 30

12
Hartmut Rosa, *Det ukontrollerbare*, København, Eksistensen, 2022, p. 31

13
Axel Salto, *Salto's Træsnit*, København, Det Hoffenbergske Etablissement, 1940, p. 33

14
Axel Salto, *Den spirende Stil*, København, Grafisk Cirkel, 1949, p. 11

15
Edmund de Waal, repeat, revise, return, p. 125

16
Edmund de Waal on Porcelain, Podcast *Material Matters with Grant Gibson*, 22.01.19

17
Axel Salto, *Salto's Keramik*, København, Det Berlingske Bogtrykkeri, 1930, n.p.

18
Edmund de Waal on Porcelain, Podcast *Material Matters with Grant Gibson*, 22.01.19

19
Hartmut Rosa, *Det ukontrollerbare*, København, Eksistensen, 2022, p. 35

20
Axel Salto, *Den spirende Stil*, København, Grafisk Cirkel, 1949, p. 36

21
Axel Salto, *Salto's Træsnit*, København, Det Hoffenbergske Etablissement, 1940, p. 26

22
Edmund de Waal, *The White Road – A Journey into Obsession*, London, Vintage, 2016, p. 24

23
Edmund de Waal, *a thousand hours*, Alan Cristea Gallery, Dapper Films, 2012

24
Hartmut Rosa, *Resonans*, København, Eksistensen, 2016, p. 323

25
Edmund de Waal, *a thousand hours*, Alan Cristea Gallery, Dapper Films, 2012

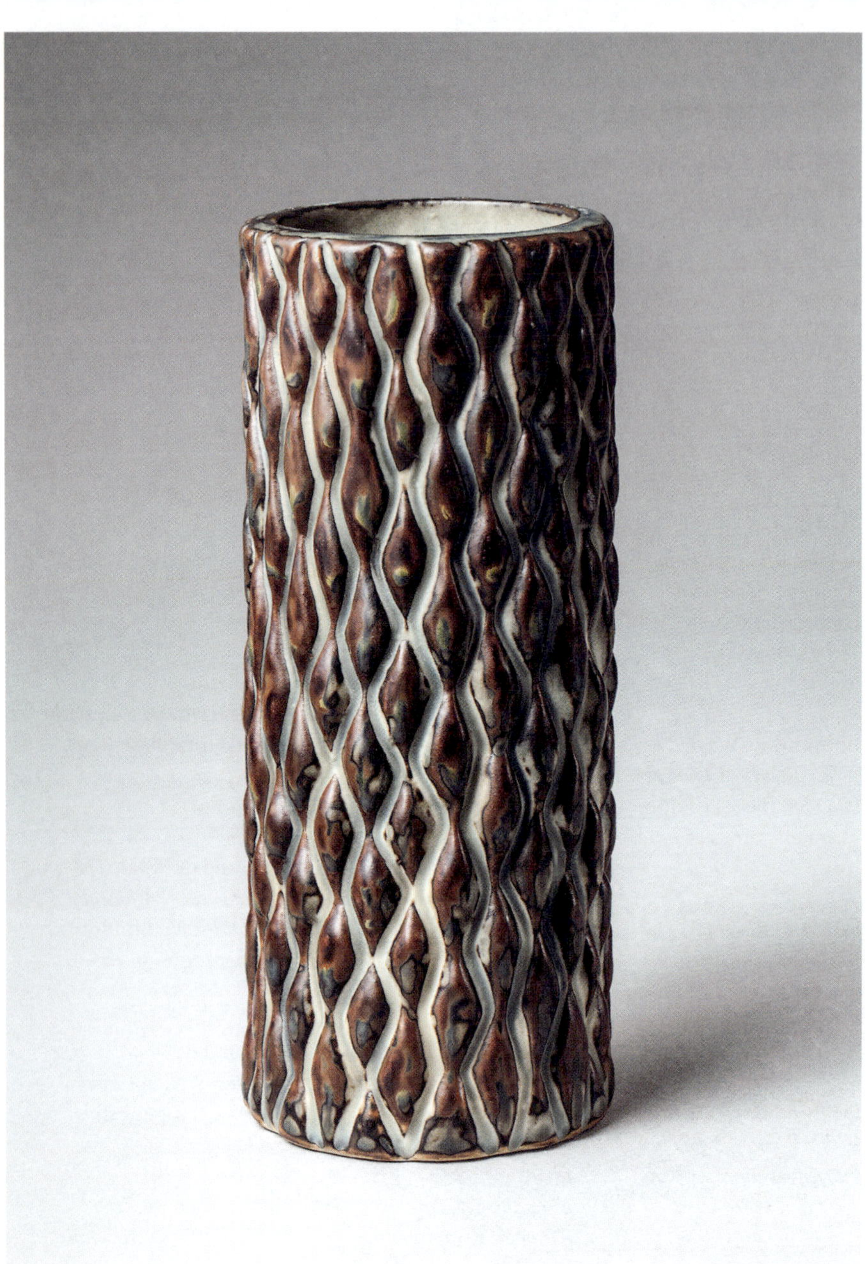

Axel Salto
Vase, 1975–79
Stoneware with Sung glaze, H: 17,5 cm
CLAY/The Royal Copenhagen Collection

Axel Salto
Textile *Energi*, n.d.
L.F. Foght
Private Collection

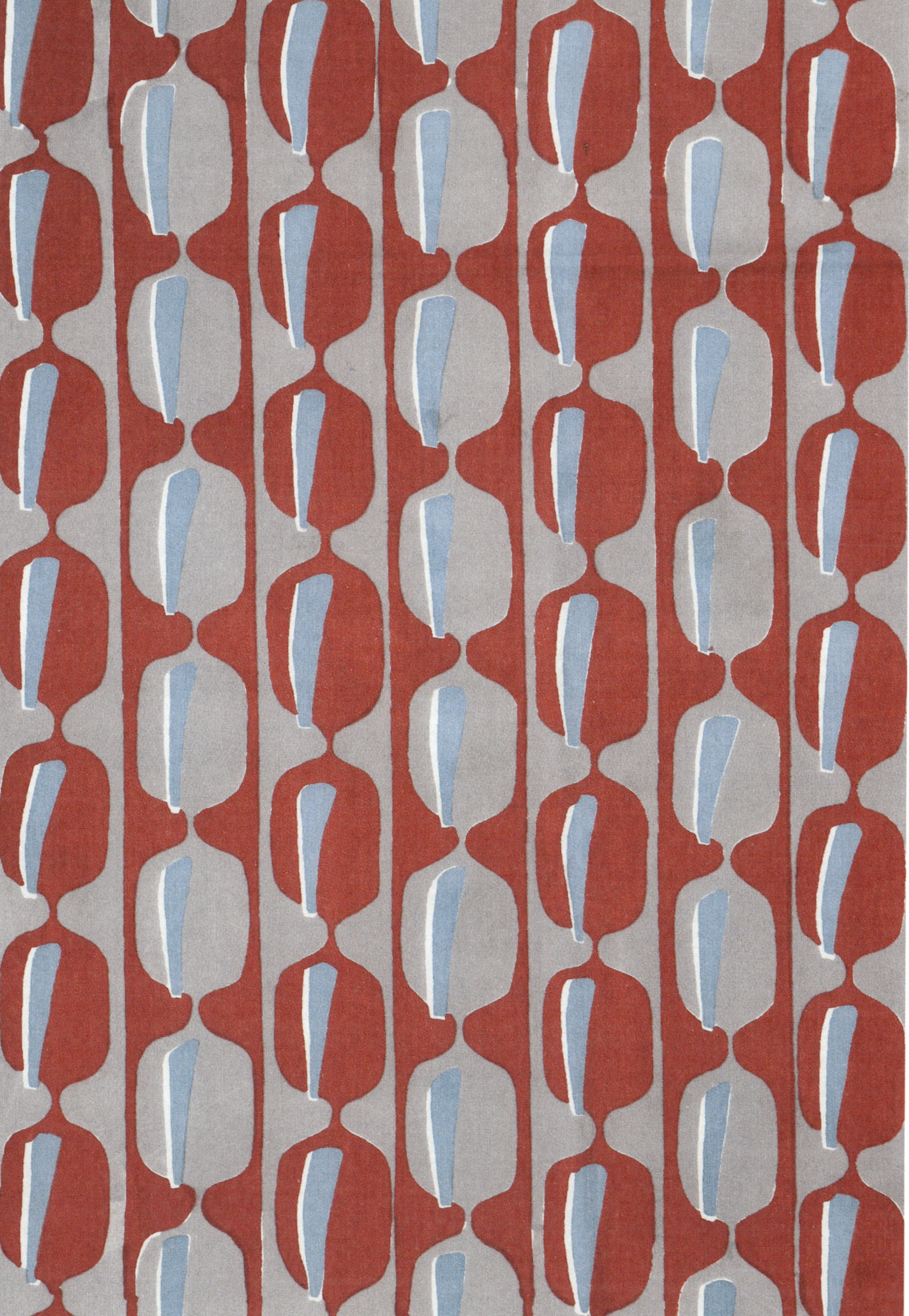

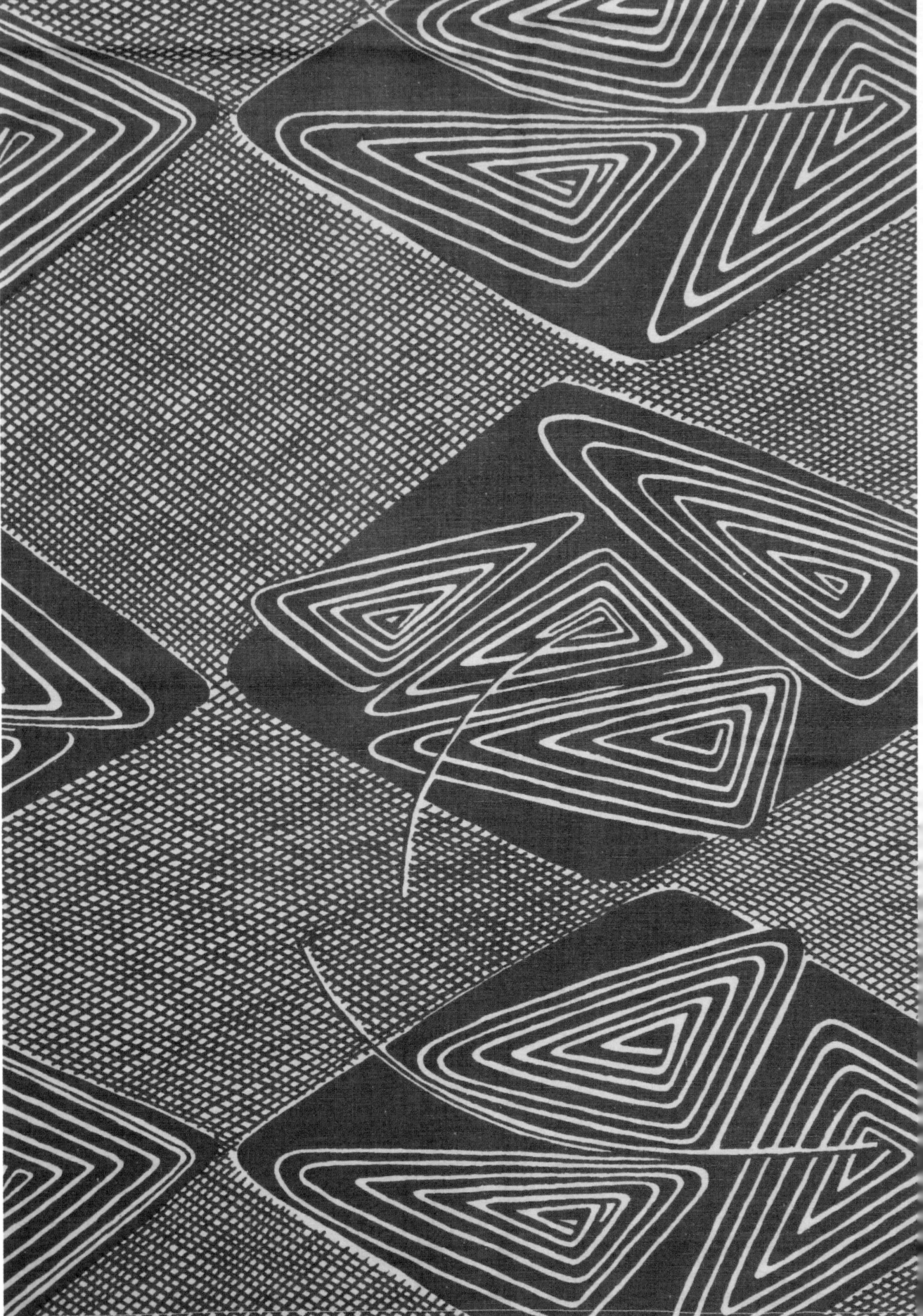

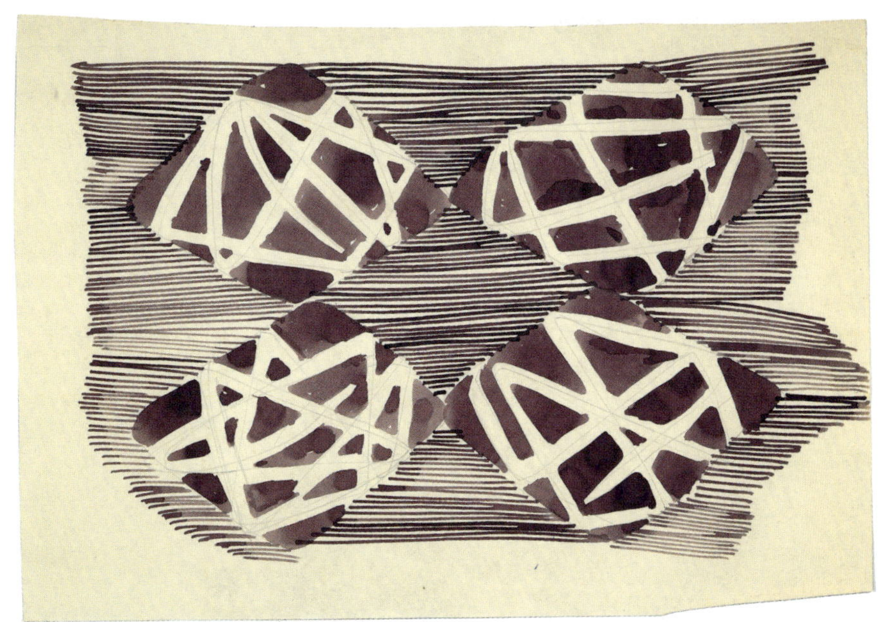

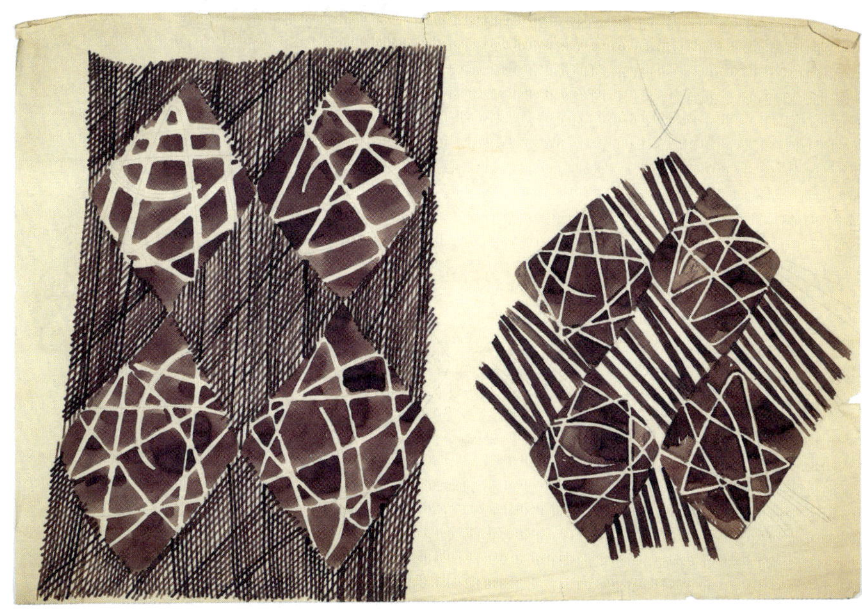

Axel Salto
Textile *Befrielse*
(Liberation), n.d.
L.F. Foght
Private Collection

Top
Axel Salto
Sketch, n.d.
Graphite and watercolour on paper, 296 × 413 mm
CLAY/The Royal Copenhagen Collection

Bottom
Axel Salto
Sketch, n.d.
Graphite and watercolour on paper, 419 × 595 mm
CLAY/The Royal Copenhagen Collection

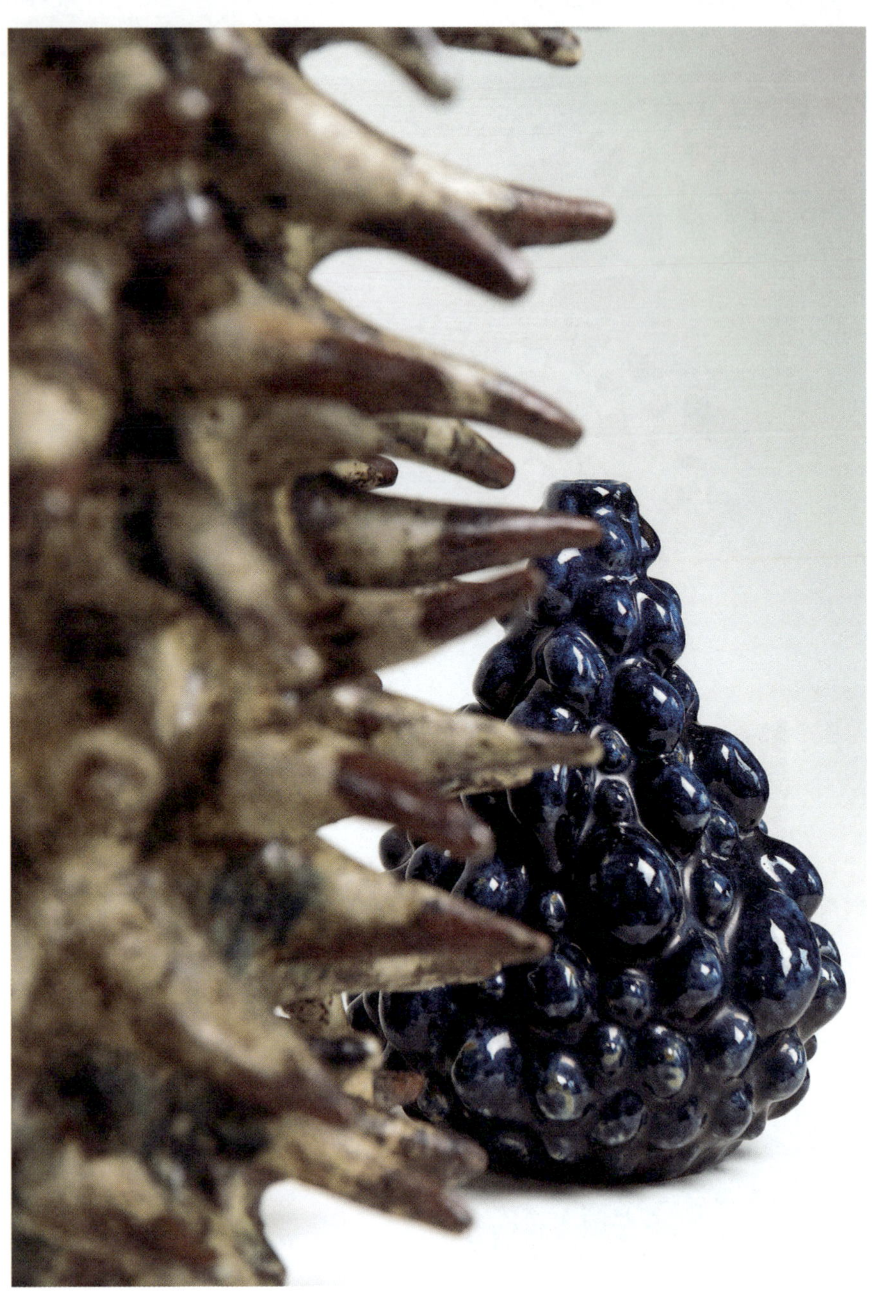

Axel Salto
Two vessels, detail
CLAY/The Royal Copenhagen Collection
CLAY/The Erik Veistrup Collection

Axel Salto
Textile *Céramique*
L.F. Foght
Private collection

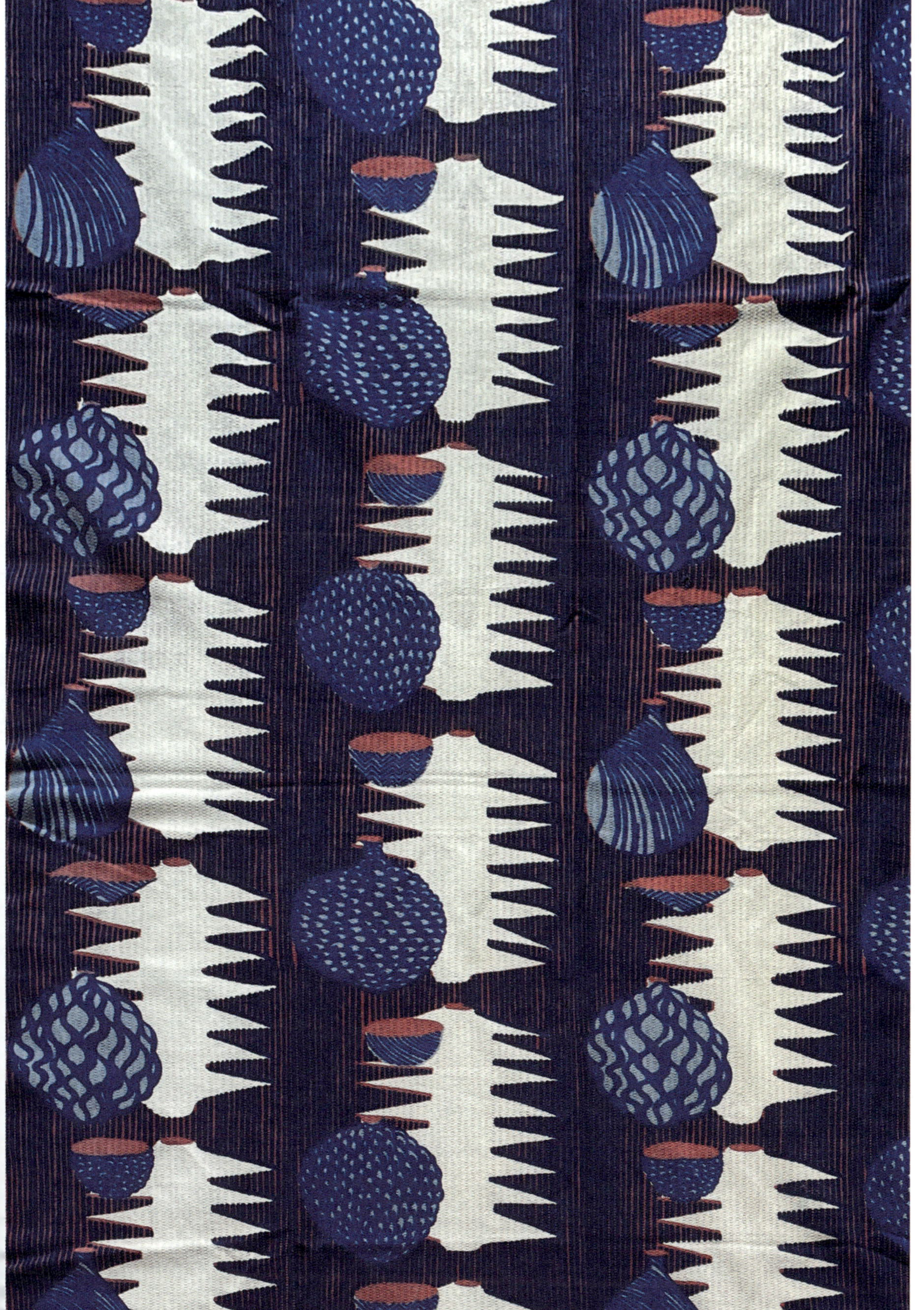

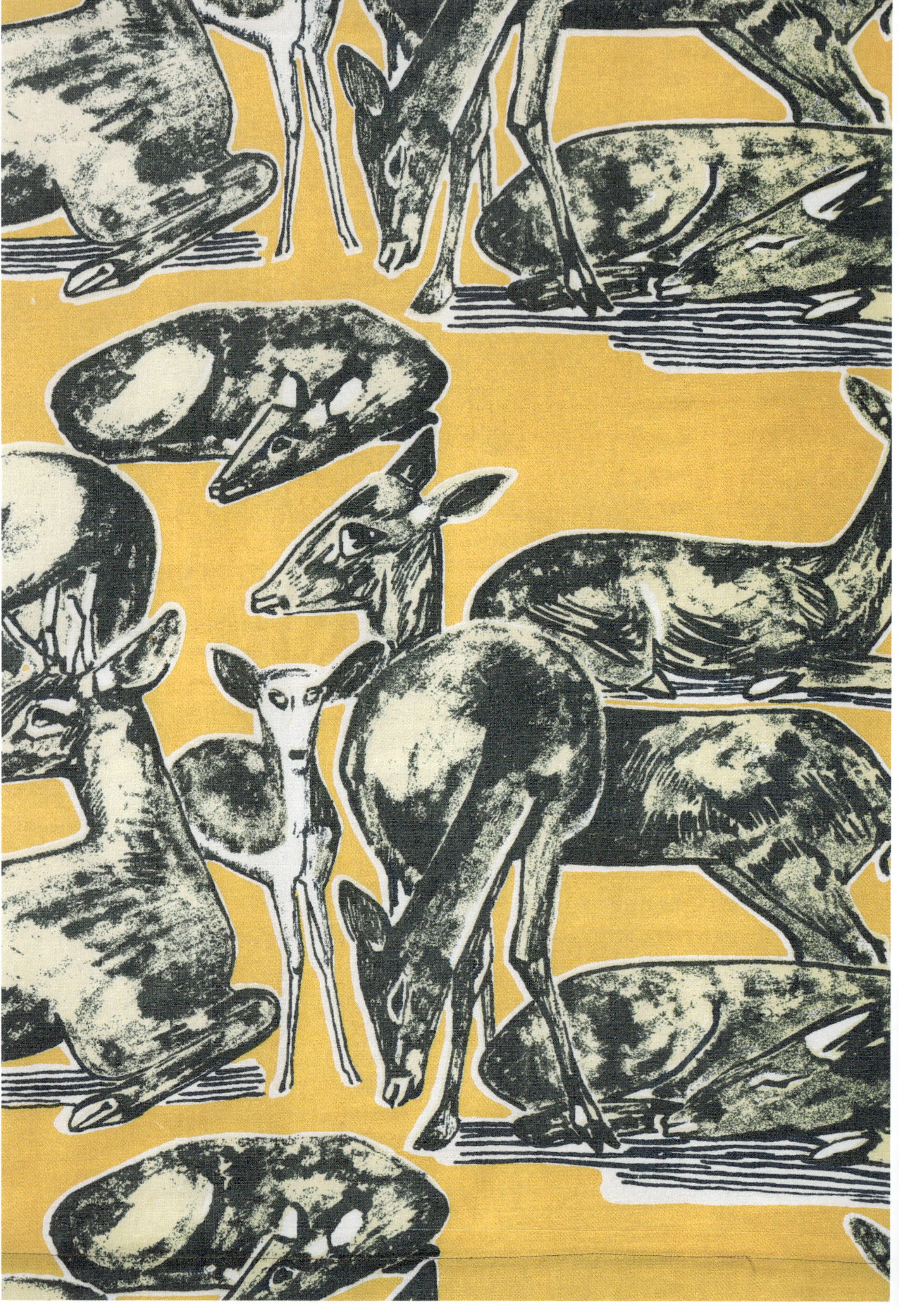

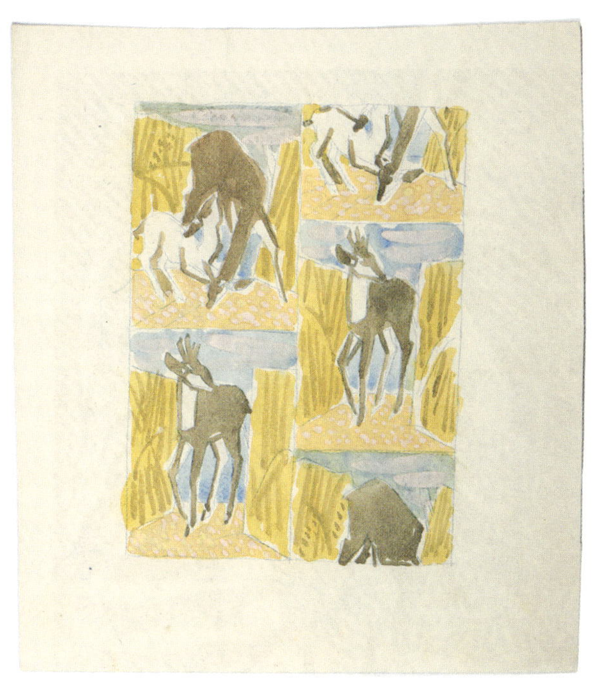

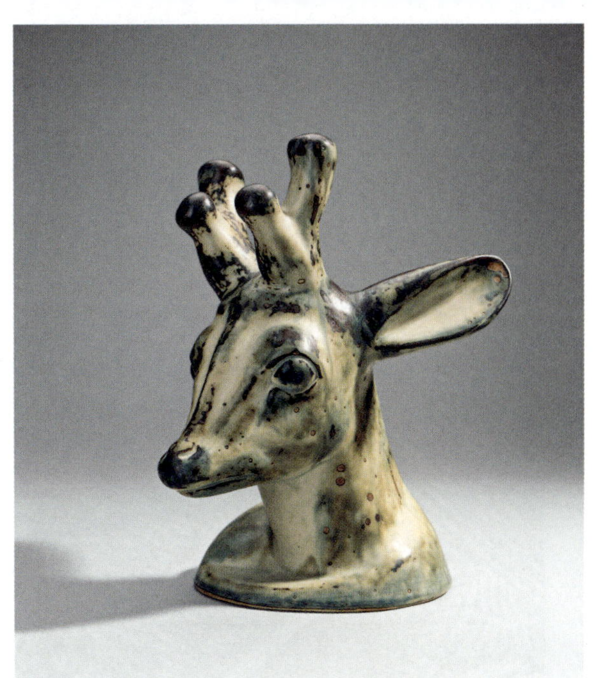

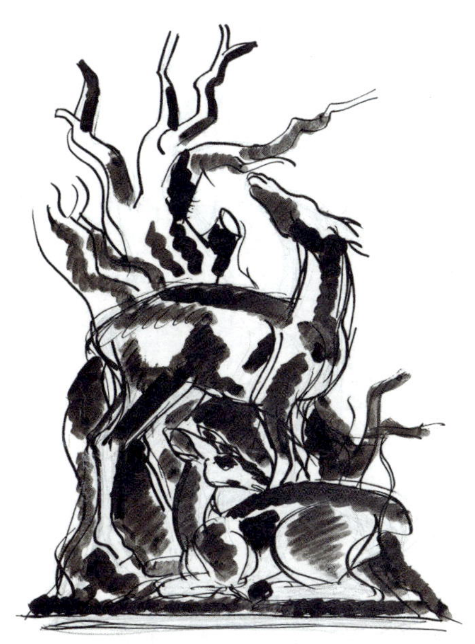

Top left
Axel Salto
Sketch of deer, n.d.
Watercolour on paper, 315 × 274 mm
CLAY/The Royal Copenhagen Collection

Left
Axel Salto
Textile *Hjorte (Deer)*, n.d.
L.F. Foght
Private Collection

Top right
Axel Salto
Deer's head, 1969–74
Stoneware with Sung glaze, H: 30 cm
CLAY/The Royal Copenhagen Collection

Bottom
Axel Salto
Motif from sketch, n.d.
Ink on paper
527 × 420 mm
CLAY/The Royal Copenhagen Collection

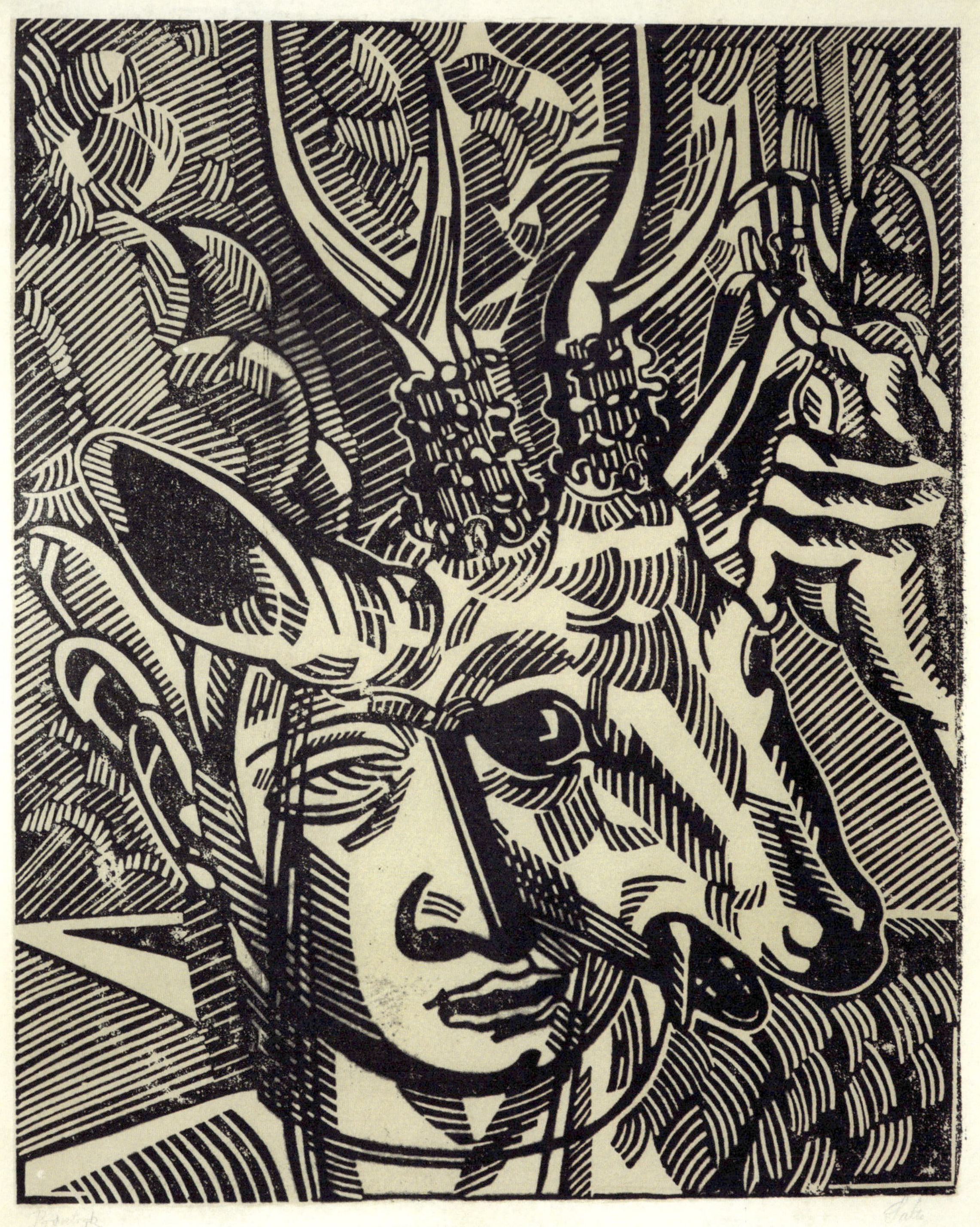

Axel Salto
Actaeon, n.d.
Woodcut on paper, 640 × 510 mm
CLAY/The Royal Copenhagen Collection

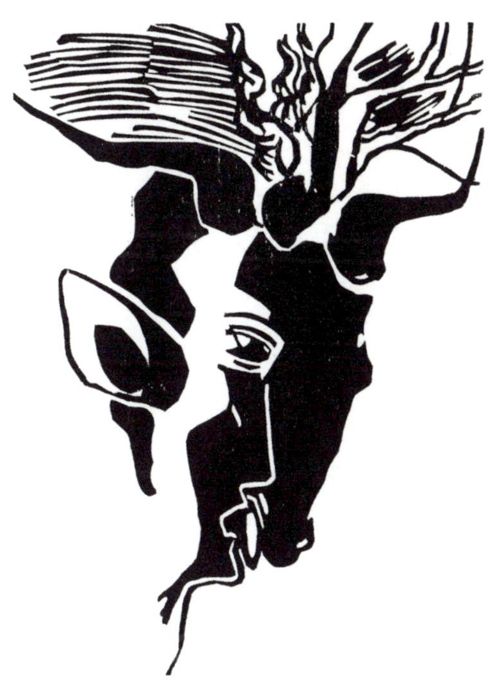

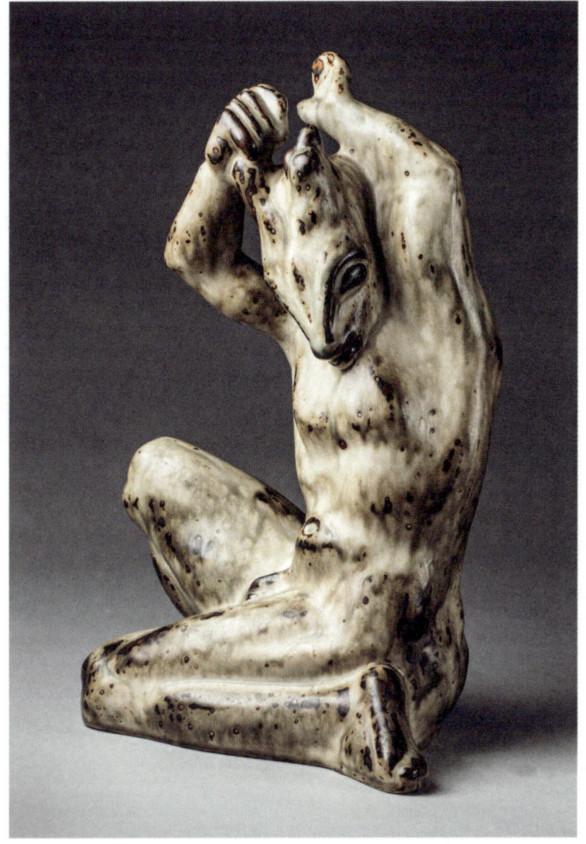

Top
Axel Salto
Actaeon, motif from illustration
Salto's Woodcuts, p. 30
Det Hoffenbergske Etablissement, København
Private collection

Bottom
Axel Salto
Actaeon, 1969–74
Stoneware with Sung glaze, H: 35 cm
CLAY/The Royal Copenhagen Collection

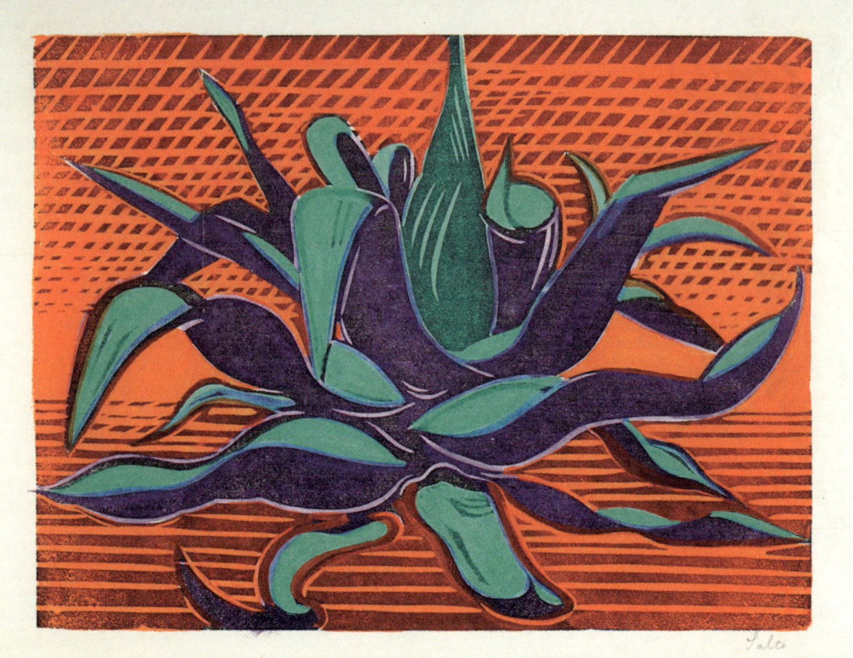

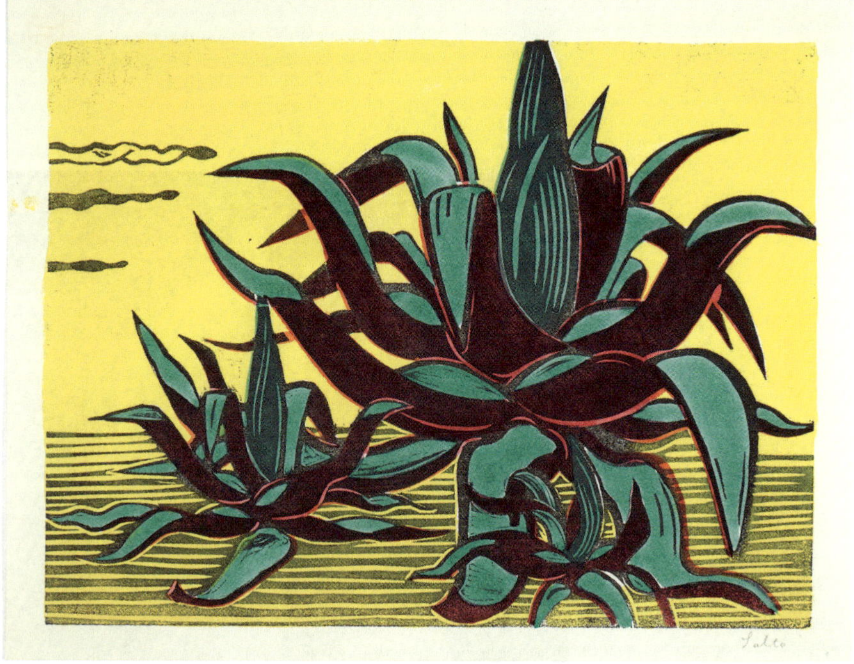

Top
Axel Salto
From the folio La Côte d'Azur, 1926
Coloured woodcut, 281 × 354 mm
CLAY/The Royal Copenhagen Collection

Bottom
Axel Salto
From the folio La Côte d'Azur, 1926
Coloured woodcut, 281 × 354 mm
CLAY/The Royal Copenhagen Collection

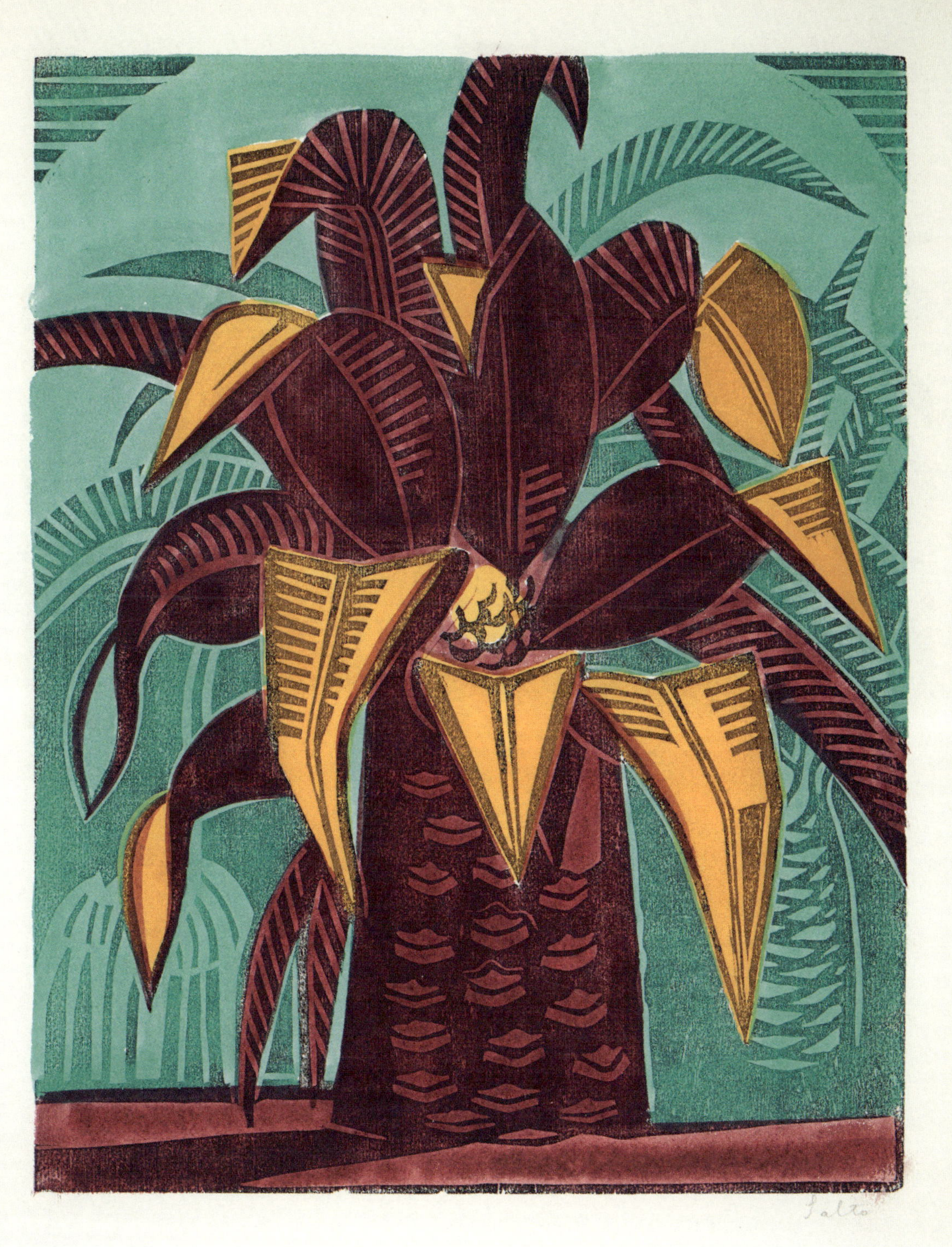

Axel Salto
From the folio La Côte d'Azur, 1926
Coloured woodcut, 354 × 281 mm
CLAY/The Royal Copenhagen Collection

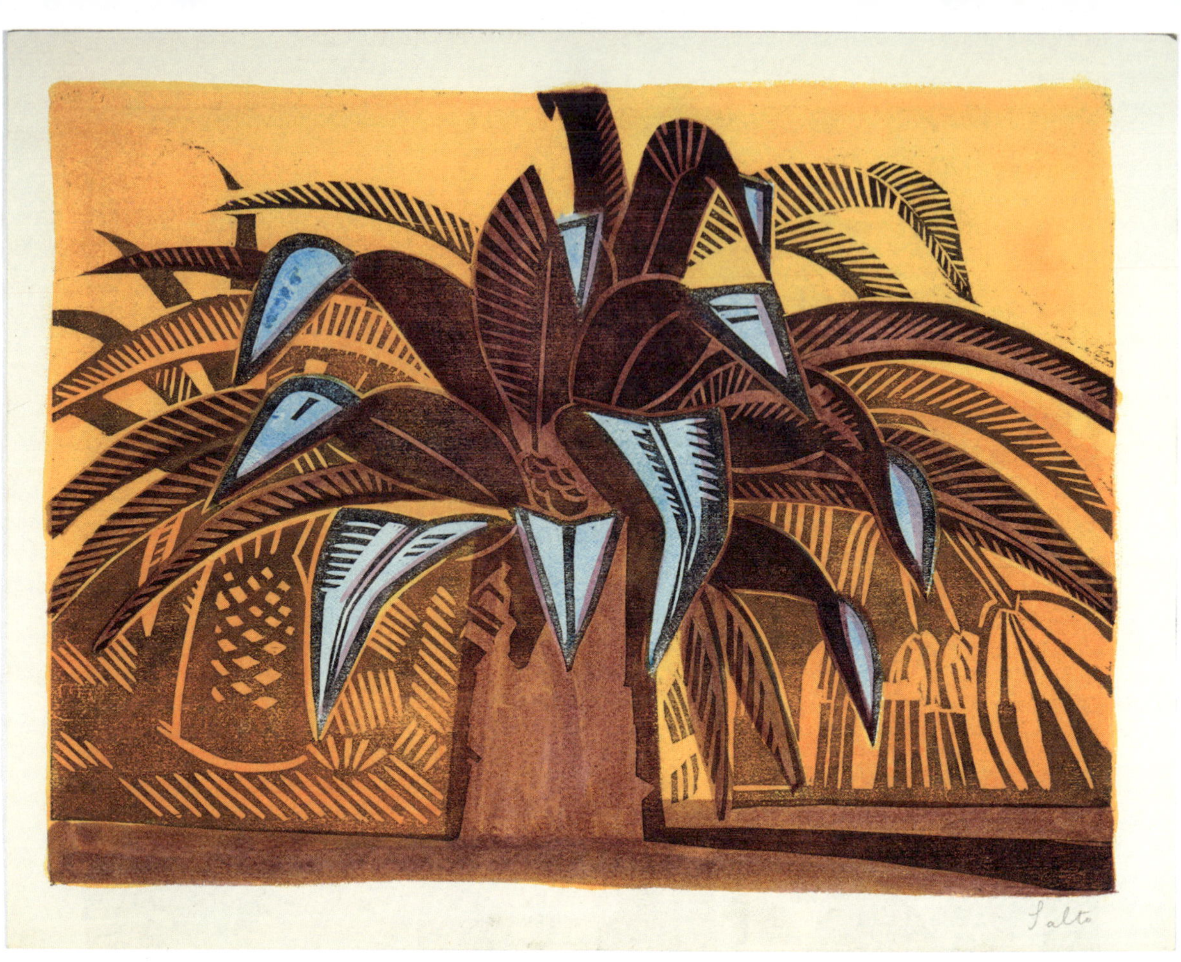

Axel Salto
From the folio La Côte d'Azur, 1926
Coloured woodcut, 281 × 354 mm
CLAY/The Royal Copenhagen Collection

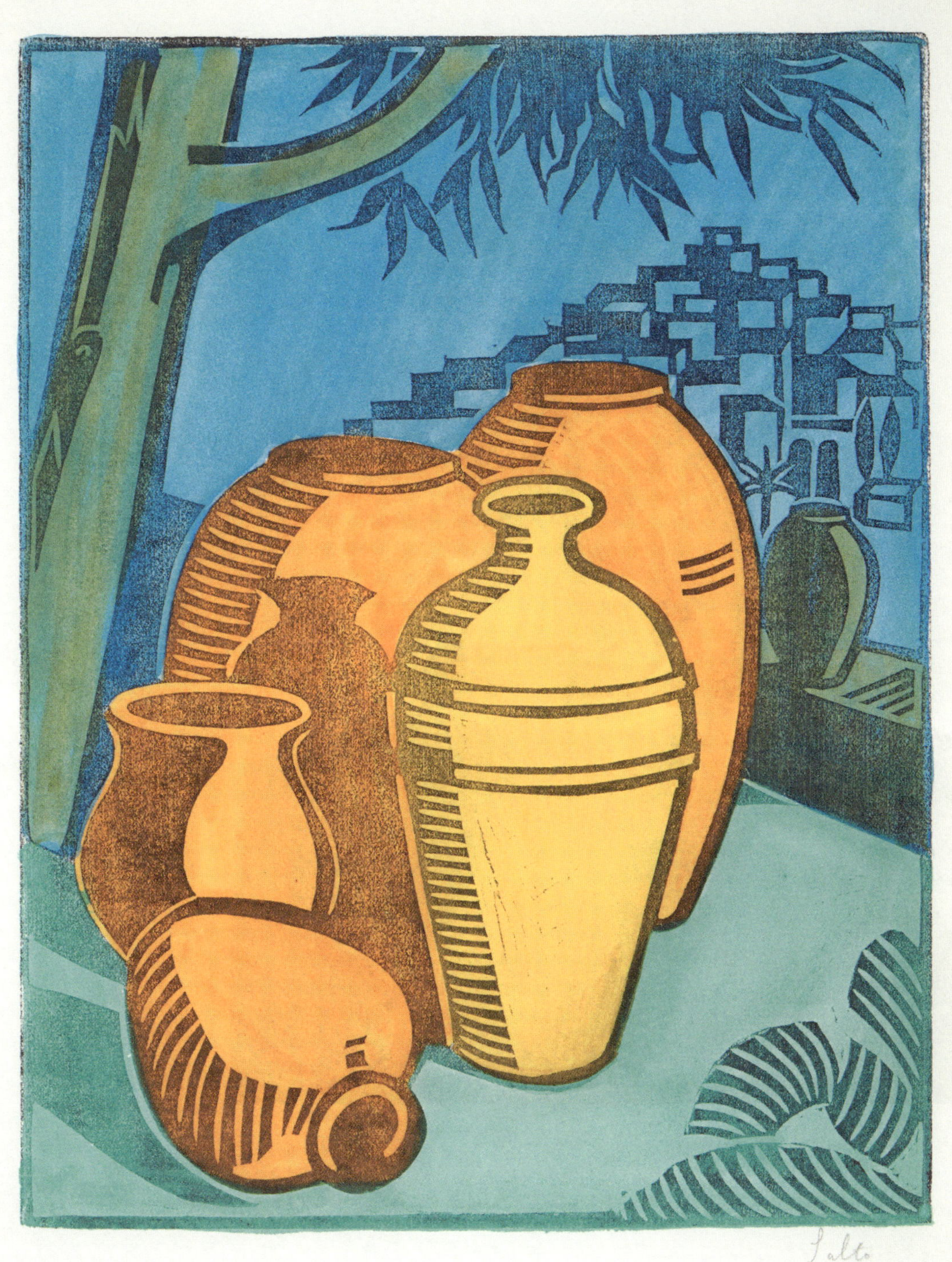

Axel Salto
From the folio La Côte d'Azur, 1926
Coloured woodcut, 354 × 281 mm
CLAY/The Royal Copenhagen Collection

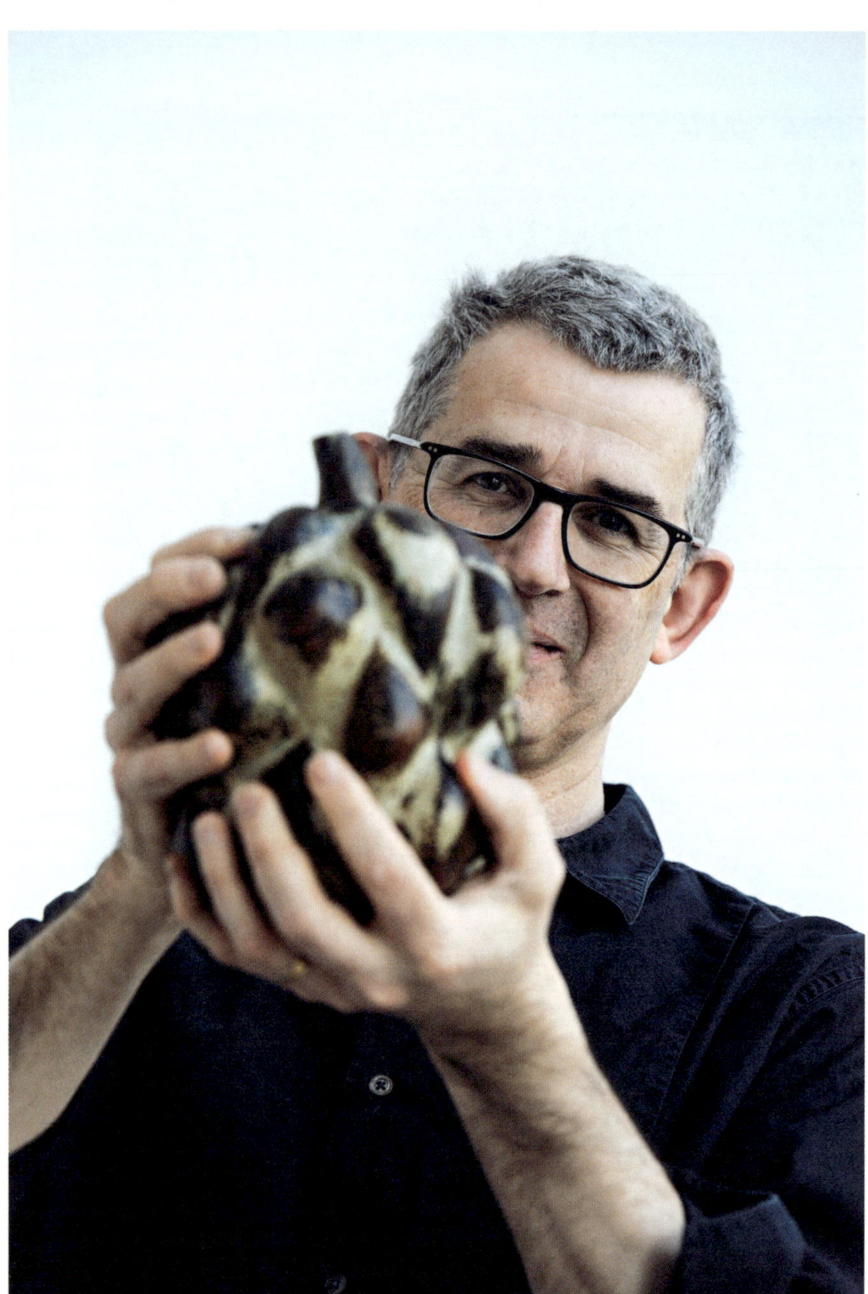

Edmund de Waal with Axel Salto vase

Afterword

A meeting of words and clay. A meeting between two high-profile artists across time. Between Edmund de Waal, interpreter of porcelain par excellence, and Axel Salto, twentieth-century master of stoneware. A meandering conversation between two of the history of ceramics' most spirited and gifted personalities who, while clearly expressing themselves differently, share a unique artistic approach.

Under the title *Playing with Fire*, the British artist and author Edmund de Waal comes together with the Danish artist Axel Salto; as curator, but first and foremost as an artist curious to engage in a conversation with Salto – a conversation connecting words with ceramics, with the kiln acting as the metaphorical starting point for a discussion about eternal movement, inherent power, transformation and metamorphosis, in 'the burning now' wherein soft clay and glazes meld together, becoming a solid body, through the tireless repetition of forms, explorations and continual return to pure artistic research.

A meeting of artists may open up great potential for special insights. It is more than 30 years since that de Waal first encountered Axel Salto's pioneering stoneware, created in collaboration with The Royal Copenhagen Porcelain Manufactory in the mid-twentieth century – a meeting both fascinating and disquieting, he recalls. In 2019, therefore, Edmund de Waal's motivation was already strong before he received our invitation to enter into an artistic dialogue with Salto – a dialogue, entitled *Playing with Fire*, now manifesting itself in an international touring exhibition, a short film, and this very book.

The idea was developed as a close cooperation between CLAY Museum of Ceramic Art in Denmark and Kunstsilo in Norway, whose collections together house a major part of Axel Salto's ceramic works. With a first showing in Denmark (2023–24) and a second in Norway (2024), the exhibition will then be presented in Britain at The Hepworth Wakefield art gallery in Yorkshire in 2025.

On behalf of The Hepworth Wakefield, Kunstsilo and CLAY Museum of Ceramic Art, we would like to first and foremost express our special gratitude to Edmund de Waal who, with courage, respect and humility, accepted the invitation to engage in dialogue with Axel Salto. Without his extremely dedicated commitment, a project of this kind would not have been possible.

We also extend our special thanks to the AKO Foundation, whose confidence has made the realisation of the project possible. With the Foundation's very generous financial support we have been able to pursue and fulfil our dreams and ambitions both for the exhibition and the film as well as this book. In addition, a very big thank you to those partners who have contributed to the project content in multiple contexts: Edmund de Waal's Studio, HK Architects, Stage One, Forlaget Press, Modest, Figure Film, Studio Claus Due, Justesen Art Pack, HIZKIA, all private lenders and not least the descendants of Axel Salto for a close and positive collaboration.

"Art allows us to think the unthinkable," Edmund de Waal writes. This is the dictum for our project. With this book it is our great pleasure to invite the reader to participate in an inspiring coming together of two of the most remarkable ceramic artists of recent times, as Edmund de Waal enters into conversation with Axel Salto.

Reidar Fuglestad – Director, Kunstsilo (N)
Pia Wirnfeldt – Director, CLAY Museum of Ceramic Art (DK)

Biographies

Edmund de Waal

Edmund de Waal is an internationally acclaimed artist and writer, best known for his large-scale installations of porcelain vessels, often created in response to collections and archives or the history of a particular place. His interventions have been made for diverse spaces and museums worldwide, including the Musée Nissim de Camondo, Paris; The British Museum, London; The Frick Collection, New York; The Scuola Canton Synagogue, Venice; The Schindler House, Los Angeles; Kunsthistorisches Museum, Vienna, and The V&A Museum, London. De Waal is also renowned for his bestselling family memoir *The Hare with Amber Eyes* (2010), and for *The White Road* (2015). His most recent book, *Letters to Camondo*, a series of haunting letters written during lockdown, was published in April 2021. He was awarded the Windham-Campbell Prize for non-fiction by Yale University in 2015. In 2021 he was made a Fellow of the Royal Society of Literature and awarded a CBE for his services to art.

Born in 1964 in Nottingham. He lives and works in London.

Axel Salto

Axel Salto was a prolific artist, designer and author who played a pivotal role in Danish modernism. Over the course of five decades, his practice broadened from painting to take in ceramics, woodcuts, graphic design, decoration, book illustration, textile design and jewellery. Nevertheless, it is without doubt his stoneware that earned him his reputation. Salto sought out interdisciplinary collaborations throughout his life and was a pioneer of many of the collective practices we see in art today.

Salto trained as a painter at the Royal Danish Academy of Fine Arts, graduating in 1914. In 1916 he travelled to France, where he met Henri Matisse and Pablo Picasso, among others. His time there inspired him to found the avant-garde art magazine *Klingen* (The Blade), which was published from 1917–20. The aim of the magazine was to promote knowledge of graphic art, and it was also a crucial forum for debate and critical thinking.

Salto's career as a ceramist began in the 1920s with his design of porcelain vases and bowls for the Danish manufacturer Bing & Grøndahl. His passion for stoneware was ignited in 1929 when he encountered the ceramist Carl Halier, who worked in Royal Copenhagen's stoneware studio. This creative alliance between artist, ceramist and manufacturer lasted almost twenty years until Halier's death in 1948. Salto's partnership with Royal Copenhagen continued for over a decade, resulting in iconic new sculptures such as *The Atomic Bomb* (1949) and *The Core of Power* (1956).

He designed wallpaper and bookbinding paper throughout the 1930s and 1940s. From 1945 onwards he collaborated with the Copenhagen firm L. F. Foght, for which he designed patterns for printed fabrics. Alongside his artistic work, Salto published a number of books of his own design. He also wrote countless essays, columns and articles. A highly influential retrospective work, *The Sprouting Style* (1949), was published in honour of his 60th birthday.

Salto's art was exhibited far and wide over the course of his life. His stoneware was presented at the 1937 World Exhibition in Paris, for which he was awarded the Grand Prix. During the 1950s, his stoneware and textile designs were shown at international exhibitions of Danish design such as Design in Scandinavia, 1954–57, The Arts of Denmark. Viking to Modern, 1960–61, and Triennale di Milano.

Born 1889 in Copenhagen; died 1961 in Copenhagen.

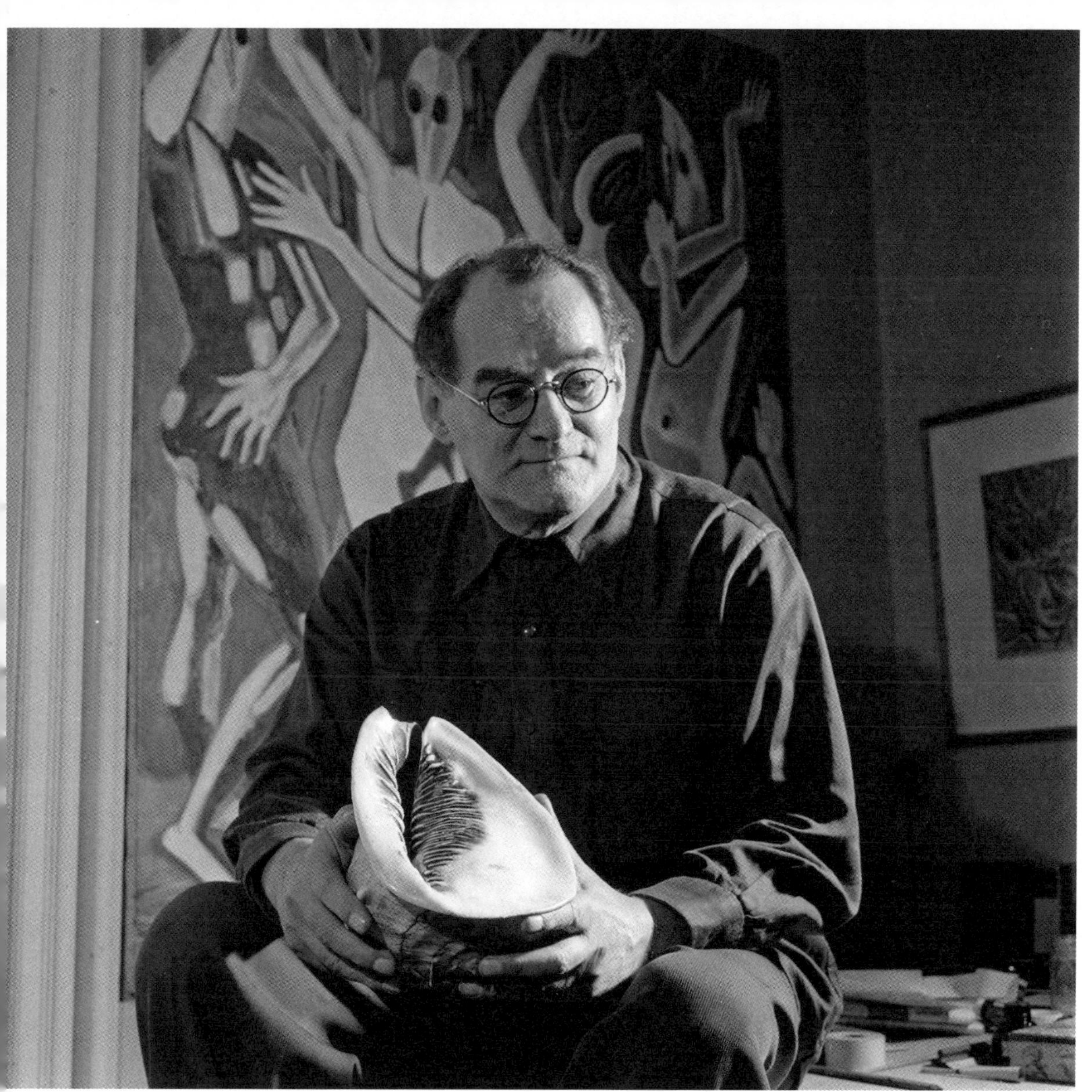

Axel Salto
1954
Ritzau Scanpix

Playing with Fire
Edmund de Waal and Axel Salto

© Forlaget Press 2023
First edition, first print run 2023

Cover and design: Modest [Rune Døli]
The book is typeset with: JJannon and F Grotesk
Paper: Munken Lynx Rough 100 gsm
Image reproduction: Italgraf Media AB, Sweden
Printing and binding: Print Best Oü via Italgraf Media AB
Cover, inside: © Axel Salto, *Salto-Paper*/BONO
© Photo/Trondheim kunstmuseum

Thanks to:
Melody Clark, Jemima Johnson, Claire Tillotson
and all at Edmund de Waal's studio

Sanne Flyvbjerg, Allan Andersen, Christina Rauh Oxbøll
and all staff at CLAY Museum of Ceramic Art Denmark

PhD Fellow Susanne Bruhn for research and support
(Area of research: Axel Salto and Royal Copenhagen)

Translation:
Annette David
Axel Salto Excerpts
A singing world, a place of fire
Afterword

Adam King
Salto biography
Book captions

All rights holders have been contacted prior to publication,
if you have any questions contact the publisher.

ISBN: 978-82-328-0588-4

Forlaget Press,
a part of Forente Forlag AS,
Bernhard Getz gate 3, 0165 Oslo, Norway
www.forlagetpress.no

Axel Salto photos
Archival footage pp. 1–2, 255–256
Stills from *Her er mit hjem*
Hagen Hasselbalch, 1956
The Danish Film Institute

Holger Damgaard/Ritzau Scanpix
4

Aage Strüwing
12–13, 24–25, 102

Teigen Foto
18–19

Allan Moe/Ritzau Scanpix
253

CLAY Museum of Ceramic Art Denmark
6–9, 14, 15, 20, 22, 30, 84–85, 92, 95, 97–99, 207-b, 237,
239, 241-tl, 241-b, 242, 244–247

Ole Akhøj
10, 17, 21, 23, 187–190, 191-t, 192, 194, 195, 197, 200, 201,
203–206, 207t, 208–210, 213, 234, 241-tr, 243-b

Even Askildsen/Kunstsilo
11, 16, 191-b, 193, 196, 198, 199, 202, 211, 212, 214, 215

Peter Leth-Larsen
185, 186, 238, 248

Private images
28, 34–38, 41, 42, 46–48, 58, 63–64, 73–75, 78, 82, 86,
90–91, 239, 243-t

Unknown photographer
51

All images on Axel Salto
© Axel Salto/VISDA

Edmund de Waal photos
Ben Boswell
135

Edmund de Waal and studio
134, 136–149, 167, 174–175, 178–179, 181–184, 235,
236, 240

Alzbeta Jaresova
133, 168–173, 176–177

Stephen White & Co
180

This book has been published with support from
the AKO Foundation

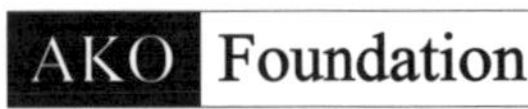

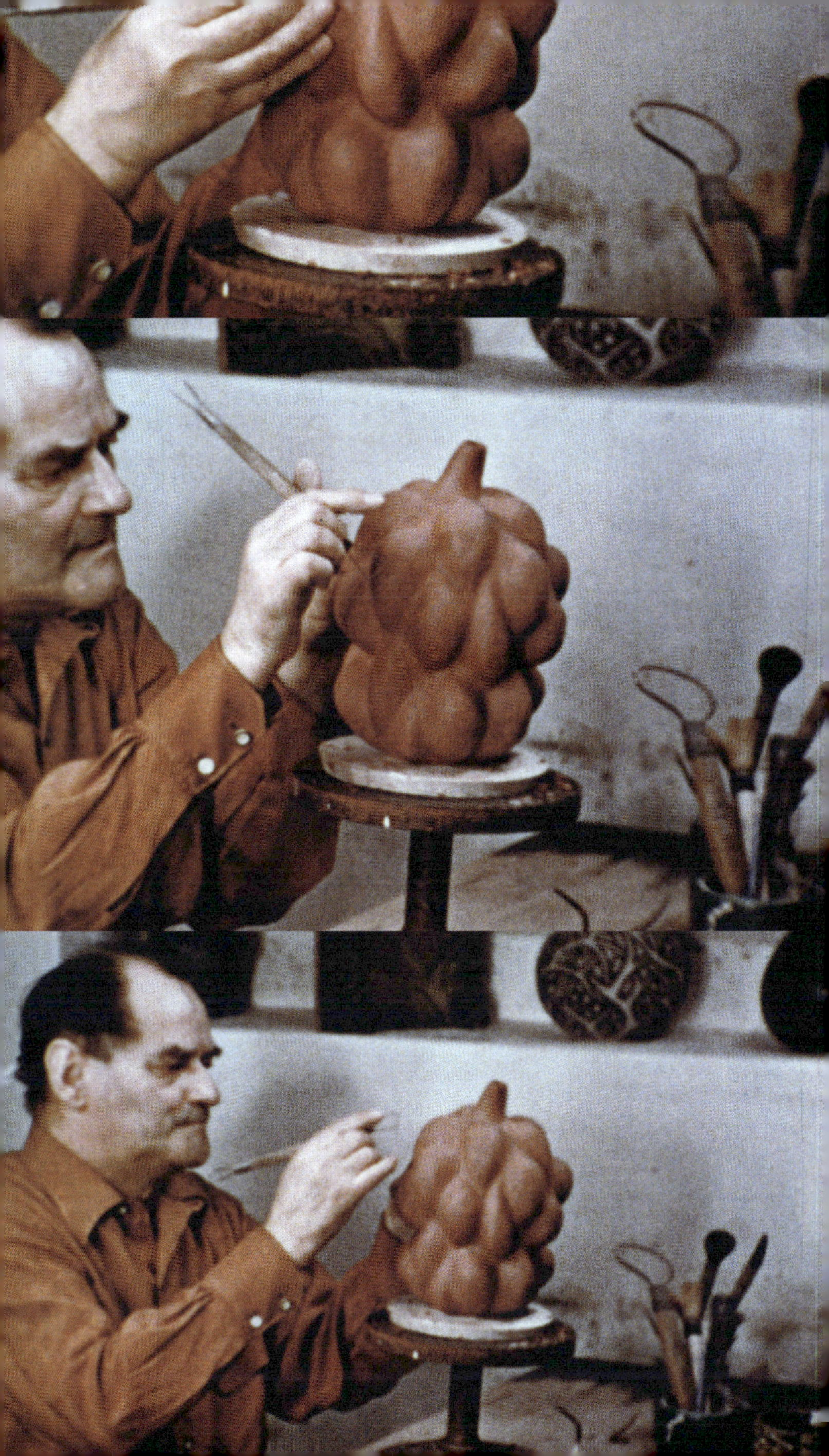

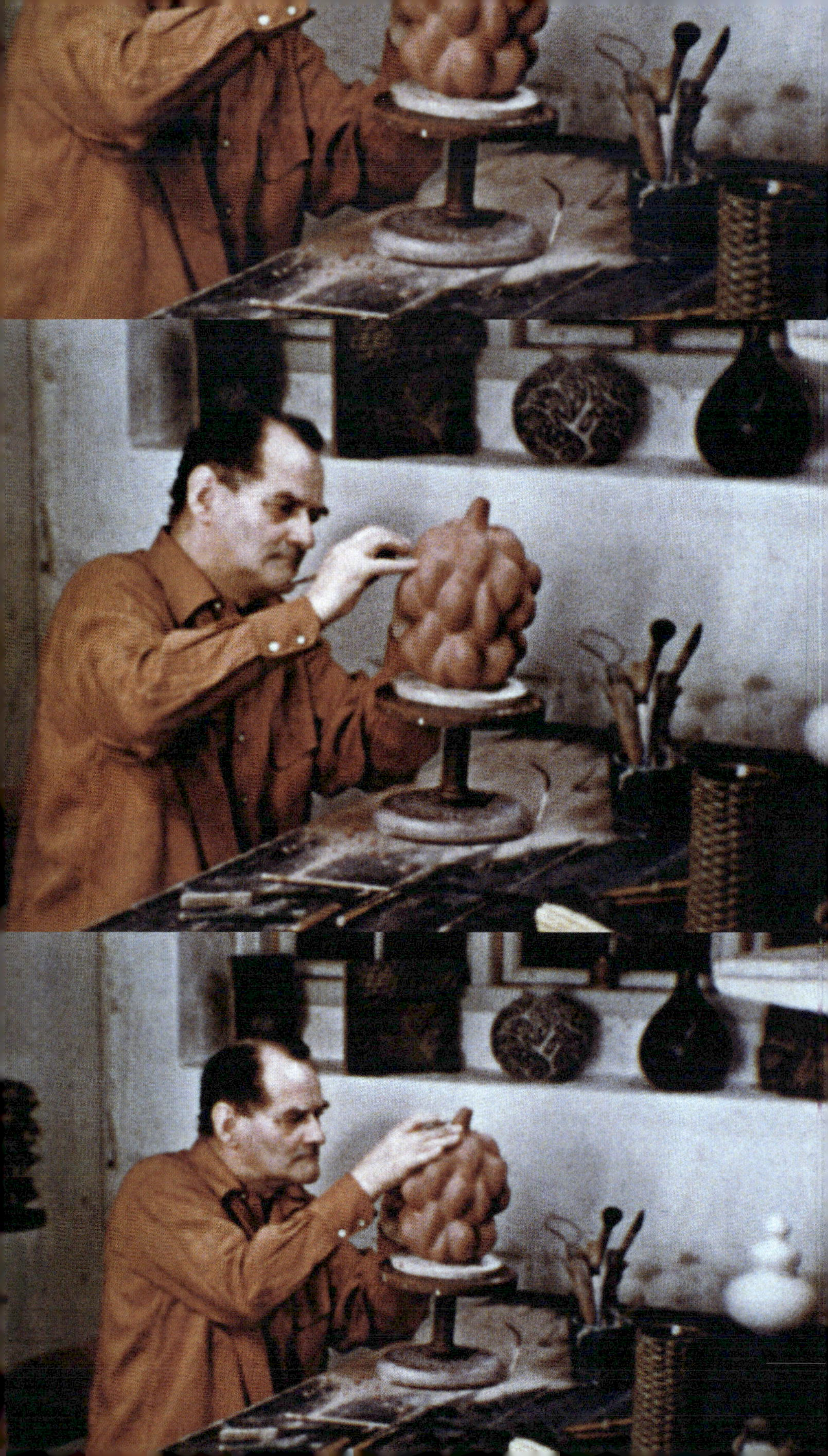